AF470871

The Man They Couldn't Gag

The Man
They Couldn't Gag

Peter Wilson

Hutchinson/Stanley Paul London

Hutchinson/Stanley Paul & Co Ltd
3 Fitzroy Square, London W1

An imprint of the Hutchinson Publishing Group

London Melbourne Sydney Auckland
Wellington Johannesburg and agencies
throughout the world

First published 1977
© Peter Wilson 1977

Set in Monotype Baskerville
Printed in Great Britain by
The Anchor Press Ltd and bound by
Wm Brendon & Son Ltd, both of
Tiptree, Essex

ISBN 0 09 128930 0

Contents

Permission to use copyright photographs is acknowledged as follows, in order of appearance in the book:
Jimmy Wilde and Pal Moore (Syndication International), Aurel Toma and Benny Lynch (Central Press), Helen Wills (Syndication International), Suzanne Lenglen (Syndication International), Golden Miller (Associated Press), Bill Tilden (Syndication International), Peter Wilson (*Daily Mirror*), Sir Leonard Hutton (origin unknown), Sir Donald Bradman (Press Association), Joe Louis and Peter Wilson (Peter Wilson), Primo Carnera and Peter Wilson (Peter Wilson), Denis Compton (Press Association), Freddie Mills and Joey Maxim (*Daily Mirror*), Rocky Marcinao and Roland La Starza (*Daily Mirror*), Jersey Joe Walcott and Rocky Marciano (Keystone), Colonel Harry Llwellyn and Peter Wilson (*Daily Mirror*), Gordon Richards on Pinza (Syndication International), Peter Wilson with Stanley Matthews and Donald Campbell (*Daily Mirror*), Peter Wilson and Reg Harris (*Daily Express*), Jim Peters (Associated Press), Herb Elliott (origin unknown), Ron Clarke and Naftali Temu (Syndication International), Emil Zatopek, Gordon Pirie and Derek Ibbotson (origin unknown), 'Spider' Webb and Dick Tiger (Keystone), Pancho Gonzales (origin unknown), Randolph Turpin and 'Sugar' Ray Robinson (Associated Press), 'Sugar' Ray Robinson and Randolph Turpin (Keystone), Peter Wilson and 'Sugar' Ray Robinson (*Daily Mirror*), Archie Moore and Peter Wilson (Peter Wilson), Mary Rand (Syndication International), Jesse Owens (Syndication International), Mary Peters (Syndication International), Lillian Board (Syndication International), Constantine, Worrell and Dexter (Syndication International), Pelé (Syndication International), Denis Law and George Best (Ray Green), Fred Perry (Fox Photos), Maureen 'Little Mo' Connolly and Peter Wilson (*Daily Mirror*), Muhammad Ali/Cassius Clay and Peter Wilson (Peter Wilson), Sonny Liston and Peter Wilson (Peter Wilson), Wilson & Wilson (Peter Wilson), 'A League of Notions' (*Daily Mirror*), Rod Laver (*Daily Mirror*), Margaret (Smith) Court and Peter Wilson (*Daily Mirror*), Peter Wilson and Christine Truman (*Daily Mirror*), Ken Rosewall (Fox Photos), Basil d'Oliveira (Patrick Eager), Gary Sobers (Patrick Eagar), Dennis Lillee (Patrick Eagar), Gary Sobers (Patrick Eagar), Joe Frazier and Muhammad Ali/Cassius Clay (Syndication International), Joe Frazier and George Foreman (Associated Press), George Foreman and Joe 'King' Roman, (Keystone), Muhammad Ali/Cassius Clay and George Foreman (Associated Press), Eddie Thomas and Ken Buchanan with the author (Peter Wilson), Peter Wilson (Peter Wilson), Red Rum (Syndication International), Jean-Claude Killy (origin unknown), Peter Wilson with Muhammad Ali/Cassius Clay (*Daily Mirror*), Billie Jean King (origin unknown), Arthur Ashe and Peter Wilson (Syndication International), Jimmy Connors and Ilie Nastase (Syndication International), Bjorn Borg (Syndication International), Evonne Goolagong (Mrs Cawley) (Press Association), Chris Evert (Syndication International), Peter Wilson and Gareth Edwards (Syndication International), Jack Dempsey and Peter Wilson (*Daily Mirror*), Peter Wilson and Amy Manning (*Daily Mirror*), Peter Wilson with Gus Lesnevich, Henry Armstrong and Max Baer (Peter Wilson), Bill Connor, Peter Wilson and Hugh Cudlipp (*Daily Mirror*), Peter Wilson with his wife Sally (*Daily Mirror*), Lester Piggott (Gerry Cranham), Henry Cooper (*Daily Mirror*).

Acknowledgements

Some of the material contained in this book appeared originally in various forms in the *Daily Mirror* and the *Sunday Mirror* (*Pictorial*) and the *Daily Express*, to whose Editors I am grateful for permission to reproduce these passages.

I cannot adequately express my gratitude to my publisher Roddy Bloomfield who at least once worked literally round the clock with me to reduce this book from over half a million words to, at least, liftable proportions; if it's still not readable that's my fault, not his.

Equally it could not have been completed lacking the devout work of my step-daughter, Susan Thompson, who bravely soldiered on with the typing, despite the fact that the decimal points in the athletics times just about drove her dotty!

P.W.

Introduction

Until I was eighteen I never dreamt of becoming a sportswriter. Writing, yes. Perhaps a job in a publisher's office. But writing about sport? No. Sport was for watching, as an enjoyment, not a profession, and, in certain specialized areas, for playing.

At eighteen, with the merciful self-confidence of youth, I regarded the world as my oyster – and if someone would kindly pass the brown bread and butter, the lemon and Tabasco, and take the champagne off the ice, oh! what a banquet was waiting! There was some talk of my going up to Cambridge; alternatively there was the possibility of my spending a year with a peasant family in the north of Italy, where I would be forced to learn the language and at the same time try to learn the rudiments of the craft of writing.

Then, in the January six months after the end of Wimbledon 1931 – I'm sorry if that sounds callous but I have remembered most of the important dates in my life through sporting events – my father died. We had never had much money, and my father, a most trusting man, had lost what little capital he had inherited through following the false advice of someone he thought a friend. I have never known to this day how he managed to pay my fees at Harrow, even though they were less than a quarter of what they are today, for *The Times* was a scurvy employer and paymaster and, although there were other publications for which to freelance, sportswriting in those days was a stingily rewarded branch of journalism, although then as now some of the best writing was to be found on the sports pages.

So I found myself committed to sportswriting, originally and urgently, to make some money. Then, as I grew to know a little more about it, gradually I found certain paramount themes and views recurring in both my columns and reports. They became the dominant beliefs of my working life.

The major one was apartheid in sport. I came late to this and my only excuse, if it can be called that, was the age in which I was born and educated when, to be self-destructively honest, I hardly even recognized the fact of the vast black majority in Africa. (As for Brazil, for instance, had anyone described to me, as a young man, the infinite gradations of colour there, I should not have believed him.)

Before the Second World War I had quite a few friends and acquaintances from sporting South Africa: Ben Foord, the first British heavyweight champion not to have been born in the UK; Vernon Kirby, the South African Davis Cup player, and 'Tuppy' Owen-Smith, who actually captained England at Rugby football. It was easy enough to envisage a black South African boxer, but a black lawn-tennis player was unimaginable and a black rugger player frankly laughable. There had never been one, you see, and except for the few men with a real vision, what you have never seen you can scarcely picture.

Apart from my introduction to Nazi racial theories in the 1936 Berlin Olympic Games – and their explosion by Jesse Owens – I became intimately involved with apartheid in sport only after the Second World War when it was suddenly brought home to me that a black or partly coloured boxer, even though born in Britain, could not fight for a British title.

Boxing, on the whole, had a good record, as far as colour was concerned. It's true that John L. Sullivan, the last of the bare-knuckle heavyweight champions, declared in his famous 'defi' of 1892: 'In this challenge, I include all fighters – first come, first served – who are white. I will not fight a Negro. I never have, and never shall.' But subsequent heavyweights never 'drew the colour line' until the then unacceptable behaviour of the first black heavyweight title-holder, Jack Johnson, prevented anyone of his colour challenging for the supreme championship from 1915 to 1937. Then Joe Louis came along, and since then there have been only two white heavyweight champions; in any case, during the long interregnum between Johnson and Louis there were black champions in almost every division other than heavyweight.

As we had then just finished a war fought, in part at least, in opposition to racial discrimination it seemed that as well as trying to entertain I must attempt to get this British colour bar removed. Before long, with the backing of the *Sunday Pictorial*, through 'polling cards', reading 'Are you for or against a colour bar in boxing?', stuck up in pubs throughout the country, and after one particularly acrimonious radio debate which ended in a slanging match between myself and the then Secretary of the British Boxing Board of Control, Charles F. Donmall – who had a pathological dislike of Negroes – we succeeded in getting first Dick and then Randolph Turpin as British champions.

Thereafter the more I travelled the less racial discrimination seemed to agree with any idea of true sport, and I fought it wherever I could – particularly, of course, on its constant appearances in South Africa, which, after the compulsory 'liberalization' of the American Deep South, became the nest of sporting intolerance. When I think that had sporting apartheid been successful I should not have seen Jesse Owens in athletics, Joe Louis in boxing, generations of West Indian, Indian and Pakistani cricketers – as well as Basil d'Oliveira – Arthur Ashe in lawn tennis, George Nepia in Rugby, Pelé in soccer, I think (morality apart) that those who tried to impose it must have been 'the afflicted of God'.

It would, of course, be untrue to say that I started as a young journalist with a burning desire to reform. Apart from anything else, youth was kept firmly in its place in the early 1930s and that attitude would soon have been kicked out of me by those who were certainly my elders, if not in all cases my betters. And anyway I had not the experience to decide what abuses should be campaigned against and what, for varying reasons, were to some extent inevitable in an imperfect world.

But as far back as 1930, even before I had achieved the anonymity of writing for a newsagency – which certainly, and rightly, would not have stood for any campaigning journalism – it seemed absurd that the great Bill Tilden, capable of winning Wimbledon at over thirty-seven, should no longer be able to defend his title in the world's best tournament in which he had proved himself the best player, simply because he had turned professional, mindful of finances with the end of his top-class career obviously in sight.

When, with experience, I appreciated the full racket of 'shamateurism' with its grimy little subterfuges, this became rather more than a windmill against which to tilt, although it took nearly forty years to effect the change.

The same hypocrisy figured in the 'cattle market' of soccer transfers where the players, on a ridiculously small maximum wage, and with no share of the fees for their willy-nilly transfers, were as exploited as nineteenth-century industrial workers.

The reforms here came from the concerted criticism of almost the entire sporting Press and it makes the veterans among us smile somewhat wryly to see the extent of over-compensation, so that in 1975, in lawn tennis for instance, Miss Virginia Wade was not only the highest-paid British woman athlete ever, but probably the highest-paid British woman of the year in any walk of life. And the more footballers are paid, the less distinctive and distinguished seem the individual skills – and the fewer the people to watch them.

Soccer, of course, in my opinion has declined more than any other sport because of the climate of behaviour which surrounds it and in which it is played. There have always been 'villains' in the game but they used to be known for what they were and the only pedestal on which they would be placed would be a pillory. And something which I personally regret not having foreseen and tried to do more about is the savagery of crowds in and around football grounds.

Yet, when it comes to the players, I still prefer (just) the temperamental outbursts of some lawn-tennis stars and the 'Achilles-sulking-in-his-tent' attitude of a percentage of soccer players to the previous living lie of the first game and the servitude of the second.

Some sports have improved out of all recognition. Despite some shortcomings, like the investigation of the true worth of foreign boxers before they appear in Britain, the boxing Board of Control, backed by those of us who love the rough old sport, has in its near half-century of existence and in my personal experience wiped out that shambling and horrifying travesty of a 'sporting figure', the punch-drunk fighter.

No longer do the 'vampire' agents, who used to call themselves managers, control a string of forty to fifty boxers from Aberdeen to Torquay without leaving their homes in London, Manchester or Liverpool. It's true that changing economic circumstances in Britain have, by reducing the total number of boxers, altered the situation materially, and that the remaining boxers are generally better educated – and hence more suspicious of 'benefactors'. But the Board, with the general support of the postwar Press, has improved conditions, although in the foreseeable future I cannot see it stamping out that monopoly of which everyone knows but which apparently is legally unprovable: so professional boxing in Britain will continue to be more 'syndicate' than sinning!

Athletics, in some ways, I have found the most depressing of all sports. Despite the fact that some of the performers have been of the highest intelligence and character – by no means the same thing – and although an increasing number have said that they wanted to compete against the best and damn the categories of amateur and pseudo-amateur, whether state-sponsored or aided by athletics scholarships, the old men (almost I wrote 'the old women') in charge have stuck to a Victorian 'morality' and mentality when almost within hailing distance of the twenty-first century. In 1957 even such a traditionalist as Harold Abrahams, who in 1924 became the only British athlete to win an Olympic Games 100 metres gold medal, commenting in the magazine *World Sports* on Avery Brundage's remark that the laws of amateurism were 'immutable', said that if this were really so an amateur could not be 'a mechanic, artisan or labourer'.

Abrahams was at his most devastating when he pointed out that the International Olympic Committee – the supreme governing body of the greatest sporting gathering in the world – is 'a collection of eminent individuals who are, in no sense, democratically elected and are responsible to no one but themselves.' He went on to stress the fact that the IOC is a self-perpetuating body which elects its new members itself. By implication he made the point that, with such a constitution and such election, it is virtually impossible to get a new and more up-to-date outlook on sport as it is conducted in the second half of the twentieth century. With the retirement and subsequent death of Avery Brundage, who seemed to have headed the International Olympic Committee since the days of Ancient Greece, there appear to be steps in the progressive direction. But the truth which has to be faced is that the world-class athlete of today cannot possibly hold down a full-time job.

Eventually 'open' athletics will have to come; the Olympic anomalies in, for instance, show jumping are there for everyone to see. And only a hypocrite or a blind man could pretend that the Winter Games have anything but the most tenuous connection with what most people understand by amateurism.

In Britain we have, at times, been badly and sadly served by our athletics administrators. Perhaps I was not close enough to the sport before the 1952 Olympic Games to realize just how badly. But over the years, although I hope the worst is past, brilliant competitors, dedicated coaches and people who wrote about the sport because they loved it, were treated with increasing lack of perception and, in some cases, ill-bred rudeness by officials, some of whom seemed to be doing more than agreeably out of the 'perks' of the sport. I shall not soon forget warning one such dolt, in a British Embassy overseas, that if he continued to be deliberately provocative I should do my very best to knock him down in front of the Ambassador. Regrettable but necessary, to try to teach him, as the figurehead of our team, some elementary manners – and how to behave in public.

One thing I regret not having achieved in over thirty-five years' campaigning is the abolition of the sadistic pursuit of hare-coursing. But I believe it will not be with us much longer. . . .

So, although as a chronicler of popular recreation the life was one of gaiety, occasional transcendent excitement and, most fortunately, getting to know better than casually a wider cross-section of the population in more countries than most people ever dream about, I and many talented and sincere colleagues were able to help along some reforms. Obstinate authority no doubt looked upon us as the spanners in the works. I like to think that although many improvements would have come anyway with the passage of the years, we did initiate some and expedite others.

In the process a lot of us grew up and became more responsible for the welfare of the sports we loved – and which had been so generous towards us – so that latterly more and more often governing bodies have come to the Press, instead of it always being the other way round, realizing that sometimes, through travel and experience at home and abroad, we might be able to provide information as well as seeking news.

Certainly the role of the sportswriter has become much more involved and – dare I say it? – more responsible than it was when I look back some forty-five years.

I Until 1935
Sometimes it was the Street of Misadventure...

My father had been so good at many sports – he was a triple Blue at Cambridge, captaining the cricket XI in 1904 and representing the University at rackets and real tennis – that it left me somewhat daunted in the playing of sport. The only one in which he hadn't seemed to excel, perhaps because he didn't esteem it too highly, was lawn tennis. So, originally as a form of self-defence, or self-expression, but later for the sheer love of the game, I began to play the somewhat despised 'lawners', as in those days it was disparagingly known.

When even stories of W. G. Grace, with and against whom my father had played, failed to encourage an interest in playing cricket, and nets during the spring holidays at Lord's proved that there was really no aptitude there, my father, bless him, made it possible for me to play as much lawn tennis as I wanted during the endless sun-drenched (well, that's how I remember them some fifty years later) days of late July, August and the first part of September.

We usually rented a house for the long summer holidays at Birchington in Kent, and despite the attractions of swimming in the sea, it was lawn tennis morning, noon, afternoon, and it would most certainly have been night too, had floodlighting then been in vogue.

I had had a little tuition at Queen's Club, London, where the secretary in my early days was E. B. Noel, a rackets and real tennis contemporary of my father. His daughter Susan, for three years women's squash-rackets champion, was an early friend but I do not remember playing lawn tennis with her. The little coaching I had was from the two Charleses – Read, a much better rackets and squash player, and Hierons. I also played very occasionally with the then senior ball-boy, Dan Maskell, who afterwards won the professional championships a score or so times, got the OBE for his services to sport, and coached Princess Anne on the private court at Buckingham Palace.

But it was on the courts at Birchington that I really learned the basics of the game, and I am glad that my father was still alive when I got to the final of the Junior Covered Courts Championships, then held at

Dulwich, in 1931. I lost that final to Alan Collins, with whom I had been at school, as I lost the other two finals in which I met him that year, at Roehampton and the West Side Club at Ealing, where Betty Nuthall, the first British girl – indeed the first foreigner – ever to win the USA women's singles, had learned the game. Alan was always a better player than I, for he had a better match temperament; but I think I was about second or third best junior of my year. I always felt that had I been able to continue playing seriously, as a senior, I might have made the doubles pair of our Davis Cup team – in a bad year . . . a very bad year.

So much for the playing days: what of watching sport? Just a few events stand out like islets in the rather placid stream of the boyhood of an only child who spent most of his time in urban surroundings.

A June day in 1921. My father had announced, as one promising a super-treat, that he was going to take me to my 'first Test match'. And it was the Lord's Test against the touring Australians and the 141st since Charles Bannerman took the first ball from Alfred Shaw on a sunny day at Melbourne in March 1877.

I remember too the first world title fight I ever saw, although it was not generally regarded as such. We were, as ever, at Birchington when my fifteenth birthday coincided with a fight billed as being for the world flyweight title between Johnny Hill, of Scotland, and Newsboy Brown, of the USA, in the open air at the Clapton dog-racing stadium. My birthday present was a trip to London and a ringside seat for the fight. I don't remember too much about the fight itself – it was, after all, in 1928 – except that I could scarcely breathe towards the end of the fifteen rounds when Hill had built up a good lead on points but, minute by fraught minute, looked as though he were going to be destroyed by the powerful Russian-born Jewish-American.

By no means all things fistic were tinged with sorrow. I had, round about this time, discovered a rather splendid place called Premierland – and that took some doing without a native guide, as it was situated in the heart of London's East End, in a hardly salubrious street called Backchurch Lane. This was a wonderful new world where everything was larger than life, and twopence coloured, too. Instinctively I felt that my mother at least would not approve of Backchurch Lane, but some of Britain's greatest boxing champions appeared at Premierland, despite admission prices of only sevenpence to five shillings and ninepence. So I invented some convenient friends to explain my frequent absences during the Easter and Christmas school holidays.

There was also, of course, that then fashionable yet hard-fought occasion, the Eton and Harrow match, which in the summer of 1931, though I had left Harrow, I had no doubt we should continue to attend in style – in a pirate, hired coach, no less!

This may all sound as though various sports were my only interest in life, but this was far from being the case. At Harrow I had shone at none of the school-accepted sports but I had made, among other friends, a special one of Lyon Playfair, son of Sir Nigel Playfair who ran the Lyric Theatre, Hammersmith, made such a great thing of reviving Gay's *Beggar's Opera* and, among other things, re-popularized Restoration drama on the London stage.

All the Playfair family had their differing enchantments. Lady Playfair, one of the earliest stage Peter Pans, seemed to have absorbed some of the fairy dust, for the more mature she became the younger she looked – and the greater *rapport* she had with young people.

Giles, Lyon's older brother, had, with John Snagge and actor Henry Ainley – one of the stage giants whom I met at the Playfairs – as beautiful a speaking voice as anyone's I have ever heard. Andrew, the younger brother, had a certain childlike refusal to accept the world as it was, and so created one of his own.

There were holiday weeks spent at the Playfairs' house in Sandwich. There were delirious nights when *Derby Day* was playing at the Lyric and Sir Nigel allowed – no, demanded – that Lyon and I should go on stage as 'extras' in the Derby crowd scene. After which, presumably to propitiate Equity, or whatever was its equivalent then, he insisted on paying us a shilling each!

It was through the Playfairs that I first heard in the confines of a drawing room that voice which could fill the largest theatre like Big Ben chiming and which belonged to Mrs Pat Campbell; and, looking at her, I wondered how it had been when, in the course of her frolicking with Bernard Shaw, she had said, 'One day someone will give Joey a beefsteak and no woman in London will be safe' . . . or so legend had it.

Had I not known the Playfairs I should never have started a poem with that most distinguished writer, Lawrence Durrell, in which each of us was to contribute an alternate line and which, scarcely surprisingly, never reached the end of its first stanza.

Best of all were the times spent at Saïd House, Chiswick, which had been specially designed and built for the famous actor-manager. I have never been quite clear what a *salon* really means, but if it implies a congregation of all that is witty and wise, fashionable and beautiful, eccentric yet basically genuine, then the Saïd House parties were the quintessence of a *salon*.

The beauties I shall omit, for I was too young and overawed to draw near to them. There were others, too, who were too alarming, in a different way, to approach. Aldous Huxley I remember once (Lyon then hero-worshipped him) standing like a lonely lighthouse of pure intellect. Who would dare to speak to such a cerebral iceberg?

A. P. Herbert, who lived nearby, was often there, full of river-lore – the house was facing Chiswick Eyot – quick as a gadfly to prick anything he suspected of pomposity, and not one to suffer fools – or young men, if they fell into that category – gladly.

Was it at Saïd House that I heard G. K. Chesterton, who, still sporting his voluminous cape, would make a point of standing next to the smallest person in the room, stoutly maintain: 'I claim that I am the most polite man here; today I got up and offered five ladies my seat in a tram!' I'm not sure?

But one character, and my one meeting with him, I shall never forget. He was an unimpressive little man, with a squeaky, high-pitched voice, and what persuaded him to devote so much time to a goggle-eyed seventeen-year-old I shall never know . . . only be grateful for it.

He was H. G. Wells. I had read much of what he had written, which was fortunate because, after asking me my age, he piped: 'Have you read my *Short History of the World*?'

I nodded dumbly. Well, I *had* read part of it.

'Then perhaps you'll accept my view that, in my opinion, this is the worst possible period, in recorded time, to be a seventeen-year-old!'

This time I could only gulp dumbly.

He went on: 'I'll tell you something else. Ninety-nine point nine per cent of mankind would be better employed spending their lives looking through a microscope at grains of sand and describing what they see than wasting their time doing whatever it is they are doing now.'

My contribution to that one was dead silence: in so far as this dialogue was concerned I wasn't even a good 'feed'.

Wells continued: 'Do you know how much life is worth in an Indian village?' Thank God, he didn't give me time to reply but pressed on: 'Or, put it another way, do you know how much it would cost to buy a strong lock for a door there? Sixpence? A shilling? Certainly not more than one-and-six. But an Indian peasant never sees that amount of money, at any time in his life. So he can't afford to buy a lock, and so a man-eating tiger can come into his hut and carry off his child or his wife . . . and he *still* can't afford a lock, in case it happens again.'

On he went, and on, and I stood there, probably mouth agape, for this was a man of two centuries – of *all* centuries – and I, at least, was content to be overcome by the exuberance of his intoxicating verbosity.

The Playfair family opened new vistas for me. I remember one morning when Sir Nigel was rehearsing to play Malvolio – in his fifties he played Tony Lumpkin better than I ever expect to see him played again – while Lyon, sitting (like his father) on my bed, was also getting me to audition *his* rendering of Malvolio. When, greatly daring, I ventured to tell Sir Nigel that some lines weren't *actually* (that awful English word) what Shakespeare had written he, quite rightly, ignored me; Lyon must have kept plugging away, with great accuracy but scarcely his father's . . . inventiveness.

Then there was a holiday in Austria when Lyon and I, travelling alone and, of course, third class – as there wasn't a fourth class – spent what seemed like days on ribbed wooden seats which threatened to leave their marks on us for ever, while our fellow travellers, breathing blasts of garlic on which you could almost hang your hat, made sure that the tethered (but live) chickens swinging from the racks, the sucking pigs and the young lambs and kids who accompanied them, were safe and well.

Unwary traveller that I was I hadn't foreseen that hours would make even the most romantic scenery pall, but Lyon, a year older, had books for the two of us in, I think, that wonderful Continental paperbacked Tauchnitz edition. Mine, I seem to remember, was *The Party Dress* by Joseph Hergesheimer, and Lyon had Hemingway's *A Farewell to Arms* which, surprisingly, neither of us had read, although it had been published some two years earlier. But then I doubt whether either of us had heard of Hitler – and he was due to make the first of his takeovers, of the Germany through which we were travelling, in two years.

Then bathing in the ice-cold Achen See in the Austrian Alps.

Even during this holiday, which had meant a unique interruption of the lawn tennis routine, I felt the choice of two worlds – the sweet and short fame of sport; the abiding consolation of a more artistic life, at no matter what level. The old conundrum of brawn versus brains, assuming you had enough of either.

But in January 1932 my father died, and my mother and I had, I believe, £40 left in the bank. That included the *ex gratia* payment made by *The Times*: my mother told me that was £5. That newspaper did, however, provide me for a time with enough work to live on, and there was occasional freelancing to be done for the Exchange Telegraph newsagency. We had moved from the medium-sized house we had rented in Westbourne Grove to a flat in Holland Park Avenue.

Working in the sports department of *The Times* was a curious and often chastening experience for an eighteen-year-old. Apart from clerical staff I don't think there was anyone much younger than my father. Some of the older men – how horrifying to think that most of them were considerably younger than I am now – were delightful. One such was 'Beau' Vincent who succeeded my father as cricket correspondent. A story typical of him, and of the more leisurely days of sportswriting, was told when he was observed one Saturday watching his old school, Haileybury, playing Cheltenham at Lord's.

Someone remarked that he had expected Beau to be representing *The Times* at the Oval where a match with some considerable bearing on the county championship was being played. Vincent shook his head tolerantly. 'No, no, old boy, I can get as much as I want on that for Monday morning out of the *Observer*.' Suddenly an expression of horror crossed his face and his chin hit his navel. 'By God!' he exclaimed. 'I'm doing it for the *Observer*!'

Fleet Street has witnessed some very peculiar scenes but I doubt if any of them could have outdone the sight of Beau conservatively dressed but wearing a solar topee and conducting an exercise in 'syncopation' – an unsteady movement from bar to bar – from one hostelry to another; and whatever else Fleet Street may be deficient in it certainly isn't bars. Invariably Vincent was asked 'Why the topee?' for, like some devout Jew in a holy place, he most certainly did not remove it in any bar which he visited.

His answer came: 'Because I'm going to Australia, old boy.'

It was true. *The Times* had finally decided to send their cricket correspondent to the Antipodes. And he, wise fellow, was trying on for size what he had been assured was obligatory headgear in that far and fearful place.

Perhaps it was only my youth but it did seem to me that there were more 'characters' in 'the Street' in those far-off days. Take, for instance, John Collett who, round about that time was, I think, editing *Lawn Tennis and Badminton*, then the official journal of the Lawn Tennis Association.

Collett was an irascible old gentleman with a limp who used a stick to aid him with his locomotion. It was his habit at the end of a not-too-arduous day to stump his way from Chancery Lane towards Ludgate Circus, crossing the Street punctiliously every few yards in order not to be guilty of omitting a single pub, local or bar. I don't know what bogey for that particular course is for, like John Collett, I have never completed it under my own steam.

A close observer of Fleet Street will notice that on the corners of some of the side streets there stand certain green-painted receptacles – that is unless the forces of progress have taken them, as well as so many other things, away. Their original function was, I believe, to contain sand and gravel to enable the horse-drawn traffic, still quite common in the twenties and early thirties, to proceed smoothly; they came into their own particularly at the Lord Mayor's Show.

However, on one occasion John Collett put on his own Lord Mayor's Show. As he set out on his nightly pilgrimage he was carrying a large bundle of letters for posting. Bang, bang, bang went the old stager until he came to one of the sand containers into which he solemnly deposited his mail. A friendly City policeman had observed Collett's ploy. He rescued the letters and caught the old gentleman just as he was about to vanish through the swinging portals of yet another of the inns, the delights of so many of which Collett had already availed himself. Said the policeman: 'Your letters, sir. Won't get very far being posted in the sand box, will they, sir? Ha! ha!'

John Collett surveyed the towering constable. Apparently what he saw did not please him. His breath came in short puffs. His eyebrows beetled. He beat on the pavement with that stout and sturdy stick.

He said: 'Officer. *Young* officer! You exceed your duties. I shall post my letters where I bloody well please.'

Whereupon he vanished into the pub leaving the unfortunate policeman to stick the letters into the nearest pillar box – or anywhere else he chose.

But back to *The Times*. The first trouble I had there was because the then sports editor's wife thought that big-time lawn tennis, certainly Wimbledon, was one of her 'perks'. I disputed this. I lost.

The sports editor had another unlovable attribute – I doubt whether even he loved that wife. This was to tell me to sit down and wait while he decided where to send me. After an hour or so of fairly alcoholic somnolence he would gaze at me under bushy brows, ask what I was doing and when I tried to tell him he would bark: 'If I'd had anywhere to send you I'd have done so by now. You can get out.'

No, this wasn't exactly the happiest period of my forty years in The Street of Adventure.

Had I known what little I know now about the mechanics of newspaper production I should have marvelled that *The Times* came out with any sports pages in it at all.

The office was the original journalistic rabbit warren, and the story goes that one night the door of the sports room opened and a distinguished gentleman came in and politely asked the way to a different department of the newspaper. That same sports editor looked up with the expression of a fighting bull when the banderillas have gone in. He inquired whether the distinguished visitor thought he was an effing information bureau and bade him betake himself off. When the door had closed behind him someone ventured to ask gently whether he knew who the 'visitor' had been. The sports editor said: 'No.'

He was informed that it had been Geoffrey Dawson. (Dawson was editor of *The Times* for over twenty years – apart from a short period when he quarrelled with Lord Northcliffe, then the owner. He was, of course, much criticized for the policy of appeasement which *The Times* pursued towards Hitler before the war.) The sports editor mulled over this information for some time and then delivered himself of his summing up: 'Well, it's bloody well time he knew his way about the building. Anyone coming out for a drink?'

Every newspaper has, of course, its share of misprints. Somehow they are funnier when they appear in so august a publication as *The Times*. The classic one was alleged to have been deliberately introduced by a disgruntled Victorian linotypist who, on the occasion of the Queen opening the Albert Bridge, amended the original story by just one letter so that it read something like: 'Her Majesty, having severed the ribbon stretched across the street with a pair of golden scissors, moved slowly forward and, with due solemnity, pissed over the bridge.'

The one I most enjoyed while I was working for *The Times* occurred on the occasion of the Boat Race. The schools and colleges of the two crews were printed in brackets after their names. One oarsman had gone to Eton and Christchurch; another to Shrewsbury and Brasenose. By some villainous trick one unhappy wight found his name followed by the declaration: 'Eton and Christnose'.

Wordage in those days was a matter of some concern to me. I was paid strictly on space and I had a strong suspicion I was not getting myself marked up for as much as I had written. I think sufficient years have passed for me now to own up to the great sports page robbery. Lying around the room was a ruler with which all stories from outside contributors were measured to the nearest half-inch. Payment was strictly on length so that if your article rapidly petered out into that size of type which needs the aid of a magnifying glass to read it you got considerably less money than the lordly ones, higher up the page, who might have written the same number of words but who, since their copy was set in larger type, got considerably greater remuneration.

There was no way of arguing with the gentleman in the contributions department, for they had a ruler and I had not. This was clearly a situation which had to be remedied. And so, late one night, when the building, and certainly the sports room, was almost deserted I purloined the ruler which gave the exact amount due for varying lengths of stories, repaired to the lavatory, stuck one end inside one of my socks, concealed the rest of the ruler up one trouser-leg and sallied forth into the night looking, I imagine, like the youngest veteran of the First World War in captivity.

Great was the search for that ruler in the sports department, but happily the news of its disappearance never reached the contributions department who, for the rest of my time, were plagued with demands for 'Half a crown more on that story; three-and-six on this one' until they would almost pay me the small extra sums just to get rid of me. Almost. . . .

Just once in my life I have felt really wealthy. It was at the end of a month in which I had taken over from the rackets, squash rackets and real tennis correspondent who was ailing. When my monthly cheque came it was for just over £90. For an eighteen-year-old to get £90 over forty years ago was unprecedented. But, by Caxton, you had to work for it, on the sheer volume of tens of thousands of words churned out. It involved going to Prince's Club, Knightsbridge, defunct these many years, perching on the little ledge over the entrance to the rackets court at Queen's Club and going to a selection of the St James and Mayfair clubs, where the squash rackets Bath Club Cup was played.

This was an example of the schizophrenia which riddled my life at that time. You would be asked into one of the big, gloomy club bars and bought a generous schooner of sherry – more than enough for a teen-ager. To be fair the members realized that you were not making much money at that time and would usually decline your offer of 'the other half'. But, of course, you had to make the offer – and if you were caught for a round it meant 'dinner' at a coffee stall and no lunch the next day. For *The Times*, as in so many other things, was niggardly with expenses.

Sometimes people ask me what I regard as my outstanding journalistic achievement. That one's easy. It was getting reports of all-in wrestling in *The Times*. To introduce such gems as 'Norman the Butcher was the winner over Carver Doone on a submission fall, gained by the application of the Boston Crab' into those sedate columns was as satisfying as it must have been baffling to 'Regular Reader'.

I even have the telegram which Atholl Oakley, a rather racy nephew of the Duchess of Atholl, who was promoting shows at 'The Ring', Black-friars, sent to the editor, deploring the decision to omit future accounts, when it was finally decided that all-in wrestling was not quite the thing – certainly not for *The Times*. It was passed on to me with a covering note: 'The Editor has received the attached communication.' You could almost see the fastidious wrinkling of the nose.

But I must say they had a point. The first time I had my suspicions that things might not be all they seemed was when I chanced to go into the dressing room at 'The Ring', Blackfriars, and overheard a conversation between two gentlemen who, only a few minutes earlier, had apparently been trying to twist one another's legs off, the better to beat out their brains with them.

One of them was saying most aggrievedly: 'You silly berk. I told you to lay orf my left leg. I've 'urt it. And why the 'ell did you go on so long before giving the submission? Now we'll 'ave to take a taxi if we're not gonna be late for our bout at the Vale 'All, Kilburn. I've got a good mind not to let you win there you're that stoopid!'

But it was not all-in wrestling that finally persuaded me that *The Times* and I were not really cut out for each other.

It was, of all acceptable sports, lawn tennis.

I had written about the drama rather than the technique of a match only to hear: 'My dear boy, we don't want *this* sort of stuff. Let's have some more of the stroke play.' And my first big story was handed back to me, almost as though the speaker had been handling it with invisible tongs. That, added to the fact that there was now a new sports editor and this one had not a wife but a brother who seemed to hanker after the same assignments as myself, made me feel that it was time for a change. I don't know whether *The Times* or I benefited more.

By 1933 I was working almost solely for the Exchange Telegraph newsagency. It was wonderful training for a young journalist.

The fortnight of Wimbledon was a prosperous time for me because, although expenses remained at four and sixpence a day in the Greater London area, instead of the fifteen shillings a day which I got for an ordinary six-day week when reporting minor tournaments, I asked for, and got, a guinea a day at Wimbledon. I seem to recollect that I also did something for the *Sunday Pictorial* on the two Saturdays. And then there was my Dutch connection.

In my early days at Wimbledon I had met a Mr Vreedenburg – I am guessing at the spelling of his name for I never saw it written – who represented a Rotterdam newspaper. For the first nine days of Wimbledon, after I had finished all my other work, I used to call him in Holland with a précis of the day's play – the only proviso being that it did not exceed six shillings' worth of time on the telephone: phone calls, even overseas ones, were, like everything else, much cheaper in those bygone days. On the second Thursday of Wimbledon Mr Vreedenburg, a delightful little man rather like Alice's White Rabbit, used himself to arrive at Wimbledon. He would pay me for the telephone calls, a grand total of £2 14s. (there were not, as I recall, any transfer charge calls at that time). Then, glory be and long live the House of Orange, nine days at fifteen shillings a day came to another £6 15s.

All in all, with the *Sunday Pictorial* payments, it would be a bad Wimbledon if I didn't manage to accumulate about £25 for the fortnight. It didn't add up to that one wonderful £90 a month – but it came in uncommon handy.

I covered, I think, three finals for the Ex-Tel., from 1933 to 1935. And what wonderful finals they were. Take the men's singles in 1933. The holder, Ellsworth Vines of the USA, was matched against Australia's Jack Crawford. The previous year in the quarter, semi and final rounds Vines had produced perhaps the three greatest victories I have seen at that stage in the championships.

Now Crawford, a man who seemed to belong to a different era, almost as though he had stepped out of the frames of some faded daguerreotype with his square-headed racket and his rolled-down flannel shirt sleeves, was up against the greatest forehand hitter and server of his age; the same man who the year before had beaten the Australian 6–2, 6–1, 6–3 in the semi-final round.

Vines was well over six feet tall and, apparently, under six inches wide! Crawford, more heavily built, his squarish face topped with light, crinkly hair, was going to have to use his brains to win this one. And use them he did, working like a beaver gnawing away at some tall pine.

The fifth set produced some of the greatest lawn tennis I have ever seen at Wimbledon or anywhere else. Vines' power and pace against Crawford's courage and cunning. In the end near-ace was parried with angled return, lob blunted smash, speed was harnessed by skill. One cross-court shot which seemed almost to brand Vines' white vest as it seared across his body to raise a puff of chalk from a side-line, was perhaps the shot of the match. It brought Crawford to match point. Vines served a fault and a sprinkling of the crowd applauded; Americans and Frenchmen had won Wimbledon every year but one since the war but this was unforgivable, particularly as the match had been played in the highest traditions of sportsmanship.

Vines just bowed ironically – and served again. Crawford returned it with a blow of iron and Vines' final stroke faltered into the net. The crowd exploded but their pandemonium did not drown the slight sigh from the fair-haired woman sitting in the players' and friends' enclosure, directly in front of my Press seat, before she slid off the bench in a dead faint. She more than anyone else knew what an ordeal Crawford had survived, for earlier in the year and in the two preceding ones she had won the Australian mixed doubles title with him – and that year one of their opponents in the final had been Vines.

She was Mrs Jack Crawford. . . .

I have devoted so much space to that match because, although it happened over forty years ago and although it is nearly fifty years since I saw my first Wimbledon final, I still believe this was the greatest.

It was indeed a vintage year for, in the final of the women's singles, an English girl, Dorothy Round, came very near to beating Mrs Helen Wills Moody. As Miss Round, having lost the first set 4–6, won the second 8–6, one of Wimbledon's mightiest cheers went up; it was the first set Mrs Moody had lost in the world's greatest tournament for *nine years*. Alas, inexperience beat Dorothy in the third.

27

I think here is the right place to tell the story, apocryphal though it may be, about Dorothy in America. As well as being one of the most truly sporting players I have ever seen, among her other activities was that of Sunday school teacher at her native town of Dudley in Worcestershire. Of course there was no question of any Sunday play in Britain, but when Dorothy went to the States she learned that some of their finals were played on that day. She let it be known that if she were fortunate enough to reach the final her principles would not permit her to play on Sunday. And then, unfortunately, she *did* reach the final. I say 'unfortunately' because it had to be postponed to the Monday, with a consequent diminution of the 'gate'. Even more unfortunately, the story goes, Dorothy was beaten 6–0, 6–1. Whereupon some bright spark on the local paper set up the headline: 'English tennis star won't play Sunday – can't play Monday!'

Incidentally, the Americans of that time must have thought some representatives of the British Lawn Tennis Association oddly named, for one of the leading lights was Theodore Michel Mavrogordato and the Secretary was Humbert Anthony Sabelli. Indeed the story goes that the latter was at a party in New York when a friend of his, wishing to introduce him to the host, said: 'I'd like you to meet Sabelli, Secretary of the British LTA.' Whereupon the American, who had clearly read his Emily Post, replied: 'Delighted to meet you, Sir Belly. And how is Lady Belly?'

And *that* reminds me of the time the Yorkshire county delegate was introduced to Sir Samuel Hoare (later Lord Templewood) then the President of the LTA. Overflowing with goodwill the sturdy Yorkshireman shook the President warmly by the hand and inquired with ferocious goodwill: ' 'Ow are yer, Sir Samuel? And 'ow's Lady W?'

But back to Wimbledon and 1934, perhaps, from a British point of view, the greatest year of all. The preceding year we had won the Davis Cup for the first time since 1912 and later in 1934 we were to defend it successfully with a 4–1 margin over the USA. But that was after Wimbledon – a Wimbledon in which Fred Perry became the first British player to win the men's singles since Arthur Wentworth Gore, and his last title had been won a quarter of a century earlier . . . in 1909, the year Perry was born!

Perry had had quite a job reaching the final, losing one set in almost record time to that singularly unpleasant Czech, Roderick Menzel, and being taken to five sets by the American, Sidney Wood, who had won the 1931 final on a walk-over. The final was something of an anti-climax. Perry was so obviously the best player, not only at Wimbledon but in the world, that even though he was meeting Jack Crawford, victor in the heroic final of the year before, scarcely anyone believed he could lose. And they were right.

Then Dorothy Round made it a glorious double by beating Helen Jacobs 6–2, 5–7, 6–3, fairly flogging herself to the net in the final set when she seemed to be dropping with fatigue but, like all great champions, knowing that her opponent was even more tired.

About this time I had my own personal cross to bear when a delightful French player, Mlle I. Adamoff, appeared in a number of British tournaments. The custom then was to use initials and not first names but as soon as I started dictating: 'I. Adamoff . . .' I would be interrupted with a low and filthy laugh and some comment like: 'I bet you did, you dirty dog.' Enough of this, thought I. I don't give a damn about custom. As far as this girl is concerned I shall use her Christian name. So the next time I was phoning something about her I began: 'Ida Adamoff . . .' only to get the familiar lecherous chuckle and this time: 'Yeah, given 'arf a chance you *woulda* Adamoff, you dirty dog, you.' You couldn't win with a name like that.

The next year, 1935, was my last Wimbledon with the Exchange Telegraph. It was Fred Perry's second win and although he lost three sets getting to the final I never had the slightest doubt that he would retain his title.

I really got the feeling about this time, and the following year, that Perry, probably the fittest man of all the great lawn-tennis players I have seen, with a wrist of steel which enabled him to 'flick' the ball on the forehand (a stroke he had adapted from table tennis where he had been the first Englishman to win the world's singles title) and a diamond-hard belief in himself, would deliberately prolong some matches, particularly those on the Centre Court, because he so thoroughly enjoyed playing there and being the dominant character on the most famous lawn-tennis stage in the world.

Once more the final, where even Perry wouldn't procrastinate, was one-sided and Fred beat that most elegant German, Baron Gottfried von Cramm, 6–2, 6–4, 6–4.

The women's singles final was one of the most memorable of all those I have seen. It brought together one of the greatest, Helen Wills Moody and her perennial and most bitter rival, Helen Jacobs. Mrs Moody won 6–3 in the final set.

Of course, there is one other player who very much disputes the title of 'greatest ever' – Maureen Connolly who won the US title at the age of sixteen. 'Little Mo' won Wimbledon when she was seventeen, eighteen and nineteen, never losing a single match there. Suzanne Lenglen was twenty before she won, although to be fair the First World War had prevented her from playing earlier. Helen Wills was beaten in her first Wimbledon final at eighteen.

Who then was the best of the three? I wouldn't be dogmatic – but I have a fund of memories of Little Mo.

However, the Wimbledon of 1935 was the end of an era – for me. The next month I joined the *Daily Mirror*.

1935-7
Mirror, Mirror — on the Ball

In some way the five years from August 1935, when I joined the *Daily Mirror*, to July 1940, when the Army joined me, were the most exciting of my journalistic life.

After the years with *The Times* and the Exchange Telegraph news-agency I was beginning to learn my craft but, not for the first time in my life, what really counted turned out not to be what you knew but whom you knew.

In this case the *deus ex machina* was Wallace D. Roome who was, I believe, Manager of the paper from its first publication in November 1903 until his death during the Second World War but who, more importantly to me, had been a close friend of my father's since they had been on the *Mirror* together in its very early days.

I still have my letter of appointment, dated 16 July 1935:

Dear Mr Wilson,

Many thanks for your letter. It will be quite convenient if you can join us on 5 August. May I just put this into writing:

This is to offer you a post on the *Daily Mirror* as a sporting writer at a salary of £10.10.0 (ten guineas) a week, starting from 5 August 1935, the conditions being the customary three months' notice on either side.

If you will send me formal acceptance of that offer I will forward it to the cashier.

> Wishing you the best of luck.
> I am,
> Yours sincerely,
> C. E. Thomas
> ACTING EDITOR

If Cecil Thomas was only the 'acting' editor I certainly never discovered who the real McCoy one was. I suppose, in fact, it was Harry Guy Bartholomew, that wayward, volcanic, vitriolic genius whose long-felt dislike of me was only equalled, if not surpassed, by my detestation of him. The only trouble was that *he* was to become the chairman.

Thomas was always most agreeable to one of the youngest members of his staff and my 'signing on' pay was very satisfactory. In those days the National Union of Journalists' minimum wage was nine guineas a week and I have an idea that the minimum for the sports staff was a guinea less.

5 August 1935 was, I believe, Bank Holiday that year. It seemed strange to be indoors instead of watching some sport or other, for, although I had been engaged as a 'sporting writer' my first few months were to be spent inside the office, learning the rudiments of sub-editing and the other complexities of producing two or three pages of sporting interest.

It was a strange – and for me, fortunate – coincidence that three youngish journalists should have joined the *Mirror* on the same day. The other two were Hugh, now Lord Cudlipp, OBE, and Bill, later Sir William Connor, known for so many years to so many millions as 'Cassandra'. Hugh was one day older than I, having been born on 28 August 1913; he has never failed to remind me how much he learned in that extra twenty-four hours! 'Cass' was two or three years older. Hugh had come to the *Mirror* via the reasonably orthodox progress from South Wales to Manchester thence to the now long defunct *Sunday Chronicle* in Fleet Street. Bill Connor had been an advertising copywriter for the J. Walter Thompson advertising agency. His undying claim to fame in that medium was, I always understood, coining the phrase for Harpic, the sanitary cleaner: 'Reaches the spot the brush can't touch'!

I realize that this was a more leisurely age, in newspapers as in everything else, but there did seem to be more camaraderie between the different branches of a newspaper in those days and some of the friends I made in the brief six months when I was 'inside' remained so until they, or I, retired.

I was extraordinarily lucky. I had no aptitude for inside work on a newspaper and on at least one occasion I nearly caused a complete stoppage. A block – the processed metal from which a picture is printed – had been mislaid and edition time was near. Wandering around idly I happily picked up something which seemed to have been overlooked, carried it across the composing room and asked, in all genuine innocence: 'Would this be it?'

A second later I was hit by an avenging whirlwind – the head printer.

'Gor-bleeding-blimey!' quoth he with some emotion, 'put the bloody thing down, will you! You wanter cause a strike or something?' All unwittingly I had offended against the rigid print union rule that journalists did not touch 'metal'.

My real luck came when, only a few months after I had joined the *Mirror*, its boxing correspondent, Stanley Longstaff, left to take up a public relations job with one of the football pool companies. Much as I loved playing, watching and writing about lawn tennis I had longed to get to the ringside to report the big fights and now I was to get my chance.

It soon proved to be a not-unmixed blessing. When you are young – brash? – you cannot believe that everyone won't see it through *your* eyes, and come to the same decision as yourself. At least that was my point of view. I was soon disillusioned.

The first 'big' fight I remember covering for the *Mirror* was in January 1936. I had been on the paper for just over five months. The gladiators in the main event were Tommy Loughran who had held the world light-heavyweight championship for two years before resigning it, undefeated, to campaign in the more lucrative heavyweight division, and Tommy Farr, who some eighteen months later was to gain imperishable fame by going the full fifteen rounds against the matchless Joe Louis for the heavyweight championship of the world.

After all these years I hope Tommy Farr will forgive me but if I were on my deathbed and under oath I would still swear that Loughran won that fight. So you can imagine my round-by-round story, each round telephoned in to be in time for the early editions going to outlying districts: 'Loughran's round . . . Loughran's round . . . Even round . . . Farr's round . . . Loughran's round . . . Loughran's round . . . Loughran's round . . .' and so on. Finally 'Loughran lands a left, and another. Farr comes boring in as he has throughout the fight but the final bell halts his advance. Loughran's round.'

Man on the other end of the telephone: 'Pretty easy for Loughran, eh?'

Me: 'Oh, sure. Just wait a second for the official verdict.'

At this stage the referee Wilfred Smith, also officiating at his first big fight, finished adding up his card and turned towards Loughran's corner. As he did so Ted Broadribb, Farr's manager, bounced up in the Welshman's corner and, in my opinion, delivered himself of the greatest whopper since Ananias came unstuck. He said, did Broadribb: 'Well done, Tommy!' He went on, Broadribb did: 'You won every round, Tommy.' He concluded, did Ted Broadribb: 'I didn't know you could be so great; you skated it!'

I was smiling tolerantly, thinking there's no tax on trying, when, to my horror, I saw the effect of Broadribb's wicked words on Wilfred Smith. The worried-looking little man had halted his advance towards the American's corner. He looked at his score card again. He seemed to shake his head and perhaps make some adjustment to the card. Then he about-turned, marched to Farr's corner and raised his glove in token of victory.

Through the earpiece of my telephone came the plaintive voice of the man dealing with my story: 'Well, come on – give us the verdict so that I can get this away.' I sat numbly, I choked. I croaked: 'Tommy Farr won on points.'

'*What?*' screamed an anguished voice, 'but you said . . . I've sent the headline up. . . . I've even written out the bills [posters] . . . you only gave Farr . . .'

'I know . . . it was all Ted Broadribb's fault. . . .' I hung up; and wondered what the hell I was going to say in my rewrite. And how soon it would be before they had me back 'inside' again. But they were very decent about it – after a time. And I was allowed to keep the boxing job. As it transpired out of evil came good – for Tommy Farr. His rise subsequently was meteoric.

It's one of my great regrets that I never saw Farr against Louis; I had been to the States two months earlier to see Louis win the title from game Jim Braddock and in those days you just didn't go to America twice in one year – or, at least, I didn't! But, years afterwards, I was interviewing Tommy on the radio and inevitably his epic stand against the 'Brown Bomber' came up. Farr looked at me with that quizzical glance of which he is a master and said: 'I just wish you'd stop writing about him, Peter *bach*. Even twenty years later I've only got to read his name and my nose starts bleeding again!'

Some critics, more patriotic than accurate, tried to pretend that Farr had been 'robbed'; never Tommy. And, surely, better to be a good and honest loser than a cheating winner.

What a year 1936 turned out to be. At the end of January I was married. We went on our honeymoon by liner (the *Oronsay*, was it?) to Majorca – an island with which I have had a love affair ever since. Don't believe people when they say everything has gone up in price. I have a programme of the pelota matches (something, but not very, like rackets) played in Palma in February 1936. Entrance was one peseta – in those days about sixpence. Today it's free! It's difficult to believe that the Majorca of those days was the same island as today's. There were only a handful of hotels outside the centre of Palma. I remember we went to Puerto Pollensa and when I turned on the hotel shower all that came down were three rather hairy spiders.

Robert Graves, the distinguished writer, had already been in Majorca for some six or seven years. He still lives at Deyá.

We lived in a tiny house in Peel Street, off Kensington Church Street. It was clearly a workman's converted cottage, for you had to go through the kitchen to get to the minuscule bathroom. At the other end of what is quite a short street there were still tenement-style 'buildings'. But our little house, which I imagine had been recently renovated, was bright and 'smart' – which meant a lot when you were still only twenty-two and the world was young and gay.

I was making ten guineas a week from the *Mirror* and an additional four guineas from a now defunct magazine, *Everybody's Weekly*, for which I did a sub-editing stint about three times a week and to which I also contributed anonymously. My wife had about £200 a year of her own so altogether we had nearly £1000 a year. If you could not live regally on that you could be very comfortable, thank you. Admittedly we had a pensioned retainer of my wife's family, who lived at the 'wrong' end of the street – our house was too small for her to 'sleep in' – and she cleaned the house, did much of the laundry and saved us a small fortune with her exquisite needlework.

But . . . we were able to holiday abroad, almost luxuriously; we ate and drank well, both at home and in restaurants; I seem to remember that Le Train Bleu was one of our favourites. It is now, I think, Le Coq d'Or. In the heart of Piccadilly Circus, almost next to the old Criterion, there used to be the Brasserie Universelle, a huge (was it underground?) restaurant where you could get a most satisfying 'dish of the day' for a shilling and a glass of Pilsner Urquell for fivepence. A threepenny tip was not disdained.

A little later we contemplated buying a very racy white – or was it scarlet? – SS car; the forerunner of today's Jaguars. It was barely a year old and was supposed to have done only 5000 miles. Price? £70. It was all a long way from four years previously when, greatly daring, I had asked my mother – who had handled all our meagre money – if I could have a pound with which to take out a girl, only to be informed sternly that I must learn the value of money and not forget that the shadow of the workhouse was perpetually hanging over us. As I was then working just about as hard as I could – three guineas for about 1700 words – the threat of the workhouse did not have quite the effect my mother intended.

But back to Fleet Street. And what a great time it was to be a young sportswriter given the freedom of Britain's pitches, rings, courts and courses.

Flat racing never appealed very much to me but I had already been introduced to the Grand National which, for most of the next thirty-five years, was to fascinate me. I didn't see the great race that year of 1936, which was a pity for it was the last time that the same horse – on this occasion Reynoldstown, ridden by an old friend of my wife's, Fulke Walwyn – was to win on two consecutive occasions until Red Rum's triumph.

I had seen Reynoldstown win the previous year when the greatest steeplechaser I ever did see, Golden Miller, unseated his jockey Gerry Wilson. In those days, before the fences were modified, you used to be able to get 3–1 against any horse completing the course; yet that year it was only 2–1 against 'The Miller' *winning!*

Then there were the 1935–6 All Blacks New Zealand Rugby touring side to thrill you. They lost only three of their twenty-eight matches, being beaten 11–3 by Swansea in their fifth match and losing 12–13 to Wales and 0–13 to England in two of the last three matches of the tour.

When the All Blacks lost at Twickenham in 1936 it was their first defeat on English soil. But it took more than Englishmen to beat them. The chief architect of their downfall was a Russian, Prince Alexander Obolensky, who had been born twenty years earlier in Petrograd, the son of an officer of the Tsar's Imperial Horse Guards. Although Alex, whom I knew well at the time, was later to be killed during a training flight while he was serving with the RAF, he had not then been naturalized and there was a somewhat awkward exchange between him and the Prince of Wales – later Edward VIII – who before the match asked him what his qualifications were for representing England.

All 'Obo' could stammer was something about being a student at Oxford. He was certainly that, for he had already scored against the All Blacks while playing for the Dark Blues, helping Oxford to come precious close to beating them. But that was as nothing to his performance at Twickenham when the second of his two tries ranks among the greatest ever scored. He first hesitated, then drew the defence, and from the right wing three-quarter position cut diagonally across to touch down wide of the left-hand post, running like an Olympic 100 metres gold medallist all the way.

Nor was that the end of our 'foreign aid', for at full-back there was 'Tuppy' Owen-Smith who had previously played for his own country, South Africa, at cricket and actually captained England against Scotland the first time England won at Murrayfield, when he got his tenth and last Rugby cap in 1937; he was also an Oxford boxing blue and a more-than-useful lawn-tennis player.

Back to boxing and on my first visit to Liverpool for a championship fight I saw Jack 'Kid' Berg lose his British lightweight title to Jimmy Walsh, of Chester.

But what was really memorable about the evening was meeting two of the finest men I ever encountered through boxing. The first drove me to the Liverpool Stadium; he was Jack Hutchinson, later to be my sports editor on the *Mirror* for over fifteen years and one of the most honourable men I ever met in Fleet Street. The second was the promoter of the fight, Johnny Best. Never has a man been better named. Despite spending his life among some of the most malodorous characters who have ever befouled sport Johnny Best *was* undefiled by the pitch.

Then it was Wimbledon time again – and three in a row for Fred Perry, the first time this had happened since before the First World War when Tony Wilding pulled it off from 1910–13; but that was not really comparable, for in those days the holder did not have to play through the tournament but stood aside, defending his title only in the Challenge Round. Perry's feat has not yet been duplicated and what is even more depressing is that apart from 1938, when Bunny Austin was beaten even more decisively by Don Budge than he had been by Ellsworth Vines, no British player has even reached the final since!

The final itself was desperately disappointing. Perry won 6–1, 6–1, 6–0 against the man whom he had beaten in the final the year before, Baron Gottfried von Cramm of Germany. At the end the umpire, having called the final score, said to the crowd: 'I have been asked to announce that Baron von Cramm pulled a muscle in his thigh in his first service game, and he much regrets that he was not able to play better.' No one thought that the injury had affected the eventual result; but it certainly ruined the match as a spectacle.

Otherwise it was one of the most successful Wimbledons for years as far as home players were concerned. All four finalists in the men's doubles were British: Pat Hughes and Raymond Tuckey beat Charles Hare and Frank Wilde; Freda James and Kay Stammers retained their women's doubles title, as did Perry and Dorothy Round in the mixed. The only title to go overseas was the women's singles – and the victory of that perpetual runner-up, Helen Jacobs, of the USA, was about as popular as if she had been British. I go into such detail only because we have never again approached such success even though more than forty years have passed.

Nor was this the end of our triumphs, for less than four weeks later we had retained the Davis Cup by beating the Australians 3–2 in the Challenge Round – Perry, inevitably, winning the fifth, final and decisive rubber by beating Jack Crawford 6–2, 6–3, 6–3. I cannot remember seeing Perry play better than he did on that July afternoon in 1936, and it was fitting that he should have done so for not only did it mean that Britain, which he had served so well, kept the Cup for another year but it was to be his last appearance on the Centre Court. Later that year he turned professional and according to the stultifying rules of that era – which were to persist for more than thirty years – he was accordingly debarred from the lawns at Wimbledon and from any competition against so-called amateurs anywhere else in the world.

Immediately after that triumphant Davis Cup Challenge Round (needless to say the last one in which Britain has figured) came easily the most impressive sporting occasion of my life up to then. The XIth Olympic Games of the modern era, held in Berlin then, of course, the capital of a unified Germany.

My first story from Berlin, which appeared on 1 August 1936, began: 'After having been nearly struck by lightning while flying somewhere over Hanover yesterday ...' Flying itself was a distinct adventure nearly forty years ago. I think we took off from Croydon and I'm sure we flew in a German plane. I know that we flew very low, and later it was said that the German pilots, later to become Luftwaffe aces, made a practice of this in order to familiarize themselves with the topography of southern England, and particularly London.

It seems unbelievable now but in those days civilian planes even had a special smoking compartment. When the urge for a cigarette became overwhelming you went into a small cabin – I can't remember whether it held two or four – shut off from the rest of the plane, and solemnly smoked your weed. There was nothing inflammable in this cabin, no curtains to the portholes, and the seats of uncovered aluminium to which one grew wretchedly accustomed later in transport planes during the war. When you had finished smoking there was bound to be a rap on the sliding door, with its glass panel, indicating that another addict wanted to steady his nerves against the rigours of flying in the thirties – as soon as you got out to make room for him.

It is almost impossible to recreate the atmosphere of a world which, please God, has vanished for ever. What you have to remember is that the Olympic Games of those days were far more remote than the modern festivals. Surprisingly enough there *was* television but it was confined to Germany. Berlin, however, was close enough to Britain, and in the same time zone, to allow you to report what happened in front of you one night and know that it could appear a few hours later.

The difficulty was that many of us couldn't quite comprehend not so much what we were seeing but the whole ambience which affected, or afflicted, all our senses. The eyes were bedazzled by more banners than I have seen before or since, flags of all the nations, the Olympic emblem with its five rings symbolic of the continents but, of course, above all, in both senses of the phrase, the red, white and black standard with its crooked cross – the swastika, sign of the Nazis, either hated or feared by so much of the outside world. The ears were deafened by loudspeakers as inescapable in the Unter den Linden as in the stadium itself. The slogan of the XIth Olympiad seemed to be a raucous, metallic *Achtung* whether to prepare you for another muscular German triumph or to warn you to keep off the grass.

The constant press of tens of thousands of bodies all around you, day after day, led to a suspicion and an almost pathological dislike of sweaty crowds, inevitably overwhelmingly German. Again it must be remembered that although there were, of course, huge crowds at football matches in Britain these were limited to a few hours once a week. These Berlin crowds seemed as though they would never come to an end. They also smelled strange – as, indeed, does any major assembly of almost any nation except your own – presumably because of dietary differences. Towards the end of the Games you could nearly *taste* the crowds.

In later years I have visited or stayed in various countries where there was a dictatorship of the right or the left, but never have I felt as I felt in Berlin in the August of 1936. In the street the uniformed Germans were almost unbelievably arrogant, 'bouncing' you off the pavement if their group outnumbered yours. Inevitably we began to anticipate these collisions and would 'bounce' back as powerfully as we could. Time after time it was touch and go – literally – whether a free fight broke out between the rival factions.

It was not difficult to find in the bookshops and kiosks the most primitive and revolting anti-Semitic books with illustrations of Jews who would have made Cruikshank's Fagin look like a knight in shining armour. I confess it was malice, and detestation of what the Germany of those days stood for, that used to make me pick up some of them and ask in execrable German what the words said and what was the purpose of producing and selling something so ugly which seemed to have nothing to do with any life I had experienced. The embarrassment of the wretched vendors was well worth the time wasted.

Even when you were off-duty – and at the Olympic Games that is a rare occurrence for a journalist – you could not get away from the feeling of constant surveillance, even if it was only by pictures in hotel lounges, bars, restaurants, anywhere you were likely to congregate, of that ubiquitous trio, Adolf Hitler, Hermann Goering and Josef Goebbels. The sleazy threesome prompted one of the most popular anti-Nazi slogans of that time: 'What should the perfect example of Aryan manhood look like? Blond, like Hitler, slim, like Goering and tall, like Goebbels.' It is easy, of course, to say that in the tense atmosphere which any Games engender you can imagine incidents and patterns of behaviour. But there was more to it than that.

The supreme irony of these racialist Games was the success of the American Negro athletes and, particularly of one – James Cleveland Owens, who got the name Jesse from a combination of the initial letters of his Christian names.

It's difficult to describe what Owens was like when he was sprinting for he was like no other sprinter I ever saw; perhaps Bobby Morrow was the nearest approach, in sheer grace, to the wonderful 'Black Arrow'. Twenty years later, at the Melbourne Games, Morrow clipped a tenth of a second off Owens' time for the 200 metres but was still two tenths of a second slower than Owens in the 100 metres dash. Moreover, although Morrow appeared in the winning US 4 × 100 metres relay, as did Owens, the white American did not essay the long jump in which Owens' world record of 26 ft 8¼ in, which he put up in May 1935, stood for just over a quarter of a century before Ralph Boston added a scant three inches to it. Owens' Olympic record at 26 ft 0½ in, which he set up in Berlin, endured until the Games in Rome in 1960.

It sounds ridiculous but Owens' legs never seemed to be coming down on to the cinder track, always lifting from it. I got the impression that I would not mind his spikes running over my body as they didn't seem as though they would inflict any punctures. He was like some athletic fakir passing unscorched along a trough of glowing ashes. He was also handsome in an uncomplicated way, his face scarcely distorting even in the throes of the most desperate competition, and he had the most perfect body of any track and field athlete I ever watched.

What Hitler thought of it all we can only guess; there have been many excuses or explanations for his failure to greet some of the black winners in the same way as he did the 'Aryans', particularly the Germans. (It was said that Hans Wollke, a German policeman who won the shot putt on the first day, went to Hitler's box for congratulations and left it three ranks higher in the police force than when he entered it.) Certainly the Führer did not wait for the end of the high jump, also on the first day, which was won by Cornelius Johnson with the silver medal going to David Albritton – both of whom were American Negroes. While most of the rest of the competitors eliminated themselves at heights below the dignity – or at least the capabilities – of the two black men, Johnson and Albritton had relaxed in their track suits shooting craps on the grass infield (unless my eyes and my binoculars deceived me). I think Richard D. Mandell gives the answer in *The Nazi Olympics* (Souvenir Press, £2·50, 1972), when he cites the Nazi youth leader Baldur von Schirach as quoting Hitler that 'The Americans ought to be ashamed of themselves for letting their medals be won by Negroes. I myself would never even shake hands with one of them.'

Things came to a head when Goebbels' newspaper *Der Angriff* ('The Attack') referred to Negroes, regarded as subhuman and therefore not to be classed as Americans, as 'black auxiliaries' of the US team. That was red-hot news in any language, and Mackenzie Porter, covering the news side of the Games for the *Mirror*, and I, made sure that the *Daily Mirror* got a full report of it. The consequences were almost immediate.

Obviously the views of foreign papers, particularly British ones whose opinions could be expected to express the outlook of the British people which Hitler was then trying to gauge, were of consuming interest to the Nazis at this period. No doubt anything we wrote on racial topics, for example, would be cabled back to Berlin. Certainly there was a reaction in this case.

Shortly after the 'black auxiliaries' story I came back to my hotel, unexpectedly, at lunchtime. We were staying in the Excelsior, then, I believe, the largest hotel in Europe, although not as grand as the Adlon and the Kaiserhof in Berlin. I went up to my room, opened the door and found everything in the most appalling disorder and a small, weaselly man *in flagrante delicto*. A kind of Keystone Cops chase then ensued around the room. I was younger and, I think, stronger. In the end nippiness prevailed, for just as I was about to collar him he pulled a chair in front of my legs . . . and base over apex went I.

By the time I got up he was out of the room and out of sight down a long corridor. Fuming with rage, I went down to the desk where the hall porter, like so many in the bigger European hotels, seemed to be equally at home in half a dozen languages, one of which certainly had been English. But when I made my complaint clear suddenly he became brick thick and we had the old routine of 'No spik English'. I left it, for it was clearly useless to pursue the affair; but two or three days later I got three letters from England, which I had read and left in my room, posted back to me at the Excelsior with German stamps on the envelope. Fortunately for me they were all completely innocuous; not like the one which I had written to my wife vouching that in three years' time we would be at war with Germany. It was typical of them to make me a liar by a month!

Of course, not all the incidents were grim, gloomy or infuriating. Some of our few off-duty hours – the early hours of the mornings – were inevitably spent in night-clubs, and one in particular, the Femina. (The atmosphere of this and similar establishments was afterwards brilliantly captured by Christopher Isherwood whom I met briefly later.) The great attraction of the Femina was that the tables, which had illuminated numbers on them, were also furnished with white telephones. The idea was obvious: if some unattached young lady caught your eye you could dial – yes, they had dials that long ago – her table number and invite her to join you.

Another humorous break in the frenetic excitement of the various events, and the almost palpable feeling of oppression engendered by the spirit of Nazism which brooded over the Berlin Games, was provided by, of all people, Hitler.

I was at the swimming stadium one day watching the usual succession of American and Japanese victories and, in some astonishment, the then brand-new butterfly stroke. Suddenly my attention was distracted as a wave of dismay swept through the swimming crowd. Somehow, unbelievably, a large, middle-aged woman, clad all in black – she was, truth to tell, a forerunner of that famous poster of later years, 'Keep Death Off The Roads' – had wormed her way through the crowds, and the perpetual bodyguard which always surrounded Hitler, and had thrown herself upon him with her arms around his neck.

I do not think I have ever heard a moan like the one which swept the crowd as a breeze sends a cornfield swaying. For a moment I think everyone believed that the impossible – but the event so longed for by so many people – had happened and that Hitler had been assassinated by being stabbed in the back.

A dozen hands wrenched the woman away – and Hitler's normally putty-coloured face went poppy red. There was a vast smear of lipstick on one of his cheeks.

Later it was said that she was an American woman, slightly deranged, to whom Hitler represented God on high. A sequel was the persistent rumour that some of the guards had been shot and others sent to a concentration camp for dereliction of duty. But Berlin was like that – full of rumours, mostly sinister, all uncheckable because of the constantly obstructive SS men.

After all these years only two track and field events, apart from Owens' exploits, remain tattooed on my memory. They were the 1500 metres – in some ways the blue riband of Olympic track races – and the marathon. I think the Berlin 1500 was one of the four most memorable track races I have ever seen, possibly one of the two best, conceivably *the* best. It had everything.

At the bell Ny, of Sweden, who had finished fifth in the 1932 Los Angeles Games made his final effort with the barrel-chested American, Glen Cunningham, lying second, Lovelock third and Luigi Beccali, the Italian who had put up the Olympic record of 3 mins 51·2 secs at Los Angeles, in fourth place. It was obvious that the winner would come from this quartet.

But no one could have foreseen how easily Lovelock, clearly discernible in the black vest of New Zealand, was to handle the opposition when he pulled out all his stops on the final back straight. Ny had already faded like last summer's tan but with some 300 yards to go it was as though Lovelock was unfolding himself telescopically, as far as his legs were concerned. With the irresistible surge that all great middle distance runners must have, he finished so effortlessly that his fair, curly hair lay like some light banner without a thread disturbed.

Old statistics are apt to bore but it's worth recording that Lovelock's time of 3 mins. 47·8 secs clipped a whole second off the then world record, held by the American Bill Bonthron; that Cunningham, who finished over five yards behind Lovelock, also beat the world record and Beccali, who got the bronze medal, ran two full seconds faster than he had to win the gold four years earlier.

Incidentally, the Berlin race produced one of the more memorable BBC running commentaries when Harold Abrahams – the only British runner ever to win the Olympic 100 metres sprint, in Paris in 1924 – forgot all about the tradition of neutrality as he saw his friend Lovelock poised for victory. As a Jew, Abrahams had been strongly criticized in some circles for having anything to do with the Berlin Olympics which were so blatantly anti-Semitic, but he forgot everything in the latter stages of the race and may, indeed, have forgotten that he was broadcasting as he shouted excitedly something like: 'Come on, Jack. You can win! You've got 'em! You can do it! By God! You can do it! Come on, Jack, come on, come on!'

I bet it made a fine commentary; there can be too many of the bloodless, over-controlled, stiff-upper-lip performances.

Finally the marathon. In 1936 Ernie Harper might well have brought it off for Britain had it not been for the camaraderie which exists between marathon runners. For afterwards Harper, the oldest man in the race, told me how he had gestured to Kitei Son, the Korean-born winner, not to pursue Carlos Zabala, the Argentinian who had won four years earlier and who set out at a terrific clip so that he was leading the Englishman and Son by a minute at the halfway stage. Sure enough at just under twenty miles Zabala 'blew up', and it was then that Son, who on Harper's advice had husbanded his strength, was able to step up the pace and win from his mentor.

Son was to say later that he had not needed any advice but I was particularly glad when, before the 1972 Olympic Games at Munich, I 'dubbed' some commentary on to the greatest Olympic film ever made, Leni Riefenstahl's *Olympia*, to see that the film showed Son and Harper running together and apparently talking – certainly the Sheffield star was gesturing to his companion to slow it down.

Only one more incident. In those days there was a more genuine innocence about the deviations of sex, though one woman sprinter certainly looked so peculiar that there were whispered queries on the lines of 'he, she or it'. But I do remember the genuine shock with which an American newspaperwoman, who had got a pass to visit the women athletes' section of the Olympic village, returned and told me how she had gone to see one girl and, coming in unexpectedly, had found the star shaving her face. Since then, of course, the tragedy of the half-and-halfs has become a widespread topic among athletes and in newspapers, and the problem of lesbianism has, unfortunately, become almost accepted in certain sports, notably lawn tennis. But as I have said there was a more general innocence in the prewar era.

Then, for the first of eight times, I saw the Olympic flame quenched after the summer Games in what remains one of the most moving ceremonies in sport, and flying back by night to London I saw, also for the first time, the great city lit up from the air. Nowadays it's an exception to find anyone who hasn't flown, but to us it was magic to see clusters of lights, diamond white contrasting with ropes of rubies and curving jade scimitars.

Even with the Olympic Games ended there was no break in daily journalism. The Berlin extravaganza was over on the Sunday and on the Monday I was at the ringside, on the Tigers' Rugby football ground at Leicester, to see South African born Ben Foord become the first overseas boxer to win the British heavyweight title by thrashing Jack Petersen, that gallant Welshman, so severely that the referee had to intervene in the third round. As an indication of how sporting values change, journalistically speaking, my story of the Foord–Petersen fight 'led' the paper, starting on the front page and turning to the back – the first time I had achieved such a distinction – and getting considerably more space than any of my Olympic reports.

So, having seen us retain the Davis Cup, having reported on the most tainted Games of modern times and seen the first and only South African ever to win the most famous prize in British boxing I came to the end of the most exciting three and a half weeks I had so far experienced. I was still ten days short of my twenty-third birthday.

Obviously it was difficult for the rest of the year to live up to this banquet of sport but there were still out-of-the-ordinary events to recall.

Boxing produced some of them. I covered my first world title fight as a journalist – although I had seen others earlier – when the greatest flyweight I ever watched, that dour, scarred Scot Benny Lynch, knocked out a game Londoner, Pat Palmer, in eight rounds with an eight-inch body punch which would not have disgraced a featherweight.

Finally there was the light-heavyweight championship of the world at Wembley between the holder, American Negro John Henry Lewis, who retained his title fairly decisively, and that master tactician, Len Harvey.

More memorable than the fight itself was the fact that I imagine it was the only time that a man had acted as matchmaker – and also 'topped the bill'. Arthur Elvin, the genius, albeit sometimes a surly one, behind Wembley, had enough nous to know that he stood no chance against some of the 'corkscrew' characters who, then as now, infested the fight game. He made the clever move of appointing Harvey, as shrewd outside the ring as he was clever in it, to be the matchmaker for the Empire Pool, Wembley. And the first match Harvey made was himself against Lewis for the world cruiserweight chmapionship. He didn't win. But it was a dam' good try.

If 1936 had been wonderfully varied, one event dominated 1937 for me. It was my first trip to the USA – and the first time for twenty-two years that a Negro had been given the chance to win the richest prize in sport – the heavyweight championship of the world. Now a *café-au-lait* coloured box-fighter, christened Joseph Louis Barrow, but always known as Joe Louis, born on a dirt farm at Lafayette, Alabama, was to get the chance denied to such stalwarts as Sam Langford, Joe Jeannette, Sam McVey and Harry Wills, all of whom had just two defects in the eyes of the white men who controlled boxing – the colour of their skins and the fact that they were too good.

Louis was going to meet Jim Braddock, a sometime longshoreman in New Jersey, who had been christened the 'Cinderella Man' by Damon Runyon in his sportswriting days, because Braddock had come back from being on 'relief' – the American equivalent of the dole – during the depression years, to beat Max Baer for the world title.

In fact, even then Louis might not have got his chance had it not been for the hatred with which the Nazis were held by the Jews of New York, who numbered more than those in Jerusalem! Louis, making one of his very, very few mistakes in the ring had, in 1936, taken the challenge of the veteran German, Max Schmeling, too lightly and had been knocked out in twelve rounds – the only time he was beaten while he was the real Joe Louis.

Schmeling had been matched with Braddock and actually weighed in and turned up in his boxing kit in an empty stadium to try to lay claim to the title. But the leading promoter of the day was Mike Jacobs and apart from his own natural loathing of what was happening to his fellow Jews in Hitler's Germany he realized that there would be a boycott by New York Jews of any fight involving Schmeling, then regarded as a standard bearer in the myth of 'Aryan' supremacy.

The New York State Athletic Commission, the governing body of boxing in the Empire State, was adamant that they would not recognize any fight for the world heavyweight title which did not include Max Schmeling, the German who had held the championship from 1930 to 1932. But Jacobs had an answer to that one. He matched Braddock with Louis and shifted the venue from New York to Chicago.

This then was the fight which was to be my introduction to the United States which, apart from the years 1940–6 I was to visit at least once annually, and usually much more often than that, up to 1972. I crossed

45

on the *Queen Mary*, that superlative ship where, particularly in prewar years, the comfort and service were unsurpassed. On board was Izzy Kline, returning to America after training ex-world heavyweight champion Max Baer for his two London fights against Tommy Farr, to whom he lost, and Ben Foord, whom he knocked out. Izzy, who was then living in Chicago, took me under his wing and made my path much easier by the number of introductions he gave me in the Windy City.

But before I got to Chicago I broke my journey in New York: that was typical of the more leisurely pace of journalism. I had been cosseted in the depth of luxury's most capacious lap for some four days on the *Queen Mary* but there was no objection by the paper to my taking a look round what is, the first time you see it, the most exciting city in the world.

New York was such a kaleidoscope of utterly foreign experience that most of it has become blurred with the years; indeed, that complete foreignness is, I believe, the keynote of a first visit to the USA, certainly to New York. I had already visited half a dozen or so European countries but despite not being able to speak a word of the language in some of them I had never felt myself so amid the alien corn as I did that first time in New York.

One thing I regret to this day. Jack Johnson was appearing in some sideshow at Coney Island and, like the inexperienced fool that I was, I didn't ask the famous old pugilist (then in his sixtieth year but looking a decade younger – he won a 15-round fight in Mexico when he was forty-eight!) what he thought of Joe Louis having broken the colour bar for which Johnson had been so largely responsible. Actually I was told later that Johnson expressed himself as not being too impressed with the young 'Brown Bomber'. This was felt to be the understandable jealousy of the veteran for the young lion, but when Johnson offered to pass on some of his matchless skills and technique to the fledgling Negro his offer was firmly, almost brutally, declined by the shrewd men behind Louis – John Roxborough, a sometime operator of the 'numbers game', a lottery popular among the poor, and Julian Black, a suave lawyer. They were both Negroes themselves and they wanted no part of the bad old Johnson image to tarnish the youngster who was to achieve, perhaps more than any other single individual, a harmony, at that time, in race relationships. And how it was needed.

Chicago was a real eye-opener. In 1937 the most notorious times of the gangsters were just past with Al Capone, the most infamous, already in jail for, of all cynical reasons, income tax evasion. It was like jailing Hitler for spitting on the pavement. But 'Chi' was still a rough, tough, wide-open town. I was introduced to two detectives who seemed to be able to have unlimited time to point out the sights, sounds and smells – the stockyard – of Chicago.

I met Frank, the man who claimed to have acted as bodyguard to the Mayor of Chicago; I think that was the famous Mayor 'Big Bill' Thompson who once, for reasons which elude me, proclaimed: 'If King George V comes to Chicago I'll punch him in the snoot!' Frank was the only man I ever met who actually carried a pistol with notches in the butt. There were nineteen of them and each, so he swore, stood for a dead gangster: 'And none shot in the back,' he would proudly proclaim. Certainly when he stripped off his shirt he had more bullet scars on his body than a Bisley target! He said there was only one type of criminal of whom he was genuinely scared – the drug addict.

'Them junkies – you just can't tell with them,' he said. 'One moment they're talking with you, nice as pie. The next – bam! They're trying to blow your brains out or slice you up like salami.'

Drug addiction was, even then, one of the major problems for the police. I met one of the top men in the Chicago narcotics squad and he told me about marijuana, already a growing hazard for teenagers, particularly as it could be grown in a window box or a disused lot. They didn't call it 'pot' then; 'muggleweed' was its name, because the smokers were inclined to get muddled in time and spatial movements.

But even with the protection of my detectives, and despite the fact that the nadir of the gangster era had passed, you didn't, if you had any sense, go into places which you were warned not to visit. One such was very near my hotel and I was advised to steer clear of it because a crooked gambling game was held there. One night I came back, as usual in the early hours of the morning, to find a whey-faced night clerk shaking behind his desk and three or four men scrubbing away at the carpet in the hotel lobby.

I asked the clerk what had happened and he told me that one of the patrons at the gambling joint had made an unexpected 'killing' – only he didn't use that word! – owing to something going wrong with the crooked wheel. In a short time he won thousands of dollars and then, instead of staying where he was and losing back some of his winnings, he made a dash for it. He was chased into the hotel lobby by some of the hoodlums and, because even they weren't prepared to start a shooting match in those surroundings, they collared the poor wretch, reversed their pistols and beat his brains out all over the carpet, took the money from him and vanished into the night.

It was in this high, wide and sometimes-not-so-handsome setting that the world's heavyweight championship was held on 22 June 1937 at Comiskey Park, Chicago, home of the White Sox baseball team. When I visited the stadium on the afternoon of the fight I found preparations for squads of police, three hundred strong, trained in military formations, to be stationed at the four corners of the 'Black Belt' on Chicago's South Side.

In the event there was little trouble either during or after the fight. Apart from the first round when Braddock came off the ropes and landed a half-hook, half-uppercut with his right, to put Louis down for a couple of seconds, it was all very one-sided until the predictable knock-out. The right-hander to the jaw, with which Louis ended it in the eighth round, remains the hardest single punch I have ever seen one man land on another. I think Braddock, who was speechless in his dressing room afterwards while a tangle of shouting journalists tried to interview him, needed seventeen stitches in his face after that horrific blow.

Joe was quite unconcerned, expressing a wish only for a plenitude of 'frahd chickun' and a desire after that to sleep the clock round.

And Joe, having won comprehensively, caused virtually no trouble by his victory so that before long they were able to stop putting sequences of him in training at the end of the movie newsreels so that the bigots of the South could cut them off without harming the rest of the film.

I did not get to know him really well that time but on the five occasions that I watched him subsequently and during the countless times that we met afterwards, both in America and Europe, I got to admire this simple man as much as any athlete I have ever met in sport.

Of one thing you can always be certain. In the dressing room of every man who has just won the world heavyweight title there will be the moment when the victor says: 'I aim to be a real fighting champion!' Somehow as the months succeed each other the words tend to get blurred. Not so with Joe. Inside ten weeks he was in the ring again to take on our own Tommy Farr and of all the heavyweight title fights which have taken place in my time this was the one which I most regret not having seen. Unfortunately in those days, as I've said, it was virtually unheard of for anyone to go *twice* in one year to America; and I do admit how lucky I was to go when I was so young a journalist.

I heard the result of Farr's gutsy struggle against Joe Louis in the most peculiar circumstances – at about three o'clock in the morning, miles out to sea, on my way back from a holiday in Brittany, with a foghorn booming eerily as we nosed our way through a Channel fog and a steward moved among the figures sleeping in deckchairs giving the news to those who were still awake.

There were two more outstanding events before the end of the year – the greatest flyweight fight I ever saw and Stanley Matthews scoring a hat-trick in an international!

In most fights you can say that one man hasn't yet reached his best

Right 'The ghost with the hammer in his hand.' Jimmy Wilde (right) outpointing, over 20 rounds, at Olympia, London, in 1919, Pal Moore the only man who had ever beaten him on points — in a 3 round Services tournament.

Below The 'wee yin's' last fight. Benny Lynch (right) knocked out, while alcoholically unfit, in what was to be his last fight, by Aurel Toma, a former chauffeur to King Carol of Rumania. Lynch, supreme in his day, was 25.

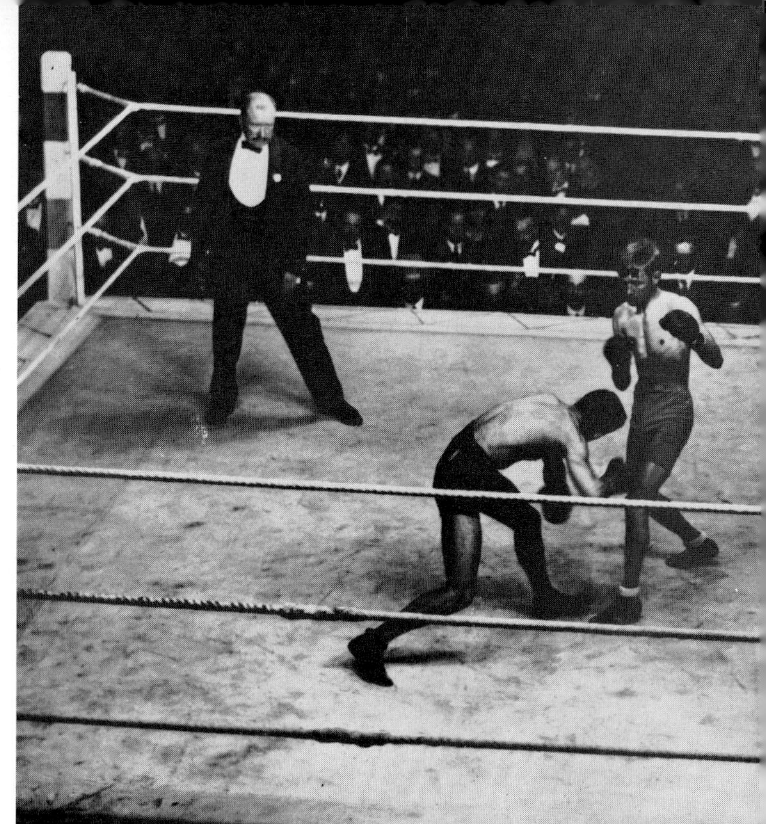

Above At 20 Helen Wills, later Mrs Moody, who was to win Wimbledon a record eight times, took part in perhaps the most famous singles match of all time, losing in two sets on the only occasion she met Suzanne Lenglen, at Cannes, in 1926.

Left The unique Suzanne Lenglen who brought the ballet to Wimbledon, and once won the singles there with the loss of only 5 games.

Opposite top left Golden Miller, the greatest horse I ever saw in the Grand National, winning the great steeplechase in 1934.

Opposite top right It all seems to be a different world: long trousers, shirt sleeves rolled down — yet there are those who still maintain that Bill Tilden was the best ever.

Opposite below At my favourite sporting centre in the world — overlooking the outside courts at Wimbledon.

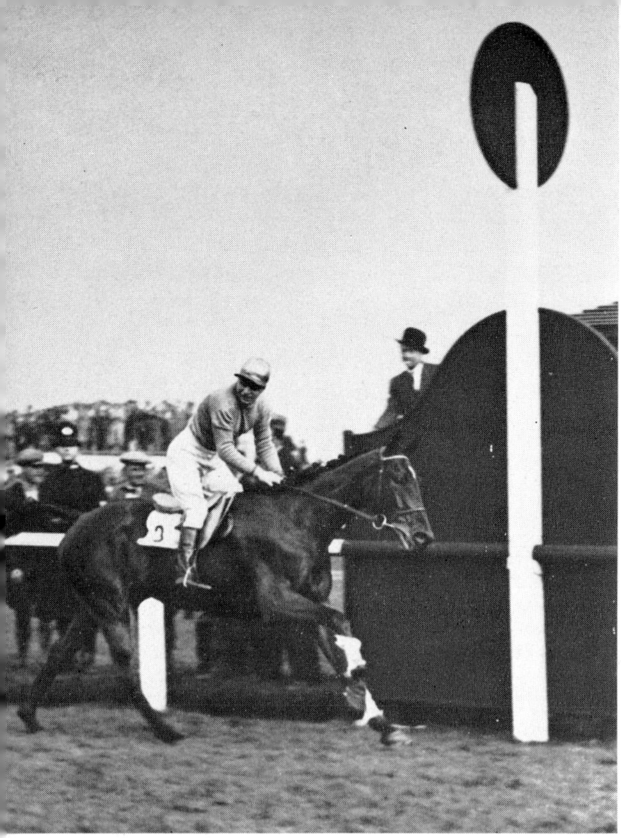

W.T. TILDEN
V
SETS

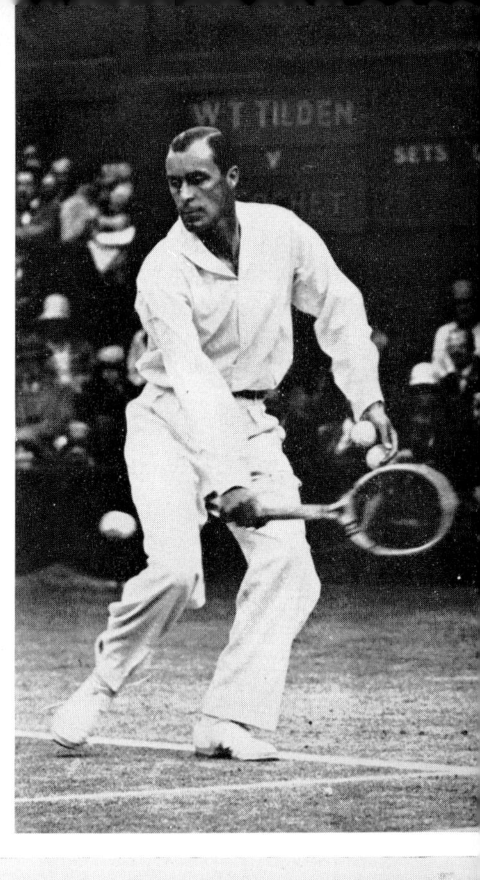

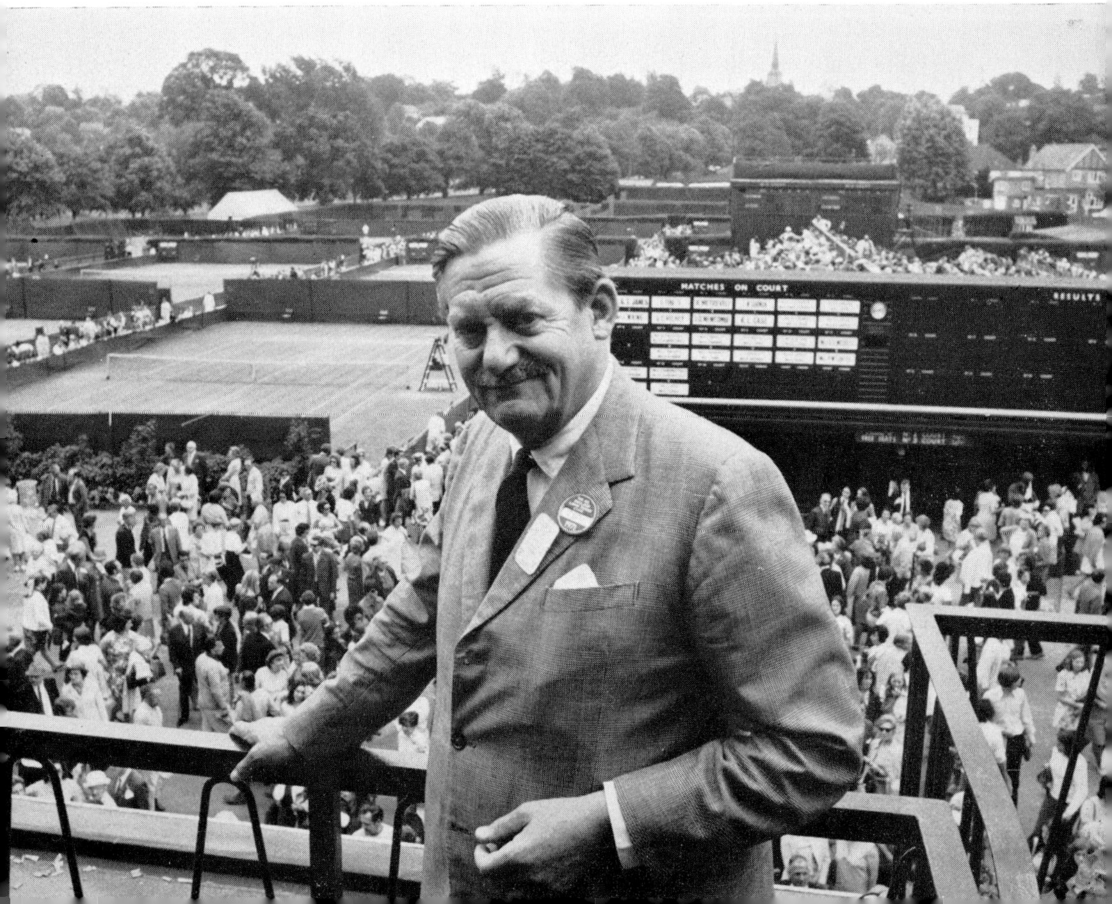
MATCHES ON COURT
RESULTS

Above If I had to pick the cricketer who gave me the most individual pleasure since I saw my first Test match in 1921. I think the choice would have to be that gayest of Cavaliers, Denis Compton.

Opposite top left A man whose back the Australians — and others — preferred to see. Sir Leonard Hutton whom I saw captaining the first team to recapture the Ashes in Australia after World War II.

Opposite top right The greatest run-making machine of all — Sir Donald Bradman dominating the final Test at the Oval in 1930, in which he made 232.

Opposite bottom left Thank Heavens he was pulling his punch! Joe Louis — definitely 'The Greatest' in my book — no matter what other mouths may say!

Opposite bottom right Fortunately Italy was out of World War II before I caught up with Primo Carnera who weighed more than any other world heavyweight champion.

Top The tenth — and 'out' — round for
Freddie Mills (left) just about to lose
his world light-heavyweight
championship to Joey Maxim.

Above The King is dying — Jersey Joe
Walcott out before he hits the canvas;
Rocky Marciano strides away as the
new world heavyweight champion.

Left Rocky Marciano punched so
hard that he used to break blood
vessels in his opponents' arms and
so bring their defence down. Roland
La Starza is the victim here.

Right Triumph at last! Gordon Richards winning the Derby in 1953 on Pinza. He was in his fiftieth year and was soon to be knighted by the Queen whose horse, Aureole, he had beaten into second place.

Below Colonel Harry Llewellyn and Foxhunter in Rome, two years after they had helped to save our Olympic bacon at Helsinki in 1952.

Above A quarter of a century or so ago — but I think Reg Harris has lasted the years better.

Left With two of the real 'greats'; Stanley Matthews, England's finest footballer, and Donald Campbell, one of sport's bravest men.

Top left The most harrowing sight I can recall in a lifetime of watching sport: Jim Peters possessed by the twin demons of exhaustion and dehydration, failing by 220 yards to finish the Vancouver marathon in 1954, although 15 minutes ahead of the next man.

Top centre Herb Elliott, the lonely eagle from Western Australia – and the greatest miler I ever saw.

Top right The majestic Ron Clarke, holder of innumerable world records, overshadows Naftali Temu. But it was the Kenyan who won the 10,000 metres in the 1968 Olympic Games.

Left Three world champions: Emil Zatopek, world record holder (3,000, 5,000 metres and 6 miles), Gordon Pirie (5,000 metres and 6 miles), and Derek Ibbotson, 1 mile world record holder.

or that his opponent is 'over the top'. When you get two boxers nearly at their peak at the same time, the contest is likely to be truly memorable. So it was with the Scot, Benny Lynch, who had confirmed his undisputed right to the world 8 st title by beating the American champion, Small Montana, earlier in the year. It's true that his adversary at Shawfield Park, Glasgow, Peter Kane, was not yet twenty, but they began earlier in those tougher days and he had had forty-one professional fights without a loss.

These were still the days of the 'hungry thirties' and the Glasgow police, particularly the mounted ones, used tougher tactics with the fans than I have ever seen from British police, before or since. Some of the crowd, obviously accustomed to this sort of thing, reacted when the police set their horses at them in a canter by bringing the unfortunate animals down, hoofs threshing, by throwing ball bearings into the roadway!

In the end Lynch's man's strength and ferocious punching – when he was fit he could hit as hard as a good featherweight – gradually wore the boyish Kane down, and after nearly pitching through the ropes into my lap he was finally counted out, on one knee, his back turned to the ring, in the thirteenth round. The ring was invaded by a platoon of fight-crazy supporters who 'chaired' Lynch from the middle of the football ground where the ring was pitched, back to the dressing room. He was twenty-four, champion of the world, the king of Glasgow.

Who could possibly guess that he was to have only six more fights? When he had that last pathetic 'fight' he was exactly twenty-five and a half. Less than eight years later he was dead.

I knew the doctor in attendance at Lynch's last fight. He had wanted to prevent him from going into the ring because the Scot was drunk! But the promoter threatened to sue the doctor if he did not pass Lynch, and as the boxer, after cramming down caffeine tablets, was able to walk a chalk line and touch his nose with his eyes closed – the standard tests for drunkenness in those days – the medico passed him.

I saw Lynch about seven weeks before he died when he was at the Glasgow ringside to see his fellow Scot, Jackie Paterson, outpoint Joe Curran in defence of the world title which Lynch had once held. 'Wee Benny' was now a bloated old-young man, weighing nearer 11 st than the trim 8 st he had been in his prime. The scar on the right side of his cheek which used to glow so lividly during the heat of a fight was now obscured by the criss-cross of premature wrinkles. Lynch's inevitable defeat by drink was one of the worst tragedies I remember in boxing, for although he could be a villain outside the ring – they said that when he couldn't afford sparring partners he used to go to a Catholic area in Glasgow and bellow 'To hell with the Pope', thereafter getting all the free fighting he wanted, and it was said the scar on his face came from a broken bottle – yet this little man, evil in drink, seemed to don an inherent sportsmanship and even a gentlemanly dignity once he entered the ring.

One incident I shall never forget. It was when he was boxing Small Montana to establish himself, world-wide, as the undisputed flyweight champion. In the latter rounds Montana was making up a lot of the leeway and Lynch must have known there was little in it. Suddenly Montana slipped and his head and shoulders became trapped between the top and middle ropes. He was wide open and, according to the rules, there was nothing to prevent Lynch from pressing home his attack. Instead he stepped forward, disentangled Montana, helped him back into the boxing area and shook hands with him before resuming the fight.

The little man couldn't keep to the rules outside the ring but never broke them inside it. . . .

Even with quite keen soccer fans you can win bets that Sir Stanley Matthews, the prince of wingers, never scored a hat-trick in an international. But he did – and I was there to see it on 1 December 1937. It was against Czechoslovakia and it was played at the Spurs ground, White Hart Lane, which towards the end, because of a late kick-off, became so dark that the heading on my piece read: 'Spot the Ball at Black Hart Lane'.

In his book *Feet First* (Ewen and Dale Ltd, 10s. 6d., 1948), Matthews writes: 'What was my greatest game?' As this was published in 1948 it does not, of course, include the 1953 FA Cup Final when, although Matthews did not score for Blackpool, he was the architect of their 4–3 victory over Bolton Wanderers. He goes on: 'I have never made up my mind whether it was against Ireland at Old Trafford, Manchester, on 16th November 1938, or when we beat Czechoslovakia 5–4 at Tottenham on 1st December 1937.'

Against Ireland – I saw that match too – Stan got only one goal himself but he 'made' no fewer than five for his inside right, Willie Hall of Spurs.

On the way back to London, on the train, I remember Jimmy Seed, the much loved manager of Charlton Athletic, saying: 'Never you forget Matthews' play today because I've never seen anything better in my life and you never will in yours.' And I don't think I ever have.

Matthews' display against Czechoslovakia was, for him, freakish, for by no stretch of the imagination could he be called a goal scorer. But on this occasion Len Goulden, I think it was, injured himself, Matthews moved inside while first George Mills, of Chelsea, and then the famous Arsenal wing-half, Jack Crayston, moved to outside right.

Even then it was touch and go, for with only a few minutes left the score stood at 4–4 when Matthews picked his way through the gloom and the Czech side and, to paraphrase a description applied to the wonderful little Jimmy Wilde, like 'a ghost with a bullet in his boot', scored the winning goal to keep intact England's home record against Continental sides.

It was a centre from Matthews which led to the last international goal I was to see for some seven years when Stan found Tommy Lawton's head at Hampden Park, Glasgow, on April 1939 in the closing minutes of the game to give England a 2–1 victory against Scotland in the last proper international to be played in Britain until after the war.

However, I am ahead of myself. . . .

3 1938–40
The End of the
Beginning

The start of 1938 saw a change of newspapers for me
which was going to last until 1950 – with, of course, the interruption of
nearly six years' wartime service with the Army.

In January 1938 I moved from the *Daily Mirror* to the *Sunday Pictorial*.

The man who was responsible for my switch was Hugh Cudlipp – who,
until his retirement at the end of 1973, was the Chairman of IPC, the
publishing octopus which controls, among scores of other publications,
both the *Daily* and the *Sunday Mirror*, the name later adopted by the
Sunday Pictorial. But in 1938 Hugh Cudlipp, at under twenty-four and a
half, was easily the youngest editor of a national newspaper – and, as far
as I know, no one younger, or as young, has ever held a similar position.

I am not going into great detail about the man who affected my career
– and therefore, to a large degree, my life – except to say without any
reservation that he was easily the most brilliant journalist with whom I
ever worked, or even met, and that when his responsibilities were purely
editorial he threw off journalistic ideas like a Roman candle discharges
sparks.

Before the war, during it, when at times we shared a bedroom – and
you have to be *very* friendly with someone to survive that – and for nearly
a decade after it we were the closest of friends, and although in the last
fifteen years that I was on the *Daily Mirror* we saw less of each other,
because of the diversification of Hugh's newspaper interests, I like to think
that the affection each had for the other is unimpaired on either side. I do
know that when I was seriously ill in 1969 Cudlipp was the first man to
whom I went for help and that, despite his responsibilities, he made it
his first priority to see that so far as lay in his power I should be looked
after.

He was a great journalist; he was – and remains – a fine friend.

But all this was in the remote, unknown future. When I went over to
the '*Pic*' I knew Cudlipp merely as a brilliant operator on the feature
side of the *Mirror*. I didn't even know him well enough to be sure whether
I liked him as a person. All I knew was that anyone who turned down a
job working with him couldn't be much of a newspaperman.

Hugh was allowed to take two people with him from the *Mirror*. Bartholomew had refused him 'Cassandra' but put no obstacles in his way when he said he wanted Stuart 'Sam' Campbell (later a brilliant editor of *The People*) and myself.

'Bart' gave his reasons for letting us go: (a) his dislike of my father – who had been dead for six years and whom I suspect 'the poor man's Napoleon' had scarcely known – and (b) the fact that Campbell busied himself too much in the affairs of the National Union of Journalists: a curious criticism, this, coming from a man who was supposed to be transforming the paper into a journal more representative of the Left! I also had an idea that Bart would not easily forgive Cudlipp for going on to a paper over which he had no control, this being largely vested in Cecil King, someone to whom it was difficult to warm on first acquaintanceship but whom you had to know really well before you realized how basically unlikable a character he, too, was.

All of this was as nothing, however, compared to the sheer excitement of getting out the *Pic* each week. You had only to put your nose into the waiting room to wonder what was coming next.

The classic morning came when, reading from left to right – but not necessarily in order of importance (to the paper, that is) – were Leslie Hore-Belisha, the Secretary of State for War, Colonel Barker, who was *not* a subordinate of the War Minister but one of those unhappy twilight-world characters who had passed for years as a retired military man until it was discovered that, legally anyway, 'he' was a woman. Next, as I recall it, was another sad, storm-tossed character, the Rector of Stiffkey (pronounced 'Stookey') who was treated in the most hideously unChristian fashion by an ecclesiastical consistory court, later figured as the biggest draw in a fun-fair, when he allowed himself to be 'buried alive', and ended up by getting eaten by a lion while appearing in a similar peep show. Finally there was a square-looking man in a squarish bowler hat, so firmly clamped on his square head that his square ears were bent down by it. In his square hands he tightly held a square envelope of a certain ominous shade of blue. Although I had not then come across his ilk – and, fortunately, personally have never since – some sixth journalistic sense seemed to tell me that here was a bailiff bringing a writ for something we had printed the previous Sunday!

Cudlipp, as he had promised, began to build me up in a fashion which any journalist of that age – or before, or since – must have greenly envied. He gave me my 'nom de Fleet Street' which endured for some thirty-five years – 'The Man They Can't Gag'.

If some pernickety characters inquired who 'They' were and what it was they wanted to 'Gag' me about they were in a conspicuous minority; and with the complete backing of the paper and Cudlipp, in particular, who said that even were I to be successfully sued for libel he would, the next day, write me a letter immediately extending my contract, I was able to say a lot of things I had wanted to for a long time, which few other more nervous, and less successful, papers would have permitted me to write.

While in Germany to see former world heavyweight champion Max Schmeling easily beat Ben Foord in January 1938 the British sports-writers explored the dubious delights of the Hamburg St Pauli district; roughly the equivalent of London's Soho. Inevitably we went to the notorious 'red light' area by the docks. It was a single street, closed off at each end by huge wooden gates which had wicket doors in them. The gates were locked at sundown, and after that no children or women (except those who lived in the street) were allowed in.

It was extraordinary in a modern European city to see groups of 'customers' strolling up and down the road – surveying the 'merchandise' which was displayed in brightly lit ground floor rooms, rather like the shop windows in the West End of London – and more or less saying: 'I'll take that blonde convertible job!'

The 'houses' were the height of respectability and I can tell the story of what happened in one of them because all my colleagues concerned are now dead. I think I might have been tempted to ascend one of the shadowy staircases, which led to who knew what questionable delights, but the dangers of such an expedition were so luridly painted to me by one of the senior members of our party – they were all fifteen to twenty years older and regarded me as being in need of care and protection – that I was content to sit downstairs quaffing schooners of the magnificent, foaming German beer.

No such cowardly considerations deterred one of our party, however. But when he rejoined us it was with the air of a man who has gone through such an experience as he hopes will never be repeated.

'Do you know what?' he asked, after we had bought him a drink and inquired of his adventures. 'My bird was a bloody acrobat! No, I'm not joking,' he added to stifle the gale of laughter which had met his revelation. 'There I am waiting for the action, as it were, to commence when she says something like "Hoop-la", turns a cartwheel – and her jumper is off – and so am I, very nearly.

'She has not got anything on under her jumper,' he mused reflectively. 'Then, before I can say anything, she comes out with another of these whoops – "Allez-oop", I think it was this time – and she does a back somersault over the bed and when she's right way up again her skirt's gone now. She didn't have anything on under *that*, either,' he added even more reflectively. 'Then its "Olé", and the splits and her mesh stockings and garters have gone. After that she started undressing me but, somehow, I didn't have any heart for it at all. I kept on wondering what sort of tricks she might get up to with *me*. So I just paid her . . . and am I glad to be having this beer! That sort of thing would never go down in Manchester!'

Five months later came the fight which, although it lasted only two minutes and four seconds, remains the most dramatic I have ever seen.

It was, of course, the return bout between Joe Louis, the Negro champion, and Max Schmeling, the idol of Nazi Germany who had once told me that Hitler liked boxing and that two pages of *Mein Kampf* were devoted to boxing; I never checked.

If ever a nation expressed sporting dichotomy it was the USA on the subject of this fight. The old guard still could not stand the idea of a Negro being the world heavyweight champion but far, far more – except some of those of German descent, or the ones who frankly favoured Nazism – were, almost literally, praying for the defeat of the German, knowing full well that if Schmeling won the title he would be on the next boat to the Fatherland; that is if they hadn't speeded up the completion of the new *Graf Zeppelin* and sent that for him so that the championship could be even more quickly wrapped up within the Reich!

Louis prepared at his usual training camp, Pompton Lakes, New Jersey, not too far away from New York City. As usual everything was done to protect Joe from any suggestion of being 'an uppity nigger'; not that Joe ever looked like putting a foot wrong but it was natural enough, when someone asked him if he were scared of Schmeling because of what had happened in their first fight, for him to answer: 'Ain't scared of nuthin' or nobody.' But immediately John Roxborough, Julian Black, or, most likely, his trainer, Jack Blackburn, would come forward saying: 'Don't ask questions like that. It makes Joe sound too smart-ass.'

Incidentally Blackburn, who did all Joe's ring thinking for him and was probably his closest friend, had long been ailing. When, in January 1942, Joe signed for a return bout with the giant Buddy Baer, brother of ex-world champion Max, Blackburn said that for the first time since Joe had turned pro he didn't feel he could be in his corner; the steps up to the ring would be too much for him.

Louis, in that black treacle voice of his, said: "Chappie, I promise you won't have to do it but once." And Joe came through with just four seconds to spare, for the fight ended after two minutes and fifty-six seconds of the first round. A little over three months later Blackburn was dead.

But now the night of 22 June 1938 had arrived. You could hang your hat on the atmosphere at Yankee Stadium where the pale faces of some 70,000 fans, tier upon tier of them, gave the illusion of the white sails of a galleon riding at anchor by night with the red exit signs, like port lights, completing the likeness of some great motionless vessel.

When the two men came into the ring it was an ironic commentary on the Nazi racialist poppycock that Schmeling, sweated out like a dried fig, was far darker than the *café-au-lait* Louis. I was seated next to a German journalist who told me with great glee that Schmeling had received a telegram from Hitler addressed to 'The New Heavyweight Champion of the World'. The newspaperman implied that this surely made Schmeling's victory inevitable.

In the event it wasn't a fight: it was a massacre. Of the 124 seconds it lasted Schmeling spent almost half either helpless on the ropes or rolling on the canvas. Louis must have launched over forty punches and I remember only one completely missing.

The really terrifying moment came when Schmeling, half-conscious on the ropes, the top one running under his right armpit and his head lolling over it, like that of a man whose neck has been broken by the hangman, swivelled round so that his unprotected side and part of his back were presented to Louis. Louis, whose normally rather thick lips seemed to have disappeared into a knife-slash of hate, swung a body punch at his hapless foe – as he was, of course, entitled to – with his full 14 st 2¾ lb behind it. (Incidentally, it's interesting that he never again weighed as light as this . . . he was lean as a whiplash and bursting with fire.) A scream like the tearing of calico razored through the uproar of the crowd. We all thought that it came from some woman supporter of the German. In fact it was Schmeling himself, screaming in mortal agony as one of his vertebrae was broken by the power of Louis' punch.

The rest was all confusion. When Schmeling went down for the last time his trainer and friend, Max Machon, flung the towel – the traditional signal of surrender – into the ring and when the referee, Arthur Donovan, kicked it aside tried to follow it on to the canvas. But Donovan had taken another look at Schmeling and, instead of completing the count, indicated that the whole thing was at an end.

Then the ring was full of little men, congratulating or commiserating according to their allegiances, and my wife, who was immediately behind the working Press seats, was helped on to her seat by a friendly neighbour and asked in some bewilderment: 'What happened?' For it had all occurred so quickly. She got her answer from a big man in the row in front who turned round, in some considerable satisfaction, to say: 'Lady! that Dutchman' – in those days, for some unknown reason, Germans were known as 'Dutchmen' in the States – 'that Dutchman is well and truly OUT!'

Schmeling was taken from the ring to the Polyclinic Hospital in New York. Eventually he sailed back to Germany on the *Bremen*, far from the triumphant 'Hail the conquering hero comes' homecoming which had been anticipated.

Yet such is the irony of sport that, looking forward, it was the vanquished who prospered and the victor who fell upon hard times. The last time I saw Schmeling he was very wealthy, having the exclusive rights in West Germany for one of America's most popular soft drinks.

He and Louis, who had fought each other twice with such ferocity, came together once again at the ringside – but this time they were on the safe side of the ropes when they did a joint commentary on the world heavyweight championship between Cassius Clay and Germany's Karl Mildenberger, at Frankfurt, in September 1966. The Negro won that one, too!

Later still Schmeling was to prove his true sportsmanship, for Joe went through a bad time and while he was in a Denver, Colorado, hospital it was reported that Schmeling had visited him and allegedly left some five thousand dollars to look after his old foe.

I still think Joe Louis as he was on that June night in 1938 would have beaten any man who ever lived. I wrote at the time: 'But I don't believe he'll ever fight like that again.' Years later when he was in London for a sports extravaganza I asked him what he thought his best performance in the ring had been. He said his four-round win against Max Baer. I cited the second Schmeling bout. He thought for a moment and then a grin like the Grand Canyon split his face. 'Well, mebbe,' he admitted, 'but it's kinda hard to get as mad as that twice.'

That was altogether a memorable trip. My wife and I had crossed on the SS *Manhattan*, the American line ship on which the US Olympic team had gone to Berlin. This was the only foreign shipping line which called at German ports and as a result the ship was crammed with Jewish refugees who, of course, were forbidden to use German vessels.

It was an affront to humanity and the brotherhood of man to see how, for the first day or two, the wretched fugitives would flatten themselves against the sides of the corridors as though they felt that they might yet be sent back to some hideous concentration camp. Towards the end of the voyage, realizing that they were truly approaching liberty, they perhaps over-compensated with explosions of 'end of term' shouting and singing; but who, in the name of humanity, could blame them?

Another passenger was the American racehorse Battleship who had won the Grand National a few weeks earlier. What a National it had been – one of the most exciting in my memory. Battleship, I was told, was a son of Man o' War, perhaps the most famous horse ever produced by the USA. It was claimed that he had actually stood at stud before winning the National, and he was the first stallion to win the world's greatest race since Grudon in 1901 – and the last to this day. Later I heard that the great little horse went back to stud and lived to a ripe old age; he certainly deserved it.

Our stay in New York, or rather Pelham, an elegant community just outside the city, was made all the more memorable by the sealing of our friendship with Burris Jenkins, America's most famous sports cartoonist, and his wife, Georgia. The Jenkins gave a wonderful party for us to which almost everyone who was anybody in New York sporting circles was invited.

Another tremendous night with the Jenkins gave me a more intimate view than I could ever have hoped for of one of my all-time greats – Ernest Hemingway. He was, I think, covering the Louis–Schmeling fight for *Colliers* magazine – and anyone who has read his short story 'Fifty Grand' knows how perfectly he appreciated the world of professional boxing. It was arranged that we would meet in some bar and go to his New York apartment. We duly had two, or half a dozen, and repaired to his place. Thereafter the proceedings might have come out of one of his own stories.

The party consisted of Burris and Georgia, my wife and myself, a boxer whose name I have forgotten but who was sparring regularly with Hemingway and claimed to have gone the distance with Mickey Walker, former welter and middleweight champion of the world; finally an anarchist whom Hemingway had brought back from Spain where the writer had been making a film of the Civil War – from the Government point of view.

I believe 'Hem' – and I use that intimacy only because it *was* such a wonderful evening and he did afterwards write a note to the Jenkins (alas! lost during the war) saying 'The Wilsons were very fine' – was between marriages. In any event he found that he had been locked out of the apartment.

That's where the 'hair on the chest' stuff began. Uttering what was in those days known as an imprecation but which is nowadays spelled out to the full extent of its four letters – I'm sure that's why four-letter words are now so popular in print because not even the most illiterate writers can misspell them – Hemingway launched himself at the barred portal.

I had often in 'private eye' thrillers read about this action but it was the first, and so far, unfortunately, the last time I have seen it done. I suppose he weighed around the fourteen-stone mark and he was in very good shape for a man just under forty. Anyway, the front door went down as Schmeling was destined to do, flat on its back. But, unlike the

German, it did not get up at all. We surged in. Then Hemingway found the drinks cabinet was locked. He put the heel of his shoe through that and produced the life-giving elixir from between the shards of shattered glass.

Thereafter everything became a montage of thoughts and emotions. The fighter re-created the highlights of his career, occasionally illustrating some particular *coup* on Hemingway. Hem talked sports, politics, writing – and gave a wonderfully precise forecast of what was going to happen to the world in the next year or two. Apart from attending to him most of us, as is the way of the best parties, did more talking than listening. The anarchist, who disdained furniture as an example of bourgeois decadence, sat on the floor and occasionally spat, after which he would look round the room disdainfully, spit again and remark: '*Capitalisti.*' Oh, it was a great evening and I just wish I could remember how it ended.

I was back in time for the final stages of Wimbledon and I believe that Don Budge, who for the second year running won all three events and this time did not drop a set in the singles, was greater than any player I saw before or since. His unfortunate victim in the final was Bunny Austin who had been able to win only six games against Vines and got only four this time!

Some of the real oldtimers consider the late Bill Tilden, at his peak, to have been the greatest ever. Fred Perry when asked his choice always says: 'Well, you think about Tilden for ten minutes and then start considering the others.' Tilden had this to say about Budge in his book *My Story*, published in 1948.

For all-round consistency, Donald Budge at the peak of his career was the finest of them all. There was no subtlety, no finesse, little grace and practically no variety to his game, but for hitting power – wow!

I have played all the greats of the past twenty-five years but no man to my knowledge ever equalled the high average of play that Budge produced over a period of fully six years – amateur and pro. I consider him the finest player 365 days a year that has ever lived.

But if the men's finals were a formality the women's produced the last appearance of Helen Wills Moody and one of the most ugly dramas ever played out on the Centre Court which, like a green-painted operating theatre, has exposed so many frayed nerves and sagging muscles, but even more heroic or inadequate spirits.

Few had thought that Helen Wills Moody would appear at Wimbledon again; after all three years earlier, when she could have been expected to be a better player, she had come within a point of defeat against the racket wielded by her perennial enemy – yes, the word is not too strong – Helen Jacobs. And now to point the drama it was Helen Jacobs who again faced her across the net; the fourth and final time they were to contest the Wimbledon final – a rivalry which had covered a full decade.

The old champion, who had not lost a singles match at Wimbledon since her first final in 1924, started well and went to 4–2 but gradually, so gradually, like grain after grain of sugar finally forcing down one side of a scale, the match seemed to be tilting in the younger Helen's favour. In the ninth game, with the score standing at 4–4, Helen Jacobs had a point to break through.

She came to the net and Mrs Moody banged in a wide passing shot. Miss Jacobs leaped to cut it off; failed to get hold of the ball properly, landed awkwardly; and that was to all intents and purposes the end. Miss Jacobs limped back to the base-line to receive service but for the first time you noticed not only the unobtrusive bandage round one ankle, required after a previous injury, but the fact that the challenger's face was now matching its whiteness.

I know that it has always been said that if the Royal Box had caught fire while she was playing Mrs Moody would not have noticed it. Not for nothing had she been nicknamed, even in her teens, 'Miss Poker Face'. Apologists for her said that she was so engrossed in the match that she did not realize she was faced by a hobbling cripple. I do not believe it. And I have two reasons for my scepticism. Mrs Wightman, donor of the Cup which is competed for annually by the women stars of Britain and the USA, came on to court to try to persuade 'Helen II' to scratch. No dice.

Secondly I am convinced Helen Moody knew against just what daunting pain her opponent was struggling because she did something which I can't remember seeing anyone else do in a singles final on the Centre Court; she crossed at the end of the net opposite to the umpire's chair where a player, even before a minute's pause was authorized between games, almost invariably stopped to towel hands and face or to sip a little liquid. Of course Mrs Moody, who scarcely had to move, had worked up neither a sweat nor a thirst as she remorselessly nailed her helpless victim to the court. But it seemed as though she were determined to ignore the other woman and certainly not to talk to her. The handshake which she finally gave to the vanquished, after winning eight hollow games in a row, belonged at the North Pole.

She had accomplished her twofold ambition, setting up an unparalleled eight victories – a figure which still stands, although Maureen Connolly, who won thrice at Wimbledon before she was twenty, would probably have eclipsed it – and she had crushed her most persistent rival.

In different circumstances her final exit from the court she had so long dominated would have been one of the great moments in sport. But the crowd, who had seen the Ice Queen ignore the plight of a plucky antagonist, let her go in a silence which, to anyone else, would have been more wounding than the loudest boos and reserved their untrammelled applause for the loser, who limped off after the victor almost like some captive foe following the chariot of a Roman conqueror.

At least let Helen Jacobs have the last word – and again I quote Tilden, who records that the following day Helen Jacobs told him: 'You know, Bill, I don't mind her being a so-and-so but I object to her being a stupid so-and-so. If she had only smiled when we shook hands at the end and said: "I'm glad you broke your damn leg", or something like that, no one would have known how she felt.'

There wasn't much more memorable – for me – in 1938. We survived the Munich crisis although even the greatest political ignoramus, after the ephemeral glow of 'Peace in our time', realized that we were only buying time – and hoped that, at last, in the eleventh hour we should make some use of it. Credit where credit is due. When it looked as though the *Blitzkrieg* might start at any moment chosen by Hitler there was just one sporting occasion which helped to lighten the surrounding gloom.

This was when Jack Doyle, quite one of the most eccentric pugilists in a sport where eccentricity is normal, matched with Eddie Phillips, a former bus driver from Bow, succeeded in knocking himself out!

He performed this remarkable feat by missing with a wild swing and sailing through the air – and the ropes – with the greatest of ease, but without the benefit of a flying trapeze. It prompted the remark, from a cynic, that the Irishman should now be matched with Buddy Baer – because they'd both knocked out Jack Doyle! (In fact while he was in the States Doyle had been knocked out in one round by Max's brother, Buddy, in a fight which that great American sportswriter, Dan Parker, referred to as 'a sub-navel engagement' – owing to some doubt about the legality of the punch which finished off Doyle.)

Towards the end of the year I was attacked by the paper Benito Mussolini had founded at the start of the First World War, *Il Popolo d'Italia* (slogans: 'Who has iron, has bread' and 'The revolution is an idea plus bayonets' – neither of them coined by Mussolini). The reason for the criticism was a piece I'd written a fortnight earlier suggesting rather strongly that it *wouldn't* be a good idea for England to play Italy at soccer in 1939.

So to 1939 – and it was as though I tried to cram everything there was in sport into the first eight months of that end-of-an-era year.

In January I was in St Moritz for the winter sports. I must say my stay started with a distinct giggle. After a somewhat dodgy flight I reached the bar of, I think, the Palace Hotel and had a brandy to settle my nerves, then one for my stomach, then one for enjoyment, then one because it was very good cognac . . . wrapped in the comfort of a capacious armchair I closed my eyes.

Something disturbed me, I opened my eyes and, so help me, the place had been taken over by midgets! There they sat, four or five of them, having clambered up awkwardly on to the high bar stools. The one on the left looked the most robust – and the most familiar. The one on the right was truly tiny; could it be . . . yes, it was, Johnny Dines and, on the left was none other than the immortal Gordon Richards, the greatest flat race jockey I ever did see.

Having mentally abjured all strong drink for ever I now ordered a *large* brandy out of sheer relief. We'd got snow white outside, all right, but the 'dwarfs' were all jockeys or trainers taking their annual winter vacation at St Moritz where, although there was, in fact, horse-racing – over hurdles, too! – on the snow covering a frozen lake, Gordon and company contented themselves with the safer pursuit of curling.

Brigadier-General Critchley, the man who introduced greyhound racing to Britain in the twenties, and his wife, formerly Diana Fishwick the international golfer, introduced me to the dubious delights of skiing. They were very kind; every time I fell over they said I showed an improved style in doing so.

But it was Johnny Critchley, the General's son, who really put the fear of heaven – which seemed altogether too close – into me when he suggested that I should brake for him in a two-man bob-sleigh.

I have never claimed to be a hero and often I have been sorely frightened; but I can't remember ever being more scared when I was supposed to be enjoying myself than I was during that bob run in and out of a pine forest. Although I don't suppose we ever went over 70 mph – and maybe it was much less – the absence of all sound except the hiss of the bob's runners on the ice, the rattling noise as you sheered off one high-banked ice wall and on to the one opposite, rather like a chunk of ice being thrown around in a cocktail shaker, and the occasional spine-shattering *bang* as you lost contact with the track and then slammed down on it again, all these together made you feel that you were going faster than flying.

I never did it again – but at four Winter Olympic Games when I saw a bob rocking, rattling, rocketing past while the logical part of my mind told me that was something I was well out of, a perverse section made me wish that I was one of the crew.

It was General Critchley who made the Grand National of that year unforgettable; it stands out not because of the way Workman won it, not because it was the centenary of the race, but for the conditions in which I saw it.

When Critch did something he did it in style – and the 1939 National was no exception. He hired a special sleeper train and the guests he couldn't accommodate on this he booked into various hotels in or near Liverpool: considerably easier said than done, for then as now Liverpool was crowded to the docks on the eve of the National. For the day Critch rented a farm in the centre of the racecourse, erected a wooden stand over a cottage on it (and insured it for £100,000), and then moved the catering staff from the White City, London, up for the day. He even acted as bookmaker so that no one had to leave his 'headquarters'. There were stars from many sports there, the champagne flowed like . . . champagne, and there was a magnificent cold buffet.

As month succeeded month in 1939 it seemed as though everyone realized that we were coming to a crisis after which nothing would ever be quite the same. It was in such an atmosphere that I went to Liverpool to enjoy General Critchley's hospitality at Aintree. The great steeplechase was run on a Friday in those days, and traditionally there was always a big fight on the Thursday at the only building in the country originally constructed specially for boxing – the Liverpool Stadium.

This year it was the fight for the British welterweight championship between Jake Kilrain, the champion from Scotland, and one of the real local pride and joys, Ernie Roderick. I was lucky enough to be only one round out in my tip that Roderick would become the next champion. Roderick fought Henry Armstrong for the *world* welterweight title later that year. For sheer nonstop going-forward-all-the-time aggression I have never seen Armstrong's like. Not only did he briefly hold three world titles, at different weights – for a comparison imagine the outcry there would be if Howard Winstone, briefly nine-stone champion of the world, had been matched with José Napoles, the world welterweight champion – but later he actually fought a draw for the world *middleweight* title.

And it's true that he started slowly for I gave the first round to Roderick; but not another until the eleventh – and that was the only other round I *did* give to the game, skilful but, in this case, completely outclassed Liverpudlian.

On my return to England from St Moritz I became involved in a campaign against what is to my mind the filthiest stain on the sporting pages of Britain – hare-coursing. In February 1939 I wrote about the Waterloo Cup – the red riband of this slaughterous sport – coursed at

Altcar and Lydiate, just outside Liverpool. Among other things I recorded:

'There's a strange hush while the tense drama of life and death is played out. The hare has a start – but in less time than it takes to light a cigarette the dogs, with their plunging speed, have eaten this up.

'Now it's the little animal's agility against the breathless pace of its pursuers. The hare seems to double back into its shadow. The dogs overrun it. On the soft soil they send up a sheet of dirt like a speedway rider broadsiding. For a moment hunted and hunters are obscured.

'In ever diminishing circles the hare tries to wrong-foot the dogs. If you have a spark of imagination you can hear the panting of the blood-crazed hounds, feel the hot breath as it creeps closer, even though you are fifty yards away. A final dizzy skid, a curtain of mud, and then the last plunge and a few frenzied kicks. The crowd gives a deep, soft sigh of satisfaction.

'The kill was some distance away. Perhaps it was not so bad, you try to reasure yourself, and in the background the mutter of conversation and the bawling of the bookies springs up again. But almost at once it stops. Another hare has flashed into sight. This one is stronger. He twists and turns coming nearer, ever nearer, to the dyke which separates the spectators from the course. Now you can see the dogs' red, drooling tongues as they close in. And the hare's eyes bulging out, like organ stops, in antic panic. My knuckles are as white as the painted fence I'm clutching. I'm praying – yes, praying – the hare will make it.

'Thiry yards to go – twenty – *ten!* But one of the dogs has headed it off. It zig-zags back, scraping across the muzzle of the other. Round in a circle into the middle of the field and back to the dyke.

'It's slower now – but there's not far to go. Weaving in and out. The dogs are tiring, too. Fifteen yards to go – then, *ugh!* One of the dogs got a hind leg. In a split-second the frantic dash became an agonized crawl. In another moment the leading dog had rolled it over. I'd always been told that the hounds went for the neck, like a terrier after a rat. I'd hoped that was so – it's the quickest way to be snuffed out.

'It isn't true. A glistening black snout was buried in the quivering mound of white fur. The greyhound goes for the entrails to try to drag them out – a steaming, scarlet mess. And the hare screams and squeals and kicks. My God! how it screams. Like a child with a hot iron on its bare flesh.

'I always thought that a woman, no matter what she may have done or what she has become, could not bear the sound of a child's scream. The Irish girl on my right lights a cigarette. "She coursed that one well, didn't she, Pat?" she says. The priest by her side nods. "She did indade.

I'll go and collect your money for you." He moves off to one of the bookmakers.

'In the meantime some of the catchers – they line the course and roar at the hare to make it keep a straight line until the two dogs are slipped – have seized the two dogs and pulled them off the carcass. Quickly and skilfully they clean the white fluff out of their mouths. Otherwise the dogs might very well be choked and, if they were left with the hare, they would almost certainly fight and injure each other, while if they gorged themselves there would be no incentive to course any more. The dead hare is slung over a man's shoulder. It hangs like a limp furry scarf. The rhythm and the blinding speed are vanished like a dowsed light. Yet, somehow I prefer it like that. They can't do anything more to it, now.

'As the day wears on the pile of hares grows. Some of them go to the farmers from whose land they have been driven. Some go to the kitchens of any owner who wants them. But for the hare which is coursed in the final a special place of honour is reserved. The owner of the winning dog, in honour bound, should take the carcass and have it stuffed to occupy a place of pride in his or her house.

'Of course there is a chance for the hare to escape. A Waterloo Cup veteran told me of the sough – pronounced to rhyme with muff – a bolt-hole at the far end of the course. All I can say is that I could not see it. Neither, apparently, could the hares. In the first nine courses that I saw there were eight kills.'

And the same veteran told me this. Even supposing the hare does make his escape through the sough, if the course has been a severe one, death is still his portion. For the tremendous physical effort and the paralysing fear are too much for one of Nature's most timid creatures. Its heart will not stand the strain – either it collapses or it breaks a blood vessel. In either event the catchers who are sent out at the end of the day's coursing find a worthwhile haul near the exits of the soughs.

I ended this 1939 article by writing: 'And I will not hear the scream of the stricken hare at Lydiate again.'

But ten years, and a war, later although it looked as though the killing Cup was to meet its Waterloo through Parliamentary legislation I still described what happened at the end of the fifth course:

'The hare, twisting and writhing like a demented thing, was twenty yards from the dyke which meant the difference between life and bloody death to it. Then it slipped and screamed with terror. It screamed again as one hound seized a hind leg.

'You could hear the harsh panting of the dogs just before they struck. Steam came from their muzzles as though their mouths were on fire. The second dog got the hare's head in its mouth. The hare's cries were

c

now muffled so that it bawled like a child left alone in a deserted house who has burnt himself and is wailing in mortal terror.

'A woman behind me said: "A-ah! I was afraid it was going to get away." Her plump companion remarked contentedly: "My bitch is a very good killer." '

I had qualified as one of the 'interfering busybodies' to whom Hugh William Osbert Molyneux, seventh Earl of Sefton, had referred while pleading for the preservation of coursing. Mind you, I hope he declared his interest.

He presented the Waterloo Cup, the Waterloo Purse and the Waterloo Plate. And it was over some of the 34,000-odd acres which he owned that the competitions took place.

I cannot understand how it can be that the House of Lords can defer or tergiversate about a piece of legislation on an issue as clearly moral as this because, as I wrote nearly thirty years ago:

'For, as long as one hears the anguished wailing of a hare as the blood gushes from its ears and its eyes come out on stalks under the pressure of a hound's teeth, then our countryside can never be the green and pleasant place of our birthright.'

But other concerns were truer to the spirit of sport, and one was a lightweight fight between two British boxers which was perhaps the greatest domestic scrap, regardless of weight, that I ever saw. This was the classic meeting for the British title between the fighter, Eric Boon from Chatteris, Cambridgeshire, and the boxer Arthur Danahar, one of the long line of Cockney kids who go back to the earliest days of bareknuckle scrapping. The referee stopped the fight eventually in the fourteenth round in Boon's favour.

This was not only the first bout ever to be publicly televised but it was also shown simultaneously in three London cinemas, the Marble Arch Pavilion, the Monseigneur and the Tatler.

The wonderful Liverpool weekend of the Kilrain–Roderick fight and the Grand National was rounded off when I went to Manchester for the semi-final round of the FA Cup to watch Wolverhampton Wanderers beat Grimsby 5–0.

I had consistently tipped the Wolves not only to win the Cup but to achieve the 'double' by taking the First Division championship as well. So convinced of this was I that before the season I had taken odds of £200 to ten shillings that they would pull it off – and I refused to lay off a penny. Two things impressed me about the Wolves of those days. The first was the shrewdness of their manager, Major Frank Buckley: he was so far ahead of his generation that although he knew nothing of the game the Americans had made him a big offer to go into baseball! The other personality at Wolverhampton whose uncompromising attitude to football, and life, made him a man whom to this day I like to call my friend was Stan Cullis who was just about the best centre-half of the lot.

So what happened? In the Cup Final lowly Portsmouth scored first and – salt in the wound – the scorer was Barlow whom the Wolves had sold to Pompey! In the end it was a rout with the underdogs winning 4–1.

Just to bring the whole gloomy saga to an end Wolves finished second in the League too, their victors, Everton, beating them by four clear points. As someone (rather unkindly, I thought) pointed out I should have backed the Wolves each way!

It was almost time to go to America again, but before I went there was a sad little story about Jesse Owens, the giant of Berlin. In 1938 at the first night baseball games in New York I had seen the great Negro sprinter running in handicaps against baseball players; elsewhere he had taken on horses. Instead of the Black Colossus of an athlete that he had once been, he had been turned into a tawdry sideshow by the American Athletic Union whose excessive demands on the man who had won four gold medals for his country to appear here, there and everywhere had virtually forced him into professionalism.

Perhaps that treatment explains, although it does not completely condone, the behaviour of some of the black American athletes in the Olympic Games in Mexico and at Munich.

Fortunately the Jesse Owens story had a happy ending for when I next met him at the Melbourne Olympic Games in 1956 he was one of President Eisenhower's personal sporting representatives. He seemed very much the same Jesse – a year earlier, when he was forty-one he said he had run 100 yards in 9·8 seconds – but when we congratulated him on surviving the years so well he said mock-ruefully, referring to his receding hairline: 'Seems as though there's more face to shave every day!' He had made a career in race relations and I have been happy to see him at subsequent Games.

The reason for my trip to the States this time was primarily to see Louis again, this time against one of those grotesque characters whom only boxing seems to be able to produce in conveyor-belt fashion. He was Tony Galento known to some, instead of the 'Beer Barrel Polka', as the 'Beer Barrel Palooka', while others preferred the 'Punching Pumpkin'. I also wanted to see Sydney Wooderson, who then held the world record for the mile with a time of 4 mins 6·4 secs, run against four of America's crack milers, including the perennial Glenn Cunningham.

But before these two events I was to meet again one of the legendary figures of all sport. Babe Ruth. I had lunch, before a preview of the sports pavilion at the New York World's Fair, with Burris Jenkins and the 'Bambino' as Ruth, probably the greatest personality baseball has ever produced, was affectionately known.

The best description of him was an image of a baked potato precariously balanced on a couple of toothpicks, for even in his prime his legs never matched the bulk of the rest of his frame. He had been retired from baseball for years, even then, and I had first met him when he came to England with his daughter Julie, who appeared in the world table tennis championships, the Babe giving her such unorthodox encouragement as: 'Swat that onion, willya, Julie honey!'

Despite his retirement he was still the idol of every man and boy who had ever been to a ball game and I don't think he was allowed to take two consecutive mouthfuls at that meal without signing his autograph.

The story which ensured Ruth's perpetual fame was very human, however. There was a kid in hospital, delirious, constantly calling Babe Ruth's name. Finally they got the big man to his bedside. The youngster looked at him with staring, disbelieving eyes. The Bambino, who could be as rough and tough and ruthless as a waterfront crimp, was as gentle as a mother with the sick boy. He struck a bargain with him. If the kid would promise to get well he, the Babe, would promise that very afternoon to go out and hit a home run specially for the youngster. He even nominated, roughly, where he would hit it.

They didn't have television in those days, of course, but the boy was almost inside the radio at his bedside when the commentary on the game began. Inning succeeded inning; then suddenly there was the crisp crack of bat on ball. The commentator bellowed: 'It is . . . no . . . yes . . . yes, Babe Ruth has done it again. A homer right over centre field.'

The kid yelled: 'He did it, he did it! The Babe did it for me – my own home run!' He closed his eyes; his temperature went down from that hour; he was cured.

Sentimental? Of course. Apocryphal? Probably. But Ruth was the kind of man around whom legends are woven . . .

Earlier I had been introduced on a coast-to-coast radio hook-up by Jimmy Walker, one of New York's most famous Mayors; I had renewed acquaintanceship with the gorgeous swimmer, Eleanor Holm; met Johnny Weissmuller, Olympic swimming star and the most famous film Tarzan – 'I don't eat fish, they're my buddies!' – and met also Gertrude Ederle, the first woman to swim the English Channel, back in 1926. They were all appearing at the Aquacade, the lavish water spectacle produced by Billy Rose whom Eleanor Holm later married.

Gertrude Ederle had quite a story. In 1926 her butcher father pledged his business to give Gertie a chance to make athletic history. She made it – but the cost was not cheap for the beating she took from the waves largely destroyed her hearing so that she had to follow most of a conversation by lip-reading.

Also there was a quiet, dignified white-haired lady whom Babe Ruth's wife introduced through a slip of the tongue to a third party as 'Mrs John L. Sullivan'. In a second the quiet, dignified white-haired lady quite changed her temperament and demeanour as, with blazing eyes and outraged fury, she burst out: 'Mrs John L. Sullivan indeed! Why, my husband knocked the stuffing out of that fat so-and-so nearly fifty years ago!'

And so he had. For she was the widow of the immortal Jim Corbett who knocked out Sullivan in twenty-one rounds, back in 1892, and so became the first man to win the heavyweight championship of the world with gloves.

The Louis–Galento fight had its moments. Twice Galento had a chance of bringing off a major upset – he was an 8–1 underdog. The first time was with the very first punch of the fight, a left hook which exposed Louis' one vulnerability – a weakness not in the jaw but on the cheekbones. I think that if Galento's aim had been better Joe would have thrown off that first punch more easily; as it was it puffed his cheek and gave him the air of a man making a monstrous slow-motion wink.

Again in the third Louis got his feet mixed up, Galento beat him to a left hook and the champion was down. He was up immediately and for the rest of the fight, which was mercifully ended in the fourth round, he looked as though he were going to dismember Galento's 16 st 9¾ lb pound by three-quarters of a pound. At the end of the fight Galento was still trying to get upright by swarming up the referee's legs.

I had been increasingly worried about the obvious imminence of war – the Louis–Galento fight was on 28 June, only a little over nine weeks before the outbreak was actually to be announced. My peace of mind was not exactly increased by a broadcast I heard announcing that London was being bombed which had me spilling my Scotch all over the bar in a very sloppy way. I do not know whether it was one of those 'funny ha-ha' programmes, like the one which announced America had been invaded by Mars and had the local citizenry in a fair old muck sweat until it transpired that this was Orson Welles' first introduction to the international scene.

I had hoped to return on the *Queen Elizabeth*, which was shortly to make her maiden west-to-east voyage but she was not due to sail for some days and I 'wanted home'. So I transferred to the *Nieuw Amsterdam*, flagship of the Dutch line. I know that as we sailed away from the

Statue of Liberty I realized that one very happy chapter of my life had come to an end.

I got back in time to see Jack Doyle fight Eddie Phillips again – well, you can't be lucky all the time! – and get counted out, on this occasion, while lying rigidly to attention like the good Irish Guardsman he had once been. I have often wondered whether it is because the British boxing public so often seems to prefer freaks and stunt fighters with 'gimmicks' that we so seldom produce world champions – never in the heavyweight division.

Finally to sport's equivalent of the ball before Waterloo. My wife and I went to Monte Carlo. There was a fight programme there with Peter Kane, by now world flyweight champion, meeting and easily beating Pierre Louis, the bantamweight champion of France. But what I had really gone there for, through the foresight of Hugh Cudlipp, was to write about the definitive end of an era.

As always, most of the people in Monte Carlo seemed to be fabulously wealthy, international playboys and playgirls – the forerunners of the jet set – and those who hadn't got titles had fortunes or were stars of stage or films.

Tyrone Power and Annabella had been honeymooning; Marlene Dietrich and Grace Moore came over from down the coast for the fight; Sir John McTaggart, famous as a builder, whom President Roosevelt had consulted on an American housing project, gave the Marquess of Queensberry a cheque for some £300 to buy tickets for French soldiers and any British sailors around, so that they could see the fight between George Markwick, ex-heavyweight champion of the British Army, and Francis Rutz, heavyweight champion of the French Army.

John Harding, general manager of the reconstituted National Sporting Club who were putting on the fight programme, took us to a ball given by Lord Patrick Crichton-Stuart at his villa at Cap d'Ail. Crichton-Stuart's father, the Marquis of Bute, had recently sold a large part of Cardiff for a reputed twelve million pounds, so it was hardly surprising that the setting was in the fantastic class.

The dancing was on a flat roof which seemed to float, like a modern hanging garden, midway between earth and sky. Higher up was a blue-tiled floodlit swimming pool, quarried out of the solid rock and nearby, also constructed out of the rock, a cinema where Crichton-Stuart could show the fruits of his favourite hobby, coloured moving pictures. Wired off from the rest of the grounds was an extra wing to the villa which made a little house by itself. Outside there was a tiny electric sign reading 'Villa Charles', for that was where Lord Patrick's baby son spent his time when he was 'at home'.

No one mentioned war yet its menace was in the jasmine scented air; they said there were concealed guns on the Italian frontier a dozen miles or so away, but amidst the perpetual sunshine, the lofty tiles, the barricade of enormous wealth, undoubtedly much more potent than even the much vaunted Maginot Line, there was a feeling of unchanging permanence which surely could not be shattered by a former Austrian house-painter.

Anyway, a favoured few of us had it right from the top. The Duke and Duchess of Windsor were at Monte Carlo.

He had always been a fight fan; I remember him attending that tough across-the-river boxing hall, 'The Ring', Blackfriars; and it was because he had been present that wonderful little Jimmy Wilde had gone through with his disastrous, last-but-one fight against the American, sometime bantamweight champion of the world, Pete Herman.

The Duke and Duchess had reserved seats in the front row which cost about £6 each but their party did not fill the whole of the row. When an American millionaire heard that they were coming he offered £30 a seat for the rest of the row. The offer was turned down.

Then, the night before the fight, a group of sportswriters was presented to the Duke. One of the things for which he had been criticized was visiting Hitler, so, greatly daring as I was much the youngest member of the group, I asked the man who had been King if he thought there would be war. His reply was unequivocal: 'As you know, I have met Herr Hitler. He assured me that he had no desire for war. I am certain he is a man of honour. I am sure there will be no war.'

That was 5 August. On 1 September the honourable Hitler invaded Poland. Two days later Neville Chamberlain announced that Great Britain was at war. The ball was over.

The next eleven months comprised a period which is about the most hazy of any time in my adult life. It was the time of the 'phoney war', but, although nothing was happening, we all knew that some day a great deal was going to – and we wanted to be part of it when the real war started.

I have a copy of a letter I wrote to Cecil King on 12 March 1940.

This letter is to inform you that I did not wish you to apply for exemption from military duties on my behalf.

I am very grateful for your offer to do so but I do not feel that I can accept it and, at the same time, carry on honestly with my work.

I should like to say how much I have enjoyed working on the *Sunday Pictorial* and that I hope to return to the paper when the War is over.

I am sending a duplicate of this letter to Mr Cudlipp. Yours sincerely.

Hugh and I had made a joint decision over a distinctly lively luncheon.

My wife had gone to stay with her family in South Devon as we were expecting our first child. On 21 June he arrived; that is the longest day so, presumably, the shortest night but I cannot say that either my wife or I felt that way about it. I could not get to Devon as the next day I was having my medical examination for admittance into the armed forces. I'm afraid I awaited the news of the successful arrival of Julian in a night-club. But at least it was called the Stork.

The following day I was passed as 'A1' for the Army – which was far from the way I was feeling.

On 19 July I received my call-up papers requiring me to report to Cowshott Camp near Woking, one week later. Clearly Thursday, 25 July, the last night of civilian liberty, had to be celebrated in a rather gigantic fashion.

I spent it with Dick Richards, already my best friend in England, while Shirley Long, who after the war helped me immensely with my first book was the third of our all-male party. Club after club succeeded pub after pub. Then, finally, while we were in a cab somewhere in Soho, we came to a dead halt. The driver tried to pass on the right; the driver tried to cut inside on the left. Hopeless. Shirley, who was rather short-sighted, got out in the pitch dark of the total blackout and reported back that there seemed to be some kind of a red lantern suspended in mid-air in the middle of the street.

Dick decided to investigate further. He got out and returned a few moments later, very silent. In the flame of my cigarette lighter I saw that he was extremely pale and swallowing frequently. He said:

'There's . . . there are . . . three bloody elephants, one in front of the other. The last one has got some sort of red light tied to its tail!'

I said I'd never heard of a red light district of that kind.

But, by God! do you know he was right? They had taken the opportunity of moving some Zoo elephants who were being evacuated to the country and they were shifting them by night so as not to tie up the traffic – except ours!

Talk about seeing things . . . well, to tell the truth, by the end of the night-morning we had all consumed enough to have seen *pink* elephants!

The next morning I duly changed my warrant for a ticket at Waterloo and set off for Cowshott Camp feeling like the wrath of God – and all the angels, too! I wasn't the only one going to the same destination – and they all looked as rough as I felt.

When I fell out at Brookwood an emery-voiced sergeant told me to get fell in. Apparently we were to march two or three miles to bloody Cowshott. There was a taxi standing outside the station. I asked if I could take it – I'd provided myself with a little more cash than the four shillings which a generous Government had sent me – and join my companions at the camp. The sergeant then proceeded to tell me what I could do with the taxi – manifestly an impossibility – and, by the time his sandpaper-voiced harangue was at an end, my head was worse than ever.

But of one thing I was very sure.

I was in the Army.

4 1940–6
It was a Long Old War

This book is not an appreciation of the war. For close on six years, like millions of others, I learned to live a different life, tried to master other attainments and, in general, attempted to be of as much use as possible so as to get the whole affair – sometimes hideous, sometimes terrifying, often funny, periodically boring and always wasteful – over.

The very day we struck camp I went down with acute appendicitis and was rushed to Aldershot. I hesitate to specify which hospital for later I was informed that, in peacetime, it was reserved for the treatment of VD! Eventually I rejoined my battalion at Selsey, and we moved on to Chichester and West Wittering, still in Sussex. Finally we made our way north, to Yorkshire, eventually arriving in Hull for a time. There I caught up with Len Harvey, still the heavy and light-heavyweight champion of Great Britain, but now a pilot officer in the RAF.

Hull provided the most concentrated bombing I experienced in England, and I was delighted to go out with Len who was full of stories of some of his comrades-in-arms who had not settled down quite as smoothly as he. Len and I used to dine always in the same restaurant, when our joint duties permitted. I was to see him only once more during the war. That was nearly two years later, on the Spurs football ground, and the last I saw of him was the soles of his feet.

He had been knocked clean through the ropes, off the ring platform and through the Press seats, by Freddie Mills who thus acquired his light-heavyweight championship. But this was not the real Harvey. He had not boxed seriously for nearly three years and he was three weeks short of his thirty-fifth birthday. Furthermore his RAF duties, which he performed conscientiously, had not given a man of his age time to prepare properly. I take nothing away from the much beloved Freddie Mills, who was only a week away from his twenty-third birthday, when I say that in Len's prime it would not have been such an easy task to catch him flat-footed.

From Hull I got my sailing orders to go to Officer Cadet Training Unit in Douglas, Isle of Man; only a few weeks after I had arrived there

I learned that the restaurant where Len and I had eaten together so often had received a direct hit, killing most of the diners. But there were so many stories like that in those days. *C'est la guerre . . .*

I still find it impossible to believe the atmosphere in the Isle of Man in the spring of 1941. That the knife was still at our throats could be observed in the early hours of the short nights when you could see Liverpool aflame. Yet, although we worked hard enough, there were so few signs of war. Rationing, apart from tea, sugar and, of course petrol, seemed non-existent. The reason for this was that the civilians were largely supplied by a weekly ship which came from the neutral Irish Free State. Beer from the Manx brewery was still selling at threepence-halfpenny a bottle; Scotch, at a shilling a nip, was plentiful. Steak and chips was one and sixpence in the cafés: as much as you liked. Add this to clean sheets, provided for the 'gentleman cadets' billeted in the peacetime hotels, and you can imagine it was hard for us to believe that we were still involved in the war at all.

The Isle of Man was also one of the main centres for detainees and other wartime undesirables – including the followers of Sir Oswald Mosley, officially known as the British Union of Fascists; unofficially the initials were, to say the least, capable of alternative interpretations. Remembering my father's instructions I had carefully avoided volunteering recklessly in the Army but when we heard of the BUF flinging their kit into the harbour and defying their guards a number of us volunteered, quite happily, to help with guard duties. It was as well, I'm sure, that this offer was refused.

I had been lucky to get my first choice of regiments, the Dorsets, and I joined my battalion at Whitstable. As a young officer I was very fortunate, my platoon was on detachment, completely on its own, and it was easy to get to know them quickly as I lived alone in a tiny cottage, near a golf course, and close to their billets. As wartime restrictions prevented the dispatch of the famous 'Whitstable natives' all over the country, I was able to eat these magnificent oysters at half a crown a dozen. My eyes – as well as my mouth – still water at the memory, even though a second lieutenant's pay in 1941 was, I think, only twelve shillings a day.

Before long the situation for which every inexperienced officer prays had arisen; the blokes in my platoon had started disciplining themselves so as not to spoil a good thing. I have no illusions that they thought overmuch of my military genius but I tried to be fair and I was fit enough to do most purely physical things at least as well as most of them. But, as I might have guessed, the idyll at Whitstable wasn't to endure long. Someone was posted to our battalion and I, as the junior officer, had to move on, to the Isle of Sheppey.

I don't think anyone unconnected with the Army before the war would credit the appalling and, in wartime, frightening difference between a good battalion and a really bad one.

We were a company on detachment and were made up of, I was told, the rag-tag and bobtail of no fewer than sixty different units. Petrol disappeared, men vanished, officers were seen swaying on parade, the constant prevailing wind, of the sort which would spare your match but blow out your life, had all the trees leaning in one direction; many of the locals seemed hopelessly inbred. It was a place to sicken you and drive you slightly mad yourself.

I managed to get a little exercise fencing – which I had not done since I left my prep school – with an officer of the RAF who had been left behind in almost a caretaker capacity. He was also very keen on hawking and had a magnificent falcon with which he used to quarter the marshes. But one day, when he had left it briefly, hooded in a shed, it was killed by a cat. It was that sort of place.

I was 'rescued' from there – if you can call it that – by being transferred temporarily to the Royal Artillery who, it transpired, were short of officers for Light Anti-Aircraft regiments.

So it was off to Yeovil. I had deliberately joined the infantry because of my complete inability to cope with anything mechanical or mathematical. Now they were trying to put us through a three months' course in, I think, a little over a month. Not only did it not work with me but, towards the end of manhandling this wretched Bofors gun in and out of action something like twenty times a day, I found that I wasn't able to walk more than half a mile or so without doubling up. I knew I was out of condition after the Isle of Sheppey, but this was ridiculous.

Finally I became due for a short leave, in London, and went to see my own peacetime doctor – the Army ones having been singularly unhelpful. It took him about two minutes to discover that I had a hernia on one side and that the other was just about to go. Armed with a note from him I duly returned to my unit and was transferred to a tiny military hospital in Dorset. I was told that it was the one in which Lawrence of Arabia died after his fatal motor-cycle crash.

I had a spinal injection and a humorous surgeon. After he had finished one side he announced jovially: 'Half-time; change sides!' But instead of tying my arms down, which would have driven me frantic, he allowed me to hold hands with a nurse who, despite the handicap of a surgical mask, gave every indication of being a very pretty girl. It was a pity that when I tired and went half to sleep she transferred my hands to a singularly unprepossessing male orderly. But the doctor was a splendid chap. When, at the end of a rather long operation, my heart apparently got rather lazy he gave me a quite remarkably large swig of first-class brandy.

Alas! I wasn't destined to stay long at this small but extremely pleasant hospital. There was an appalling accident in the course of a massive military demonstration exercise in which one of the supporting aircraft fired into the close ranks of soldiers who were there to observe the manoeuvres. There was a wild rumour that the free Polish pilot who was supposed to have caused the carnage, in which there were many killed and wounded, was in fact a Luftwaffe pilot who had been infiltrated into the RAF. I think this story was given credence because among those attending the exercise was Field Marshal, then General, Montgomery who was, of course, alleged to be the main target.

Whatever was the truth of the whole affair all of us, except the critically ill, found ourselves summarily scooped up into ambulances to make room for the shattered bodies of the victims of the exercise. I was taken to the Cornelia Hospital, in Poole, and it's not a journey I care to recollect too vividly. Jolting along in an Army ambulance without the stitches in your stomach having been removed is not a form of travel which I would recommend.

After convalescence and sick leave I had a most peculiar spell with a detachment of 'crocks' guarding a factory where, so we were told, most of the cordite for the Navy was manufactured. It was brilliantly camouflaged – if that's not a contradiction in terms! – but as the head chemist had, we were assured, been a German, who had left only a matter of months before the outbreak of war, it struck me that the enemy might know pretty well where the factory was situated. I know that on the rare occasions when there was any bombing we didn't worry too much about the bombs themselves bursting: everyone was waiting for the louder 'echo'!

I saw a medical board in a big rambling hospital in Devon. While I was waiting my turn the matron told me how one night a fleeing German plane had dropped a random bomb on it. By ill luck it fell on the mental wing, where there were a few homicidal patients. Most of the inmates were trapped but one man, who had been a civil engineer before being admitted to the mental ward, organized pulleys, hoists, makeshift cranes, and allowed for stresses and strains so successfully that, by the time the official rescue services arrived, there was little for them to do but tidy up the mess. Everyone was considering a re-examination of the rescuer's mental health, when, without a moment's warning, he made a murderous attack with a razor-sharp sliver of thick broken glass which he had secreted under his coat during the rescue operations; the matron told me that the doctor, about whom the patient had a persecution mania, was lucky to escape with his life.

The result of my board was that I was permanently physically down-graded to 'B'. Later I was told that this meant that I could never be posted overseas. In the meantime I was transferred to an Infantry Training Centre, with a new intake of recruits every six weeks and the job of turning them into semi-trained troops.

To add to my general misery I went down with infective hepatitis – a particularly catching and utterly depressing form of jaundice.

Then came deliverance in the form of Hugh Cudlipp. Winston Churchill had decided that the British Army needed its own newspaper. The Americans already had *Stars and Stripes* which had been started with, I believe, the assistance of such brilliant writers as Alexander Woollcott in the First World War, and which promptly restarted when America entered the Second World War. The story was that Churchill, after his meeting with Franklin Roosevelt at Casablanca in January 1943, saw a copy of *Stars and Stripes*, which reported the President virtually verbatim and then, more or less as an afterthought, added something on the lines of: 'A Mr Churchill also spoke'! Whatever the true reason Hugh was summoned out of the desert, where he was fighting with the infantry, and called upon to start a Forces newspaper. It was called, perhaps not very originally – but succinctly – *Union Jack* and when it started, at Constantine, North Africa, it was the beginning of the British Army Newspaper Unit.

Hugh got to hear of my malaise, found out that there was nothing in the war that I would have preferred to do than join a Forces newspaper – where at least I would roughly know what I was doing – and pulled strings, via the Adjutant-General's office, so that on my release from hospital I was accorded combined convalescent and embarkation leave and then instructed to make the best time possible for North Africa.

That leave was a real race against time for my wife was about to go into a Devon nursing home to have our second child. The night before I was due to go north, to join a North African convoy, we tramped up and down some steep steps in the village to hasten the advent of our latest arrival. It worked. I stayed in the nursing home until the early hours of the morning; no joy. A few hours later I rang up. Yes! I had a second son. I had, I suppose, about a couple of hours with the two of them. Then I had to leave for Liverpool and embarkation for North Africa. When I next saw Rodney he was nearly three years old.

Constantine, my eventual destination, was famous for two things – its defiance of the ancient Romans and a deep ravine with a bridge and a viaduct. The story goes that when the Romans were besieging Constantine the ladies of the town paraded up and down the ramparts, flaunting their charms and, in the language of the day, more or less saying: 'Come and get it – if you can.' In the end, as they always did, the Romans managed to outflank the gorge and, as they stormed the town, the honest burghers of Constantine hurled the unfortunate ladies over the city wall to the river bed, nearly 1000 feet below, so that they should be denied the conquerors.

This custom had not completely died out by 1943. During the feast of Ramadan, when the pious Muslim each day eschews food, drink and women during the time of day a white thread can be distinguished from a black one, tempers are inclined to run somewhat high. It was unfortunate that some American troops picked this particular period to start tormenting some of the priests outside the Sidi-el Kattani mosque, getting hold of the loose end of their turbans and twirling them round like so many teetotums. The next morning three American bodies were found at the foot of the ravine.

There was an incident involving our Arab brethren which more or less illuminates the irreconcilable differences between East and West. My viewpoint was from an open-air café in one of the steeper streets in Algiers.

At this stage civilian motor vehicles, even those burning coal or in some cases what appeared to be hay, were in such short supply that if you had one you ran it until it disintegrated, for there was not the slightest possibility of getting any spares for it, except on the black market, where the cost was prohibitive and the penalties Draconian.

On this occasion one large solid-rubber tyre of a BF – Before Ford – vehicle finally gave up the unequal struggle and parted company with its parent contraption. The wheel rolled down the street, under its own power, at an ever-gathering pace. Down the same street, oblivious of the hooting of cars, the braying of donkeys and all the other noises which made wartime Algiers such a lovesome thing, God wot, came one of those Arabs, apparently juggling invisible objects as he walked. He also was oblivious of the rubber Juggernaut, which was bearing down on him in much the same way as that fiend in the famous Thurber drawing captioned: 'You and your premonitions.'

Finally one voice more raucous than the rest apprised him that while it might be true that the year was at the spring, day at the morn, morning at seven, the hillside dew-pearled, the lark on the wing, the snail on the thorn and God in His heaven – quite clearly all was not right with the world. I suspect the warning voice was *not* that of one of the Arabs who had come to a jostling halt, to see what would be the outcome of the meeting between this irresistible force and that, clearly, very movable object.

The strolling Arab turned his head. At what he perceived his jaw fell agape, his eyes stuck out like old-fashioned coat pegs, his swarthy complexion turned a suety, dirty shade of grey. Yet he was in no immediate peril. It is true that the solid-rubber tyre, as though possessed by some malevolent *Efreet*, had now gathered such momentum that it was progressing in great thudding bounds down the street. But there was plenty of time for the perambulant to exercise that primitive manoeuvre which, in the prize-ring, is known as side-stepping.

What was hopeless was to do what he tried, which was to predate Roger Bannister and the sub-four minute mile by some ten years.

Substituting the juggling motions of his arms for the controlled frenzy of the pistons of the *Flying Scotsman* at full pelt, he behaved as does the hapless rabbit caught in the headlights of some advancing car. Straight he ran and fast he ran. But he did not run fast enough. His *tarbush* flew off and was crushed by the remorseless monster now at his heels. A moment later the same fate befell him. As he was struck firmly between the shoulder blades and left flattened in the macadam like some gigantic fly forever trapped in amber, his flowing white *djellabiyeh* showing the passage of the wheel, he gave one final despairing ululation to Allah.

I have never seen so many people falling about in chunks, gripped by uncontrollable laughter, as the Arab onlookers. This was definitely the funniest thing since the last earthquake, murrain or sudden death. It was left to a representative of Western man to establish that the smitten was not, in fact, mortally injured and to set him right side up and restore his *tarbush* to him.

The war in North Africa was over, and our job was to start printing different editions of *Union Jack* on such French presses as were available. As well as at Constantine the paper was printed in Algiers and Tunis. Sport began to get organized and one of my first jobs, as well as getting home and local sports news into the paper, was to go round talking sport to various isolated units.

Gradually we moved on. First of all to Sicily where, in Catania, we took over a newspaper office which would have graced Fleet Street.

From the slopes of Etna, where so many brave men died, we flew over Vesuvius, glowing faintly like a gently puffed cigar, and so to Naples.

In wartime the old sneer about Naples being 'the only Mediterranean port without a European quarter' seemed justified. The basic poverty and centuries-old filth were intensified by the attitude of so many of the local citizens who, if they were not involved in the black market, gave themselves over to a feeling that as it was hopeless to do anything, they might as well do nothing.

Most of the streets off the Via Roma were out of bounds, rightly, to servicemen, but looking down them you could see the old women sitting on what passed for the pavements, cooking their poor, pathetic scraps of food – when they had any – over charcoal braziers which they kept glowing with wooden fans. This sort of cooking couldn't have changed in centuries; but now the food had got worse and more scarce.

Venereal disease became a tremendous military problem; at one time it was incapacitating more troops than the enemy were able to. The Americans summed up the situation succinctly, if savagely, with a poster showing a swarthy girl peeling a stocking off one hairy leg, with the caption: 'If she's game she's got it!' You could not walk down the street without being pestered by kids of six, seven or eight, tugging at your sleeve and jabbering: 'You want jig-a-jig? My sister very loving, very clean. Only one tin bullee beef.'

We got into the most Godawful – and I use the word advisedly – row in our attempts to discourage these pedlars of dubious delights. We printed, in Italian, a tasteful little notice which said, roughly: 'We are here to win a war as quickly as possible. We are not interested in the black market or in your syphilitic sister.'

Unfortunately a soldier with what I can only describe – in print at least – as a warped sense of humour, showed it to an English-speaking priest who had meant only to pass the time of day. And we had the fury of the Church, backed by the higher military echelons – a formidable combination – thundering round our collective heads. Maybe we were stupid: after all, most of the kids couldn't read anyway!

I do not care overmuch for amateur philosophers, but it does seem to me that in the middle of the organized beastliness which is war the Church, which sanctions the breaking of the sixth commandment, is hypocritical to a nauseating degree when it somes to the question of sexual problems. Of course prostitution is evil. Of course men should be continent; of course married men should be faithful. But equally men were never intended to be away from their homes and wives for year after heart-wearying year. Professional soldiers who, God knows, are not generally the brightest of men, know these things and, no doubt wickedly, but sensibly, arrange for brothels, controlled for cleanliness, by the Army. But the Church always puts its pious foot down – and armies continue to be ravaged by VD.

We had been at war for over four years now and 1943 gave way to 1944. Sport began to assume big-time proportions behind the lines, either as an outlet for surplus energy for the performers or as an entertainment for the uniformed spectators.

Early in the year there was a tremendous boxing tournament, embracing the eight generally recognized weights, both amateur and professional. Easily the outstanding star was Marcel Cerdan, who had held the French welterweight title at the outbreak of war and was now a *matelot* in the Free French Navy.

Later I met Jack Sharkey who had not only refereed in Algiers but was the only man ever to fight both Jack Dempsey and Joe Louis. As he was only twenty-four when he met Dempsey and still on his way up – but not that night! – whereas he was nearly thirty-four and taking part in the last fight of his career when he met Louis, he refused to say who was the better performer in the ring. For the record he was knocked out in seven rounds by Dempsey in 1927, and in three by Louis in 1936. But he did opine that if the two men had been locked alone in a room, with the key on the mantelpiece and no interfering referee around, it would have been Dempsey who would have unlocked the door. From the films I've seen of the old 'Manassa Mauler', who is now 82, I'm inclined to agree. Dempsey thought rules were written by fusspots to protect cissies.

There was more top-class boxing later, after Rome had been liberated, and I hereby confess that I entirely failed to spot a future heavyweight champion of the world in the form of an ebony light-heavyweight, Ezzard Charles, who did only enough to win on points, without ever seriously inconveniencing his opponents.

I remember the athletics meeting at Florence not only for my first sight of Harrison Dillard, winner of the 100 metres in the first postwar Olympics, but because I was sharing a room with Geoffrey Dyson, possibly the greatest athletics coach Britain ever produced. What an enthusiast that man was. At the end of the war the Americans were sending some of their top track and field coaches over, to give instruction to any British or French instructors who were interested.

Dyson made such an impression on one of the most famous of all the Americans, the coach from Princeton, that he more or less guaranteed that Geoffrey would be his successor when he retired and that in the meantime, as his assistant, he could make something like 10000 dollars a year – a tremendous sum for a British coach in those times. Dyson turned him down politely but firmly. He explained that his one great ambition was to make Britain great in athletics.

It gives a clue, perhaps, as to why our world-ranking performances have not been more frequent to say that Dyson, after spending a lot of his own money – and, of course, unlimited time – was treated so scurvily by those in charge of British athletics that there was no honourable course left open to him but to resign as National Coach, which he did, in the middle of an international meeting abroad, when an attempt was made to interfere with the order of the runners, whom he had rehearsed in the tricky job of baton-passing in the relays.

My own favourite story connected with Geoff was when, at the end of the war, he was running an Inter-Allied Sports Centre at Udine, in the north of Italy, not far from Sequals, birthplace of Primo Carnera.

The idea was that the French should teach racing cycling, the Americans vouchsafe some of the mysteries of baseball and the British lay bare the inner secrets of Rugby football. On the surface a bright idea. But . . .

It came to pass that a very high ranking British officer (I believe it was General Sir Oliver Leese) was to pay a visit to the Centre. For hour after weary, sweaty hour a group of forlorn Americans were made to practise scrummaging. Finally the great man arrived. He went up to one unfortunate who had been jammed in the second row, with the man behind exerting nonstop pressure on his backside, while his own head was sandwiched between the two backsides in front of him. The General clapped him on the back and inquired: 'Well, m'boy, and how do you like rugger?' To which the long-suffering American could only reply wearily: 'It's kinda innimate, ain't it, General!'

Gradually as the spring of 1945 mellowed it became obvious that the end, at least in Europe, could not be much longer delayed.

There was more and more sport. I chatted with Andy Beattie, the Scottish international whom I had seen in the famous FA Cup Final of 1938, playing for Preston North End against Huddersfield. Beattie told me of a youngster who had started to make his name before the war, had narrowly escaped being 'brewed up' in his tank and would, said Beattie, make even Stan Matthews fight to keep his place on the right wing, once he recovered from his experiences. His name was Tom Finney.

Somehow it became more and more urgent to get back to some normality. But even when the war in Europe did come to an end there was nearly a year to wait before I was demobilized. However I was lucky enough to get a brief trip back to Britain. I had about six months' service still to go when I returned from London to Rome.

It seemed a very long time since I had joined the troops liberating Rome in July 1944 and found myself part of that delirious throng which figured in the freeing of the first European capital to be rescued from the Nazi yoke. A few days after the liberation I attended what I'm certain must have been one of the most extraordinary audiences ever accorded by a modern Pope. It was given by Pius XII to assorted correspondents and photographers, military and civilian.

We were a motley throng. Dirty (there were no laundry services and water was short); some unshaven; some of the women correspondents in slacks – an unbelievable sight in the Vatican – almost all the men in shorts of varying degrees of griminess. And the attitude of the company was, in many cases, frankly hostile. When the Pope gave us his blessing and welcome a harsh voice rasped in reply: 'And I suppose last week you were saying the same thing to the bloody Germans!' Pius replied that all Catholics were his children.

An RAF photographer in a pair of very short shorts found something wrong with his camera and knelt on the floor, almost standing on his head, and unwittingly exposed his genitalia, crying out: 'Hold it, hold it.' One of the beslacked American women correspondents to whom the Pope had addressed a few words remembered, after he had passed her, that she wanted to say something and caught the Pontiff by his robe saying: 'Just a minute, Your Holiness.' Free fights nearly broke out between some of the men muttering four-letter words and others, devout Catholics, to whom this was the supreme moment of their war.

I am not competent to decide whether Pius was a good Pope, as I am not a Roman Catholic, but I do know that he was a supreme diplomatist for when I looked at my notes later I found that there was not a single controversial headline to be extracted from what he had said.

I spent a brief period at Milan where we shared a newspaper office with the local Communist Party. It was a point of honour with me to throw up a salute of which a Guards officer would have been proud while my Italian opposite number responded with a clenched fist salutation, straight from the Kremlin. Already it was obvious that peace was going to have problems just as complex as those of wartime.

I also had a few weeks in Athens where we had opened another edition of *Union Jack*. It was impossible not to be disgusted when you saw how the supplies provided by the United Nations Relief and Rehabilitation Organization never reached the starving thousands who so desperately needed them, but were sequestered by the wealthy few. The cradle of Western democracy was not a happy place at the end of yet another war to save democracy.

At last I got the longed-for signal to report back to Milan for the start of demobilization.

Having been back in England so recently I realized how any supplement to the rations would be welcomed, and before embarking on the train which was to take us to Calais I managed a crafty trip from Milan to nearby Gorgonzola, where I got one of the largest and most imposing pieces of that ferocious cheese that I have ever seen. Alas! I had overestimated the speed of our train. After a couple of days of stop and start that cheese was beginning to make its presence known throughout the length and breadth of the train. In fact, if I hadn't kept it on a short leash it would, I am sure, have outdistanced the train.

In the end the officer in charge of the train tracked down the overwhelming odour to my carriage and sternly ordered me to get rid of it forthwith – if not sooner. At some station in central France I regretfully bowled that noble cheese down the main platform. It is my sincere belief that the local inhabitants thought that, at last, perfidious Albion was using the deadly poison gas which for years had been such an awesome threat.

But they got their own back on me when we had to spend a last night at Calais. We went into a local bar and ordered what purported to be Calvados. I took one sip, then poured a liberal dose on the zinc on the bar and applied a match. The blue flame seemed to lick hungrily at the ceiling, and when it finally died down there was a circular black mark and a distinct indentation in the zinc. The proprietor wanted me to pay for it. I offered to do so if he would provide me with a new stomach. Mine had survived the rigours of war for nigh on six years, but, I was convinced, would never be the same after his hell-brew. We parted with imprecations and expressions of mutual ill-will.

A few days later, in the spring of 1946, at long, long last, I was demobilized.

5 1946–50
The Road Back

I had been very lucky in the Army but now the real struggle was going to start – the battle to re-establish myself in Fleet Street, to come back to what had been my normal life before a break of nearly six years.

To complicate things the *Sunday Pictorial*, to which I returned in May 1946, was limited to twelve pages and for the first six months or so after my demob its circulation was limited to, I believe, what it had been before the war. Writing only about fifty times a year, in a midget-sized paper with a restricted circulation, was hardly the easiest way to make a come-back.

Sport itself was booming. The first really big event I remember was the fight for the world light-heavyweight title in which Freddie Mills challenged the American holder of the championship, Gus Lesnevich, at Harringay Arena.

People today who talk about galloping inflation – and who doesn't! – might remember that well over a quarter of a century ago promoter Jack Solomons was charging £21 for ringside seats, and the whole thing was nearly over in the second round! In that hectic three minutes Mills was smashed to the canvas four times and, as I wrote in a preface to one of Freddie's books:

I wonder how many people appreciate, or even remember, that it was Freddie Mills, more than any other individual who quite literally saved big-time British boxing.

Had Mills stayed down in the second round there would have been an out-cry against over-matching our champions against the better trained, better fed, and more skilful Americans. Yet no one could have blamed the man himself for he had stood up to the one-man firing squad which was Lesnevich – and had disdained a bandage round his eyes.

In the end the fight was stopped in Lesnevich's favour in the tenth round, but only after the winner had sustained a broken nose, his left eye rendered non-existent and his hairy torso bespattered with his own blood.

Then came the first postwar Wimbledon. Obviously outsiders have won the championships, but I think you could have got pretty large odds against the Frenchman, Yvon Petra, who looked like a mobile lamp post, taking the men's singles. I seem to remember being surprised that he was seeded as high as number five.

But, on a Centre Court with some 1200 seats railed off because of war damage, the lanky Frenchman with the big serve triumphed where the hot tip, Jack Kramer, went out, largely because of a blistered playing hand, after a 17–15 second set against the Czech, Jaroslav Drobny. The following year, however, Kramer won an undistinguished Wimbledon, including the Australian Dinny Pails, taking the shortest postwar final against fellow-American Tom Brown.

But there was no mistake about the women's singles. This title was won by Pauline 'Bobbie' Betz, a gay strawberry blonde with a backhand which was the feminine equivalent of Don Budge's magnificent stroke. Miss Betz won the title with the loss of only twenty games, one fewer than Alice Marble had lost the last time Wimbledon had been held, in 1939. Incidentally, Bobbie, excluding the lady who won the first women's title in 1884, was only the third girl to win at her first attempt, and there has been only one since – Maureen Connolly.

I always thought that Pauline Betz could have been one of the very great women players, but after winning the US Championships – for the fourth time – later in the year, she turned professional which, of course, in those days virtually finished her career.

After nearly three years overseas it would have been reasonable to expect a fairly extended stay at home, but within six months of getting back to civilian life I was off to Norway for the European athletics championships.

The currency restrictions of those days could have their funny side as I had learned on the flight to Oslo. I thought one of my fellow-passengers looked slightly familiar and, during the flight, he came up to me, addressed me by my right name, and reminded me that we had been at school together – and asked if I could lend him a pound. In the normal way you learn to discourage that sort of approach a bit on the sharpish side but I felt fairly confident about this borrower. His name was Rothschild! If I had to point to a summit moment in my whole life I think that would be it. . . .

Although this was so long ago and was my only visit to Oslo I remember it vividly for the British in the immediate postwar era achieved a popularity in Norway which, alas, we have seldom subsequently equalled anywhere.

It was also one of the most alcoholic sporting occasions I have ever attended. You had only to open your mouth and speak English for some magnificent Norwegian, so many of them wearing those jaunty little woollen caps which had been a proscribed symbol of the Resistance movement during the war, to close it with a slug of aquavit, that fiery northern liquor, administered straight out of the bottle.

There were one or two splendid incidents which spotlighted how out of touch everyone was with organizing big-time sport after seven years. For instance, there was a mistake in the timing of the 10,000 metres and the marathon, which was, by the way, almost certainly over half a mile short! The winners of the two events were actually on the track at the same time – but running in opposite directions!

Then there was the starter who set fire to himself. He had started one race and put his pistol back into his blazer pocket. About five seconds later it went off again in some mysterious way. Despite looking distinctly shaken the official tried to carry it off, strolling away with a would-be nonchalant air. Another five seconds later and he had broken the European record for the standing long jump: the pistol had set fire to his pocket which, in turn, had burned through his slacks.

But the real highlight of the whole championships was Sydney Wooderson's last great international appearance in the 5000 metres – a little over 3 miles 188 yards.

On 23 August, just a week before his thirty-second birthday, the wispy little man who had broken the world record for the mile *nine years* earlier with 4 mins 6·4 secs and who had gone through the war, first with the National Fire Service, then in the Pioneer Corps and finally with REME, ran, in some ways, the race of his life. Four days earlier Wooderson had told me that he thought the race would be won in 14 mins 10 secs. This was surprising enough for, apart from Gunder 'The Wonder' Hagg's time of 13 mins 58·2 secs, which the Swede had set up during the war, no one had beaten the 14 mins 8·8 secs established by the Finn, Taisto Mäki, just before the war.

On the day of the race itself the little man told me that on further consideration he thought the winning time might have to be a little faster. It was. For as he slammed through the tape to end, the colour of a candle that has burnt out and collapsed on itself, in the arms of the British team's masseur, Wooderson had returned 14 mins 8·6 secs – the second fastest time ever for a distance he had never run before! As soon as Wooderson had recovered sufficiently to speak he gasped that he would never run this sort of race again – and he kept his word.

From triumph in Oslo to tragedy in Cardiff for Welsh lightweight Ronnie James who got his shot at the world championship against one of the greatest body punchers I have ever seen, Ike Williams. James had to boil down to make the lightweight limit of 9 st 9 lb and Williams cut him in half with an alleged 'bolo' punch – nothing very different from a right upper-cut to the body.

The last time I was in New York I was in the office of Teddy Brenner, who succeeded Harry Markson as director of boxing at Madison Square Garden, when a portly, grey-moustached, middle-aged Negro came in. There was something vaguely familiar about him and when he went out I raised by eyebrows interrogatively at Brenner. 'Ike Williams,' he said. Then he added: 'There may have been better lightweight champions before him, but them I didn't see. Williams was the best I ever watched; they didn't come any better.'

By 1947 the long war years had, at last, begun to fade and George Casey, the sports editor from whom I had learned so much, was doing more than his fair share to help me back.

About this time I felt a yearning to return to the USA. It was nearly eight and a half years since I had last been in New York and with Joe Louis back in the ring I wanted to be at the centre of world boxing action. However, I did point out that Jersey Joe Walcott, Joe's opponent, was over three months older than Louis who himself was nearer thirty-four than thirty-three; I admitted it might not be much of a scrap. Never try to 'con' your employers if you hope to last.

I don't think I can improve on the first paragraph I wrote about the fight after seeing Louis floored in the first and fourth rounds: under the heading of 'I'll Swear On Oath That Joe Louis Was Licked!' I began my story: 'Have you ever attended an execution and seen the condemned man turn round and shoot the firing squad?'

It was one of the most noteworthy upsets in heavyweight history – and certainly one of the most controversial decisions of all time.

The fight ended as sensationally as it had begun, for while the referee's and the judges' score-cards were being collected Louis tried to leave the ring before the decision was given. It was my impression then, and it remains the same over 10,000 nights later, that Louis, a supremely honest athlete, thought that he had lost and wanted to get back to the anonymity of a locked dressing room before the announcement was made.

Then back to England. But not to my home. For my marriage had broken up.

It was one of the delayed wartime casualties. My wife had always been shy. Before the war I had been able to introduce her to a new world, for her, of sport and headlines and the constant pressure of a deadline which was none the less urgent even when it did come only once a week. But during the war, with two young children to bring up and marooned in the middle of the country in an otherwise elderly household, with no means of travelling even a few miles, she had lost touch with the brash but stimulating, ephemeral but effervescent world which we had grown to enjoy together a decade or so earlier.

There is no doubt that the fault was mine. I was so determined to try to get to the top in sportswriting that I pushed myself a little hard. As a result I was drinking fairly heavily to keep going day and night. And, when my wife did not care to share this somewhat hectic existence, obviously I was inclined to play around.

Curiously enough we separated, in the end, because of the children. I have always viewed with the greatest suspicion those lachrymose drunks who claim that their wives do not understand them and that had it not been for 'the kids' they would have separated years ago. One morning after a more than usually bitter wrangle I noticed one of the boys was red-eyed. I asked him what was the matter and eventually it came out that he had heard the two of us 'saying nasty things to each other'. How can it benefit children to grow up in an atmosphere of hostility and acrimonious animosity I completely fail to see. A clean cut is surely much better.

So it proved with us. My wife, all praise to her, always allowed me to see and to take out the children whenever it was possible. I like to think that because of her attitude they were able to adjust better than most to a situation which must always be traumatic for uncomprehending youngsters.

There was no question of a divorce. I do not think my wife ever wanted to marry again and although I had one or two fairly serious affairs there was, when I was honest with myself, at that time no one with whom I wanted to share the rest of my life. Instead, after a year or so of misery on my own in furnished rooms, my prewar friend Dick Richards, then show-business writer of the *Sunday Pic*, and I shared a succession of flats ranging from Marble Arch to Berkeley Street and some eight years of fun, games and general hell-raising which was probably very bad for both of us but not a minute of which, with my hand on my heart, can I honestly regret.

In the meantime, at the beginning of 1948, I remember one dinner party in particular. Joe Louis had come to London as one of the major attractions of an exhibition with a sporting theme which was being held in London's giant Earls Court Arena, and I persuaded Hugh Cudlipp to throw a dinner party for him at the Albany Club, that most entertaining of postwar rendezvous.

One way and another it promised to be an evening of more than somewhat explosive dimensions. To begin with Hugh kept on flirting with Joe's then wife Marva, a most attractive brown-skinned girl. I kept on trying to point out that with umpteen million girls in the world it seemed to me the height of folly to play Romeo with the wife of the world's heavyweight champion – she, incidentally, wasn't doing anything to damp Hugh down. Why not juggle with gelignite if he was out for kicks, I suggested.

But I confess my thoughts became less altruistic and more concerned for the safety of my own skin when, during the meal, Joe leant across to me and said: 'So you thought Walcott whupped me?' Blimey! This looked like turning into the sort of dinner which only the Borgias really appreciated. I had no idea that he would have seen my story printed in a British newspaper. But apparently some bastard had cut it out, the full back page of the *Sunday Pictorial*, and mailed it to Joe.

Frantically I tried to remember what I had written. The headline was enough: 'I'll Swear On Oath That Joe Louis Was Licked!' Meanwhile Joe was waiting for an answer. I licked lips considerably drier than my palms which were damp with apprehension. In the end I nodded. 'Yes, Joe. I did think he won.' What else *could* I say?

Big Bronze nodded his head slowly. Here, I thought, it comes. For years I had been writing that a clean, quick knockout does not hurt the recipient. Now, by God, I was going to get a first-hand – yes, you could say that again – demonstration which would prove whether I had been telling the truth or not.

Louis spoke. 'Well, mebbe you was right and mebbe you was wrong. *But there ain't gonna be no argument when we meets again!*'

That conversation explains why, for one of the only two times since 1929, I missed the finals of Wimbledon.

For on 25 June 1948, Louis met Walcott in a return bout, and I flew over to see it.

It was, except for the result, a desperate disappointment for all Louis' supporters. Again a right-hander dropped the champion in the third round but he scrambled up before the count could begin. Yet, try as he did, he could not recover the co-ordination and the reflexes, the timing and the thunderbolt power of the punches of a decade before. Of the first seven rounds I gave six to Walcott with one even.

Then the tide turned and big Joe started reaching the grimacing, clowning opponent who mopped and mowed like some brown monkey in a pair of white silk shorts as he tormented his opponent.

Still the end was unexpected. Walcott backed to the ropes to get Louis to lead to him so that he could cross his right hand over the champion's left – the sort of punch with which he had previously dropped his man. But this time Louis landed with his right – three times. Instantly it was obvious that Walcott was badly hurt. He threw one very good right which halted the big man; but one thing Louis hadn't lost was his ability to finish off a man once he had him in real trouble.

Once more Walcott was on the ropes and Louis landed on his jaw, following him with pinpointed punches as he slid slowly down the ropes. For once the gods had remitted the years and Joe, for a glorious half-minute, was allowed to be what he was when he became the youngest-ever heavyweight champion of the world up to that time. I thought I had seen him often enough to follow the movements of those great brown hammers which were his fists. But, in all, I counted no more than half a dozen blows in that final assault whereas when I saw it on film in slow-motion, there were at least eleven punches. Joe's hands could still move fast enough for you to miss nearly half the punches – but they didn't miss his opponent.

Then came the statement which everyone who liked boxing and who liked Louis wanted to hear. Over the radio Louis said: 'This was for you, Mom. This was my last fight.'

Later, still supremely honest, he commented: 'Five years ago I would have come out in the first round and got it over in a hurry. But I am not the fighter I was.'

As, of course, we were to see in the tragically inept performance against Ezzard Charles over two years later, and the final obliteration by Rocky Marciano in 1951, when Louis was nearly thirty-seven and a half. But as long as he could lift his fists he tried to go on, endeavouring to pay back the millions they said he owed in back taxes and which seemed to grow to a more impossibly enormous total with every breath he drew. I read in one American magazine that his indebtedness was going up by the equivalent of £97 10s. *a day!*

Before that, however, there had been plenty of excitement in the year. I had returned to St Moritz to see my first Winter Olympic Games – and come across the perpetual 'Mr No' of the Olympic movement, Avery Brundage. The sweep and pageantry of the Winter Games is the most sparkling, I think, in the whole wide tapestry of international sport. But of course they are no more 'amateur' than top-class lawn tennis used to be.

A month later and I was to see an accident unique in my experience of even that most testing of races – the Grand National.

It concerned Lord Mildmay who was riding his black gelding, Cromwell. It looked as though he were going to be unlucky yet again as he had been twelve years earlier, on Davy Jones. Then he seemed all set for victory until, at the fence before the last, the buckle of the reins broke in his hands and, with the reins dangling free, Davy Jones ran out at the final fence.

This time the same sort of thing happened – not to Cromwell but to Zahia, one of the only two mares in the race, who also ran out before the last obstacle. This left Mildmay the consolation of at least getting third place. But as he took the last two fences his old-fashioned upright style, like some ancient sporting print that had jumped out of its frame, seemed more awkward than usual. What we did not know until afterwards was that after Cromwell had jumped the canal fence for the second time an old riding injury to Mildmay's neck reappeared and caused his head to drop towards his chest. He was unable to get his head up again and he took the last two fences virtually blind.

My favourite, if apocryphal, story about this ill-starred sportsman was the time when he had been having a bad run and a lot of the professionals decided it was up to them to see that this immensely popular amateur had a change of fortune.

So they arranged for him to win a race. One rider fell off, another's mount seemed to refuse, a third baulked a fourth and couldn't get disentangled himself. In the end there was only one jockey left contesting the race with Mildmay, for it had been decided that for the sake of appearances *someone* had better at least finish.

But Mildmay was having one of his worse days. He zigged and he zagged, weaving all over the course, nearly coming off and plodding along at the pace of a snail while his unfortunate 'opponent' was having the devil's own job to hold his horse back.

Finally the other 'jock' managed to come topsides with his lordship and, arms almost wrenched out of his shoulders after his exertions in holding back his mount, who was rarin' to get on with it, he gasped: 'For Gawd's sake, m'lord, come on or we'll *both* be up in front of the stewards.' Of whom Mildmay was one!

But if sport can produce some of the closest friendships between the widest variety of people in every walk of life it can also establish feuds which only death can end.

I was invited to Australia House to a reception held for the Australian cricketers who were touring England, for the last time under the captaincy of Don Bradman, and for the first time for ten years.

A decade before I had sat through that marathon 364 by Len Hutton, parts of which, to be truthful, made one feel that a record as inconsequential as pole-squatting was being set up. Bradman, before he broke a bone in his ankle, reputedly said that if Hutton could make so many, he, Bradman, would make more. I had not seen him since.

As my taxi drew up outside Australia House two others arrived simultaneously. Out of one stepped my cousin on my mother's side, Douglas Jardine. Out of the other Don Bradman. We entered the building and walked up the stairs together, myself in the middle. It was over fifteen years since Jardine, with the rocket attack of Harold

Larwood, had proved that Bradman, even on his own doorstep, could be found vulnerable. Now I felt that I was accompanied by two invisible men – as far as each of them was concerned.

Douglas chatted to me, asking about my mother, but his Red Indian-style profile never inclined a fraction of an inch in the direction of Bradman who, face as clenched as a conker, ascended the steps as though neither of us had been there, or even existed at all. Everyone was asked to sign a visitors' book. I often wondered which of them got his name on top of the other's. I did not wait to see.

After my trip to the States for the Louis–Walcott fight I came back to see the return fight between Freddie Mills and Gus Lesnevich. The fight was nothing like their first epic battle but Gus got cut over both eyes very early on and when the exchanges became so dull that they were not worthy of a world title fight another great British referee, Teddy Waltham, famous for years as an incorruptible Secretary of the British Boxing Board of Control, asked for more action.

That was in the tenth round – and Freddie Mills supplied the action. He dropped Lesnevich twice for counts of nine, and although the contest was reasonably close at the finish there was only one possible winner; for the first time since dear old Bob Fitzsimmons, back in 1903, a British-born fighter had won the world light-heavyweight championship.

In less than a week the XIVth Olympic Games of modern times were upon us.

It's a curious thing that of all the eight summer Games I covered the London ones made least impression on me. Partly this was because, being on a Sunday paper, these were the only Games I wasn't reporting day by day. Additionally these were still days of 'mass austeria' which meant that Britain bidding for, and getting, the Games was one of the worst things, in the long run, that ever happened to British sport. I am looking at this from a long-term view. Every country staging successive Games has derived some permanent benefit from acting as the hosts. New sports stadia have been built, Olympic villages, subsequently to be occupied by ordinary tenants, have been erected, new roads, flyovers, carriageways, even underground railway systems have been installed for the lasting benefit of the host nation's citizens.

In 1948 London got nothing, but nothing. I know that it is contrary to the Olympic tradition for anyone to derive benefit from the Games, but I still cannot understand why it was necessary for us to bid for them when Finland rightly said that she could not stage them so soon after the war.

The result was that the bulk of the competitions were held at Wemb-

94

ley, either in the football stadium or in the adjoining Empire Pool. Competitors were put up in existing Service establishments. The staging of the Games by that superb showman, Arthur Elvin, was a masterpiece of improvisation, a classic example of British 'muddling through'; but to get not even a new national stadium, after being hosts to the 'Greatest Show on Earth', was a bitter pill from which sport in the United Kingdom is still suffering.

Of course there were great races and great moments and one distinction which was unique; the outstanding track and field athlete – and athletics is the very spine of the Games – was a woman, Fanny Blankers-Koen, a Dutch housewife.

Had it not been for the war I'm sure Mrs Blankers-Koen would have been the most famous woman athlete of all time. As it was, between 1938 and 1951, when she was thirty-three, she put up official world records in no fewer than seven separate events – 100 yards, 100 metres, 220 yards, 80 metres hurdles, high jump, long jump and pentathlon. When you realize that she was also a member of the Netherlands women's squad which twice set up a world record for the 4×110 yards relay, and of the team which established a world record for the 4×200 metres relay, the imagination boggles at the talent of this warm-hearted, golden-haired woman who won four medals at the 1948 Games.

I was covering the Olympic boxing for BBC TV. I remember writing earlier that year, about another event, that: 'You can be a "televisitor" to this match if there's a set handy.' Times do change!

In fact, although to be absolutely honest I don't remember them making a great impression on me at that time, there were two outstanding gloved gold medallists.

The flyweight title went to an Argentinian, Pascual Perez, who was later to hold the world professional title for some five and a half years and was certainly one of the three best eight-stone men I ever watched. The middleweight division was dominated by a Hungarian, Lazslo Papp, who was later to set up a record which might stand for ever – the winning of boxing gold medals at three successive Olympic Games.

There was however one boxing story which, as far as I'm concerned, provided the best headline that has ever been put on anything I've ever written.

In September Jack Solomons, easily the outstanding British promoter of that era, brought over an American, Lee Oma, who had learned his boxing in jail, to fight the British heavyweight champion, Bruce Woodcock. I had been tipped off in the States about Oma – that he wasn't, as it were, exactly the sort of man to whom you would rush if you wanted to buy a second-hand pair of boxing gloves – and I wrote a distinctly critical piece, thereupon being soundly taken to task for being unfair in bringing up his past, hitting a man after he had paid his debt to society, etc., etc. In 'training' lackadaisical Lee seemed more concerned in dealing cards than throwing punches.

Came the night of the so-called fight. Inside three rounds the crowd, to the sound of the chimes of Big Ben, was chanting: 'Lie down, lie down, lie down, lie down.' In the intervals between rounds members of the public who had recognized me at the ringside came up, said they had previously criticized me for being biased but now wanted to apologize. I have never known anything quite like it.

The sorry farce came to an end in the fourth round when Oma, having apparently been tapped on the chin, clasped his stomach and flopped all over the ring like some great landed fish. But it was the public who had been 'landed'. We had a 'brains trust' to produce a headline, including Hugh Cudlipp and Stanley Halsey, then the soccer writer and, under a 'strap' line which read: 'PETER WILSON ON THE big FIGHT' there appeared just three words: 'OMA? COMA? AROMA!'

They told the whole story.

After the excitements of 1948 the following year was comparatively tame. I paid my by now regular visit to the States, this time in June, to see two world title fights, the middleweight and the heavyweight.

First came the middleweight, in which Marcel Cerdan, the Frenchman, lost his title against Jake La Motta, known as the 'Bronx Bull' – to those who liked him – but as a variety of other things by the infinitely larger number of people who detested him.

It was staged at the Briggs Stadium in Detroit. The fight itself was a sad let-down. In the very first round La Motta, a very tough egg indeed, half-hit, half-wrestled Cerdan to the canvas. In Europe the American would certainly have been warned, conceivably disqualified, for wrestling. For, although it was not immediately obvious, Cerdan, who had fallen awkwardly on his left shoulder, was reduced to only one effective hand, being unable to raise his left even to guard himself.

There had to be a return. And it was fixed for 28 September. If it had taken place then Marcel Cerdan might still be alive. But La Motta injured himself in training and the return bout was postponed until 2 December.

There must have been a jinx on the Frenchman. In the normal way he would probably have finished his serious training in France and then gone over to get acclimatized about three weeks before the fight. But Edith Piaf was opening at, I think, the Versailles in New York – and the wonderful little French singer was the *chère amie* of the great French middleweight. He persuaded his manager, Jo Longman, who had been with the Free French under General Leclerc during their astonishing march in the Second World War to Lake Chad and who thereafter, his eyes affected by the desert glare, always wore dark glasses, to fly back with him to New York earlier than they had intended so as to surprise the 'little sparrow' on her opening night.

But they never got there. For on 27 October 1949 the plane with Cerdan and Jo Longman aboard flew into a mountainside in the Azores and all were killed.

At the start of 1950 I travelled behind the Iron Curtain for the first time. I went to Budapest where the world table tennis championships were held. There was nothing especially memorable about the play but the ambience, although in a different way, was almost as oppressively overwhelming as Berlin had been some fourteen years earlier.

The hall where the championships were held was so draped with scarlet banners that it reminded me of a slaughter-house dripping blood. Slogans appeared in four languages – English, French, German and Russian – although there were no Russians playing. There were no Americans either, on the order of the US State Department.

Under a huge picture of the then Deputy Prime Minister, Matyas Rakosi, who had spent many years in prison under the old Hungarian regime, there was the following 'uplifting' thought for the day, and every other day: 'Our example in sport is the great Soviet Union, led by the great Stalin, the chief fighter in the peace camp.'

Well, I suppose you could take that two ways.

I was staying in the Hotel Gellert and the first thing anyone saw there was a larger-than-life-size picture of a bearded man, draped in blood-red, with, underneath, the inscription: *'Lenin elt; Lenin el; Lenin elni fog'* ('Lenin lived; Lenin lives; Lenin will live forever').

We were lucky enough to be assigned, as guides and interpreters, the last batch of university students to have been allowed to take any foreign language – apart from Russian.

One of the British players got the greatest offer (and one of the biggest shocks) of his young life when he went into one of the shops and asked for something cheap to take back home, only for the pretty girl behind the counter to say, in perfect English: 'How about taking me?'

I was dining in my hotel one night when a huge notice started to get on my nerves. I asked my elderly waiter, who had already told me proudly how he had been a *commis* at the Savoy in London before the First World War, what the Hungarian placard said. Deadpan, he translated: 'Do not insult the citizen waiters by offering them tips.' Then, *sotto voce*, he added: 'Mark you, sir, we do not insult easily.'

Everything should have been going wonderfully well; but it wasn't, for me, on the *Sunday Pictorial*. Indeed, for the first time in nearly fifteen years, I wasn't happy with the Mirror group. The unpredictable Bartholomew had got his way and ousted Cudlipp from the editorship of the *Pic* – a piece of inanity which, personally, I found, and still find, unmatched in my experience of journalism.

I had been one of the 'traitors' who had left Bart's aegis for the new-found delights of the *Pictorial*. That had been a dozen or so years, and a war, before but Bart's memory was as long as his temper was short. If he could get rid of Cudlipp he could most certainly obliterate me.

There was some office 'do' at which the shock-headed Bart shouted down the table to me: 'Why don't you get your hair cut?' And in only a slightly lower tone added: 'He's the only one on the whole staff with longer hair than me.' Answering his question to my neighbour at the table I muttered: 'I don't get my hair cut because I'm too bloody scared of getting my throat cut, too!' But I didn't mutter it very quietly.

I was warned that Bart was 'gunning' for me. If watching boxing had taught me only one thing it was the importance of beating the other fellow to the punch. I heard, through Hugh Cudlipp who had joined the Express group, that Arthur Christiansen, the famous editor of the *Daily Express*, might be interested in hiring me, as boxing writer and joint sports-columnist with John McAdam.

I wasn't supposed to start writing for the *Express* until August but 'Chris' got in touch with me and said that he needed an article that week and another features-style one the next. It was a good way of getting a new recruit to realize the urgency of working for the *Express* and, perhaps, to get him just a little bit off balance at the start; always a useful ploy for an editor.

I turned them in without too much difficulty. Perhaps psychiatrists would have said that I had a built-in defeatist complex, but I had never believed I was indispensable, for a columnist without a paper is like a high-diver without a platform. So, some time earlier, I had written two or three articles which, with a minimum of 'updating', could be topical and provocative.

The first one did the trick, with a selection of readers calling for my blood – or announcing that they were going to cancel their subscriptions. When the latter happens you know that you have a reader for life, because he or she has got to see if you take any notice of their criticism, or if you are going to annoy them further.

Anyway Chris, who had used a legitimate editor's trick to see if I could be caught on the wrong foot, would, I am sure, never have grudged a writer's legitimate riposte. But, I admit, I never did tell him how I was able to deliver those two columns quite so quickly.

6   1950–3
Expressure

A newspaper has as much individuality as the different journalists who make up its whole. The *Daily Express*, while it was as successful at this time as the Mirror group, aimed at a different market.

I would say that the *Mirror* was genuinely concerned about the plight of those lame ducks who, if I understand some of today's politicians aright, must be left to sink on their own. As we all know God must have loved the common people because He made so many of them, and I'm not denying that their very numbers made it profitable for the *Mirror* to be solicitous on their behalf; but it was not just an exercise in circulation. Honest compassion entered into it, too.

The Express, or so it seemed to me, was addressed to the successful – or, at least, to those who had aspirations and the probability of achieving material benefits. Their readers already had a car but were planning on another or, perhaps, greatly daring, thinking of some sea-going craft. It was not so much that the *Express* was Conservative-orientated whereas the *Mirror*, although allegedly independent, was obviously canted to the Left. There was an overt feeling of the just-acceptable face of capitalism in Fleet Street's 'glass house'.

Perhaps it's easier to sum up anyone through their weaknesses rather than their strengths. As far as the general editorial staff of the *Daily Mirror* and *Sunday Pictorial*, of those days, was concerned the temptation which they found most difficult to resist was drinking. At the *Express* it was gambling.

I realize that all such generalizations are bound to miss many targets – as well as wounding some innocent bystanders; but this was my first, superficial if you like, feeling of contradistinction between two popular and successful newspapers.

I always regret that I did not meet the late Lord Beaverbrook, except fleetingly. On one of these occasions in the early fifties I did learn how one of the facets of genius is an infinite capacity for noticing apparently inconsequential details.

He had financed a fairly lavish party for the staff at one of London's more expensive hostelries. Whisky was still in somewhat short supply and this particular establishment bottled its own which was not, I suppose, more damaging to the constitution than diesel oil. It just tasted worse. In those happy, far-off days I was better than a raw hand when it came to ingesting 'Scotland's finest', but when I tasted this particular hell-brew I imagine that my face scrunched up in a mixture of supreme distaste mingled with fury that an alleged five-star joint could get away with this kind of licensed larceny.

I was contemplating my drink, certainly through a glass and indubitably darkly, when I was recalled to my immediate surroundings by a tap on the shoulder. Like one of Lars Porsena's messengers someone had been bidden to escort me to the Presence.

I could not believe that Lord Beaverbrook wanted to discuss the great problems of sport with me. He was a good enough newspaperman to know that sport did, in no inconsiderable way, help to sell his journals. But I believe that he had no interest in it himself and, more than that, regarded as somewhat juvenile those who made it a main concern. This attitude may have been caused because, so I was told, he had not been too fortunate in a flirtation with that callous jade, the Turf.

But there was no time to speculate deeply on the reasons for my summons. The horns of Elfland were, not so faintly, blowing in the form of that rasping, asthmatic, Canadian-inflected voice. He said: 'Mr Wilson, I understand that you are a considerable authority on whisky.' Now if ever there were a 'Have you stopped beating your wife?' remark this was it. If I said 'Yes' I was a self-confessed tosspot. If I gave 'No' as an answer I was telling the proprietor that, at best, he was ill-informed and at worst that he was a liar; and, anyway, had I said 'No' I would have been lying in my, at that time, not false teeth.

I inclined my head. You can never go far wrong that way in the presence of God.

The interrogation went on: 'Then why did I see you make a grimace when you took a drink just now?'

I thought: the hell with it. It's his party and, although I'm sure he can afford it, I don't see why he should be taken for a financial ride and the rest of us for an indigestible one. I said: 'Lord Beaverbrook, the stuff which is being provided for your guests under the guise of whisky is sailing under a flag of convenience, certainly not that of Scotland.' (At least, with *esprit d'escalier*, that's what I like to think I said. Probably it was more like: 'The management is getting away with murder in what they're giving your guests as whisky.')

Anyway the message got through. The baronial fingers clicked like pistol shots. From the wainscoting, or wherever they vanish when not on public view, a banqueting manager or two appeared. Lord Beaverbrook indicated in short, sharp, pungent words what the matter was, and in a matter of minutes the 'house Scotch' had vanished and we were drinking something more palatable.

You don't become a millionaire in your twenties, and stay that way until your eighties, by putting up with second-best or letting people sell you the second-rate.

Some time later Arthur Christiansen told me that following a column of mine which he had liked he tried to arrange a visit to Beaverbrook for me. But the next piece I wrote was so disappointing to him that Chris managed to cancel the whole thing in case it was a bad column instead of a good column day! Perhaps it was all for the best.

The only person with whom I had to come into close contact and whom I cordially disliked was Harold Hardman, the sports editor. He was a miserable, mean-spirited, narrow-gutted little man with little talent and less milk of human kindness. It was largely he who so bedevilled dear John McAdam, with whom I originally alternated columns, that John was finally constrained to resign. This Scot, by the way, was one of the last of the genuine sporting 'characters' in Fleet Street. Like some perky sparrow, hopping from cobblestone to cobblestone, you could see him fluttering in and out of the side-roads and alleys which branch off Fleet Street and all of which contain their own intimate 'locals'.

It was a good time to start on a new paper – and to get back to daily journalism. Among the characters I particularly enjoyed writing about was MacDonald Bailey, the Trinidad sprinter, who really set the tracks in Britain and the rest of the world alight, but who found it hard to gain recognition from the stuffier than stuffy officials who have always done their damnedest to damage British athletics.

Time after time Mac Bailey would break a record only to find that the track was seven inches short or there was anemometer (wind-gauge) trouble or an insufficiency of stop-watches. All these 'hindrances' were discovered *after* Mac had run and broken records and it was hard not to believe that certain officials weren't conducting a witch hunt against him.

Another great runner of this period was the toughest marathon man I ever knew – Jack Holden from Bilston in Staffordshire. I had seen him have to give up in the 1948 Olympic marathon when a blister formed under the horny outer skin of the ball of one big toe and, smash down as he would – and did – mile after mile he could not break it so that it was like running on an open nerve.

Owing to the ignorance and inefficiency of Hardman, the sports editor, I did not get to Brussels to see Holden complete the epic double

of the Commonwealth and European marathon titles but I was told
how he paraded in front of his most dangerous rivals saying grimly, and
with the appropriate gestures: 'Take a good look at this,' pointing to
the number on his chest, 'because once the race starts all you're going
to see is this,' indicating the same number on his back! It was not boast-
ing, and I doubt whether Jack could have spelled 'psychological warfare', but this iron man of forty-three just wanted everyone to know who
was boss.

And he won the Commonwealth race, running the last ten miles of
the 26 miles 385 yards in his bare feet, over rough ground and in
atrocious weather. Not only that but after twenty-three miles, when the
mind has to take over from a body pleading for relief, Holden was
actually savaged by a Great Dane which left his legs scarred.

Round about this time everyone was talking about a new sensation
in British boxing – Randolph Adolphus Turpin who was destined to
scale the supreme heights and plumb the ultimate depths all inside
fifteen years.

Turpin was only one fight away from winning the British middleweight title by knocking out Albert Finch, one of the only two men who
had beaten him, as a pro, up to that time. Ever since he had been an
amateur it was clear that Turpin was going to be something special.
Now it was obvious that he was going to be outstanding.

In the meantime I was off to the States to cover one of the great
sporting tragedies of my time – the eclipse of Joe Louis.

Two and a quarter years had elapsed since Joe had announced that
he would fight no more having, in the eleven years during which he
had held the world title, vanquished everyone who had earned the
right to be in the ring with him . . . and many who had no such right.
If a man put up a good fight with him the first time he always, with the
exception of Tommy Farr, gave him a second crack at the championship
and always won more decisively the second time around.

But there was this one opponent he could never lick – the Income Tax
man. And because he was an honourable man, he decided he must fight
as long as he felt he could go through the motions of putting up his fists.

I felt a curious affinity with Joe. We had been born within nine
months of each other, he on a dirt-poor farm near Lafayette, Alabama,
I in a Bayswater flat. I was an only child; he was the seventh of eight
after three brothers, Alvanious, Deleon and Lonnie, and three sisters,
Susie, Emmarell and Eulalia, while Vuennies was the youngest.

Joe's paternal great-grandfather was a mulatto whose wife was a
full-blooded Red Indian. Like Ezzard Charles, whom he was now to
meet, Louis was the descendant of slaves (Charles' grandmother, still
alive in her nineties when he won the title, had actually been a slave).

My paternal grandfather had been a property owner in London and my maternal grandfather a Scottish solicitor.

No two men could have had more different backgrounds and up-bringing or represented more differing cultures; yet I always felt, above all the other athletes whom I watched and admired over the years, a special empathy with Joe. Perhaps it was because he had, at twenty-three, been the youngest man up to that time ever to win the most famous sporting title in the world and I, at the same age, had been the youngest writer ever to be sent from Britain to cover the event.

That's why watching him cut to shreds by Charles, a decent man and a talented but colourless fighter, was one of the saddest things I ever saw.

The only thing I liked about the fight was the final bell which meant that Joe had managed at least to last the distance. I had feared, during training, that the greatest pitcher – of punches – was taking himself to the well just once too often. In between his sparring rounds he occasionally gave a curious little stiff-legged jump into the air as though to re-assure himself that the spring was still in his muscles and that, even at nearly thirty-six and a half, his youth had not all gone. It was rather like an ageing Peter Pan trying to prove to himself that the fairy dust which had enabled him to fly had not turned into dandruff.

After it was all over and we were in his dressing room, only it was more like a funeral parlour, Louis, to whom words never came easily but who always seemed to say the right thing when it mattered, uttered his own epitaph. Looking round those of us who had seen him during the thirteen years since he had first won the title, who had seen him overseas serving his country, who had thrilled to the years of unparalleled supremacy and bitterly regretted the years when a shadow had been boxing, Big Bronze said simply: 'Thank you all very much. Ah done ma best.'

Then he was gone.

One footnote: twelve years later, when Emile Griffiths regained the world welterweight title from Luis Rodriguez – there was desperately little difference between those two in the 10 st 7 lb division – a fan at the ringside rushed up to Joe Louis saying: 'You're the greatest, you're the greatest! Can I have your autograph?'

The old 'Brown Bomber' gave him his autograph, all right, but before doing so he also gave him that famous, lazy grin of his and said: 'What do you want me to sign? Joe Louis – or Cassius Clay?'

As far as Europe was concerned no sooner had the sun of Joe Louis set than a new comet from the USA began to light up the skies – christened Walker Smith, known as 'Sugar' Ray Robinson.

One of my abiding regrets in boxing is that I never saw Robinson as a welterweight. Up to the time (9 August 1950) when he last successfully defended his 10 st 7 lb title which he had won in December 1946, against Charlie Fusari, he had been boxing professionally for just under ten years, had had 113 fights, almost exactly one a month, had lost just one decision and boxed two draws.

To a generation familiar only with the antics and gyrations of Muhammad Ali/Cassius Clay it's difficult to believe that Robinson was, in some ways, more of a sensation in Europe in 1950–1.

He had a seventeen-foot-long heliotrope-coloured Cadillac embellished with 'Sugar' written in his own handwriting on the door. He travelled with a retinue which included his manager, a big, black man called George Gainford and known as the 'Emperor'; a trainer; an assorted number of sparring partners; a masseur; a golf professional; his private hairdresser; a male secretary called June; a North African dwarf whom he called his 'Arabian knight' and, usually, his beautiful wife, Edna Mae, and one of his sisters.

Robinson stayed in the finest hotels, ate at the smartest restaurants, dressed like a king – and fought like a demon.

In his first fight in Europe he stopped Jean Stock who, two years earlier, had been the first man to beat Randolph Turpin inside the distance. If ever a man seemed surrounded by the aura of invincibility it was Sugar – inevitably nicknamed 'Death' – Ray. He also added a new dimension to lives which, more than five years after the war, were still too often drab.

He was not in every way a sterling character. But a 'character', in the racier sense of the word, he certainly was.

At last the inevitable meeting between Robinson and Turpin was promoted at the Earls Court Arena in London, which holds more than 18,000. The betting gave a clear picture of how people fancied the two men's chances. It was 3–1 against a Turpin victory; 7–2 on Robinson; 66–1 a draw, and 20–1 against a Turpin points victory.

And, of course, the 20–1 shot came off. I think it must rank as the biggest upset I have ever seen in a British ring. The decisive turning point came in the seventh round when the two men's heads came together – the fault of neither – with a sickening click like two billiards balls colliding. Turpin came away unmarked but Robinson was so badly gashed that after the fight Dr Vincent Nardiello, himself an ex-boxer and well-known around Madison Square Garden, whom Sugar Ray had invited to England specially for this fight (did he know something?) had to insert fourteen stitches near Robinson's left eye.

But it would be unfair to Turpin to suggest that it was only the accident which brought him victory. His strength, his long left leads and the fact that 'Robinson had Paris in his legs', as American fight agent, Lew Burston, said, all contributed to the defeat of 'the unbeatable'. Robinson himself summed it up as well as anyone when he commented: 'Turpin does everything wrong – right.'

For the Robinson–Turpin return I made one of my longer trips to the States for, including the voyage, I was away for nearly five weeks. And it gave me a chance to be one of the first of three British journalists to see the girl, who, had it not been for her tragic injury and even more tragically early death, would have been incontrovertibly the greatest woman lawn tennis player of all time.

I am talking, of course, of Maureen Connolly.

When I first saw her playing and winning in the third singles match of the Wightman Cup, just outside Boston, she was twenty-two days away from her seventeenth birthday. Less than a fortnight later 'Little Mo' – named after the famous American battleship, the *Missouri*, which, like the state of the same name, was shortened to Mo – had beaten Doris Hart in the semi-final and Shirley Fry in the final to become the second youngest US title holder since the women's championships were first played in 1887.

After the final when the photographers asked her for 'A great big smile, please, Maureen' she could only sob, with tears sprawling down her cheeks: 'I can't smile – I'm too happy!'

It was about this time that the ineffable Hardman and I exchanged a couple of cablegrams. He, the idiot, didn't seem to realize what a discovery this youngster was – she lost, I think only four more competitive singles matches in her life – and what a shot in the arm for lawn tennis she was going to be for the next three years.

His cable read brusquely: 'All I want from you is boxing, boxing, boxing.' My reply was a little longer, as, fortunately, neither Turpin nor Robinson was sparring that day. 'Regret neither man working working working today today today Regards regards regards Wilson Wilson Wilson.'

And that, thank the Lord, shut him up – for the time anyway.

But one story which I had not omitted to send and which was to have, in my opinion, a decisive effect on the outcome of the Robinson–Turpin return concerned a preliminary fighter called Georgie Flores.

He had appeared in the chief supporting bout before the world welterweight championship between Kid Gavilan and Billy Graham and he had been knocked out by Roger Donoghue in the eighth and last round. Five days later he died as a result of his injuries.

This was the age when the gangsters were truly dominating boxing. Men like Frankie Carbo and 'Blinky' Palermo virtually controlled huge chunks of the fight business.

Not for the first time it struck me how desperately slowly justice seems to move in the States. When I publicly attacked the gangster-controlled set-up of boxing in the USA, and particularly in New York, I was in turn attacked in some New York papers, defended in others, assailed on the radio and threats were passed on to me that I'd do well to 'keep my nose clean'.

Nearly nine months later, writing in the American magazine *Life*, Robert K. Christenberry, then the Chairman of the New York State Athletic Commission, the body responsible for professional boxing in the State of New York, had said: 'Below that surface lurks another, more arrogant, infinitely more outrageous influence: the underworld's. Against this evil we *have* declared war. The full extent of the invasion of the game by its ringleaders, a clique of hoodlums, racketeers and sure-thing gamblers, is being examined by our own and other investigators.'

Yet it was not until there was a Federal investigation, headed by Senator Estes Kefauver of Tennessee, held in Washington in December 1960, that things really started to move, and in the end such villains as Frank Carbo and 'Blinky' Palermo got long prison sentences.

I had written about the sinister underworld influence before the Robinson–Turpin return – indeed it was about this time that I had a shouting row with the revolting Palermo who threatened to 'get' me and did, I was told, point me out to some of the rats who were his only willing companions. The trouble was that Blinky 'put the finger on' another British sportswriter, Cliff Webb, who, like myself was burly, reddish-faced and sported a generous moustache! I'm happy to say that no ill befell Cliff.

But the way the rules could be flouted came out about a fortnight after the big fight. It turned out that the New York State Athletic Commission rule which forbade a boxer who had been stopped in a bout from fighting again for thirty days had been ignored. Flores, it was revealed, was technically knocked out in five of his last six appearances and had, in fact, been stopped in the same fatal eighth round only two weeks earlier by Roger Donoghue, the man who finally brought him to his tragic end.

So we came to the Robinson–Turpin fight in the shadow of tragedy with the anti-boxing lobby calling for the banning of the sport in New York State or, indeed, the whole Union. This wasn't as good a fight as their first one had been – perhaps because the element of amazement that anyone could give 'Sugar' Ray as good, and better, than he got from him was missing.

About halfway through the tenth, with the fight still very much in the balance, Robinson came out of a clinch with his left eye – the one which had proved vulnerable sixty-four nights earlier when he had lost his world title – streaming with blood. It seemed clear to me, and it must have been even more devastatingly plain to Robinson, that he could not fight another five and a half rounds with such an injury.

Like the superlative champion he was Robinson flung himself into an all-out attack, committing all his reserves, realizing I think that he had to win *now*, so there was no point in husbanding his strength and trying to 'pace' the fight for fifteen rounds. A scything right hurled Turpin back into the ropes, badly hurt, and another right cross dropped him on his back for a maximum count of nine.

When he got up Robinson swept him to the ropes again and hurled bomb after bomb at his sagging jaw. To begin with Turpin, supported by the ropes, moved with the punches, swinging like a great brown pendulum and taking much of the force from the blows. But, inevitably, some of the punches did get through full-bloodedly and when a final right smash to the jaw landed, leaving Turpin like the dummy in a bayonet-practice session, the referee, Ruby Goldstein, stepped between the two men indicating that the fight was over and Robinson had regained his world championship in just over nine weeks.

The supreme irony was reserved for the end when it was announced that 2 mins 52 secs of the round had elapsed. That meant that had Turpin gone down again then there would not have been time to count him out as, in those days, the count did not continue once the bell had sounded.

But no one could fairly blame Goldstein for this. He was there to see fair play and to protect either boxer if, in his opinion, he couldn't protect himself. A referee doesn't have a built-in stopwatch. Additionally Goldstein, although he subsequently denied this must, at least subconsciously, have been thinking about Georgie Flores and what the effect of another fatality – and one which would get much more publicity because of the importance of the contest – would have on the sport which he had practised professionally as a young man.

Nearly nine months later it was back to New York once more to watch Sugar Ray Robinson in his most ambitious project so far, as middleweight champion (11 st 6 lb) in an assault upon the world light-heavyweight title (12 st 7 lb) held by Joey Maxim who had knocked out and ended the career of Freddie Mills.

Maxim and Robinson were due to step into the ring on Monday, 23 June but, as one New York paper headlined it, 'Jupe Pluvius Jinxes June Joust' – which, being translated, meant that a downpour caused the postponement of the outdoor bout – and for forty-eight hours because, on the Tuesday, there was an important baseball game which could not be rearranged.

The delay was expected to harm Maxim more because of the difficulty of keeping his weight down.

Came Wednesday night and the highest temperature ever recorded for that date in New York City. It was 99 degrees and under the ringside lights that went up to 104. With New York's typical humidity I have never felt so hot in my life. I went into a nearby saloon and after drinking three or four beers, with salt in them, I weighed myself on a pair of scales in the bar. Then I went to my ringside seat. Even with my jacket off and my tie removed I could scarcely breathe.

I thought I recognized a man sitting in the row behind me in the Working Press section; I imagined that he was an out-of-town newspaperman whom I had met on some other trip and I leaned back to say: 'My God! Aren't you glad you don't have to live in this bloody awful climate?' He gave me a sickly grin and a New York sportswriter nudged me and murmured: 'That's telling him, British. He only happens to be Thomas Dewey, the Governor of the State!'

The only man who seemed totally unaffected by the inferno was General MacArthur who, if you please, was wearing a light top-coat apparently forbidding himself to sweat like the common people.

I still believe that Robinson could have won that fight – although I had tipped Maxim – if his innate sense of showmanship and his feeling for a great occasion had not overcome him.

You could see it when the two men got into the ring. Robinson, despite the scorching heat, was in two robes, one of white towelling and one of royal blue and during the inevitable protracted introductions he kept bouncing up and down in his corner while Maxim, under the tutelage of that old fox, 'Doc' Kearns, sat quietly in his.

Robinson very nearly dropped his man in the seventh but, apart from heavyweights, hitting a world champion who is over a stone heavier than you is a fruitless pursuit and although he had hurt Maxim it was Robinson who slumped into the ropes at the end of the round, burnt out through his own exertions and the searing heat. I think he knew as early as this that he couldn't win.

But the next sensation concerned not the fighters but the referee. Round after round Goldstein's eyes had been growing bigger and bigger, black saucers in the sallow pallor of his face. It was no good. The black patches of sweat on his grey shirt grew ever larger. His face began to come apart like a jigsaw puzzle being broken up. At the end of the tenth round he had to be led from the ring.

His score card was handed to another ex-fighter referee, Ray Miller. Years afterwards I read an interview with him in which he said how glad he was that he did not have to give a points verdict as he had been unable to read Goldstein's figures for the last few rounds.

By the thirteenth Robinson was fighting on instinct, boxing from memory. The bell ending the round went – and so did Robinson, to what he thought was his own corner. But it was a neutral one with no stool, no friends, no hope. His handlers raced across to bring him back to the haven of his own bivouac but it was too late. Miller spoke to him, asking him if he was all right. Sugar Ray mumbled disconnectedly. The sixty seconds sped by.

Came the bell for the fourteenth. Maxim, moving fast for almost the first time in the fight, came racing across the ring. Miller halted him. There was no more for 'Pal Joey' to do. He had won.

I managed to totter to the same saloon that I had visited before the fight. Although I have never wanted a drink more in my life I disciplined myself to get on the same set of scales before I started to guzzle some ice-cold beer. I had lost exactly half a stone! Later it was printed that Robinson had lost eleven and a half pounds and Maxim nine, which meant that by the end a heavy middleweight was fighting a welterweight for the light-heavyweight championship of the world!

Back in England I had the satisfaction of seeing Little Mo Connolly fulfil the prophecy which I had made about her a month earlier and become the second youngest winner of the women's singles at Wimbledon during this century. She was still over two months short of her eighteenth birthday.

But the curious thing was that Maureen, an object lesson for any player in behaviour, was never really popular with the crowds. Perhaps it was that sergeant-major walk along the base-line with a racket instead of a pace stick. Or the way, when she was in the depths of concentration, that she would seem to bob her head, like a chicken pecking at a row of corn. Perhaps it was just that British trait, so inexplicable and infuriating to foreigners – and logical people generally – which makes a domestic crowd appreciate a good loser more than a brilliant winner.

In the final Maureen met Louise Brough who had been there four times previously. It was a good game up to 5–4 in the first set, with Miss Brough leading, but after that growing fatigue was no match for the youth and power of Maureen who won 7–5, 6–3.

The whole fortnight had been a particularly great victory because Little Mo had injured her shoulder; had been called upon to scratch by her coach, Eleanor Tennant (nicknamed 'Teach'), and had a final and irremediable breach with that formidable woman who proclaimed to all and sundry that Maureen would now lose. For a seventeen-year-old to take on all this – and the cream of the lawn tennis world – was asking rather a lot. But Mo did it.

Now it was time to prepare for the XVth Olympic Games of the modern era which were held in Helsinki, the Finnish capital.

In some ways this was the most enjoyable of the eight summer Games which I covered. One reason was simple enough: track and field, the essential part of the Games, is to Finland as totally consuming and fulfilling as soccer is to Britain.

The Finns were still very much under the domination of the Russians who actually had an enclave stretching into the outskirts of Helsinki. Additionally, and quite disgracefully, the USSR, which was competing in the Games for the first time since the Russian Revolution, was allowed to set up a separate Olympic village for its athletes and those of some of its satellites – a complete breach of the whole Olympic ideal which is that the youth of the whole world, irrespective of ideologies, race, colour and creed, should live together and strive against each other in harmony for the duration of the Games.

The opening ceremony was certainly one of the most memorable of all time. What made it so was the identity of the runner who carried the torch on its final stage into the stadium and up the steps leading to the bowl where the Olympic Flame was ignited, not to be extinguished until the last event of the Games had been completed.

For a few seconds there was silence, compounded of surprise – for, untraditionally, this was no golden boy symbolizing the athletic youth of the world – and unfamiliarity with the lean middle-aged figure who stepped out so bravely, belying his fifty-five years. Then the Finnish crowd came to its feet, exploding like a rocket at its zenith, for the older fans had recognized the runner as Paavo Nurmi, the most famous athlete Finland has ever produced and arguably the greatest middle and distance runner the world has ever seen.

Perhaps the selection of Nurmi as the final torchbearer was an omen, for rarely has one man so dominated the Games, in my experience, as did the greatest competitive long-distance runner of modern times – Emil Zatopek, the Czech.

He won the first event on the track, the 10,000 metres, and he won the most famous one to finish there, the marathon; in between he had run a heat and won the final of the 5,000 metres. Thus in eight days he ran 38 miles, 1137 yards, 2 feet, 7 inches to secure three individual gold medals against the world's greatest runners.

The 10,000 metres was easy for him. He finished something like a hundred yards ahead of the second man, Alain Mimoun, the French-Algerian. In his heat of the 5,000 metres the Czech could actually have been disqualified, for so anxious was he to see the Russian Anoufriev qualify that he shooed him home like a mother hen, actually pushing him across the finishing line, making himself guilty of a technical foul by deliberately touching another competitor.

But the final of this event was one of the great races of all time. Apart from the winner the hero was a twenty-one-year-old Chris Chataway who, until the last bend, was never out of the first four. Then, the salt-white of his fatigued face contrasting with his carroty thatch, he hit the kerb and fell half off the track while Zatopek, Mimoun and the German, Herbert Schade, streamed away from him to finish in that order, the incredible Zatopek chopping eleven seconds off the Olympic record.

But his other efforts paled in comparison with his marathon victory – all the more incredible because this was the first time he had ever run this distance competitively.

Hot favourite when the runners wheeled out of the stadium, like a scattering of confetti, was Jim Peters, the Chadwell Heath optician, who set a cracking pace which gave him a lead of nearly 100 yards after the first of the twenty-six miles.

At the halfway mark Gustave Jansson, of Sweden was leading by a couple of yards from Zatopek with Peters right up there third.

After that it was all Zatopek. He was alleged at one stage to have come up to Peters, as the favourite, and asked: 'Are we going fast enough – this is my first marathon!' Whether this is true or not I don't know, but after about twenty miles the Englishman was attacked by cramp, and, although he made another plucky effort to finish, he had to be brought back by car after sitting at the roadside exhausted. Zatopek sped on to beat the best Olympic time for the marathon by 6 mins 16 secs – considerably over a mile!

Apart from our show jumping team the Games were bleak for Britain. MacDonald Bailey could get only a bronze medal in the 100 metres which I am still sure was won by Jamaica's Herb McKenley, although the gold medal was given to Lindy Remigino from the USA.

But the disaster was in the 1,500 metres where the runners included Roger Bannister who was so put off his schedule by finding that he had to run three, instead of two, times that he finished only fourth. However, there was consolation in the eventual winner, the little-considered Josy Barthel, who stood on the winner's rostrum with tears streaming down his face as the band frantically searched for the National Anthem of – the Grand Duchy of Luxembourg. I haven't checked but I imagine this was the only time that tiny country ever won a gold medal at anything – and Barthel had beaten not only Bannister but Lueg of Germany, who was at that time co-holder of the world record for the distance.

After the athletics, boxing provided most of the stories, and what happened in Helsinki might well have changed the whole history of the

professional world heavyweight championship. Two new weights –
light-welter and light-middle – were introduced for the first time and
Lazslo Papp, the Hungarian who had won the middleweight gold
medal at Wembley in 1948, found that he could make the new light-
middleweight limit.

At Helsinki Papp was at this greatest. In one of the preliminary
bouts he met Spider Webb, who later was to give Terry Downes,
future middleweight champion of the world, a savage beating. Webb
lasted just twenty-nine seconds against Papp who went on to win the
gold medal without ever really being extended.

This left the middleweight division clear for a seventeen-year-old
coloured fighter from New Jersey, by the name of Floyd Patterson. He
was very light on his feet and extremely fast with his hands. Indeed, I
wrote at the time: 'Put him in the book as a potential professional
champion of the future.'

But I still believe if he had met Papp then, the ferocious punching of
the twenty-six-year-old Hungarian would have been too much for the
boy whose jaw was never the most robust part of his make-up. And had
Patterson been badly beaten then would he have subsequently become
the youngest-ever world heavyweight champion – and the first ever to
regain the title after losing it?

And unless you had used a crystal ball to try to discern the first man
to dethrone Patterson the very last person you would have expected
would have been the Swede Ingemar Johansson, then less than twenty,
who was disqualified after two dreary rounds in the final of the heavyweight class against the American Ed Sanders, 'for not giving of his
best' – and was denied even a silver medal.

Social life in Helsinki was mixed. I was lucky in not being in the
students' hostel where most of the Press were accommodated, but while
our flat was comfortable enough it was very difficult to get any sleep in
a town where you could read a newspaper without the aid of any artificial light almost up to midnight and again shortly after three a.m.

I was really sad to say goodbye to Helsinki for this was truly one of
the few Games where, in most sports and especially in the track and
field events, the true Olympic spirit illuminated the proceedings like a
second flame.

My next major job was covering the world professional sprint cycling
championship. It is bad luck to be born British if you are a cyclist for
you will never receive from your fellow countrymen anything like the
acclamation which is the meed of the Continental stars, some of whom
are better known than the most famous footballers and better paid than
some champion boxers. Thus it becomes one of the toughest jobs in sport

for a British cyclist to take on the Continental *maestri* on their own tracks and conquer them.

Such a hero was Reg Harris who won the world amateur sprint title in 1947 and in 1949 in his first year as a professional became the first man ever to win the world professional title at his initial attempt.

Harris had the same sort of 'damn-your-eyes-I'm-better-than-you' temperament which had served Fred Perry so well on the lawn tennis courts of the world. He trained as hard as any man I have ever known. For ten months he had trained and raced, raced and trained. With training spins of anything up to seventy miles he had gone the equivalent of three-quarters of the way round the world on his bicycle. Naturally he was tough physically – but he was even tougher mentally.

Alas! For Harris this was not his year. In the semi-final he had a slow puncture and although he appealed his plea was turned down. His final chance came in the four-man *repêchage* in which he seemed chiefly concerned with Arie Van Vliet, the 'Flying Dutchman', while Sid Patterson of Australia was keeping an eye on the French outsider, Georges Senfftleben. Strategy as much as speed was the keynote of these cycle sprints.

Somehow Patterson let his attention wander, and in a flash the Frenchman was off and away to a lead which even Harris with his typical final 'buffalo charge' – head lowered, legs pistoning – could not wipe out.

But like the great champions in any sport, Harris 'picked himself up, dusted himself off and started all over again'. Two years later at Cologne he regained the world title at the age of thirty-four; and, incredibly, regained the British title in 1974.

I wish there were a few more like Reg Harris today. I find their point of view infinitely more understandable, and acceptable than, say, the philosophy (so-called) of a George Best.

After Harris came my first meeting with a man who, if anything, trained even harder than he did and was, perhaps even more determined to become, and remain, champion of the world – Rocky Marciano.

Marciano was meeting Jersey Joe Walcott who – having lost twice to Joe Louis and then, with the world heavyweight title vacant after Louis' retirement, lost twice to Ezzard Charles – had finally, in a third meeting with Charles, caused a 6–1 upset by knocking out the 'Wizard of Ezz' in seven rounds.

Marciano trained at Grossingers, the huge Jewish resort in the Catskill mountains where more and more fighters were preparing. He did his sparring, bag-punching and callisthenics in an aeroplane hangar attached to Grossingers' private airfield. A ring was rigged up in it, and the coiling mist and cloud which wreathed the Catskills the first time I went to see Rocky made the hangar appear like an execution shed, while the timbered cottage in which the challenger lived looked, through the driving rain and in the half-light, like something out of a horror movie.

But Marciano himself was refreshingly down to earth. He was easily the smallest heavyweight champion I have ever seen for, although the record books give his height at 5 ft 11 in I am sure he was something like an inch short of that, and his heaviest-ever fighting weight was 13 st 7 lb. For Walcott he was to weigh 13 st 2 lb.

Marciano belonged in the noisy, practical-joking, schoolboyish yet barrack-like life of a lonely training camp, smelling of steak cooked with garlic, as a sailor belongs in a ship.

Walcott was very different. In repose his face, carved by hundreds of gloves but even more deeply graven by the rigours of life for a Negro during the depression years (he admitted to having celebrated his thirty-seventh birthday and unkind people said he had celebrated it three or four times) looked as though he could play the title role in *Uncle Tom's Cabin* without benefit of make-up. There was a strange affection between him and his manager, Felix Bocchicchio – he used to hand out cards with his name spelled out phonetically: Bo-key-key-o! – who looked like George Raft playing a tough gangster part.

Walcott, who had six children, had quit the ring on more than one occasion and in 1945 he had decided to make it permanent. His coal-bin was empty and there was precious little food for the family. Then, as in all the best fairy stories, at the moment of deepest gloom, the good fairy, in the unlikely guise of Felix Bocchicchio, arrived to paint a rosy picture for old black Joe. Walcott heard him out and then said: 'If you'll keep that coal-bin filled for me I'll fight for you.' And that was their contract.

I have seen over thirty fights for the world heavyweight title and in-controvertibly the most exciting, the one most in balance right up to the final punch, was this one in which Marciano became the first white heavyweight champion for fifteen years.

It started with a sensation when the 'Brockton Blockbuster', as they called Marciano, was caught with a barrage of punches to the head and dropped in the very first round. Afterwards he was asked what he thought while he was on the canvas and he answered: 'I wasn't thinking much then but when I trotted back to my corner at the end of the round I said to myself, "This is only the first round, it's scheduled for fifteen, and this old pappy guy has put me down already. This figures to be one hell of a fight!"' If ever I heard the words of a born fighting man these were they. And it certainly *was* one hell of a fight.

Nevertheless, at the end of the twelfth round I had Walcott ahead by seven rounds to four with one even. The officials had him so far ahead that if the champion could stay on his feet for the next three rounds he couldn't get worse than a draw – which would mean that he retained his title.

But the thirteenth round was the unlucky one for Jersey Joe. Rocky backed the champion to the ropes as he had scores of times before but this time, before Walcott could eel his way along them, Marciano landed the hardest single punch, a right-hander, that I'd seen demolish a man since Joe Louis had torn the crown from game Jim Braddock's bloody brow fifteen years earlier.

Walcott went out like a light bulb being switched off. He was out before his left knee touched the canvas and the rest of his body followed like some toppling chimney. The force of that terrifying blow seemed to turn Walcott from black to grey while he was falling.

Marciano's dressing room and the party thrown for him at one of Philadelphia's swankier hotels by 'Jimmy Tomato', a millionaire tomato grower and Marciano's No. 1 fan, was like breaking-up day at a boys' school, but back at the stadium Felix Bocchicchio said gently to old black Joe: 'Come along, champ', and they vanished together in the shadows.

The other thing which made this evening memorable for me was meeting A. J. Liebling for the first time. Joe Liebling, gourmand, gourmet, civilized and cultured man, wrote about boxing just about as well as anyone ever has. Liebling and I had to walk a long way back into the city – an exercise which both of us despised. Joe used to walk on the outside of his soles because his feet constantly hurt him. In his bowler hat, with his chest and stomach puffed out, and shuffling along with a kind of rolling waddle he was like nothing so much as a king penguin in an overcoat! Stopping at any saloons, hostelries or taverns which looked inviting we set up a friendship which endured until his death some years later.

By now it was 1953 and before long it was time for me to make my last move in Fleet Street. I was finding Hardman ever more tiresome – indeed, had it not been for the friendship and encouragement of Bob Findlay, that prince of good fellows, who was later to become sports editor of the *Express*, then the *Sketch* and finally the *Mail*, a truly remarkable record, I don't think I could have put up with things.

But before parting from the *Express* I did have a final, very painful scene with Arthur Christiansen.

Both of us were going out to lunch and we met, of all places, in adjoining stalls of the lavatory. As both of us were getting rid of our overmatter Chris remarked casually: 'You'll be glad to hear that I confirmed a rise of' – and he named what was then a very considerable sum – 'for you this morning.'

I almost had a stricture. All I could say, foolishly, was: 'Oh! you shouldn't have done that.' Chris probably thought this was a pretty hypocritical remark but I have never meant anything more sincerely. What he didn't know was that I had already written a letter of resignation, which was due to be put on his desk at three o'clock that afternoon. Hugh Cudlipp, who had gone back to the *Mirror* group, had insisted on this so that the man I was to replace on the *Mirror* could be told by him of the rearrangement of jobs, and not hear of it through the Fleet Street grapevine.

Of course, Chris sent for me, when he got my letter, and we had a blazing row in which he accused me of I know not what. What made it worse was that I had recently been a guest of his at his country home near Clacton, but I had been unable to talk of my imminent departure because of the promise I had given Cudlipp, and out of consideration for the *Daily Mirror* man who was being offered my old job on the *Sunday Pictorial*.

Although Chris and I later made up our quarrel and he was almost unfailingly very fair to me in print he would, nevertheless, have made me work out the rest of my contract and, understandably, I should have been played down gradually for, obviously, no newspaper is going to boost someone who will shortly be leaving.

However, almost at once I got my release and, which I neither expected nor deserved, full payment from the *Express* until the end of my contract, which fortunately was nearly concluded. It was one of the most generous gestures I have ever experienced in Fleet Street or anywhere else.

1953–6
Back Home Again

The *Daily Mirror* gave me a right royal front page welcome back – and, for a time, a room which meant picking my way across the flat roof of the old building in Fetter Lane when I needed to get to the main building. The journey reminded me of my first (and virtually last) poem, written at Elstree, my prep school, which began:

> Chimney pots, chimney pots
> In London there are lots and lots!

Shortly afterwards, however, I got an office on the main editorial floor which led to one of my rare confrontations with Cecil King. He had taken over the Chairmanship from Bartholomew who, it was rumoured, had gone berserk and with a fireman's axe had chopped up one of the panelled *sancta sanctorum*, built in a more leisurely age for more leisurely directors.

My room had for years been occupied by a massive old-fashioned safe, weighing heaven knows how much but certainly standing taller, and considerably wider, than I did. I imagine even a second-rate cracksman could have picked it in about five minutes flat but it had become a fixture, in every sense of the word, and it was the special pride and joy of an old servant of the firm. Only when he was pensioned off by death was it possible to remove it and make room for me and my absolutely invaluable secretary, June Drysdale.

One afternoon when she and I were about our lawful occasions the door opened and the bulk of Cecil King appeared in the doorway. Typically he did not address either of us but, in equally typical Olympian tones, announced: 'The safe has gone.' This was too much for me. I got up, spread my jacket wide and remarked: 'Search me!'

It was one of the very few occasions when June was overcome by the often peculiar occurrences in my office and dissolved into giggles.

King made no comment, turning on his heel. But of course I can hardly pretend that it improved our relationship.

The day after I had rejoined the *Mirror* I was in France covering, among other things, the French lawn-tennis championships. I remember it because of the conversation I had with 'Little Mo' Connolly. When she had won the French title she held all four of the major championships, Australia, France, Wimbledon and the USA, at the same time. She was still only eighteen.

But she brushed aside my congratulations at being the first woman ever to accomplish this. She said: 'I won Wimbledon and the American championship last year. I have to win them again this season to make it count. All four in the same year is what matters.'

On 2 June, shortly after I got back to England, Queen Elizabeth II was crowned and on 6 June the Derby was run with the Queen's colt Aureole (a name meaning 'the gold disc surrounding the head in early pictures') starting as second favourite. You can imagine what a 'housewives' choice' the Royal colt became; in fact there was even the ridiculous rumour that, as no owner would want to be the one to deprive the Queen of her moment of supreme triumph on the Turf, there would be a gentlemen's agreement to allow Aureole to win! And there were even idiots who believed it.

Alas for romance and tales of fairy queens! The second favourite finished . . . second. For at last, in his fiftieth year – amazing how long the top jockeys can go on – Gordon Richards, on Pinza, won the one truly outstanding prize which had for so long eluded him.

I had got to know Richards towards the end of 1949 and even then his record was almost unbelievable. Apart from being as likable and surely as admirable and honourable a character as the British Turf has produced, since 1925 he had been the champion jockey every year except 1926 when he was ill, 1930 when he was beaten by the smallest possible margin on the last possible day, and 1941 when he was put out of business by a broken leg.

But the 1953 Derby win was the climax of his career, and it was one of those supreme strokes of irony which give a piquant relish to sport that the win on Pinza over the Queen's horse Aureole coincided with her award to him of a knighthood in that year's Honours List. I always thought that if anyone had had any sense of occasion they would have produced a sword from somewhere so that the Queen could have dubbed Gordon on Epsom Downs instead of waiting for a more conventional setting!

There was a sad postscript to all this. The following year, shortly after his fiftieth birthday, Gordon was still well ahead in the Jockeys List when his mount reared up and went over backwards with the little champion underneath. It turned out that he had fractured and dislocated his pelvis, and these injuries brought his riding career to an end. With an irony which was savage this time the filly which fell on him belonged to the Queen.

It was in 1953 that for the first and last time in my life I acted as un-official manager to a boxer.

The fighter was Don Cockell, sometime British and Empire heavy-weight champion, a man cursed with unwanted weight – as a light-heavyweight he had been extraordinarily skilful – but one whose courage didn't fail when it came to his supreme ring test.

His manager suffered from a bad heart and, on this occasion at least, he did not feel he could face the 12,000-mile round trip to Seattle where Cockell was to meet Harry 'Kid' Matthews. He asked me if I would stand in for him. After I had made it clear that my prime job was that of a newspaperman and that if Cockell merited any criticism he would get it, I promised to do my best for a British heavyweight in a foreign country.

As stand-in manager I succeeded in getting the rules amended and, through the good offices of Emmett Watson, the local columnist, who with his wife Betty later became a great friend of mine, I managed to get a cut under Don's eye stitched by a doctor who refused a fee after Don, quite reasonably I felt, had turned down one doctor who looked as though he were going to sew the lower to the upper eyelid!

Cockell did us proud by just shading the fight – I gave it to him by the narrowest possible margin, a quarter of a point – and he went home some £6,000 better off.

I just had time to see England win the decisive Test match against the Australians at the Oval, before 'retracing my footsteps', so to speak, by returning after seventeen years to the Olympic Stadium that Hitler had built in Berlin in 1936; now it was to hold the first postwar athletics meeting between Britain and Germany. Then it was on to Stockholm, for the match against Sweden.

It was here I realized how comparatively small nations could, and can, successfully challenge us.

The British athletes were housed at Boson, a permanent athletics camp, ten miles from the centre of Stockholm. It had every facility necessary for top-class preparation and intensive training, and I was told that scores of smaller towns throughout the country had these magnificent permanent training centres. What made the contrast with Britain, then even less well endowed with similar centres, all the more galling was that the money came from the state-controlled football pools – decided on *British* football matches!

That was nearly a quarter of a century ago; but we still don't seem to have got the message.

Ten days later I was off to New York again, this time to see Rocky Marciano defend the world heavyweight title against Roland La

Starza. It was good to catch up with 'the Rock' again, for, apart from some of his tactics in the ring, I have never known an athlete I liked more.

Then there was his perky little trainer, Charlie Goldman, who although in his mid-seventies, used to be very upset if you didn't ask, when you met him for the first time on every trip, whether he was married yet, for when you did so he was able to reply, with a wicked gleam in his eye: 'Naw! I'm still living *à la carte!*'

Marciano and La Starza had, as a matter of fact, met some three and a half years earlier, before Marciano had won the title, and La Starza had not only lasted the full ten rounds but had received one of the three votes of the officials in charge of the bout. Their meeting this time was the first heavyweight title fight between two white boxers since 'Cinderella Man' Jim Braddock, a 10–1 underdog in the betting, had outpointed Max Baer for the championship more than eighteen years earlier.

The fight was, like so many of Marciano's title defences, more like a massacre. Unlike, for example, Joe Louis, Rocky didn't take his opponents out with a single punch. Instead he left them looking like the sole survivor of a multiple road crash.

They covered La Starza with a sheet, after he had been stopped in the eleventh round, and there was a doctor on each side of the slab-like rubbing table on which he was laid. But all the 'corpse' was concerned about was his manager, Jimmy Di Angelo, whom he'd put into hospital with a heart attack after demonstrating to him his skill at stunt flying. Through his pulped lips he asked: 'Are *you* all right, Jimmy?'

The courage of boxers never ceases to move me.

Ten days after I got back to England I was in New York again for the Turpin–Olson fight. I have rarely attended an unhappier training camp. Less than ten days before the scheduled date of the fight Turpin threatened to walk out. Neither his manager nor his brother Dick, who had won the British title before him, could give any reasonable explanation of his behaviour.

I was due to do a half-hour 'live' broadcast to Britain on the Saturday before the fight – and I can't remember a more nightmare experience. 'Sugar' Ray Robinson didn't turn up. I had to play a tape of an interview someone else had got with Turpin, without time to hear what was on it before it went on the air. Only the assistance of Jack Solomons and singer Eddie Fisher got me through – just!

The fight was a disaster. Had it been over the amateur distance of three rounds Turpin would have been a unanimous winner but over the professional full distance of fifteen I gave him only one round after the first three. Olson's superior fitness nullified the greater skill of the

Englishman who afterwards could only say: 'If I'd been right I'd have stopped him in eight rounds. I've had a lot of domestic trouble.'

The tough New Yorkers were even more succinct in their summing up and I shall never forget how, as Olson, overcome with the emotion of winning the world title, wept quietly in the ring, a cameraman shouted to one of the Swedish-Portuguese-Hawaiian-American's handlers: 'Turn him round so we can see the bum crying!'

No wonder America turns out so many champion fighters; you've *got* to be tough to win there.

The more I recall days that are past the more I realize that there really is nothing new in sport, for I was no sooner home again than I was embroiled in a controversy which seems to have continued ever since: the allegation that the forward play of the All Blacks, then touring under the captaincy of Bob Stuart, was too ruthless.

Yet, as had happened in 1905–6 and in 1935–6, Wales were still too good for the iron men, with Cliff Morgan playing the kind of defensive game which only he could achieve at fly-half, and Olympic sprinter, Ken Jones, favoured by the bounce of the ball, taking a cross-punt from Clem Thomas to score the winning try. Somehow there wasn't so much talk about roughness after that, and even that great full-back, Bob Scott, didn't have things as comfortably his own way as usual.

But if some things seem to endure how very different, and more pleasant and profitable for the players, certain sports have become.

At Wembley the professional lawn tennis players, as carefully screened from the 'amateurs' [*sic*] as if they were lepers, were producing some wonderful play.

It was in this tournament that I saw one of the most memorable single matches I have ever been privileged to watch when Frank Sedgman won the £2,000 championship in front of some ten thousand 'live' spectators at Wembley and an estimated two million television viewers; as a footnote, you can't stage the minor professional meetings nowadays for less than £12,000!

In the final Sedgman took just forty-nine minutes to beat Pancho Gonzales 6–1, 6–2, 6–2 and his play was better than any I had seen from him before and comparable with the best I had seen from any other player at any other time.

To be fair to Gonzales, owing to promotional disputes with Jack Kramer, he had competed in only one tournament after winning this same championship the previous year. But, since the palmy days of Cochet, I had never seen anyone take as early a ball as Frank did that night; he even appeared to *see* it a yard faster than anyone else.

Four days later I was back at Wembley – the outdoor stadium this time – to see the most crippling stroke that had yet been delivered to English soccer. You have to remember that up to 25 November 1953 England had never been beaten at home by any overseas team, except by Eire on one occasion.

Then we met Hungary. Inside ninety seconds we were a goal down. After ninety minutes we were beaten by the 'tennis score' of 6–3.

You could see what was going to happen even before the game started. While our players were performing orthodox 'shooting in' exercises before the referee's whistle sent them on their way one of these magical Magyars – Hidegkuti it was, later to be known as 'Hat-trick Hidegkuti' – trapped the ball, flipped it on to his instep, rolled it up his shin, steadied it on his knee, jerked it on to his shoulder and nudged it on to the top of his head. Then he repeated the whole process in reverse.

England had come out to meet a team of footballers and were now, apparently, to be faced by a side of booted prestidigitators.

And so it turned out. I was sitting next to that old stalwart of Sunderland, Arsenal and England, Charlie Buchan, and it was within five minutes of half-time that one of his horny elbows dug into my ribs and he exclaimed: 'That's the first one of their passes to go really astray.'

The names – Hidegkuti, Puskas, Bozsik, Czibor, goalkeeper Grosics – resounded like a bell tolling for English football. The post-match comment which made most sense to me, as it expressed what so many had thought for so long and even more were now accepting, appeared in the Belgian paper, *La Dernière Heure*: 'It was a triumph of youth over old age; the triumph of a team playing as such for months, if not for years, against a formation of elements from different clubs and brought together only in the last three days.'

That gave me an idea for a competition. I offered prizes for the best letters on the theme: 'Would you be prepared to let your favourite players be called upon by England for maybe a month at a time in order that the old country should regain its former unchallenged superiority?' I pointed out that if you were, for instance, a Blackpool supporter you might have had to sacrifice four players, Stan Matthews, Ernie Taylor, Stan Mortensen and Harry Johnston, all of whom had played against the Hungarians.

I received 13,300 letters in answer and the overwhelming majority said that they *would* be prepared to put country before club. I wonder if they really meant it.

A British runner was very much in the news at that time – and for a long time to come. He was Gordon Pirie whom the Americans had tried to 'poach' by offering him one of their athletic scholarships at Oklahoma

University. In the end I was able to get him a job with a paint firm in Britain which enabled him to keep his amateur status and, at the same time, gave him more time for training than his position as a bank clerk allowed. What a lot of nonsense all this fiddling around with amateurism is in the second half of the twentieth century.

For no particular reason that reminds me of the time a Springbok rugby team on a tour of Europe – I think it was Avril Malan's side of 1960–1 – were invited to a banquet at Lambeth Palace.

To the skipper's horror the table was smothered with gold and silver salt cellars, sugar sifters and various precious pieces of plate all, of course, irreplaceable but all the most shining temptations to any rugby side, almost all of whom are notoriously addicted to the habit of 'pouching' souvenirs.

But ashtrays and tankards from a public bar are one thing and precious Church plate is something else. So, before they sat down, the quick-thinking Malan is alleged to have asked the Archbishop if, seeing that most of the team belonged to the Dutch Reformed Church, he might be allowed to say grace in their own language.

The prelate, obviously thinking what well behaved young men he had invited to the Palace, of course gave his assent. Whereupon Malan is supposed to have said, in Afrikaans: 'The first beggar I see as much as coveting any of the plate on this table will find himself in the next plane home so fast he won't know what's hit him!' A pause, then: 'Amen.' The Archbishop beamed benignly.

My own next trip was to South Africa in January 1954. Once more Don Cockell, this time defending this Empire heavyweight title against Johnny Arthur in Johannesburg, was the reason for my journey.

When I got to Johannesburg the trip had a hilarious beginning. A sportswriter from one of the South African papers rang me at my hotel and asked if he could come to interview me on boxing matters. We arranged to meet in the bar.

After we'd had a drink he asked me his opening question: who were my choices as the best champions at the eight different weights? Well, that wasn't too difficult, as far as my time went. I answered: 'Heavyweight – Joe Louis; light-heavy – Archie Moore; middle – Sugar Ray Robinson; welter – Henry Armstrong; light – Ike Williams . . .'

'Stop . . . stop,' cried my interrogator. 'They're all niggers!'

Of course I knew all about apartheid, although it had not then become so notorious, and I swear I was not deliberately trying to be provocative. Even two decades and more later I am not positive that I would make any alterations to the above list.

But if my interviewer had 'seen black' I must say the use of that odious word made me see red.

I replied, rather tersely, that he had asked me who I thought were the *best*, not the most ethnically acceptable, and one word led to a few dozen more, culminating with the gentleman who had been sent to interview me eventually inviting me to step outside.

I was extremely happy to say that, as far as he was concerned, I drew the line not at colour but at the idea of meeting him at all; and then, I admit, with the greatest possible pomposity, added that I wouldn't dream of soiling my hands on him!

God! they make you as childish as they are.

The only memorable thing about the fight was the weigh-in, for they put Cockell on one of the gold assaying machines and his weight was announced as fifteen stone and half an ounce! They don't mess about with their gold.

Apart from the fight, in which Cockell, hampered by a poisoned right thigh, took fifteen rounds to beat a man he should have defeated in a third of that time, I don't think I've ever disliked anywhere, except Calcutta, as much as Johannesburg with its corrosion of race oppression and the ghastly conditions of the nearby shanty towns.

It was therefore good to be back in time to see the last official match of the All Blacks' tour of Britain, against the Barbarians at Cardiff, which they won by nineteen points to five to bring their tally to twenty-four wins, two draws and two defeats.

It is, as I've said before, desperately difficult to compare the great stars of one age with those of another, but I still wonder whether I have ever seen a much greater full-back than Bob Scott, although he was now at the end of his international career. As so often happens, without the tension of an international, the match against the Baa-Baas was probably about as exciting a performance as the New Zealanders produced during their entire tour of Britain.

My next destination was Rome where I was going to see, first, Foxhunter, with Colonel Harry Llewellyn the British show-jumping star combination of the 1952 Olympic Games; secondly, Randolph Turpin defend his European middleweight title, and, thirdly, the Italian lawn tennis championships.

It was one of the most disastrous trips I have ever made. Foxhunter refused three times at one of the early obstacles, and was disqualified in the international show-jumping competition.

Turpin was stopped in sixty-five seconds by the Italian, Tiberio Mitri, in a fight of just three punches.

And not a British player survived the second round of the lawn-tennis championships!

Just so that my cup was sure to overflow I had no sooner finished phoning the details of one of these disasters to London than the copy-taker remarked, *en passant*: 'I don't know if you're interested, but Roger Bannister has just broken four minutes for the mile!'

A postscript to this whole disastrous episode came a few days after we had returned to England. During the Foxhunter débâcle it had come on to rain very heavily. Once our entry had been eliminated I decided there were better things to do in Rome than sit and watch a succession of sodden nags, and borrowing from, I believe, the late Robert Benchley I said: 'I don't know about you, but I'm going to get out of these wet clothes and into a dry Martini.'

This obviously stuck in my companion Dennis Rowe's mind, but, as a raconteur he was very much less talented than he was as a photographer. One evening I was having a contemplative drink in dear old Barney Finnegan's pub in Fetter Lane. In those days it was divided, in the old-fashioned way, by thin partitions of wood and clouded glass, into little cubicles. I was in one and Dennis and some of his mates were in the adjoining compartment. I heard Dennis talking. He commented: 'That Peter Wilson's an amusing bloke. You know when we were in Rome it started pouring with rain and he turned to me and said: 'I don't know about you but I'm going to get out of these wet clothes and into a gin and tonic"!' I've heard some jokes fall flat but that one absolutely squelched.

Dennis it was, too, who was asked the riddle: 'Do you know who sleeps with cats?' To which the answer is: 'Mrs Katz – and sometimes Mrs Greenbaum.' Dennis thought this was the funniest thing since the General Strike and he couldn't wait to pass it on to his cronies. Unfortunately it came out as 'I bet you don't know who sleeps with Mrs Greenbaum!' There's no recovery from that sort of thing.

Shortly after this my favourite boxing manager in the world, Jack Hurley, who had promoted Don Cockell's fight in Seattle – as well as managing his opponent! – came to London. Most fight managers I can take or leave alone, preferably the latter, but Hurley was something rather special.

He used to 'cut his fighters down the middle' – i.e. take 50 per cent of their purses – but when I suggested that this seemed somewhat excessive he countered by saying: 'Well, what's half of nothing, then? And I tell you a lot of the guys I looked after in the past were strictly nothing guys until I conned some poor slob into paying good folding money for them!'

Not all Hurley's boxers were 'nothing guys'. He managed Billy Petrolle, the legendary 'Fargo Express' who lost only twenty bouts out of 157, including meetings with six world champions, and who must have been one of the best lightweights who never won the world title. His three battles with Jack 'Kid' Berg are still talked about by those who were lucky enough to see them.

The last time I saw Jack Hurley he had a new worry; if he hadn't at least one major worry he would have worried about that. Someone had given him a vicuna overcoat which had cost several hundred pounds. We were sitting in a bar and he complained bitterly: 'I always thought this guy was a friend of mine. I never did him a smidgeon of harm and now he's like to worry me to death. Now you, you there, watch it; don't spill any of that garbage on my new coat' – this was to a waiter with a heavily laden tray who was passing the coatstand where Hurley had hung his coat. He sighed deeply: 'You know what? That coat takes up about four of my waking hours every day. I have to jump around like a cricket to see that no bum with a cigarette gets close enough to burn it. I always have to sit where I can see it in case some lousy thief tries to swipe it. Then there's the brushing and general maintenance – I swear it takes more looking after than a new Cadillac. Oh, that guy who gave it to me! What a stinking trick to pull on someone you call a friend!'

It was Jack who was associated with one of the great con tricks of all time when Pete Rademacher, who had just won the Olympic heavyweight title in 1956, was matched *in his first professional fight* against Floyd Patterson, then the world professional heavyweight champion.

Hurley summed up the whole affair succinctly. He said simply: 'We should all have gone to jail!'

Instead he has, I am sure, gone to heaven, where, unless the surroundings are even more beneficial than they are claimed to be, I'm certain he is trying to cut the leading harpist down the middle!

This was the year of Lester Piggott's first Derby win, at the age of eighteen, on the 33–1 outsider, Never Say Die.

I confess that despite his outstanding skill, Piggott has always been too cold a fish for me. After his victory they came to invite him to appear on television. 'Not interested,' he said.

I did manage to have a few brief words with the young man. But quietly, almost as an aside, he said: 'Why all the fuss? After all the Derby is just another race. . . .'

If the summit is such a barren plateau, even at eighteen, life must be a lacklustre affair.

He had, and still has, to watch his weight stringently and at one time it was widely rumoured that he would outgrow the weight for flat races and if he wanted to go on racing he would have to turn to jumping.

But more than twenty years later he's still winning classics all over the world.

It is said that he's worth round about a million pounds, but he is one athlete whom I don't envy, for a cup of black coffee and a cigar is not my idea of a sparkling way to start the day. . . .

There followed another trip to the States to see Rocky Marciano defend his title, for the third time, against a previous heavyweight champion, Ezzard Charles. To get to Grossingers where, inevitably, Rocky was training, I flew in a specially hired helicopter for the first time.

During this trip Marciano made a most revealing remark. He told me: 'I wish that I wasn't undefeated.' Up to that time he had forty-five professional fights without a loss and, in fact, he was to finish his career, and his life, without ever losing a pro fight.

But he expanded on a remark which, on the surface, was a remarkable one to be made by the heavyweight champion of the world. 'Don't get me wrong. I don't mean I want to lose now. I don't intend to lose, and I will fight harder than ever to keep the streak intact, because as long as I'm unbeaten I'm still champion of the world. But I often wish to myself that somewhere along the line, before I won the title, I had lost a decision. I can't explain it, but I would like to have been beaten only to know what the feeling is like.'

Well, Rocky didn't lose, putting Charles through the 'Marciano mangle' so that, like so many other fighters, he was never quite so good again. The great punchers do that to their opponents.

But Charles, underrated because of his lack of glamour and, illogically, unpopular because he had been the first to beat Joe Louis on his comeback, fought with tremendous courage to take Marciano the full fifteen rounds – the only time 'the Rock' had to travel that distance – only to end up with a face so swollen that it resembled nothing so much as one of those huge water-melons which have a skin of such a dark green that it looks almost black.

The 1954 Empire Games at Vancouver will always live in my mind for two races – the only meeting between Roger Bannister and the Australian John Landy who, forty-seven days after Bannister had registered 3 mins 59·4 secs at Oxford, had reduced the time to 3 mins 58·0 secs at Turku, Finland, helped (as Bannister had been) by Chris Chataway. The other never-to-be-forgotten race was Jim Peters' marathon.

The Empire Stadium in Vancouver had a magnificent setting, girdled as it was with blue waters and rimmed with the high mountains which were still veined with snow even in August. And here, on a fateful Saturday afternoon, two memorable athletics events finished within minutes of each other.

Bannister ran the mile, which he knew would be the only one in which he would ever meet Landy, as though he had been computerized. One picture summed up the whole race. Landy of the shuffling stride was in the lead. Normally Bannister used to make his 'kick' some 300 yards out on the last lap. On this occasion, with the greatest self-control, he delayed his burst until something like seventy yards from the tape.

And just as he slid into top gear the temptation to look back to see where his Nemesis was overcame John Landy, and he turned his head to glance inwards, over his left shoulder, at the precise moment when Bannister raced past and outside him on the right. Landy described that fleeting glance as 'taking a hopeful'!

In a way the whole racing careers of these two great athletes were fused into that split second, for, of course, there was no catching Bannister at this stage of the race and he finished first in 3 mins 58·8 secs to Landy's 3 mins 59·6 secs – a little under six yards, but it might as well have been sixty as far as poor Landy was concerned, and it was small comfort that he still held the world record . . . by 0·8 secs.

Afterwards the Englishman ascribed his victory to 'not letting anyone else make me run any way except the way I had planned'.

Then Bannister, whom I had sometimes found to be rather aloof, did a most endearing thing as far as I was concerned. He had, as he always did, run himself out until his 'bank' of oxygen was exhausted. He had just finished a mass Press, radio and tape-recorded interview when he must have been physically and mentally spent. But he took time to turn to me and say: 'I'm sorry you missed the time when I was the first to break the four-minute mile, Peter, because I remember you saying on the radio that if you had the choice that was the sporting event which you most wanted to see.'

But if the Bannister–Landy mile was an Everest of human endeavour it was soon to be eclipsed by what I still think of as the Hades of sport – Peters' marathon.

There was nothing to warn anyone about the macabre ending as Peters, to the ragged roar of the crowd which always lines a marathon course, came from the street, down the precipitously steep ramp leading into the stadium where, of course, he had to do a final lap. Progress reports had put him ahead almost all the way and it seemed even more of a certainty for him when Stan Cox, the other English entry, between whom and Peters there was some considerable rivalry, was reported as having collided with a telegraph post, ending up in hospital.

It was a blazing hot day and later it was suggested that Peters had contributed to his own undoing by setting too fast a pace; another theory was that the extremely steep descent from the road outside to the stadium had finally unsettled a man who was just about at the limit of his endurance anyway.

This is how I described the grisly scene at the time:

You have heard of someone running like a drunken man. Peters is not running like that. He is running – no, meandering – like a rather bad comic on the stage burlesquing a drunk.

Two steps forward, then three to the side. So help me, he's running backwards now. The roar of the crowd dies to a hushed whisper and then to a silence in which you can hear a pin drop – only it isn't a pin that drops, it is Jim Peters.

The first time he falls it's forward on to the grey ashes which are no greyer than his face. Red stars appear on his knees.

He's up again. He's running in grotesque, sprawling S's, so that one moment he's nearly on the grass centre field, and the next he's lurching up against the trackside seats.

Anyway he's only got about 300 yards to go – anyone can do that, surely. But – oh, he's down again. This time he's in a sitting position, gaping up at the blazing, implacable sun which is screwing the juice out of his featherweight body and the marrow out of his bones.

Ah, there's the announcer over the public address system telling everyone in the infield to sit down. That's right. The cash customers have paid up to thirty-five shillings to see this. They mustn't miss an incident in this X-certificate movie.

To be sure he's not taking the shortest way home. He's fairly weaving all over the track on those funny, wavering, magnificent, wonderful, plucky legs of his, like white pipe-cleaners. But that's his problem – no one's making him do it, are they?

Oops! he's down again.

But nobody stops it. Later they say the doctor who is empowered to pull any runner out of this crucifying race at any time has been hauled back by officious officials who don't want to see Peters disqualified from the race.

I suppose they don't reckon it matters if he's disqualified from living.

Now it's getting quite farcical. He's up, he's down. He's up, he's down. He's up, he's down.

So Jim Peters pitches over the line, a white scarecrow, and Mick Mayes catches him and a stretcher is brought and people remember to take a deep breath again.

And then they announce that the real finish is on the other side of the track, 220 yards away, and so Jim Peters – what does he remind you of, a landed fish with a gaffed jaw heaving for water and dying in the sun, a trapped and bloody fox which has gnawed its own leg off for freedom, a rabbit with infected myxomatosis beating its own brains out? – so Jim Peters has lost, anyway.

I went down to the first-aid room and I was there when they brought Jim

E

Peters in on the stretcher. There was a collar of foam streaming from one corner of his twisted mouth, over his neck and down his chest.

Once he asked: 'Did I make it?' and mercifully the nurse who was with the three doctors said: 'You did all right, Jim', and so he thought he had won.

Without exaggeration, except for hare-coursing and bull-fighting this was the most nauseating spectacle I can remember in all my years of sport – a semi-conscious man being allowed to destroy himself progressively while no one had the power or the gumption to intervene.

Fortunately Peters did not suffer any permanent ill-effects from his ordeal but he never ran again. It was a happy touch when the Duke of Edinburgh sent him a special gold medal inscribed: 'To J. Peters as a token of admiration for a most gallant marathon runner.'

There was one man for whom, in the end, I felt almost as sorry as for Peters and that was Joe McGhee of Scotland – for he was the winner whom no one ever remembered.

The next major overseas event I covered – a fortnight or so later – was the European athletics championship at Berne, Switzerland, which also resulted in some memorable races. One was the 10,000 metres in which Zatopek ran with such imperial ability that he was like a wild stallion scattering donkeys. Then there was Bannister's best competitive race in which he won a pretty rough 1,500 metres; one competitor was hit so badly that he was not only floored but subsequently collapsed during the race.

What a finish to Bannister's career. In little over three months he had become the first sub-four-minute miler at Oxford, had beaten Landy in their sole confrontation at Vancouver, and had proved himself the best man in Europe at the European distance of 1500 metres. It was good to see Bannister, that most cerebral runner, go out at the top.

The final outstanding event was the 5,000 metres and the first view, for most of us, of a new star – Vladimir Kuts. There had been rumours of this blond Russian ex-sailor running distances at impossible speeds and collapsing long before the tape, so no one paid any particular attention when, against a field which included Zatopek and Chataway, he was leading by at least fifty yards at the halfway stage.

When, with only three laps to go, he increased his lead to 100 yards eyes began to pop. In the end the event split into what were virtually two races – as so often happens, but rarely so dramatically.

Kuts won as he liked by a little over eighty yards, clipping 0·6 second off the world record which I had seen Zatopek put up in Paris only three months earlier, and Chataway finished some nine yards ahead of Zatopek! In the normal way he would have been turning cartwheels at having beaten the mighty Czech.

Incidentally, Berne provided a sad indication of the decline of British athletics today, for in those European championships, although Britain was outclassed by Russia, who scored 269 points, we were a good second with 100½ points, finishing ahead of nineteen other European nations.

Chataway didn't have to wait long – under seven weeks, in fact – for another chance. The next big athletics meeting was the international between London and Moscow at the White City.

Those who were there saw perhaps the most memorable two-man race ever. As this was an international, only four runners – two from each country – started; but everyone knew that neither Peter Driver nor Vladimir Okorokov was going to affect the race in any way.

Sure enough Kuts jumped into the lead right away but Chataway, Berne very much in mind, never let him get clear. Every time the blond Russian accelerated or slowed down the pace the red-headed Englishman stayed a constant distance behind him, as though hauled along by some invisible umbilical cord of athletics.

The 5,000 metres is approximately 3 miles 188 yards, so in this race of races the Russian, still leading, broke the essentially British three-mile record, which he had taken from Chataway in the course of the Berne race, while Chataway's final burst, within fifty yards of the tape, reduced Kuts' world time for the then essentially Continental 5,000 metres by exactly five seconds – an astonishing margin at that time. Kuts, too, broke his old record, to finish, after those 3 miles 818 yards, just *one-fifth of a second* behind the Englishman.

No wonder the crowd of over 40,000 were cheering, roaring, some even crying – and I was told the same thing happened in front of millions of TV sets – and I really did see men literally throwing their hats into the air despite the chill of a London October night.

The final picture of this floodlit encounter, in which the shadow finally passed the substance which was throwing it, was of a wide-eyed, gasping but ecstatically happy Chataway being helped off the track by – inevitably – Roger Bannister. And the gallant Russian whose efforts had ensured that they *both* broke world records? Well, the crack was: 'Kuts? He went Chataway!'

People often ask me who were the best fighters at the various different weights whom I ever saw. It's impossible, of course, to give a scientifically provable answer, but one of my all-time greats for the featherweight would certainly be the Negro Sandy Saddler.

About that time I flew to Paris to see him meet the European nine-stone champion, Ray Famechon, the Frenchman who in exactly a hundred fights spread over ten years had been outpointed only three times by European boxers. Never has there been a more painful demonstration of the vast gulf between the top Americans and the best Europeans, for after five rounds Famechon looked like a man who had tried to stop a hand grenade with his face or catch cannon-balls with his teeth and the fight was halted in Saddler's favour.

The most unexpected trip I ever made came in the first three weeks of 1955. I was summoned to see Hugh Cudlipp. The interview was brief. Cudlipp asked: 'Do you know anything about cricket?'

I nodded. 'I haven't been able to devote myself to it full time so I can't claim to be among the top experts, but I've followed it pretty closely for years.'

'Good. How soon can you leave for Australia?'

After the desperate period for English cricket of the postwar years public interest had suddenly soared during the tour of Australia when the English side captained by Len Hutton had made a great comeback after a disastrous start in which we had lost the first Test by the shattering margin of an innings and 154 runs. Back in 1953 we had at last triumphed at home – the first time we had won the Ashes since 1926 – but the margin had been the narrowest possible: one win to us and four draws. To triumph in Australia was something very different, and again something which had not been achieved since my cousin Douglas Jardine, aided by the thunderbolts of 'Lol' Larwood, had tamed even Don Bradman and won the 1932–3 series 4–1.

But now Hutton had his jet-propulsion too, in the form of Frank Tyson (nicknamed 'Typhoon') who, with six for 85 on the last morning at Sydney, had won the second Test for us by the uncomfortably close margin of 38 runs. At Melbourne in the third Test Tyson had been even more devastating, taking seven for 27, and on the fifth day having a spell of fifty-one balls in which he took six wickets for only 16 runs!

Everything therefore depended on the fourth Test at Adelaide. Australia had to win it, and the final Test at Sydney, to regain the Ashes. A draw and England would hold on to the Ashes; a win for us meant the series was ours.

Such was the background to Cudlipp's command.

On the way to Australia I had the grim experience of stopping off at Calcutta, the saddest, grisliest city I have ever visited, where men and women are literally born, live and die on a patch of pavement, where the screeching of carrion birds wakes you at dawn and where a corpse, covered by a threadbare blanket which will later be retrieved, is carried at a jogtrot by stretcher-bearers to the burning ghats. I saw a corpse inserted into a hollowed-out pyramid-shaped erection of logs. After one foot had been burned off and the skull had exploded in the heat I left.

When people express their wonder at the spread of Communism I wonder if they have visited places like Calcutta – for I suppose there must be others as ghastly, although fortunately I have not seen them.

I arrived in Australia just before the MCC's match against South Australia at Adelaide. I can't remember more continuous, searing heat than the weather there, the more obvious coming from an English winter. Day after day and night after sleepless night the temperature soared up to 98° and, even in the early hours of the morning, never dropped below 78°.

On the last day of the ensuing test twelve wickets fell for 139 runs before England gained the five wickets' victory which ensured her retention of the Ashes and the winning of the series.

I managed to take in some other sport while I was in Australia. I saw what was on the whole a rather lacklustre Australian athletics championship at the Kensington Oval, which used to be Bradman's home ground, but I was particularly impressed with the determined, courageous and brainy running of young Herb Elliott, a sixteen-year-old West Australian from Perth, who took the junior mile in 4 mins 20·8 secs. To return that time at sixteen is magnificent running and if ever I saw a moving signpost of a future champion this was it.

Before I left Sydney I managed to spend one evening at the nearly fifty-year-old stadium at Rushcutters Bay where a fighter called Johnson was topping the bill.

Nothing remarkable about that, of course, but this was the stadium where boxing history had been made when Jack Johnson became the first Negro to win the heavyweight championship of the world, winning the title uniquely – on the intervention of the police in the fourteenth round – from the French Canadian, Tommy Burns, born Noah Brusso. Appropriately enough this happened on Boxing Day in 1908.

The memory of that epoch-making fight still seemed to pervade the dingy old stadium. In the lobby there were pictures of it: Burns, a little Napoleon-like man beside the colossal black; Johnson's head shaved like a cannon-ball, his lips like blunt black razor blades. I can remember nothing of the other Johnson and the fights I saw that night, for my mind was full of the championship of long ago about which I had read so much that I felt as though I had actually seen it.

I came back with John Arlott, distinguished in print and on the air-waves as a cricket critic, via Fiji and San Francisco. In Fiji John had an introduction to one of the Paramount Chiefs who, although he had run to fat and must have weighed something like twenty-five stone, had clearly been a most powerful man. It was said that in his prime he could throw a cricket ball well over a hundred yards!

There was a ceremonial reception with everyone, except John and myself, in native dress. We were handed half coconut shells full of kava, a local brew made by pounding (or chewing – ugh!) the root of a Polynesian shrub. Ours was, at least, pounded, with metal bars in gourd-like containers, in front of our eyes. Then this witches' potion was given to us and we became the focus of all eyes. Kava is allegedly intoxicating or, some people say, a mildly stimulating drug. Well, speak as you find – that's what I say – and to me this hellish concoction looked like dirty dishwater and, by God, that's what it tasted like too. After a preliminary and premonitory sip I checked, in some distress. Out of the free corner of his mouth John, that much publicized connoisseur of the finest wines, whispered: 'Go on! You've got to drink it down in one otherwise they'll be insulted; and they can't drink until we've finished.'

To whisper at such length with one side of his mouth while the other was concerned with vintage kava seemed to me the cleverest trick of the week – or, perhaps, it was just that he had a paralysed palate! – but clearly there was nothing for it but to follow John's courageous example.

When we had finally downed this nauseous draught, closely observed all the while by the Chief and his attendants, there was a deep-throated 'Aa-ah!' and everyone set to quaffing their own potions, not forgetting of course, to refill our containers. I don't know about a cricket ball but by the time it was all over I felt I could throw a half-coconut shell much farther than a hundred yards – like clear off the island, for instance.

Less than seven weeks later I was back on the Pacific coast of America to chronicle the short life and hard times of Don Cockell against world heavyweight champion, Rocky Marciano.

There is little to record about the Marciano–Cockell fight which went exactly the way anyone who had seen both box-fighters expected it to.

By this time I had got to know Don fairly well and before the fight he asked me what advice I could give him. I fear the Marquess of Queensberry would not have approved of what I told him – but the Marquess had never seen Rocky Marciano and I had. In effect, I told Cockell that anything would go (including himself!) under American rules and that at the first sign of anything illegal by Marciano he must reply with a harder head, a lower punch or a total disregard of the bell ending a round. I assured him that under the American 'no foul' rules he would not be disqualified but I warned him not to wait until he was half-crippled before he tried to retaliate.

The fight was halted by the referee in the ninth.

Joe Williams of the *New York World Telegram* summed it up: 'Marciano violated practically every rule in the book. He hit after the bell, used his elbows and head in close quarters, several times punched below the belt and once hit Cockell when he was down. . . . If Cockell should get the idea that anything goes in the American ring, short of wielding a knife or pulling a gun, you couldn't blame him.'

Afterwards Don told me: 'You were dead right, Peter. Of course, I should have butted him back and hit him low when he did it to me. The trouble is that you have to do these things at once, otherwise the opportunity has passed. And if you're brought up under our rules you have to force yourself to break them – you can't do it instinctively.'

Marciano said: 'Cockell took some of my best punches. I do not know why the American public underestimated him. I don't think I have ever fought a braver guy.'

Before you dismiss Marciano as just a villainous plug-ugly with truncheons for hands, let me show you a glimpse of the reverse side of the coin.

It happened at Rocky's training camp at Calistoga in the Napa Valley, famous for its Californian wine and immortalized more than forty years earlier by Jack London (himself more than a bit of a fight fan) in *The Valley of the Moon*. Before I had left London, a cripple, whom I knew as a great boxing enthusiast, had written to me begging me to get Marciano's autograph for him.

I had just completed a taped interview for the BBC with Rocky; even in those few days before a fight when a boxer gets to his edgiest it was always a delight to talk to Rocky. He seemed so genuinely interested in the whole affair that he made every interview alive and he was so modest a person that when we first met he could not believe that I had come all the way from England to see him.

The weather was broiling in the Napa Valley and I was just about to leave when I remembered about the autograph. Rather diffidently I explained the circumstances to the world champion and produced a notebook in which he could inscribe his name.

He shook his head: 'No, that's not good enough.' Then in the blazing sunshine he ran well over a quarter of a mile to his own chalet to get a magnificent action picture which he autographed to 'My pal, so-and-so'. In all sport I have never met a more ambivalent character than 'the Rock'.

Later in 1955 I made my first trip to the USSR for an athletics international, Russia *v.* Britain. A few days earlier we had been at Bordeaux warming up against the French men's and women's teams.

There with my old friend Sydney Hulls I sampled the joys of one of the world's great restaurants, Le Chapon Fin – now, alas, I believe destroyed to make way for yet another block of office buildings – where, for the first time, I really knew what King Henry I felt like after his famous surfeit of lampreys. Sydney and I distinctly overindulged ourselves in delicious *lamproies* and what with sampling as many of the clarets as we could lay our lips to – hoping that our pockets, too, would stand the strain – we were rather a sickly couple by the end of various feasts. I was told that at the time Le Chapon Fin had over 1000 varieties of Bordeaux in their cellars.

I doubt if you could have found more of a contrast with Bordeaux than Moscow.

The arrival of our athletes unfortunately coincided almost to the hour with the state visit of the veteran West German leader, Konrad Adenauer. When I was driven to the airport to meet our team we were suddenly faced with the longest cortège of menacing black limousines since the days of the great gangster funerals in the Chicago of the early thirties. Our taxi was unceremoniously forced off the road.

Before the meeting on Sunday there was time to see some of the attractions of Moscow. Having an Intourist guide we were able to circumvent the great line of devoted pilgrims which snaked its way through Red Square to file past the vault containing the funeral biers supporting the embalmed bodies of Lenin and the still honoured Stalin.

There was one slightly macabre circumstance. The bodies lay side by side and the eye of Lenin on Stalin's side was half-open in a kind of grisly peek-a-boo, as though to say: 'You may be God the Son but don't forget God the Father of all the Soviets is keeping His eye on you!'

The meeting itself was a disaster for Britain: in thirty-one events – twenty for men and eleven for women – we won a grand total of five for the men and two for the women. Our outstanding performance came from John Disley in the 3,000 metres steeplechase in which he broke the then ratified world record with a time of 8 mins 44·2 secs. Chris Brasher was second.

Chataway did win the 5,000 metres in a slow time but Gordon Pirie in the 10,000 metres was destroyed by Kuts who must have won by about a furlong from Pirie and Ken Norris.

The highlight of our social side was to be a visit to the Bolshoi Ballet. Lainson Wood, one of the great all-round sportswriters of my time in Fleet Street, and I accounted ourselves fortunate in being able to buy a couple of seats for approximately £4 each – even though that was quite a sum of money in those days – to see the incomparable Ulanova dancing in *Romeo and Juliet*.

How it happened I shall never know or begin to understand. When we arrived we were shown into an enormous box, in what the decadent West would have called the royal circle, *which was next to the one occupied by Khrushchev and Adenauer.*

Our box held sixteen and besides Lainson and myself there were seven whose middle name might have been Siberia and another seven whose eyes, apparently constructed of ice-blue diamond chips, spelled Belsen – or its modern equivalent. The Russian and German secret services were taking no chances: but *we* were!

It is now necessary – but not easy – to describe Lainson. Get the idea firmly into your mind that he was a *huge* man, though his height was no more than six foot, if that. Among other peculiarities – and you have to take my word for it that he would have provided one of those mammoth footnotes in the works of the late lamented Herr Jung – Lainson was the only man I know who could go to sleep between forkfuls of Lobster Thermidor; nor was that all, for when he fell asleep he snored – snored with the sound of stout calico being rent in twain. And when he was awoken he would return to the sentient world with a great cry and the whirling of burly arms.

All this I had forgotten as we took our seats at the Bolshoi and waited for the performance to commence, Lainson growling incomprehensibilities in his ursine way (it always seemed as though his tongue were far too large for the cavern of his mouth) while I looked apprehensively at the next box where chunky Khrushchev and the aloof Adenauer were regally seated.

Ulanova was then, I believe, forty-seven but the delight of her dancing, what little I saw of it, could have come from a bud-fresh girl of sixteen. The house was stilled, as though we were all at the court of the Sleeping Beauty. And then it happened.

It was oppressively hot and, unobserved by me, Lainson had gone to sleep. No Sleeping Beauty he. As his eyes closed and the first ripple of chins sank on to his rhythmically heaving chest one of those mighty snores ripped through the Bolshoi. I froze in my seat but in as slow and menacing a fashion as the hood of a cobra dilates, so fourteen pairs of eyes – half of them slit and Slav, half Prussian blue – swivelled in our direction.

Like the fool I am, I jogged Lainson in the ribs and whispered: 'Wake up, wake up!' With a mighty shout he did so and one of his tree-trunk arms knocked me half-askew in my seat. I could see – or felt I saw – seven KGB men feeling for pistols and seven Germans fumbling for the handcuffs.

There was no way of cutting short this appalling situation. Instead of being able to admire the incomparable art of Ulanova I had to sit slewed round in my seat, keeping one and a half eyes on Lainson with only half of one to spare for the great ballerina.

Every time the tip of Lainson's leading chin threatened to spread on his chest I had to put a forefinger, shaking with apprehension and rage, under it and support that great lolling head so that no more Stromboli-like eruptions should shatter the theatre.

I couldn't get him out because, just as the curtain had risen, some blockhead had locked the door of the box from outside. But, by golly, as soon as the interval came and I heard the click of the lock I had Lainson out in the corridor before either the Russian or the German guards could show any unwanted interest in us. Down the stairs we sped – I swear for all his twenty stone Lainson's feet scarcely touched the steps – and I was able to relax only when I had got him into a droshky, troika or, more likely, a humble taxi.

He made only one comment: 'Tha' wash a bloody short show,' he grunted, as though feeling he had not had fair value for his four pounds.

Another episode involving Lainson I remember equally clearly.

We were attending a fight at an ice rink where, because of fire regulations, a large proportion of the hall had to be left untenanted. As there was no percentage – or, anyway, no profit – in insulating this part of the rink, the ice was left virtually uncovered and you can imagine what *that* was like on a cold winter's night.

In the event Lainson, wearing an enormous overcoat constructed on the lines of a bell-tent and fitting about as well, was a little late and had to push his way to his seat, bordering the edge of the ring.

As ill luck would have it, next to him was a venerable sportswriter who, for some years, had been wearing what must have been the original wig ever constructed – no doubt thrown away by the aspiring *perruquier* with the disappointed inventor's resigned cry: 'Oh, well! Back to the drawing board.' But of this the venerable sportswriter had no idea. It was his pretty conceit to imagine that he was fooling the world, that no one knew that every solitary hair on his head was not his own.

As I have said, Lainson was seated next to him and, as Lainson insinuated his twenty-odd stone into a place designed for a man of much more modest dimensions, the corner of the bell-tent caught the world's oldest wig – and swept it into the ring where bloody combat was going on.

Now, apart from missiles thrown by the disgruntled citizenry – which normally do not sail through the ropes until the end of a fight after an unpopular decision – there is only one object, apart from the fighters, which drops to the canvas. And that is the gumshield of one of the boxers, which has been dislodged by his opponent's efforts. In this case the practice is standard. The referee kicks the gumshield to the nearest corner occupied by one of the boxers. If it's the wrong one a member of the opposing entourage will be round right smartly to collect it. If it belongs in the corner to which it has been kicked, one of the seconds there will rinse it in the bucket of ice-cold water used to revive his principal between rounds.

When the wig landed in the ring the action was fast and furious. The referee, without looking down, kicked it to one of the corners. I had, in fact, witnessed the full sequence of events, but I was like one of those characters in an ancient Greek tragedy, in the grip of remorseless Fate. There was nothing I could do. I could only observe.

Observe I did, paying, I regret to say, scant attention to the fight which was waxing so furious above my head. I observed one of the seconds in the corner to which the wig had been kicked, by reflex action dunk it wholly and completely in the bucket of icy and slightly blood-tinged water. He hadn't actually *seen* his man lose his gumshield but then he hadn't seen the other boxer lose his. Better to be prepared. The minute interval between rounds was all too short for the manifold tasks which had to be accomplished. The fact that the object he had doused in the water was furry rather than rubbery made no impression on him in the heat of vicarious battle.

At that moment the bell signalling the end of the round rang. The two boxers went to their corners. The one in whose the wig had landed pushed his gumshield forward with his tongue and another second took it and went to rinse it. He came across the sopping wig.

'Wha's this then?' he inquired holding up the disgusting object.

'Ah dinna ken,' replied another handler. 'It lukes lak a droonit rat.' That was enough for second number one. With some strange Scottish oath he hurled it from him far, far under the ring platform.

Meanwhile the action shifted to the venerable sportswriter. I have said how patches of ice had been left uncovered and now the considerable nip in the air was reaching the V.S.'s dome which already resembled the skating rink in which we were all seated. Slowly one of his hands reached the crown of his head. With horrified incredulity he began to tap his skull, in the way a man who is not sure of the freshness of a boiled egg gingerly taps the shell.

Nothing. Instead of the familiar fuzzy covering, he found – nothing. With a great shout he leapt to his feet and delivered himself of the immortal lines: 'By Go-ad! Ah've bin scalpit!'

And the consequence was . . . that, as a lunatic ending to a maniacal incident, when he pieced together what had happened he reported Lainson, who remained oblivious of the whole affair, to the local branch of the National Union of Journalists – for unprofessional conduct!

I flew back from the Moscow athletics with David Burghley, now the Marquess of Exeter, his vivacious wife, and Chataway. We broke our journey in Stockholm and the four of us had a hilarious dinner party, watching the pretty Swedish girls go by; that, curiously, was the first impression after leaving Moscow – how pretty and well dressed the girls were 'in the outside world'.

A couple of days later I was in a cold, wet cemetery, normally known as the White City, to see what was virtually the end of Don Cockell in the ring. His 'executioner' was a giant Cuban, Nino Valdes, who forced him to retire after three rounds, but of course, the real architest of his downfall had been Marciano who had effectively finished his career, as he did that of so many others.

Another three days and I was back in New York to see the long-awaited fight for the world heavyweight championship between the heavyweight champion, Marciano, and his most persistent challenger, the world light-heavyweight champion, Archie Moore.

It's curious to look back on those days – the first time I met Moore who was to become one of my closer friends in boxing – and to remember how this international ambassador of goodwill was quiet, suspicious, almost sullen; probably he had had to wait so long, and had been pushed around so much, that he had become disillusioned with the human race. He did, in fact, claim that it had cost him the equivalent of some £20,000, spent on various publicity devices, to secure the fight with Marciano.

Up at Grossingers was the same old Rocky – primitive, menacing to any other heavyweight in the world, but of the earth earthy and always unaffectedly glad to see you. This was how it was to meet Rocky in those days, as I described it then.

High up in the Catskill Mountains, only one hundred miles from the concrete caverns of New York, the world is still very young.

Early in the morning, before the sun has lifted itself into the wide sky, the grasslands are white with frost like the stubbly beard of an old man. The morning mist ascends thinly like smoke from a burning ghost town.

Out of the mist lumbers a squat, swart man. For a mad moment you get the idea that you are seeing the first primitive man learning how to walk upright.

All at once you see clearly that it is the heavyweight champion of the world, Rocky Marciano, returning to the lonely cabin in the hills after his morning pre-breakfast routine of seven miles on the road.

There *is* something primeval about the most dangerous unarmed man in the world. He lopes up to you and gives you that lopsided grin of his. His face is a briar patch of black beard. He is formless in baggy woollen pants and heavy leather boots.

He says: 'Hi ya, Pete, Nice to see ya again. How ya been?'

We follow him into the tiny bedroom. It is unbelievably spartan. A not very long, but very broad, bed fills almost all the space. The monastic atmosphere is intensified by coarse white sheets and grey army-style blankets.

This is the man who for the first time in nearly ten years may bring back the million-dollar gate to boxing. The man who has run something like 500 miles over the hills and trails of the Catskills, who has already boxed something like 120 rounds – the equivalent in time of eight full championship fights.

The fight, destined to be Marciano's last – he retired undefeated after it, one short of his half-century of victories – was as good as any I ever saw him in, apart from the one in which he won the title.

It started amusingly and I don't think I can do better than quote from dear Joe Liebling's book, *The Sweet Science*: 'The referee, a large, craggy, oldish man named Harry Kessler, who, unlike some of his better-known colleagues, is not an ex-fighter, called the men to the centre of the ring. "Now, Archie and Rocky, I wan' a nice, clean fight," he said, and I heard a peal of silvery laughter behind me from Mr Wilson, who had seen both of them fight before.'

On what constitutes a 'nice clean fight' I wouldn't care to hazard an opinion; a good fight it was; a clean fight it was not.

The real sensation came in the second round when Moore feinted his man into position and then beat him to the punch with a right-hander which landed flush on Marciano's jaw and knocked him down for only the second time ever in a serious fight. Marciano walked over to the ropes and referee Kessler, apparently forgetting that the compulsory count of eight was not in force during this championship bout, impeded Moore from getting at a man whom he knew he had sorely hurt.

Those few precious seconds when he was not able to get at the wounded 'Rock' cost Moore what chance he ever had of winning boxing's supreme prize.

What one always forgot about Marciano was his superhuman strength, which led to an almost instantaneous recovery, no matter how badly he had been hurt. Instead of 'boxing clever' in the third he came out like an ice-breaker ploughing its way through polar waters. And he won the round.

By the fourth Marciano was really pouring it in and, just for good measure, he hit Moore after the bell had gone. Then he dropped his hands and Moore, stepping back a pace, hit him very hard in the mouth before pushing him away furiously.

It was then I knew Marciano was going to win again. For, as he trotted back to his corner, he was grinning like a kid on his way to a sweet shop. This was the sort of stuff he understood and revelled in.

Moore won the fifth but after that it was merely a question of how long it would last. Archie was down twice in the sixth, went down again in the seventh and was 'aided' by the bell when it interrupted the count over him in the eighth. Finally, in the ninth, a left hook dumped Moore in his own corner like a great brown seal, beached by a hurricane and transfixed by the hunter's harpoon.

By Saturday I was back in London interviewing Marciano via transatlantic radio. The question I wanted to ask him was about the incident
in the second round. Fortunately the connection was good, but when I
asked Rocky why he had seemed to walk away to the ropes, almost
without trying to protect himself, he replied in the patient terms of
someone explaining something which should already be clear: 'But,
Pete, you've been in the States before and you know we have this
mandatory count of eight if you're knocked down.'

'Yes, I know that. But as this was a world title fight that rule was
waived, and once you were on your feet again you were a legitimate
target for Moore. You were lucky that Kessler didn't let Archie get at
you right away.'

Now Marciano's tone was definitely that of someone explaining how
two and two made four – to the idiot child: 'Yeah, Pete. But he couldn't
let him start in on me again until he'd got to eight. That was why I
walked towards the ropes and . . .' Suddenly the penny dropped.
'Omigarsh! I see what you mean. Of course they don't have that eight
count in a title fight.'

In his dressing room after the fight Rocky had hinted that he might
retire.

He had been twenty-nine when he won the title – only Bob Fitzsimmons, Jack Johnson, Jess Willard, Jim Braddock and Jersey Joe
Walcott had been older when they first became champions – and he had
only just passed his thirty-second birthday when he had his last fight.

In 1969 came the brutally unbelievable news: Rocky had been
knocked out for the first time in his life – but permanently. A small
plane in which he had been travelling crashed near Newton, Iowa, and
Rocky was killed. It was the day before his forty-sixth birthday.

The year 1955 came to an end with the usual variety of sporting
occasions and one – bull-fighting – which made me as nearly sick as anything I have ever seen in public 'entertainment'. I was given the space
to write two really venomous articles on this 'stench of sport'.

Yet it goes on – nurtured, I am certain, by the holiday tourists who
want a cheap thrill and for whom it is made easy by the package-deal
firms who organize special trips to the bull-ring. How a nation like the
British who claim to be animal lovers can tolerate what happens to the
picador's horse, quivering with fear as he smells the blood and battered
by the horns carried by half a ton of bull, passes my understanding.

Prominent sportsmen in Britain were showing increasing intelligence
– particularly the track and field men. Two of the leading 3000 metres
steeplechasers of that time – John Disley and Chris Brasher, who had an

equal passion for mountain climbing, both went into print about this time, putting forward their views on contemporary athletics both in Britain and overseas.

Four months after the international between Russia and Britain in which we had been outclassed, Disley wrote:

Finally, I think that Geoff Elliott, the pole vaulter, had a valid reason for our defeat. He said that the Russian athletes really put everything into their efforts, they gritted their teeth, swore to themselves and concentrated all their nerves on a determination to win.

'Our chaps,' said Elliot, 'just went through the motions!'

I wonder if years of preaching that 'the game's the thing', 'be a good loser', and 'the important thing is taking part and not winning', has not built up a psychological barrier to winning in British youth. . . .

We in this country can only stay in striking distance by adopting a more realistic attitude to our sport and to our sportsmen.

Brasher, almost coincidentally with Disley, was writing about the ever-vexed question of amateurism and stating firmly that no potential opponent should be declared professional and excluded from competing. He wrote:

If those athletes in my own event were excluded on these grounds from going to Melbourne, I – for one – would immediately cease training. One of the major reasons for still competing would have disappeared.

These reasons are as complex, and very akin to, the reasons why people climb mountains.

With the present situation an athlete who has, through an immense amount of hard work during the winter, acquired the necessary toughness to gain selection to his national team and a place in the final of his event knows that he will be competing against the athletic élite of the whole world, not against only certain classes of people from certain countries.

The winner of a gold medal at Melbourne has proved to himself that he is the best athlete in the world at that event. This was certainly not true of any Olympic celebration before the war.

Brasher put the average athlete's – as opposed to the official – attitude towards professionalism when he said:

He does not mind if his opponent has been playing hookey with the amateur laws, for who can effectively define those laws? He does not mind if his opponent has no real job or profession except that of sport.

Late in January I arrive in Cortina d'Ampezzo, a fairyland village set high in the Italian Dolomites where the Winter Olympic Games were to be held.

Whether there is really a case for entering British competitors for the essentially alien Winter Games I am not sure, despite the occasional brilliant successes of our competitors in the skating and bobsleigh events. Clearly other people at Cortina shared my views for I remember Sir Arnold Lunn, who was knighted for his services to British skiing, saying: 'Our trouble is that with ferocious taxes, our boys are holiday skiers. I think it is time to study whether we should continue to enter. It's bunk to say people come here only to compete – nine out of ten come to win. And Britain is not doing any winning.'

The 'Man of the Games', as outstanding in his medium as Jesse Owens or Emil Zatopek, was Tony Sailer, a twenty-year-old Austrian plumber who was a triple gold medallist, winning the slalom, the giant slalom and the downhill – the latter, I suppose, the blue riband of Alpine skiing.

He was an extremely handsome youngster, as well as having an immaculate skiing style – unlike the 'flapping rooster' method of Jean-Claude Killy, whom I was to see succeed him as a triple medallist twelve years later, at Grenoble. I believe Sailer afterwards made quite a success in Continental films; he certainly had the looks and the personality for it and he was already apparently making a good thing out of his skiing through the endorsements which used to bring Avery Brundage to a point of apoplectic – but not, alas, speechless – fury.

What a year 1956 was. Next on the calendar of the memorable was the most dramatically tragic incident I can remember in that most dramatic of all horse races – the Grand National.

The National consists of sixteen obstacles – all but two are taken twice – spread over 4 miles 856 yards of Aintree heathland.

The 1956 race was led, with literally no more than a cricket pitch to go, by the Queen Mother's ten-year-old bay gelding, Devon Loch. The Royal Box was jumping, the Queen Mum had switched on that wonderful smile when, inexplicably to this day, in the last stage of the run-in, with Devon Loch surging towards the winning post, the horse half-reared up as though to clear an invisible barrier and then, when he settled again he seemed to be tethered like a rocking horse, his rear legs stretched out grotesquely, belly to the ground, as though the sawdust had run out of some artificial animal. Or, as one awestruck spectator put it: 'As though he meant to curtsey to the Royal party as he passed and could not recover himself.'

An indelible memory was of jockey Dick Francis, who has never introduced any incident so unbelievably freakish into his now world-famous racing thrillers, trying desperately, uselessly, to get his mount, which seemed to have suffered petrification, to start again. As he failed, Francis sobbed, covering his face as though in the very pillory of shame,

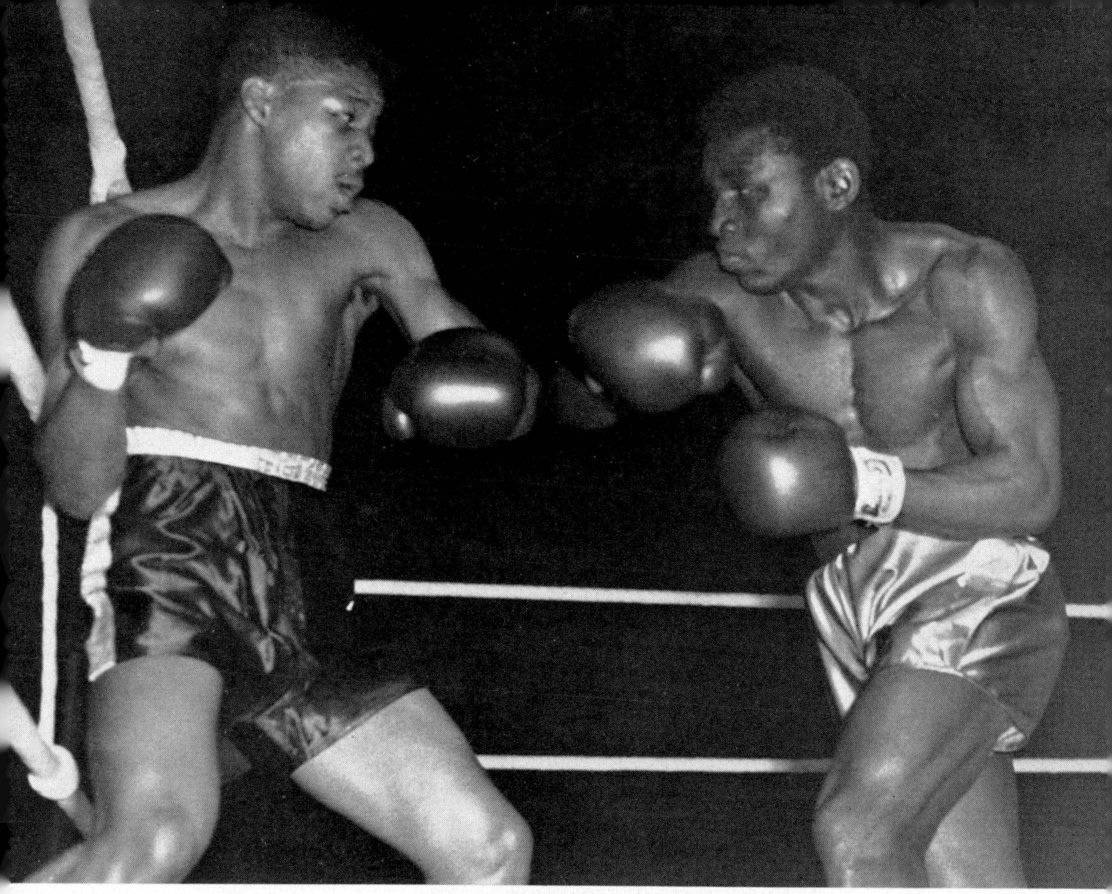

Above Dick Tiger (right) the Nigerian who came very high on my list of all-time great middleweights and later joined the exclusive 'club' with fewer than a score of members, composed of world champions at two or more weights. His opponent here was 'Spider' Webb.

Right Even as a veteran Pancho Gonzales retained much of his power and speed of service which, at his peak, made him one of the all-time greats of the game.

Left Randolph Turpin (left) looked a size bigger than 'Sugar' Ray Robinson when he took the world middleweight title from him.

Below The heart of the matter! Randolph Turpin (right) makes 'Sugar' Ray Robinson's mouth fly open in pain as, in the greatest upset seen in a British ring in my time, Turpin takes the world middleweight title from the American.

Opposite top 'Sugar' Ray Robinson undefeated world welterweight champion; middleweight champion on five separate occasions. Not a bone out of place in his hand and minimal marks on his face.

Opposite bottom Archie Moore was great, but I, too, knew the ropes — and which side of them to keep with Archie!

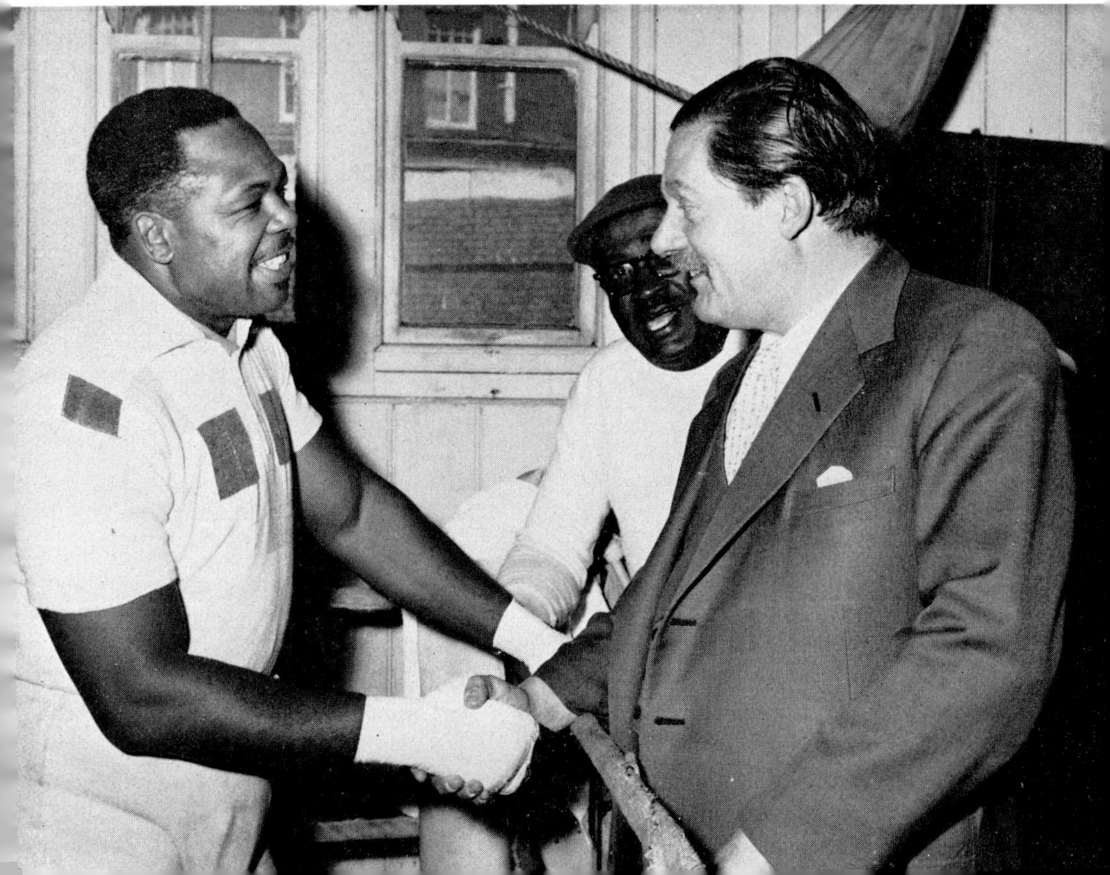

Top She flew through the air with the greatest of ease — and grace. Mary Rand, later to win the 1964 Olympic long jump gold medal.

Above When Irish eyes have a golden glint in them. Ulster's Mary Peters with the gold pentathlon medal she won in the 1972 Olympic Games.

Left 'I seem to have more face to shave every day!' Jesse Owens 36 years after he had won four gold medals in 'Hitler's Olympics' of 1936.

Opposite The overworked phrase 'the poetry of motion' is beautifully portrayed by Lillian Board whose death, 13 days after her 22nd birthday, was one of the greatest sporting tragedies of modern times.

Opposite top Lord 'Learie', Sir Frank and 'Lord' Ted. Captains all: Constantine, Worrell and Dexter.

Opposite bottom left Arguably the greatest soccer player of all time, Brazil's Pelé seems to have the ball, and the field to himself during a 'friendly' against Scotland at Hampden Park in 1970.

Opposite bottom right Two stars but what different styles — in everything. Denis Law and George Best training.

Right Fred Perry, the outstanding British lawn tennis player for, at least, 70 years whose record of three-in-a-row at Wimbledon has yet to be equalled and had not been achieved for over 20 years before his first win in 1934.

Below So young — so great — so unforgettable. Maureen 'Little Mo' Connolly. The greatest woman player in the past thirty-five years.

Left A smile on the face
of the tiger, Super —
MACC — Muhammad
Ali/Cassius Clay.

Below Sonny Liston,
almost looking happy,
as he is presented with
a Boxing Writers' Club
tie and a miniature
silver ring.

dismounting from his 'dead' horse as ESP, the eventual winner, and the other commoners, the nine horses who did finish the course, streamed past him; he walked, bowed, a few faltering steps; he flung his whip to the turf . . . and still he cried.

A week after the Grand National I had arrived for the first time in Japan. The occasion was the world table-tennis championships and, incidentally, it was my first meeting with Ann Haydon, then seventeen, who was later to forsake table tennis for lawn tennis and whom I was to see as Mrs Ann Jones, winning the women's singles at Wimbledon thirteen years later.

Tokyo was immense fun. I had been booked into one of the former royal palaces which had been turned into an hotel. It was Japanese-style; rooms made up of paper and wooden partitions on rollers, a bed on the floor (surprisingly comfortable), a kind of vertical bath in which you stood, up to the neck in water, and various other refinements which I didn't discover until later – usually too late.

This was the first time Japan had staged the world championships and she could be well pleased with her players for they won the men's and women's singles, the men's doubles and the Swaythling Cup, the team competition for men.

Just ten days after the end of the table-tennis championships I did the most sensible and happiest thing I've ever accomplished in my life.

I married Sallyann Meenan Thompson.

My own first marriage had long been at an end and had finished in, fortunately, a quiet divorce.

Sally was a widow. I had, in fact, made a good friend of her husband, C. V. R. 'Tommy' Thompson, while I was on the *Express* for whom he wrote a distinguished column from New York, where he was head of their American bureau. Then, a desperately ill man, he had come to Britain with Sally, and the three of us, with Arthur Christiansen and his wife, had gone greyhound racing one night. It was hardly an auspicious first meeting for Sally and myself. Frantically distressed about Tommy's health she developed a migraine – and was sick all over me in the car coming home!

After Tommy died – having put up a typically courageous fight against lung cancer – I began to see more of Sally, both when she brought her two children to England so that their grandmother could see them, and also in New York when I was there covering sporting events.

I used to stay with the wonderful Burris Jenkins in their apartment at Peter Cooper Village, overlooking New York's East River. Most of my trips at that time seemed, fortunately, to be in the summer when it was too hot to sleep – but not too hot to sit out on the grass squares enclosed by the apartment buildings.

That was not much more than twenty years ago but it might have been another world with the river flowing silently like molten tar and the intermittent mournful hooting of the tugboats interrupting the ceaseless susurration of the traffic in the distance. In those halcyon days there was no fear of muggers, except perhaps in Central Park; violence and hatred did not stalk the streets.

Also there were the splendid New York licensing laws which permitted you to drink until 4 am. And the taverns in nearby Third Avenue were a rich and rare collection.

One in particular was our favourite and often after we had (to misquote W. J. Cory) 'tired the moon with talking and sent him down the sky' we would repair to this nearby air-conditioned hostelry until even the benevolent bartender would be compelled to interrupt, saying: 'Look – you're swell people and I love ya but . . . will ya get th' hell outa here before I lose my licence!'

Even four o'clock in the morning isn't late enough when you have so much to tell each other and so much to find out about love, life and the pursuit of happiness. Luckily you do not need much sleep in New York . . .

We were married at Caxton Hall; Dick Richards, with whom I had shared flats and apartments for some eight years, looked after all the details like some unlikely but admirable Jeeves, and we went on our honeymoon to – Broadway! No, not the one in New York City but the village on the borders of Worcestershire and Gloucestershire, in which counties we had also done some of our 'courting'.

It was rather a strange honeymoon – in fact we were not due to take our real one until later in the year in our beloved Majorca – because on the fifth night Sally drove me down to London where I reported the final fights of Don Cockell and Jack Gardner, both of them sometime British heavyweight champions but both now in a sad twilight of their careers.

Then we drove back again to Broadway in the early hours of the morning, to a truly superb 'feast in the dorm' laid on by the Lygon Arms where we were staying with, as I recall, a wonderfully agreeable waiter who had stayed up to serve us and made light of our apologies for the lateness of the hour.

That honeymoon driving was an omen of things to come: altogether Sally has driven me, either to assignments or for fun, through England, Scotland, Wales, Northern Ireland, Eire, Andorra, Austria, Belgium, Denmark, France, Germany, Italy, Lichtenstein, Luxembourg, Spain and Switzerland – as well as the USA.

Never has a man had a better helpmeet or one who has better put up with the peripatetic life of a sportswriter.

From Zanzibar came the news that Stanley Matthews (by now well into his forties) had appeared on the spice island and within minutes a deliriously happy mob of African and Arab kids had mobbed his car. Stan the gentleman got out, led the way to a bare patch of ground and said: 'Let's have a game.'

Afterwards with his usual modesty he said: 'I never dreamed that football – and my name – were so familiar in such a remote corner of the world. I have played in front of millions throughout the world but I shall never forget Zanzibar. Before I retire I want to come back here to play properly.'

I think it was sheer love of the game which kept Stan so young for so long. After Zanzibar he was due the next day to go on to Nairobi to turn out for a multi-racial Kenya FA team against a Combined Services side drawn from British troops fighting the Mau-Mau.

If Matthews had been playing in this day and over-priced age he would, on skill and entertainment provided, have retired a millionaire.

With Cockell and Gardner at the end of their careers we started hearing more about a young fighter who was to become the most famous and arguably the best British heavyweight of the century – Henry Cooper.

He had a particularly devastating set-to with one of the native fighters who was to be one of his perennial, and unsuccessful, challengers, Brian London, destined to win the British heavyweight championship less than fourteen years after his father, Jack London, had done so, the only father and son to have achieved this distinction.

This occasion, the first of the three times they met, was the most disastrous for London. It was his thirteenth professional fight, he weighed 13 st 13 lb and he was stopped – no, not in the thirteenth but in the very first round!

In Windsor Archie Moore, the world's light-heavyweight champion, who had already been fighting for over twenty years was preparing to defend his title successfully against the English-based West Indian, Yolande Pompey. It was typical of that suave – and most delightful – *boulevardier* of the world's rings that when I went to see him training he took time out from losing about a stone and a half to get me to send, on his behalf, a bouquet of roses to Althea Gibson who had just started to scale the lawn tennis peaks by becoming the first, and only, black girl player to win the French championships. (Later, of course, she was to add the Wimbledon and the US championships to the French title.)

In due course Moore successfully defended his title although Pompey gave him a rough time of it for the first half of the fight and 'Mongoose'

Moore – so called because of his lightning counter punches – agreed with me that when he finished the fight, on the referee's intervention in the tenth round, Pompey had been ahead on points.

Archie was to fight again just seven weeks after beating Pompey, in a contest against James J. Parker of Canada, quite unjustifiably billed as being for the world heavyweight title – left vacant, of course, by the retirement of Rocky Marciano, which had been announced three months earlier.

There was nothing in any way memorable about the affair, which was entirely one-sided, Moore being so much in command that more than once he asked the referee to stop it before the official finally did so in the ninth round. The best summing-up of the fight before it happened came from 'Squire' Bill Daly who was looking after Parker and was a man practised in the ways of the fight world. Parker was the local pride and joy but he was also 3–1 underdog in the betting; as Daly commented, 'There ain't no sentimental money in boxing.'

Bill it was too who, on meeting Sally for the first time at Toots Shor's original splendid hostelry with the palindromic address of 53 W 53 Street, New York, remarked, after giving me the lowdown on various characters and situations nonstop for about an hour and a half: 'That's a great broad ya got there. Ya wouldn't hardly know she was there at all, ya wouldn't.' Sally, who is as much of Irish descent as the 'Squire' himself and had the red hair to prove it, nevertheless accepted this, in the strange new world in which she found herself, as being the compliment it was certainly intended to be!

A couple of days before my birthday Joe Erskine gave me the best present I could have asked for when, in his thirtieth professional fight, he took the vacant British heavyweight title which I had predicted he would win before he had ever had a money fight. He outpointed his fellow Welshman Johnny Williams over fifteen rounds at Maindy Stadium, Cardiff, and no sooner had Williams sportingly anticipated the referee by raising Erskine's hand in token of victory than the skies opened. But if it had been wet at the ringside that was as nothing compared with the celebration later that night in Tiger Bay, where Erskine had grown up knowing how to look after himself.

It was a vintage Wimbledon in 1956 as far as the men's singles champion was concerned. Lew Hoad, sleepy-eyed but with tremendous power, beat his 'twin' – actually Ken Rosewall is exactly three weeks older, and they were born within a few miles of each other at Sydney in November 1934.

It was a splendid final with Hoad coming back to win the fourth set,

148

and with it the match, after trailing 1–4, with a display of hitting reminiscent of Ellsworth Vines at his best. Afterwards Rosewall cracked: 'I was quite pleased with the way I played. But the next time I meet Lew I hope I'll do a little better – like winning two more sets.'

We thought he was joking but, as it turned out, about a couple of months later in the final of the US championships, Rosewall, who had been beaten 6–2, 4–6, 7–5, 6–4 in the Wimbledon final, turned the tables on Hoad, winning those 'two more sets' and the match 4–6, 6–2, 6–3, 6–3.

As well as taking Wimbledon Lew had already won the Australian and the French championships that year and Ken's triumph in the finals at Forest Hills prevented the powerful blond slugger, who looked more like a light-heavyweight boxing champion than a lawn tennis player, from being the second man to achieve the 'Grand Slam', which used to be the most prized accomplishment in the sport.

At the end of September I attended the athletics meeting between Great Britain and Hungary. Being in Budapest then was like watching the lid of a kettle clattering up and down as the water inside it boils. I claim no gift of clairvoyance when I say that on my return to London I told Sally that something would have to blow up soon. Students and some journalists had been almost unbelievably frank – or foolhardy – in giving me inside information while I was in the Hungarian capital. Little more than three weeks later came the Hungarian uprising against the USSR.

On 31 October British bombers based on Cyprus began attacking Egyptian military installations in connection with the dispute over the Suez Canal.

On 1 November I left for Australia!

It was, I promise you, a coincidence. I was not in the confidence of the Prime Minister, then Sir Anthony Eden, and once it was decided that the Olympic Games were to go on, despite the tragedies of Hungary and Suez, I was very much on my way.

There was no jet flying to Australia in 1956 and my original schedule was London, Zürich, Istanbul, Beirut (which we flew over because of the Suez trouble), then Karachi (where we missed a riot by six hours), Calcutta, Singapore (where we were supposed to have a day to recover from the amount of flying we had done but where, in fact, they hustled us on for fear of further trouble), Djakarta (flown over for the same reason as Beirut), Darwin, Sydney and finally, blessedly, Melbourne.

My travelling companion was the late Jim Manning, one of the outstanding sports journalists of my time and, as usually seemed to happen, we were on completely different sides of the fence on the subject of Suez,

Jim vehemently supporting the British action and I being as bitterly opposed to it. I swear we scarcely stopped talking about it for the three days or so that the trip took.

But although there was light illuminating the run-up to the Games there was plenty of shade, too. Some nations, including Egypt of course, had withdrawn. Others sent only skeleton teams. Already some of the Hungarians had announced that they were not going to return to their homeland after the Games. Some of them did not know whether their closest relatives had been killed in the second stage of the uprising.

The Games, which were supposed to glorify the free association in athletic competition between the youth of the world, were overclouded by the threat of impending tragedy which was to explode into the savagely repressed student rising just before the Olympic celebration in Mexico City twelve years later, and the ghastly massacre of the Jewish athletes during the 1972 Games in Munich. W. S. Kent Hughes, famous in Australian politics and chairman of the Games organizing committee, came out with what was on everyone's mind when he said: 'Never before in the history of the modern Olympics have the Games been staged in such difficult conditions.'

The *chef de mission* of the combined West–East German team, Gerhard Stoeck, was at great pains to say that sport, as represented by the Olympic Games, could perhaps teach the politicians of the world a lesson. Yet, dredging back in my memory, I remembered Herr Stoeck winning the javelin-throwing event and finishing third in putting the shot in those 'non-political' games of 1936 in Berlin, when racial hatred was at its most odious. And Stoeck was one of the first two German medal winners to be taken to Hitler's box for congratulations on the first day of the 1936 Games.

The wired-in Olympic Village was, of course, the potential tinder-box of the Games. As it gradually filled up tension mounted daily when teams, or splinters of them, arrived daily from the trouble spots, the festering boils, of Europe and the Middle East.

The Hungarian *chef de mission*, Gyula Hegyi, telephoned from Darwin asking for the old Hungarian flag to replace the Soviet-style banner. But, before the Village Commandant was able to accede to this request some of the Hungarian athletes already in residence had torn down the hated Communist flag of their country and ripped it to shreds. Amid cheers and cries of 'Long live Free Hungary', they ran up the revolutionary flag of 1848, with the Hungarian colours crossed with a black stripe of mourning. Olympic officials tightened the regulations in the Village and orders were issued that all Press questions about race, religion or politics were to be blocked.

But there *were* some heart-warming examples of the Games as they should be, and there were occasions I felt that it was very well worth while coming halfway round the world to see sport without being tormented by the sad agonies of politics. One such was when I watched Emil Zatopek, probably the greatest active runner in the world, spending an hour circling the practice track with runners of almost every nationality. As he ran the Czech never stopped giving advice, and if he could not speak the language he explained with signs. Many of his tips went to John Joseph Kelley, the Connecticut schoolteacher who could be one of 'Zat man's' most dangerous rivals in the marathon.

Then there was the incident when Audun Boysen of Norway, former holder of the world's 1,000 metres record, came off the track limping slightly after a solid workout. Almost before he was off the cinders an American trainer trotted over to him and gave him a ten-minute massage. Nearby Italian cyclists, perhaps the best in the world, were coaching Ethiopians (then known as Abyssinians).

These sorts of incidents made the Games come alive – as did the people who had travelled thousands of miles with not the remotest chance of winning, but just for the great glory of taking part in the Olympic Games.

It was good to re-establish contact with Jesse Owens twenty years after 'his' Games. At Melbourne he was one of the personal representatives of President Eisenhower. The great Negro athlete talked gaily of those far-off days in Berlin, saying 'I didn't have a chance to shake hands with Hitler. I didn't go to Berlin to do that. But *I* had a good time. I'm sorry he didn't stop. Furthermore, I'm enjoying myself here – and I'm not sure where he is!'

Then he became serious: 'For me there is a real Olympic spirit. It began when I jumped in Berlin against Long, of Germany. When I beat him on my last jump by just $7\frac{5}{8}$ ins he shook my hand and congratulated me. From that moment onwards we wrote to each other until 1939 when Germany invaded Poland. Last year I was in Germany, meeting some people, and I saw a boy among them and at once I knew it was Long's son. Now I write regularly to the son of the man who was a fine sportsman in defeat. That's the way the Olympic torch is carried on.'

Just before the Games started there were incidents to take some of the tension away.

One contretemps to raise a globe-girdling giggle occurred actually on D-day minus one. An official of the Australian women's team was deputed to take a look at the women's dressing rooms to see that the appointments were shipshape and Bristol fashion. Shipshape and Bristol fashion they may have been, but from the ladies' point of view there was one thing uncommon awry. The Australian official came out from her tour half-laughing, half-crimson-cheeked. She said: 'I don't know about th'others but *my* gurls are owld-fashioned. They lyke ter squat dahn w'en they do it!' The plumbers had installed the stand-up stalls favoured by gentlemen!

As a result, up to the early morning hours of the day of the Opening Ceremony, plumbers and their mates were labouring mightily to make sure that the women competitors should not have yet one more handicap to their success.

The Opening Ceremony itself went off without any hitch – thanks to the fortitude of the nineteen-year-old Australian who was accorded the honour of carrying the torch into the stadium and lighting the Olympic flame despite the fact that it was spattering his arm with burning magnesium. We were to hear a great deal more of this youngster in the future. His name was Ron Clarke.

The Games started with a bang, when Vladimir Kuts succeeded Emil Zatopek as the 10,000 metres champion and thus became the first man to win an athletics gold medal for the USSR. Running is supposed to be a non-contact sport but if ever I have seen someone crush, pulverize and strangle an opponent it was Kuts against Britain's Gordon Pirie.

Infuriating though he could be on so many occasions it was to Pirie's credit that he tried so desperately hard to beat Zatopek. A lesser athlete would have settled for a silver or bronze medal but Pirie was out to win – or bust. And in the end, after twenty-one of the twenty-five laps, it was bust. The English runner's face turned duckweed green, his stride turned into a hobble. He slipped back into the ruck of runners and in the last four circuits he lost three-quarters of a lap.

Incidentally, the confusion at the end was indescribable; the wrong placings were at first given out and there are those to this day who swear that the final positions of the whole field never were properly elucidated. It seemed to me to bear out a theory which I had held for a long time, that once a man is lapped he should drop out of a race.

One truly great British performance was in the 800 metres when Derek Johnson, another athlete who often seemed to find himself in trouble with the authorities, ran the race of his life and one of the best over this distance that I have ever seen.

The Englishman, who had seemed to be boxed in, nipped through a gap in the middle which must have looked to him like the first gleam of sunlight to a man trapped in a mine. With forty metres to go Johnson was ahead . . . thirty . . . twenty . . . he was still leading, sallow face now snowball-white. But one must never underestimate the fighting spirit of the Americans. The towering Tom Courtney rallied his thirteen stone and 6 ft 2 in to rein Johnson back and, with the very last of his cinder-gobbling strides, won by perhaps thirty inches.

After the race Courtney commented: 'When we got through the tape

I had to ask Johnson who won. He replied: "You did, Tom." ' Johnson said simply: 'By coming second I have now committed myself to another four years of running. If I had won I think I would have retired.' That's what the Olympic Games means to true athletes.

As far as athletics was concerned it was a toss-up who was 'Man of the Games'. I suppose most people would have plumped for Vladimir Kuts but I have a vague hankering after Bobby Morrow who, although he did not manage four gold medals, as Jesse Owens had, captured three, taking the two individual sprints and anchoring the winning team in the sprint relay, all the time moving as smoothly as running water.

The British still had hopes for the 5,000 metres; at that time Pirie was the world record holder with a time of 13 mins 36·8 secs which he had put up five months earlier at Bergen, Norway. In addition there was Chris Chataway, who had held the record briefly the year before, and Derek Ibbotson, who was destined to break the world record for the mile the following year.

I suppose we had never had a stronger team for a distance race but all to no avail. The first to crack was Chataway. Four laps from home he had been in second place, trailing Kuts, but from the seventh lap onwards he fell back to finish last but one. For ten and a half laps of the twelve-and-a-half-lap course it was still a race; after that it turned into the 'procession of protracted death' in which Kuts specialized once the Russian bear began to dance.

Kuts won by 11 secs – about 75 yards – from Pirie with Ibbotson third. The Russian had clipped 27 secs off Zatopek's Olympic record but was still 2·8 secs outside Pirie's world best time – small consolation really to the Englishman.

Then came the biggest British track sensation of all – Chris Brasher's triumph in the 3,000 metres steeplechase. It was doubly dramatic, first because Brasher had been the outsider of our threesome, behind Helsinki bronze medallist John Disley and Eric Shirley, secondly because Brasher had to appeal against disqualification before he got the victory he so richly deserved.

This was the first time in twenty-four years that a British athlete had won an individual gold medal on the track.

The British contingent was cheering itself hoarse when someone, cooler and sharper-eyed than the rest, asked, the words dropping like lumps of ice down our spines: 'Why did that official hold up a red flag when they were going over a hurdle at the top bend of the last lap?'

We soon got an answer. First an announcement was made: 'The result is withheld pending the umpire's report.' Then the official list was read out: 'Rozsnyoi, Larsen, Laufer, Rzhischin, Disley, Robbins

Shirley . . .' What had happened? Why had Brasher, who had won by some fifteen yards, been omitted? Again the answer came quickly: 'Number 226, Brasher of Great Britain, is disqualified because of interference in the last lap.'

It was as though a giant hand had been clasped round 100,000 throats. To lose is bad enough but to lose, after thinking you were the undisputed victor and with the slur of a disqualification smearing you as well, is about as shattering a blow as any athlete can sustain. My one thought, above everything else, was: 'Why did it have to happen to Brasher?'

Brasher, one of the pacemakers who unselfishly helped Roger Bannister explore the unknown possibilities of the sub-four-minute mile. Brasher, who once wrote that he did not care what ideologies his opponents had or whether they were state-sponsored or not. He had said that if any attempt was made to exclude certain classes of athletes he would not wish to compete because all he wanted was to prove himself the equal of the best in the world in his event. Now he had not only proved himself the peer but the superior. And they were making something squalid out of his victory.

I shall not forget his face as he sat in the interviewing room, after British team manager, Jack Crump, had registered his appeal with the jury of the International Amateur Athletic Federation. He looked a bad ten years older than his true age of twenty-eight. His face was the colour of cigarette ash and his cheeks were sunken. The complaint was that when he, Ernest Larsen, of Norway, and Rozsnyoi (the Hungarian world record holder) had come up to the fourth last jump he had allegedly interfered with Larsen. But Brasher said neither he nor the other two runners recalled any sort of incident. More than that he would not say while his appeal was being considered.

It was one of the best examples of dignity under great strain and, obviously, crushing disappointment that I have ever seen given by an athlete. The minutes and the hours passed.

Finally the official verdict was announced. It read: 'The jury of the IAAF considered the appeal against the disqualification of C. W. Brasher in the 3,000 metres steeplechase. After hearing the evidence of all those concerned, including the two athletes affected, the jury decided unanimously to allow the appeal and Brasher is therefore placed first. The jury consider that Brasher and E. Larsen came into contact with each other but that it was unintentional and both runners stated that it did not affect their running.'

It was the climax to a largely selfless career. Though both Brasher's contemporaries, Bannister and Chataway, were generally much better known to the ordinary public it was the 'work-horse' who had brought himself to the peak of condition at the peak period – in Australia just before the Games he knocked thirteen seconds off his best-ever time for two miles on the flat – who won the coveted gold which had eluded his famous contemporaries.

To the delight of the Australians Betty Cuthbert won gold medals in three of the nine events then in the women's Olympic programme, the 100 and 200 metres and the sprint relay in which she ran the anchor leg. Betty, who ran with her mouth open – as someone said, 'as though she were trying to catch flies' – provided one of the best front pages I have ever seen, devised by Bob Nelson, editor of the *Melbourne Argus*. The only words which appeared on the front page were 'Betty You Beaut!' And they stuck to her throughout her career.

There was a piquant footnote to the athletics section of the Games with the finish of the marathon, won by Alain Mimoun, the French-Algerian with the shuffling, economical style.

It was interesting to see Mimoun's behaviour at the end. He was fresh enough but looked furious. He did not want a blanket to wrap round himself. He did not want officials, photographers, anyone or anything round him. He just wandered about angrily on the grass centre. Until a great roar went up as Zatopek, in his familiar sweat-drenched red vest, toiled into the stadium, in sixth place. Then Mimoun nodded, as though to express some private satisfaction, and finally left the track.

The North African who had followed the Czech as inevitably as 'u' follows 'q' – he had been second to Zatopek in the 10,000 metres in London in 1948 and second to him in both the 5,000 and 10,000 metres in Helsinki in 1952 – now, at last, had got his revenge on the other side of the world. But in a way Emil had the last laugh, for his Helsinki time of 2 hrs 23 mins 3·2 secs was still 1 min 56·8 secs faster than Mimoun's at Melbourne.

The outstanding success of the Games, from the British point of view, was the boxing team. We had sent only seven competitors, although there were now ten weights, and we won two gold medals – 40 per cent of the total golds won by all British competitors at Melbourne – one silver and two bronze medals.

Terry Spinks, an eighteen-year-old who was later to win the British professional featherweight title, had the kind of wit which you expect to find honed in his native Canning Town. Earlier, when he had boxed in Moscow and had been met with bouquets on arrival – an old Russian custom – he had remarked *sotto voce*: 'Blimey, don't they bury us first!'

However, it was not until our boxers had done so well that some of the more upper-crust of the British Olympic establishment really wanted to know them. Earlier they had been very much on their own under the supervision of their quite brilliant trainer, Jack Roy, and it was nauseating later to see some of the high-and-mighty visiting the fighting men, with a revolting mixture of insincere, fawning admiration barely overlaying their inborn patronizing attitude.

Britain's other winner was Dick McTaggart, who not only took the gold medal in the lightweight division but was also awarded the special trophy for the best stylist in the whole competition. Curiously enough McTaggart never turned professional. He was a southpaw and I think he was wise enough to realize that his scientific style of boxing would not go down really well with the pro crowd who prefer more blood and thunder.

We now had won four gold medals but there was still one more to come, captured by seventeen-year-old Judy Grinham in the 100 metres backstroke, with Margaret Edwards, three weeks younger, third.

But there was a reverse side to the Olympic medal. The water polo match, which unfortunately brought Hungary and the USSR together, almost literally turned into a bloodbath when a Hungarian, Ervin Zador, was hit so viciously over the right eye by one of his opponents that his brow was split and the water stained red. No wonder he said later: 'I've never been in a game like this. It wasn't a water polo match – it was pure boxing under water.' In the sabre event again a Russian and a Hungarian met; this time the Hungarian knocked his opponent off his feet and had to be restrained as he tried to slash at him while he was on the floor.

To go to the Hungarian section of the bravely conceived Olympic Village was to visit a funeral parlour. Athletes sat around in groups, talking in church whispers. Some still wore a black ribbon across the Hungarian flag on their track suits. Officials said that about 60 per cent of the men were married and because of that they would return to Hungary. And those who had made up their mind to risk the road from which there could be no return believed – or was it hoped? – that there would be no reprisals against members of the Olympic team.

Britain had done well in the Games. But our reasonably encouraging haul of medals and the always moving Closing Ceremony with the Olympic flame, which a fortnight before had looked as though it were going to burn for ever, suddenly and silently doused, was eclipsed when I stood in the draughty departure-shed at Melbourne airport to watch the Hungarians leave. Some of them got halfway to the bus for the chartered aircraft and then, blinded with tears, turned round and ran back to 'new Australian' Hungarian friends or relatives. To be present while someone renounces his country for ever is as devastating as seeing a young mother deliver her baby to an adoption centre.

When the first party left, nine seats in their plane were vacant. At least twenty athletes, swimmers and fencers were to remain in Australia, or proceed to America or parts of Europe other than their homeland. Eight of the eleven water polo players did not plan to return to Hungary. They hoped to have an exhibition tour of the USA to raise funds for Hungarian relief.

I saw Laszlo Tabori, sometime 1,500 metres world record holder, saying sad farewells to men and women who had been his team-mates all over the world and whom he might never see again – for he was one who did not plan to go back.

I talked to Mihaly Igloi, one-time prisoner of war of the Russians and perhaps the greatest athletics coach in the world at that time. Later he stated: 'I will stay here in the village for a few days. Then I hope to get a job in Melbourne as an athletics coach. It would be utter madness for me to go back.' And an English-speaking Hungarian said to me: 'You can say that Igloi now looks on Tabori as his son.'

Earlier the coach had broken down when the holder of the 1,500 metres world record, Istvan Rozsavolgyi, caught the bus to the plane. As well as those who remained behind it was said that some twenty or thirty of the 110 athletes scheduled to fly back would end their journey at Milan and would proceed from there to Austria One of them was the world record holder for the 3,000 metres steeplechase, Sandor Rozsnyoi, who had finished second to Chris Brasher in the Games. He had received a telegram from his wife in Vienna, saying that she was safe there with their baby. Others, because of wives and children, decided at the last moment that they *must* go back. Little Jo Kovacs, who had often run in England and who had won the silver medal in the Melbourne 10,000 metres, was one who finally made up his mind to return to Hungary only on the morning of the flight. He said: 'I have a sixteen-month-old-baby waiting for me. I cannot let her down.'

And so one stood and watched, helpless to do anything, as the men and women going back lurched along, tears sprawling down their cheeks, features convulsed, some speechless, others almost hysterical.

The only ones who were equally devastated were those who stayed behind. . . .

8 1957–60
The Pace Quickens

Sport was growing ever more international, and with the increase in speed of communications – corporeal, verbal and cabled – the pace for the worldwide sports correspondent grew in intensity. Apart from 'local Derbys', and the FA Cup Final in soccer, almost all the other top sports had to introduce an international angle really to draw the crowds.

Incidentally, the International Table Tennis Federation taught many of the more prestigious sports a lesson for, from the start, they refused to allow the white-only South African Table Tennis Association to be a member while other, more selfish, sports were gibbering about 'building bridges'.

An example of the pigheadedness of some sports' officials came to light when, in 1957, the Council of the Football Association again voted against the use of substitutes. This happened twenty-four hours before the FA Cup Final between Aston Villa and Manchester United which was turned into yet another lopsided contest when Ray Wood, United's goalkeeper, was injured after only six minutes.

The diehards insisted that soccer was a game of bodily contact – a man's game – ignoring the fact that the goalkeeper was often in a position where he could not defend himself, and it was scarcely 'a man's game' to hit someone who was virtually handcuffed. There had been enough examples of injured keepers at Wembley. The giant (in every sense of the word) Frank Swift was sickeningly smashed by the centre-forward in an England–Scotland international there; the year before Bert Trautmann, the German-born Manchester City goalkeeper, had finished the Cup Final with a broken neck. Earlier in 1957 Jack Kelsey, the Welsh keeper, had been injured in the international against England.

But . . . no substitutes for injured goalkeepers nor any protection for them, ruled the FA.

Of course both substitutes (not only for goalkeepers) and protection for the custodians were introduced eventually. But, as usual, it took such a long time.

All over the world the amateur governing bodies of different sports were now making themselves look more and more idiotic. Marlene Mathews, whose 10·8 seconds for the 100 yards was not going to be beaten for over a decade, was solemnly warned by Australian AA officials that she must not compete *in a three-legged charity race*. It might, they said, infringe her amateur status!

From a professional point of view my colleagues and I were finding the spread of television, both domestic and overseas – although we were not yet harassed by satellite communications or colour – a new and dangerous competitor.

There was, of course, no doubt that more and more people were going for instant sports news to TV. But with a communication form even more ephemeral than newspapers it is, despite the spate of quite appalling expert soccer panellists, still easier to argue things logically in print rather than in spontaneous 'unthought-out' words.

It probably must sound like sour grapes but I am still glad that most of my career was concerned with writing rather than talking. Conversation is one of the civilized arts, as is writing, informed with some kind of style; breathless monologues, rising to a point of vocal near-hysteria, are not.

In this connection I am reminded of the time Freddie Mills and I joined forces for a commentary on the first out-of-town professional boxing tournament to be televised. At his first defence of his world title against Joey Maxim, Freddie had lost both his title and some half-dozen of his front teeth, and, hideously encumbered with a new set of false 'choppers', he got appallingly tied up while trying to say that two of the boys in a preliminary bout were boxing 'amateurishly'. After a couple of stabs at it, getting his tongue tied up with his tonsils, he sat silent for a moment and then, addressing himself with some petulance, demanded: 'Why do I try and say words like that? I couldn't pronounce them even when I had my own teeth!'

I thoroughly enjoyed doing a couple of largely autobiographical programmes on TV, as well as providing the commentary on 'Today On The Centre Court' for ten years or so. It is also incomparably the best medium for having a flat-out, no-punches-pulled, knock-down-drag-'em-out row with anyone whom you really dislike.

But although it creates immediate celebrities 'TV's a stuff will not endure' and prejudiced (before you say it) though I undoubtedly am, I believe the best of journalism does. For a time, at least.

Plus ça change, plus c'est la même chose. Even then there were disputes between the sporting bodies and the BBC about the merits, and otherwise, of televising sport live. The Football League was viewing the gogglebox with increasing – and not unjustified – alarm, whereas the BBC, in those days far superior to commercial TV in the field of sport, had a spokesman saying jauntily: 'If we don't put on sport on a

Saturday afternoon, we would put on something else. That something else – a leg show, perhaps – might prove more popular than sport and keep even more people in front of their sets.'

For, paradoxically, television has no greater interest in sport than to persuade the people most interested in it not to take part in it, nor to watch it 'live', in order that the TV ratings may continue to soar. And the ratings matter more than the sport – or the sportsmen.

One of the few, the very few, 'scoops' – that word so beloved by the chroniclers of fictional journalism – which ever came my way in Fleet Street spotlighted one such iniquity. Tommy Little, who had spent a lifetime in boxing, first as a schoolboy star, when he received his first award from the late Princess Marie Louise, at the age of ten; then as a pro at the old 'Ring', Blackfriars, where he appeared in front of the Duke of Windsor, then the Prince of Wales; and finally as a referee, got in touch with me to tell me that he had made up his mind to quit.

So – what was the reason for a man, whose whole life had been involved with the sport, calling it a day? He was due to referee, at Olympia, a bout involving Billy Walker and Joe Bygraves, and another ten-rounder featuring Frankie Taylor, for the princely sum of eighteen guineas – which meant, that if both fights lasted the distance he would be paid less than £1 a round.

The cost of the programme was around £8000 plus a television fee of £1500. As Little said: 'The *Radio Times* claims that BBC Television has landed one of the best "live" fight scoops for years with its coverage of the Walker–Bygraves scrap. But apparently this, plus another fight, is worth only eighteen guineas for the referee.'

Even at the expense of my 'scoop' I did my best to try to make Tommy change his mind. But Little said: 'It breaks my heart to go out of the game like this. But if, after spending a lifetime in it, I am not worth more than this, then there is something wrong with boxing today. Recently I was offered only five guineas to referee two fights at the National Sporting Club, where they throw pound notes into the ring as "nobbins" for novice boxers.' ('Nobbins' is the money tossed into the ring by a crowd appreciative of the efforts put into a particularly hard fight provided by down-the-bill fighters.)

Of course Little was quite right. There is a tremendous burden on boxing referees – and not only those in charge of title or top-of-the-bill fights. For a good referee, by judicious and unobtrusive warnings to a young boxer, can ensure that a novice doesn't get into the bad habits which are later so difficult to eradicate. . . .

1957 had started sadly. On 11 January the death of one of the outstanding figures of the past quarter of a century was announced.

This 'sportsman' was Golden Miller, the greatest four-legged steeple-chaser ever I did see. The end of his trail came when he was put down at the fine old equine age of thirty. 'The Miller's' greatest run of successes was in the Cheltenham Gold Cup which he won five times in succession. But, to a public not primarily interested in racing, he really made his name in the Grand Nationals of 1934 and 1935. In 1934, carrying 12 st 2 lb, he put up a record for the 4 mile 856 yard course with its thirty obstacles. His time – which was to stand for nearly forty years – was 9 mins 20·4 secs, the equivalent of 28·82 mph.

The fact that his National time was finally eclipsed meant nothing, for many years earlier they had so modified the fences at Aintree that any comparison with the past was impossible – or, at least, pointless.

The changing tastes – and the ever-rising costs – plus, thank heavens, a higher standard of living compared with prewar days, led to some interesting sporting statistics – particularly with regard to professional boxing, then crippled with a 33⅓ per cent entertainment tax which had been introduced in September 1952.

In January 1935, 245 professional tournaments were held in the United Kingdom.

In January 1950, there were still seventy-six shows.

By January 1955, there had been a cut of more than 50 per cent, and only thirty-six tournaments were promoted.

In January 1956 the number had dropped to twenty-eight and in the same month, in 1957, there were just seventeen promotions – not one of them, by the way, in Scotland.

British boxing was indeed passing through a lean spell.

Meanwhile Joe Erskine, the British heavyweight champion, was matched with Nino Valdes. He was to do even worse than other British heavyweights for he was stopped after 2 mins 3 secs of the first round – thirteen seconds of which he had spent on the floor! I cannot remember feeling worse at the ringside, on behalf of Joe, of British boxing and, to be honest, because I had tipped Erskine with some confidence.

All this while I was inveighing against the idea of Dai Dower challenging for the world flyweight title – but all to no avail. So, at the end of March 1957, I found myself in Buenos Aires where Dower and the champion, Pascual Perez, were to clash two nights before All Fools' Day.

If ever an event pinpointed the casual attitude which characterized the British approach towards professional sport and the tough, hard modern methods employed by other nations, it was this fight. Dower seemed to spend much of his time resting before the day of the contest while Perez sparred with Carlos Miranda, ranked second only to himself in Argentina, and Juan Romo.

Perez was not an elegant sight as he sweated through his dingy black knickers and spat on the dirty ring floor. He landed a low punch on Miranda and apologized briefly, and he looked a rough, tough, mean hombre. His big, red-headed wife, Herminia, who would have had difficulty in making the welterweight limit, impassively smoked a cigar through his work-out. No elegance – but the fans liked it. The boys who one day hoped to emulate Pascual, in ruling the fighting roost, clustered round the ropes, while in the ring Seguara, Perez' trainer, was stripped to slippers and shorts, his grey pelt from neck to navel glistening with sweat.

There was quite a scene at the Lorenzo Stadium on the night of the fight. Three hundred police, equipped with pistols, swords, tear-gas canisters and with hosepipes ready, patrolled up and down, on the ground and were silhouetted against the towering rim of the stadium. I was not surprised, for it was announced that the crowd was 80,000 – easily a record boxing attendance for the Argentine and about the largest one in which I have ever been.

The fight was unbelievably brief. Dower was knocked out in the first round, but the whole thing was such a shambles that the time was given variously as 2 mins, 2 mins 48 secs, and 2 mins 58 secs. If the first figure was right Perez was paid approximately £5,000 per minute for his night's work.

Perez himself made, perhaps, the most cynical summing up of the whole sorry affair when after the fight, he said: 'I overstepped myself. Usually I just weigh up my opponent in the first round. This time my hand slipped!'

Stockholm was my destination when I went to take another look at Ingemar Johansson. The last time I had seen him was nearly five years earlier when he was disqualified for not giving of his best in the final of the 1952 Olympic Games and booed out of the ring. But what a difference there was now.

Now Johansson held the European professional heavyweight title, and at the towering open-air Johanneshov arena, 10,000 of his countrymen, including members of the Swedish Royal family, cheered him home as he put the skids under Henry Cooper in five rounds.

It had been a rather dull encounter, with Cooper fractionally ahead on points, up to the moment that Johansson let go with the straight right (he called it his 'toonder and lightning') which, just over two years later, was to win him the world championship.

It was true that there was a lot of sunshine and Cooper had been so manoeuvred that the sun was shining directly into his eyes; hence his rather sad summing up: 'I didn't see the punch coming.' But even here Johansson had the edge when he retorted tartly: '*That* was the idea.'

It anyone had said, at that time, that 'our 'Enery' would, nine years later to the week, be contesting the world title he would have been advised to get his brains tested, for the Englishman was going through an appalling slump in which, in successive fights, he was stopped in five rounds with cut eyes by Peter Bates, knocked out in nine by Joe Bygraves, then in five by Johansson and then outpointed for the second time by Joe Erskine, this time for the British championship.

Stockholm was followed by one of those mad-dash periods, a fight in Cardiff, the next night another in Doncaster, then one in Rome.

The next day it was on to Paris to see the Grimsby girl, Shirley Bloomer, add the French lawn-tennis championships to those of Britain and Italy which she already held. Women's lawn tennis had been far more successful than men's in Britain since the war. It is not so much that the girls had more talent, but in application and sheer guts they were a long way ahead of the men.

Shirley, later to marry another epitome of guts, Chris Brasher, wriggled her toes on the cool concrete beside the red frying-pan of a Centre Court at the Stade Roland Garros in Paris. The barefoot Contessa of the courts had a strip of loose skin slapping on the ball of her left big toe, and under it was a raw patch, big as a baby's mouth. Another half-dozen blisters were distributed over both her feet. In addition the thumb and the first two fingers of her playing hand were taped to prevent the splits which had developed in earlier tournaments from spreading.

Yet Shirley, twenty-two and blonde, was grinning. When I asked her how she had been so successful in tournaments from the Caribbean to Rome she gave this candid and commonsensical answer: 'There's nothing remarkable about me. I'm a very ordinary girl. People tell me to do various things but I know I'm not good enough for certain shots. But I do keep fit. When I get on these hard courts where, of course, it's nothing like so easy to hit outright winners as it is on grass, I just make up my mind I'm going to *stay* there. If it lasts three hours I'm still going to be there – and, perhaps, my opponent won't be.'

Determination – of the best kind. For if you can find your destiny in sport it's surely worth while to give it all you have got – if it's going to give you all it has got. Small wonder that sixteen years and three children later Shirley was still ranked in the top ten in Great Britain.

Back from Paris to London to see Dave Charnley, who had just won the British lightweight title, dispose of a scar-browed Californian, Johnny Gonsalves, in eight rounds.

I think southpaw Charnley was probably the best fighter Britain produced, in the postwar era, not to win a world title. Twice he challenged Joe 'Old Bones' Brown who held the world lightweight title for over five and a half years, and twice he was defeated. When he finally caught up with Brown, beating him in six rounds, it was too late, for the black Louisianian had already lost his world championship.

Now on 17 May 1966 Randolph Turpin made the headlines for the last time: dead by his own hand and one of his children sorely wounded. It horrified a wider world than the sporting one, for Turpin's defeat of Sugar Ray Robinson had done more for the image of British boxing than any other of the thousands of fights I can remember and, at the same time, had raised the *amour propre* of the ordinary man-in-the-street.

It was as though he were doomed from the very start. Of all places for a youngster of mixed ancestry to grow up Leamington Spa was the least suitable. His father died before he was born and his indomitable mother had to fight, semi-blind, like a tigress to bring up her brood. Randolph, slightly deaf, withdrawn, suspicious – and with cause – of many people in the boxing world had a sad growing up. It was said that a sadistic police officer had paraded him through the streets in handcuffs after an earlier abortive suicide attempt. His first marriage went wrong. The huge purse monies just went.

This is not just hindsight: at the pinnacle of his fame and fortune there was always the sombre feeling that the gutter from which he had clawed his way would one day reclaim its own. . . .

Over to Paris again, this time to see Hogan 'Kid' Bassey become the first Nigerian to fight for – and win – a world title; the featherweight.

The solemn-faced little Negro's opponent was a French North African, Cherif Hamia, with skin the colour of old ivory. In the tenth round, after Hamia had just managed to survive one knockdown, the referee intervened to save him from further unnecessary punishment, and Bassey was the world champion.

But that did not conclude the night's hostilities. As soon as the fight in the ring was over scores of shouting, sweating, sobbing Nigerians, some of them in their native costumes, gleaming like ankle-length nightgowns, stormed into the roped square. They were hysterical with joy and excitement, and they defied the efforts of the tough, club-twirling gendarmes to remove them before they had saluted their little champion.

Outside the ring, as Bassey managed to slip away to the dressing room, there were more confrontations between the Nigerians and the Algerians. But someone made the mistake of picking on a burly figure – and a bonny fighter. It was Bessie Braddock, MP, in whose constituency Hogan lived and who was at the ringside with a party which included John Moores, a partner in the famous Littlewoods pools firm and a Steward of the British Boxing Board of Control. If Bassey had shown his prowess so Bessie was able to demonstrate *her* power of punch when one of the Algerians became a little naughty – and no powder-puff slap but a proper bobby-dazzler delivered with the knuckle part of the fist!

Wimbledon was coming up and the men's matches were increasingly dominated by the Australians. This was deserved if only, when you came to think of it, because Australia was the first nation to make lawn tennis a major sport.

This was the year when perhaps the most popular British player of all time, Christine Truman, appeared for the first time at sixteen – and got to the semi-final!

But that Wimbledon belonged to Lew Hoad, the first man to win the men's singles two years running since the incomparable Don Budge had done so in 1937 and 1938. Hoad's 6–2, 6–1, 6–2 victory over his twenty-year-old compatriot, Ashley Cooper, took only fifty-seven minutes. And it was proof of Hoad's genius at that time that Cooper was good enough, the next year, to succeed him as champion.

One of the ever-developing chapters of Wimbledon was added when Althea Gibson became the first black woman champion. She had not lost a set in the championships and conceded only thirty games in six matches.

Then I was off to the States. My purpose this time was twofold: to see Floyd Patterson defend the world heavyweight championship which he had won against Archie Moore eight months earlier, and to see how Lew Hoad, who, only a fortnight before had so completely dominated Wimbledon, would fare against the professionals.

The championship of champions was played at Forest Hills, traditional home of the US championships – still, of course, officially amateur then. Despite Hoad's pre-eminence among the allegedly amateur players of the world he – and his sponsor, Jack Kramer – got a rude awakening when, in his first pro tournament he was beaten in four sets by his old 'cobber', Ken Rosewall, in five by the American who had preceded him as Wimbledon champion, Tony Trabert, and finally, again in four sets, by the towering Pancho Gonzales.

Gonzales was the lawn-tennis champion of the world. No one had ever been able justifiably to claim that title before. But Gonzales (who got only approximately £900 for his epoch-making victory, whereas a quarter-final loser at Wimbledon today gets more) was a legitimate claimant to the distinction of being 'the world's best'. In this all-play-all tournament he had beaten Frank Sedgman, the 1952 Wimbledon champion, Tony Trabert, who won the title in 1955, Ken Rosewall, the 1954 Wimbledon finalist, Pancho Segura, the tenacious Ecuadorian who had been even more successful as a pro than as an amateur, and finally Lew Hoad, Wimbledon champion in 1956 and again that year.

Later, behind the stands at Forest Hills, when I asked Hoad what he really thought of it all he said: 'Peter, I've got to begin all over again. This is a different league. They may make mistakes, but never on the easy shots.'

So on to one of the most pathetic characters who ever challenged for the world heavyweight title – Tommy 'Hurricane' Jackson.

The only reason Jackson got the fight was that, in the contest before he won the world title, Patterson had been awarded only a split verdict over the 'Hurricane'. Jackson, whose mother dominated him – she was one of the very few 'Moms' to share a training camp – was a figure of fun; but after you had laughed for a little while you felt that perhaps you should be crying. True, he had almost inexhaustible energy and a capacity to soak up punishment – but boxing, fortunately, is something rather more than that.

Patterson who, at twenty-one, was the youngest man ever to win the world heavyweight title, had already assumed some of the dignity of a champion without yet having developed the introspective side of his nature which later prompted me to call him 'not Floyd but Freud Patterson'.

The atmosphere of slap-happy razzamatazz which had characterized the whole Patterson–Jackson build-up continued right up to the weigh-in which was held, of all places, on the stage of the famous Winter Garden Theatre on Broadway where show-girls – I imagine in every sense of the phrase! – took champagne baths in the days of the fabulous Ziegfeld Follies.

But what laughter there had been stopped when it was time for the fight to begin, for this proved about the worst of the thirty-odd world heavyweight championships I have seen, although it lasted much longer than many of them. It was not until just after halfway through the tenth round that the referee, Ruby Goldstein, did the compassionate thing and stopped the public flogging which Patterson was administering to Jackson. On my score card the challenger had not won a round and only two had been even.

Patterson ended up with more than the £65,200 he had been guaranteed and as for Jackson ... he ended up in hospital with a suspected bruised kidney. It was, for all serious purposes, his pugilistic finish for although in the next three and a quarter years he was to have eight more fights – actually winning five of them – he was never a serious contender again.

So ended one of boxing's shabbier chapters.

In South Africa the even shabbier policy of apartheid was pursued when a Transvaal official of the South African Cricket Association said that if the Rhodesian Union altered its rules to allow the inclusion of non-white players it would probably face expulsion from the Association. Coming events cast their shadows before and this was a forerunner of the later, disgraceful Basil d'Oliveira affair.

Now it was farewell to Denis Compton, perhaps the cricketer who gave me more unadulterated enjoyment than any other.

Even though it is over four decades ago I can remember some of his shots in the third match he played for Middlesex – the first time I ever saw him – as though they had been made yesterday afternoon. Particularly do I remember Nobby Clark of Northants bowling him some whistling bumpers and the young Denis hooking them off his eyebrows as you or I would brush away a troublesome fly. And well do I remember the rubbery smile of satisfaction which creased the seamed features of dear old Patsy Hendren, who had taught young Denis this shot – and so much more.

Compton's record was written in gold: seventy-eight Test appearances against Australia, South Africa, the West Indies, New Zealand, India and Pakistan. Yet perhaps the reason for Compton's unique popularity was that he wasn't always the golden boy floating on a pink cloud of success. There was that disastrous 1950–1 tour of Australia when he played eight Test innings in four matches – he was unfit for the second Test because of an increasingly painful knee – and made a grand total of 53 runs.

They said then that Compton was through. But it was after that that he produced perhaps some of the greatest performances of his life, considering the pain that he was always in with his damaged knee. He finished his last Test series against South Africa, in his thirty-ninth year, with only one kneecap, and was still good enough to end up fifth in the batting averages.

Technically I have seen greater batsmen than Compton but never one who seemed to get more enjoyment out of the game, and return it a thousandfold to those who watched.

My next 1957 trip was to the Poland *v.* Great Britain athletics international held at Warsaw – a sad capital even over twelve years after the Second World War had ended and eighteen years, to the week, after its bombing had sparked off that same war. What made the state of the city all the more poignant was that the one completely new and towering building – others had been rebuilt with rubble from the bombed houses – was a gleaming Russian edifice, whether a war memorial or a bureaucratic centre I cannot now remember. It seemed unbelievably callous to have such a showpiece in the midst of desolation – and shortages such as I can never remember in peacetime Europe.

Typical of the mismanagement which has bedevilled British athletics

administration for the greater part of my adult life was the way Geoff
Dyson, in my opinion the best coach Britain ever had and one of the best
in the world, was treated during the Polish meeting. He was relegated,
as far as I could judge, to weighing discuses, javelins and hammers and
generally running the sort of errands which an office boy – not too brilliant an office boy, mind you – might be required to do.

The final straw came when, without consulting the technical coach,
officials changed the order of running in the men's sprint relay. Both
teams returned the same time – but the Poles won by inches. Yet, in the
Melbourne Games, using the team running in the order which Dyson
had rehearsed with them for fifteen consecutive weekends *we* had beaten
the Poles. I wrote at the time: 'If we are to be serious about athletics we
must have coaches. If we are to have coaches they must be treated
better than native bearers.'

Unfortunately, it was too late as far as Dyson was concerned and
some time later he resigned as chief coach to the Amateur Athletic
Association and took up a coaching job in Canada. When he returned
it was to coach in the limited surroundings of Winchester College. So a
man who turned down the highly lucrative offer of a coaching job in the
States at the end of the war because he wanted to make Britain a significant force in world athletics was virtually lost to the sport in Britain.

When people wonder why we do not do better sometimes in international athletics competition I answer that with treatment such as that
handed out to Geoff Dyson – not a unique case although an outstanding one – it's a wonder that we do as well as we do.

I was soon back in the States again to see the fight which was probably
one of the best I have ever watched and which certainly contained the
toughest round I ever saw.

It was for the world's middleweight title, which had been won for the
fourth time by Sugar Ray Robinson, and his opponent was Carmen
Basilio, then the world welterweight champion.

Robinson was his usual self, very much the suave *boulevardier*, and
always with the quotable phrase. For instance, he said bitterly: 'I wish
I were defending my title not against Carmen Basilio but against
Governor Orval Faubus.' Faubus was the State Governor who had
called out the troops to prevent Negro children from going to a white
school.

To listen to Robinson on boxing was fascinating, as it is always
fascinating to listen to a real expert, no matter what the subject. And in
his tough trade he had forgotten more than most fighters, including
world champions, had ever learned. For instance: 'I don't believe in
studying an opponent too much before you meet him. I did once with
Artie Levine. They told me to watch out for his left hook and he knocked

me down with a right-hander. Although I'm not a strong man – I win my fights with my wits and by outguessing my opponents – I've never found eight or ten pounds too much to give away.'

Harking back to the first time he lost the middleweight title he said: 'Randolph Turpin was a very strong man – you felt it in the clinches. But me – I don't think I'm a hitter. I rely on co-ordination, surprise and speed of hand. I think the hardest blow I ever delivered was when I regained the title for the fourth time, from Gene Fullmer who had previously beaten me. Just before the end I hit him with a really hard right under the heart; it didn't knock him out, but it helped him get the message.'

On the Basilio fight he observed that it was the first time he had ever been the bigger man. But there had been times when his opponent wasn't the only adversary he had to beat: weight came into it when he had to sweat to retain the world's 10 st 7 lb title which he relinquished undefeated and which Basilio now held. He said: 'I used to get a big wad of chewing gum and chew and spit for two hours – that way you can lose a pound.'

Rarely have two fighters presented more of a contrast than Robinson and Basilio. The Negro could have been delicately chiselled by some master sculptor – anyone would have had to be a master to 'chisel' Robinson! – but Basilio looked as though he had been quarried and hewn out of solid rock by a novice using a pickaxe. I christened him 'the Gnome of Granite' for, although he was ruggedness personified, he was very small in comparison with Sugar Ray, being three and a half inches shorter, outreached by five and a half inches, and over half a stone lighter.

I went to see him training in a mid-town gymnasium at Syracuse towards the north of New York State. And even in sparring, wearing fourteen-ounce gloves – more than twice the weight of the ones used in actual combat – and with his sparring partner fitted with a heavy leather headgear, Basilio broke his jaw. I got to know and to like Basilio – but, by Castor and Pollux, you earned your money if you were his sparmate.

He was an ex-US marine – and they might have coined the phrase 'leather-neck' just for him. His childhood had been almost unbearably savage, working on his Italian parents' onion farm. He was one of ten youngsters, all working on their knees, cutting the heads off onions just as quickly as they could. And learning the hard way. Because when you missed you gashed your thumb to the bone.

Few fights outside a world heavyweight championship have ever created more interest than this one when, for one of the very few times, Robinson was a 4–6 underdog. He was also thirty-seven – antique for a man who had had nearly 150 pro fights as well as eighty-five amateur ones. Basilio was seven years younger.

The betting was phenomenal. One of the bartenders at Toots Shor's restaurant, then the great hang-out for sports stars and fans, told me that it was the heaviest betting fight since the war, while Eddie Borden, who ran a book in London for a time, assured me that about £3¾ million had been wagered on it.

From the first bell to the last it was one fight which really lived up to all the preliminary ballyhoo. The skill and envenomed artistry of the matador all belonged to Robinson. But the guts, courage, stamina, durability and most of the best body-punching were Basilio's currency. Pride is a great spur – and no fighter had greater pride in himself than Sugar Ray – but hunger sinks a deeper rowel than even pride: and Carmen never forgot those days of 'slave labour' (his phrase) on his knees in the onion fields of Canastota.

The climax came in the eleventh round with three occasions when, for each man, one more punch would have meant that he was floored and exhaustion, I am sure, would have prevented him rising. But neither man could raise that one punch.

It was that rare fight where, at the end, you have to look at your score-card to be certain who has won, so often have the fortunes of war shifted. Indeed that great boxing writer, George Whiting, left the ring-side thinking that Robinson had won and it was only when he got back to his hotel, from where he was going to file his story, that he added up his card and found that, after all, he had made Basilio the winner.

I never expected to see a better fight and, so far, I never have.

The way of the reformer, if not hard, is often unrewarding. For years I had been advocating the addition of two judges outside the ring to help the referee inside the ropes score a fight. By now I had the support of top promoter Jack Solomons who wrote to the British Boxing Board of Control asking to be allowed to try out the system at one of his Harringay shows.

The Board replied through its secretary, Teddy Waltham, himself a good enough referee to have controlled world title fights in such disparate cities as London, Bangkok, Rome and Frankfurt. 'The stewards, after careful consideration of your suggestion, directed me to inform you that they regret they cannot recommend to the Board that the suggestion be implemented. As you will appreciate, even to permit an experiment with the proposed suggestion would involve a drastic change in our rules of boxing, and the Stewards feel that such a change should be made a matter for discussion at an annual general meeting.'

Well, I can't remember what the discussion, if any, achieved but we still don't have judges in British professional boxing.

The irony was that when we had a European championship in Britain it was conducted under the rules of the European Boxing Union – and *they* believe in the use of two judges as well as the referee. Then, just to confound confusion, on the rare occasions when Britain got a world title fight we reverted to our own rules and it was governed and scored only by a referee.

I am not stupid enough to suggest that the addition of two judges would make bad decisions disappear overnight – amateur boxing disproves that little theory – but I do think there might be fewer outrageous decisions if three sets of eyes were employed rather than one. Cricket has two umpires, in soccer and rugger there are linesmen and touch judges to aid the referee, lawn tennis has a proliferation of officials – and boxing is a much less precise sport, when it comes to a points decision, than any of the others I have named.

Perhaps the most shattering sports story for years as far as British fans were concerned happened at the start of February 1958. It will always be known as the Munich disaster. Or, as my long-time colleague, Frank Taylor, himself one of the horrifically injured survivors, put it in the title of his most explicit book, *The Day A Team Died* (published by Stanley Paul in 1960).

The team was, of course, Manchester United and the eventual death toll was twenty-three – insignificant, numerically, in these days of jumbo-jet cataclysms but shocking because so many gifted youths were wiped out in, or even before, the high noon of their physical prowess, and especially poignant for those of our craft as eight of the victims were sportswriters.

The one to whom I had been closest was Henry Rose, the best-known sports journalist ever to function in the north. Manchester had been playing in Yugoslavia against Belgrade's Red Star team and had managed to hold on to a draw which meant that they had qualified for the semi-final of the European Cup, having already won the first leg at Manchester. Thus, most of the sportswriters were representatives of the northern editions of national newspapers or worked for northern publications.

As a result Manchester was a city of mourning in a way which I have never seen duplicated in a similar metropolis. And, without exaggeration, apart from a Royal funeral or that of some outstanding statesman, I can never remember anything to equal the farewell paid by Manchester to Henry Rose, its favourite chronicler of the sporting trivia which nevertheless make up the warp and woof forming the pattern of the everyday man's life.

Two hundred taxi-drivers had volunteered the use of their cabs free, to transport mourners across the centre of the city – where all the traffic lights were switched to green so as not to delay the cortège as it passed – to the Jewish cemetery where Henry was to be buried.

Foolish things stick in your mind at life's most sombre moments. I remember I trapped my thumb in the jump-seat of the limousine in which I was travelling and it bled persistently. I wrapped a crisp handkerchief round it and somehow the dazzling white of the handkerchief seemed almost an impertinence amid the surrounding black.

So the procession flowed like a river of Indian ink through the centre of a Manchester brought to a halt; the pavements were crowded three and four deep with mourners who had never met the man but who had welcomed him at their breakfast tables, morning after morning, year after year. As for me I felt as though a part of my youth had gone to the grave, too. I had travelled both sides of the Atlantic with Henry for more than twenty years. I had seen him less than happy working from London and then, disproving the old sporting adage 'they never come back', making a triumphal return to the Manchester he loved – and which was now showing how much it had loved him.

There was sympathy in plenty for Manchester United and, naturally, for their wonderful manager, Matt Busby, one of the sorest injured. Red Star, their last opponents, suggested that the United team should be declared 'honorary winners' of the European Cup. The following Saturday flags drooped at half-mast at every League soccer ground in the country. Players wore black armbands and stood in silence for two minutes before the start of the afternoon's matches.

But things were soon 'back to normal'. On the day of the memorial service held some ten days after the crash, in St Martin-in-the-Fields, London, Mr Bob Lord, a wholesale butcher and chairman of Burnley Football Club was quoted in the *News Chronicle* as saying that he was very sorry for Manchester United but that they would 'have to fight their way out of trouble' and that Burnley's star winger, Brian Pilkington, would not be joining United. 'If United want to pick up other clubs' best players,' he said, 'so that they can win the League Cup, European Cup, Central League, and Youth Cup, they had better think again. I am just sick and tired of the whole business. If they think they are coming to Burnley to take any stars they had better have second thoughts.' Incidentally, Lord became one of the senior officials in the game.

At the time I commented: 'This is the cold-blooded attitude which is driving so many people to look on professional sport as a despicable business.'

Three weeks later and it was off to Chicago, Los Angeles and White

Plains, New York. The first stop was for the inevitable return match for the world middleweight title between Carmen Basilio and Sugar Ray Robinson.

I am often asked why the States produce so many more world class boxers than any other country. Part of my answer is the unbelievable toughness of a lot of the fighters who accept that despite the damage they may suffer in the ring they can be equally hard-used outside it – and without the same financial assuagement.

A history of the United States in the last century and a quarter or so could be written round first prize-fighting and then professional boxing. At first pugilists and then boxers were Irish immigrants, fleeing the famines of their native land. The persecuted Jews soon followed. Negroes, of course, were always there – not that they were always permitted to box white men. Then came the impoverished Italian immigrants, and particularly their Italian-American descendants for whom boxing was an honourable alternative to near slave-labour or organized crime. Nowadays the Mexicans, the Puerto Ricans and the Panamanians have taken over. As long as there are underprivileged peoples there will be professional boxing.

Basilio was the toughest of the tough.

If their first bout had been one of the greatest I ever saw the second contained some of the dirtiest fighting I had ever watched in a ring. Actually the fighting started before the first bell – as well as continuing after it.

But the first hostilities were concerned with Frank Sinatra, whom cameramen were trying to photograph in his ringside seat when some of his 'bodyguards' intervened. Show business was particularly well represented, as many of the stars had previously attended the funeral of air-crash victim Mike Todd before going on to the fight.

Frank Sikora, the referee, gave the usual instructions about wanting a good, clean fight, with a ban on kidney, rabbit and low punches. Maybe both fighters had gone stone-deaf or perhaps they just weren't paying attention, but if a low left from Basilio wasn't the first punch then a swinging left from Robinson to the kidneys was. After that they *both* used the rabbit punch as though equipped with guillotine blades instead of boxing gloves.

At first Sikora attempted to do something about the general mayhem, but after a time, seeing that both were equally guilty, he more or less declared himself neutral and allowed a total *blitzkrieg* by each man. The bell didn't stop them for several seconds and when Basilio finally got back to his corner there was another 'war', with his manager, Joe Netro, pushing one of Robinson's entourage, who had been established as an observer near Basilio's corner, off the ring 'apron'.

So it went on – inside the ring at least – for the full fifteen rounds, but from the sixth Basilio was a winking, blinking, one-eyed gnome and, although Robinson was tired unto death, there was no doubt in my mind that he had regained the title for an unprecedented fifth time.

Yet even the decision wasn't unanimous.

The decisive incident was the closing of Basilio's left eye – exactly how this was accomplished no one was quite sure – and at the end of the fight he was taken to a Chicago hospital where he was expected to stay for two or three days although a specialist confirmed that nothing was seriously wrong with the eye.

As for Robinson he had to be supported between two of his handlers, his legs perished rubber, the tips of his boxing boots scraping in the grit of the corridors leading to the dressing room, his head sagging on his breast; it was a scene all too reminiscent of those old-time gangster pictures where, at the last moment, the 'killer's' courage fails him and he has to be carried by guards to the death chamber. No outsider was allowed in his dressing room for an hour and when I saw him an hour after that, back in his hotel, a priest had just left him and all he could whisper was 'Mr Wilson, I don't know whether I shall ever fight again. I'm tired, so tired. I shan't make up my mind about anything for days . . . maybe a week or more.'

In my opinion that fight really finished both men even though Robinson continued for seven years and Basilio for three.

Often these long-drawn-out punishing battles leave one man missing the vital spark which distinguishes the triumphant fighter from the resigned plodder, but it is rarely that you can put your finger on the fight that finishes two outstanding battlers.

From Chicago I went to Los Angeles to see Hogan 'Kid' Bassey defend his world featherweight title again Ricardo 'Pajarito' (Little Bird) Moreno, from Mexico.

The fight itself was something of an anti-climax. After an even first round, in which Bassey was hit so hard that he had to cling to 'Little Bird' closer than a wet bathing dress, the Nigerian outboxed the Mexican and knocked him out with a right cross after two and a quarter minutes of the third round.

On the way back I broke my journey in New York to find out what it was like to play a man-to-man 100-match tour against the greatest lawn-tennis player in the world – Pancho Gonzales. Lew Hoad told me.

At the halfway mark Gonzales was leading by twenty-seven matches to twenty-three at the end of the first week in April. The tour had started in Australia on 2 January, moved on to New Zealand and then across to the USA. Already they had travelled 35,000 miles and the confrontation was due to continue until 8 June, when it was scheduled to end at La Jolla, California.

I had asked Hoad if he thought he would catch Gonzales again, and the answer was: 'I don't know. He's playing terrific tennis. When the conditions are perfect I can usually win, but he knows the circuit and I don't. When the lights are bad, he'll lob into them – he knows all the tricks.'

The match was set against a background very different from those of the great amateur championships of the world. There were neon signs at the back of the court in the community centre at White Plains, extolling in purple and red the virtues of hamburgers, hot dogs and beer. Instead of the green lawns of Wimbledon, the coarse grass of Forest Hills, New York, or the red rubble of the Stade Roland Garros, Paris, there was a wrinkled canvas court which had been transported round the world, and instead of the creeper-covered towers of Wimbledon, a white-painted organ in a hall where basketball was played, concerts held, and food exhibitions or bazaars staged.

Here also were the two greatest lawn-tennis players in the world at that time: Pancho Gonzales and Lew Hoad. And they produced great lawn tennis. Gonzales beat Hoad 6–2, 6–4 in something under three-quarters of an hour to lead 28–23 in the series, and his play was probably as good as any I had seen since I had watched my first Wimbledon nearly thirty years before.

Hoad needed miracle lawn tennis to overhaul 'Big Pancho' then and, of course, he couldn't do it; although, to be fair, I'm certain no other player of that era could have.

In the Italian championships in 1958 I saw the birth of a new champion, Maria Bueno, an eighteen-year-old bombshell from Brazil, who had her toughest match in the semi-final against the holder, Shirley Bloomer.

La Bueno saved one match point in the second set and two more in the third in which she nearly collapsed on the court with cramp before winning 1–6, 9–7, 8–6. It was the first match for twenty-one months that Shirley had lost on the red rubble courts of Europe but, although the Italian crowd was unfairly biased against her, she never 'lost her cool' – although the sun temperature had been in the high nineties! Maria went on to win the final against Australia's Lorraine Coghlan.

Girls were really making the news in lawn tennis these days for, with the Wightman Cup approaching, a dispute as bitter as that over Jenkins' Ear – but much more attractive – broke out over the colour of Karol Fageros' panties!

Karol Kristin Fageros was a New York-born player, good enough at lawn tennis to represent the USA in the Wightman Cup but infinitely more famous for her vivid blonde hair – with panties to match. It was about these that I was constrained to write:

I have to record, with almost overwhelming regret, that Colonel Duncan Macaulay, Secretary of the All England Lawn Tennis Club, Wimbledon, announced with suitable gravity that Karol Fageros, the golden girl of the courts, would not be allowed to wear her twenty-two carat gold lamé (rhymes with balmy) panties on the sacred turf at SW19.

Like the wise military man he is, the not-so-gallant Colonel relied on protocol for his veto, saying: 'It is a matter clearly covered by the rules.' (What is covered by the rules, Colonel? Kindly make yourself clear!)

'The rules state that players must wear white and this applies to the Wightman Cup as well as the championships. If all the colours of the rainbow were allowed there would be the danger of putting an opponent off.'

I don't know about putting the opponents off but I bet it would pull the spectators in. However, the edict has gone out – no gold in them thar frills.

Final comment from K.O. Karol: 'I guess I'll have to leave them off – I'll wear white.'

I'm glad she added the last three words!

But one mighty victory Britain did gain in lawn tennis that year – achieved, of course, by our girls. We regained the Wightman Cup (after a break of twenty-eight years!) by the narrowest margin, four rubbers to three, nine sets to eight and eighty-one games to seventy-eight.

The great individual triumph was for Christine Truman, then seventeen. She beat the Wimbledon champion, Althea Gibson, 2–6, 6–3, 6–4. When, on the first of her match points, she served a double fault I swear a score of people round No. 1 Court fainted clean away!

That year's Wimbledon saw the closest a British player has got to winning the men's singles since the war. I know that Mike Sangster and Roger Taylor have reached the semi-finals and that, in 1958, Bobby Wilson was beaten in the quarter-finals, but the man who beat him, Ashley Cooper, went on to win the title, and this was how close Wilson got to victory.

The Englishman had a point for a 6–5 break in the fifth set. He played the point audaciously, seemed to have won it with a volley – only to see Cooper pick this up and slide the ball past him to land plumb on the side-line. Three inches more and, I'm sure, the match would have been Wilson's, and he was playing well enough to go on to take the title.

It was on the start of the first day's play in the Lord's Test against New Zealand that the announcement came that Douglas Jardine had died at the age of fifty-seven. I mourned him not only because he was a relative of mine but because, unlike so many British practitioners, but like the Americans and Australians, he played to win – curious how Don Bradman disliked him, largely for this.

That he conducted a feud against the Australians there could be no doubt. Once I asked him how it all started. He told me.

When he was at Oxford and Warwick Armstrong's side was touring here, in 1921, no one had made a hundred against them. The Australians came to Oxford, and Jardine had made 96 not out, with a quarter of an hour to go on the final day. Suddenly Armstrong announced that the next over was to be the last. The Oxford captain protested, pointing out the agreed hours of play. Armstrong was adamant. He led his team off the field – and left behind an implacable enemy.

That was Jardine – all man. He never forgave an enemy. He never forgot a friend. Quarter he never gave, and quarter he would have disdained had it been offered him. A great cricketer – and, again, a *man*.

Of all the sporting festivals I found the Empire (later renamed the Commonwealth) Games the most enjoyable. The Duke of Edinburgh hit upon a felicitous phrase when he named them 'The Friendly Games'. I covered them in Canada, Wales, Australia, Jamaica and Scotland and I have no hesitation in saying that the happiest of all were those held in Cardiff in July 1958.

Rather than stay in the inevitable hotel Sally and I had managed to get the use of half a house near to the centre of the city. I thought we could do more entertaining there, necessarily late at night because of the hours of the Games, without disturbing other hotel residents.

We loaded up the car with a crate or two of Scotch, gin, brandy and various other mellifluent unguents designed to soothe the leisure hours of what promised to be a fairly vigorous assignment. I was glad that there was no Customs post on the English–Welsh border or we should have had to pay a rajah's ransom to get our precious cargo through.

As we drew up outside the house I was afflicted with considerable alarm and apprehensions and I voiced some of these to Sally. 'What,' I asked, 'if these are strict chapel folk who think that the Devil lurks in every pint pot and wouldn't even have a twopenny packet of wine gums in their house?'

But as it turned out, from the moment we were in, a kinder, more hospitable hostess I have never met; she could have made no profit from us, for she charged little enough in all conscience, as she insisted on giving us the most enormous 'brunches' before the Games started each day, and she was more than happy to join us in some of our late-night revelry.

The most impressive athlete in Cardiff was Herb Elliott. He won the half-mile first, outfoxing Brian Hewson with a time of 1 min 49·3 secs – a dawdle compared with 1 min 47·8 secs which the English runner had achieved twice earlier in the year.

But it was in the mile that the hawk-faced Australian really came into his own. I had watched the great milers of the world for over twenty years, including New Zealand's Jack Lovelock and England's frail, bespectacled Sydney Wooderson. I missed the Swedes, Gunder Hagg and Arne Andersson, because of the war, but I had seen some of the great runs of the first sub-four-minute miler, Roger Bannister, Australia's lone wolf, John Landy and, more recently, Derek Ibbotson and Ireland's Ron Delany. But Herb Elliott was the greatest I had seen.

With Lovelock one expected probably only one peak race a year, but Elliott had then already run seven sub-four-minute miles, more than any other man, and all within that one year. When he was physically and mentally at his summit, it was hard to envisage Elliott running a mile in *over* four minutes.

There is a quality of inevitability about the truly all-time greats in all sports. A feeling of invincibility which approaches perfection. Joe Louis had it as a fighter; Don Bradman on the cricket fields of the world; Don Budge in lawn tennis. Herb Elliott had that quality as a miler.

Only once did the Welsh fall down in their organization of these gay games. It was over the marathon.

The trouble was the traffic. For the first ten miles and the last six the runners had to thread their way through some of the densest traffic on the Welsh and English roads. Lorries, buses, cars, motor scooters surrounded them, threatening either to run them down or choke them with fumes. Innumerable cyclists weaved their way round the panting, sweating, blistered, heat-dazed black, brown and white men. The confusion was indescribable, the conditions fiendish. It must have been like running up an exhaust pipe sixteen miles long.

Dave Power, Australia's iron man and almost the answer to the incomparable Emil Zatopek, was the winner. And he swore he would never run a marathon again!

Power's time was 2 hrs 22 mins 45·6 secs which clipped 8 mins 4·2 secs off the Games' best time for the event; and 46 mins 12·4 secs later the last man to finish crossed the line and collapsed. He was tiny, dusky Dass who had led the runners out of the stadium over three hours earlier.

Incidentally, in the boxing we had our first international look at bantamweight winner, Howard Winstone, who, nearly ten years later, was to win the world professional featherweight title.

From Cardiff on to the rural track at Santry, just outside Dublin where I saw one of the most memorable miles of all time in which the first five runners, Herb Elliott and Merv Lincoln, both of Australia, Ireland's Ron Delany, New Zealand's Murray Halberg and another Australian, Albert Thomas, all finished inside four minutes. Elliott's time of 3 mins 54·5 secs not only broke the four-year-old official record set up by his countryman John Landy, but also the unofficial time of 3 mins 57·2 secs established by Derek Ibbotson, which was still waiting ratification.

The following night Albert Thomas, who had already broken the world record for the three miles, in Dublin thirty days earlier, and the night before had finished fifth to Elliott, showed the world mile record holder the way home in a two-mile race in which he clipped 1·4 secs off the world record held by the Hungarian, Sandor Iharos! These magnificent Australians.

The man who made all this possible was a Dublin optician named Billy Morton. He had the nous to acquire, from a Dublin mental home, what was virtually a quagmire. The ground was too near the airport for the home's purposes.

The impression he made on me – I had often met him at athletics meetings in England but only to chat to at the bar – was vivid. Picture a man under medium height, with a big head (in the literal sense of the phrase) covered with a waterfall of white hair, looking almost as though someone had shaken a salt cellar over his skull. He had eyes which snapped and jumped like the keys of an expert's typewriter – but even the speed of his eyes could not keep up with his deliberate 'Irishisms'. For instance, when the Santry track was opened and he was announcing a famous American military band as a forthcoming attraction, he used the unforgettable phrase: 'This is the band which must be seen to be heard.'

Before the mile race, with everyone keyed up for a possible world record Billy, who took part more energetically in every event than all the competitors put together, read off the list of starters. Then he announced at the top of his not inconsiderable lungs: 'Now, me bhoyos . . . up and at it.'

That was the sort of thing which made this meeting so memorable. We are accustomed to travelling the air routes of the world to the great stadiums of the five continents and to seeing superlative performances achieved in front of cantilever stands, encircled by the prison grey of reinforced concrete, the times blazoned forth with the latest stereophonic sound equipment. But at Santry, an unknown suburb about three and a half miles from the centre of dear, dirty, delightful Dublin, the nearby goalposts on the hurling fields were uprooted limbs of trees, still sprouting foliage, with the birds nesting in them. And I felt that, at any moment, an event might be held up while the cattle went home to be milked, or the sheep found a new grazing pasture on the grass centre of the track. I reported then:

You see the greatest mile race ever run – or, I suspect, ever dreamed of – and at the end a wildly excited Irishman with a stop-watch rushes up to Billy Morton, the oculist, with his watch registering the incredible time of 3 mins 54·5 secs, and shouts:

'Billy I'm never going to start that watch again!'

And Billy, his eyes out like organ stops and the fingers of his hand darker than the black notes of a piano with, I would guess, the nicotine of something like eighty chain-smoked cigarettes, answering:

'I can't see the figures.'

And the fan replying in all seriousness: 'Begob, you ought to go and see a good optician!'

Great sporting achievements may pall if they happen too frequently, but to see them achieved in a bog-drained dream of one little man made the whole thing the fairy story that sport should always be.

How different soccer was in those happier days. At Wembley in 1958 England beat Russia – which was good – and by a score of 5–0 which, nowadays, would seem like a misprint!

But there was a sad occasion the following week when Harringay Arena, which had been staging some of the biggest fights ever seen in Britain, for over twenty years, closed down as a boxing arena.

Jack Solomons, the promoter, had got together an incredible number of world, European, Commonwealth and British champions, all of whom had entered the ring in Harringay, and the following day I went to a lunch with a lot of them, including the former world heavyweight champion, Max Baer, who, long before Cassius Clay was nicknamed the 'Louisville Lip', was known as the 'Livermore Lip', from his home town of Livermore, which nudges San Francisco.

On 12 January 1959 Henry Cooper took the British and Commonwealth titles from Brian London. It was an extraordinary bout for while I didn't give a single round to London and made only the fifth, seventh and eighth even, it was remarkable to see two British heavyweights both on their feet at the end of fifteen bruising damaging and all-out sessions.

Science was taking more and more of an interest in sport by now. One man who, as a result, was 'cleared' was the German sprinter, Armin Hary, who was always having to face charges that he got unfair 'flying starts'.

Scientists examined Hary's reaction time to the starter's pistol, and special films were taken showing that in each of six consecutive starts he got moving exactly three-hundredths of a second after the 'off'. That was less than a fourth of the average time – and faster than the time it takes to blink your eyes.

Some specialists said the German must have a 'sixth sense' for the starting gun, claiming that it was physically impossible for nerve impulses to travel so fast in the human body. Hary was the first man in the world to register ten seconds exactly for the 100 metres – a record which was not broken for eight years.

Gradually the man who did 5·9 secs for an indoor 60 yards – even more remarkable, in some ways, than his outdoor 10 secs for 100 metres, because always it is overcoming the initial inertia of a standing start that slows down the overall time of a sprinter – came to be acknowledged as a phenomenon.

Herb Elliott was still running sub-four minute miles and collecting more medals as 'Athlete of the Year', and was going in for a diet which would not have been regarded as excessive by John the Baptist who, it may be remembered, kept himself alive in the desert by eating locusts and wild honey.

Elliott had been lecturing American runners for being 'too soft'. He said: 'A lot of chaps could run the first half-mile in two minutes, but running the second half is the real test. US runners can't do it because the body wants to stop. And if the Americans want to run they will have to deny themselves other things the body wants – like chocolates, for instance.'

I don't know whether American athletes consciously absorbed what the hawk-like Australian had to say but it was an American, Jim Ryun, who reduced the world record to 3 mins 51·1 secs. And it was Ryun, who broke Elliot's own world 1,500 metres record – after nearly seven years.

But diet was not the only thing with which Elliott found fault in the American training system. Warming to an old theme of his, he said:

'There is too much emphasis on team-winning in America.'

This was anathema to Elliott. I remember the first time I had met the great runner. We were both on radio at Broadcasting House.

He was complaining about the noise made by excited spectators during various rounds of the tug-of-war at the White City where he had been competing, saying that they should be banned during championship meetings.

I disagreed, saying that, apart from relay races, this was the only team sport which had a place in athletics. The lean, bronzed Australian turned on me, almost angrily, to lay down his philosophy of the sport.

'Athletics is an individual sport,' said Elliott. 'You should be on your own when you're on the track. You shouldn't expect any help. It's up to you to prove that you're better than the others by yourself.'

Everyone was getting rather tired of the ever-shifting but ever-similar permutations of the world's leading heavyweights – Floyd Patterson,

Ingemar Johansson, Eddie Machen, Zora Folley, Nino Valdes, Willie Pastrano, Henry Cooper, Brian London and Joe Erskine.

I think I was the first one in Britain to introduce a new one – Charles 'Sonny' Liston – and I'm still wondering whether I should have been prosecuted for doing so! At that stage Liston had had twenty-four fights, winning twenty-three, fourteen of them inside the distance.

We knew that he had run away from an area of racial hatred where he was born, near Little Rock, Arkansas, to St Louis where, with holes in his shoes and a hollow in his belly, he grubbed for food in dustbins and slept where he might.

Inevitably, he joined a gang, was caught after robbing a restaurant and landed in trouble with the police which culminated later in his getting the first of two jail sentences. Not all of this came out at once, and a lot of Liston's early days are still wrapped in mystery – as you would expect of a big, black kid born of a second marriage with twelve half-brothers and sisters by the first one, and he himself one of thirteen from the second.

But we were to hear more of Liston – much, much more over the next decade or so.

In March 1959 I was off to California to see Hogan 'Kid' Bassey put up his world featherweight title, this time against a tough little man, Davey Moore, nicknamed the 'Springfield Rifle'.

In a very tough and good fight Bassey, who had to have five stitches over his left eye, four over his right and tape to cover a deep gash in his cheek, was forced to retire against Moore after thirteen rounds.

Americans say there's no such thing as a good loser but little Bassey gave them the lie that night when he said softly, after we were alone in his hotel room: 'I'm sorry, Mr Wilson, if I let you down.'

He had lost his precious world title; he had, temporarily, lost his sight through a red blindfold of his own blood but he was apologizing to a critic who had also become a friend.

There was only one snag about California from a newspaperman's point of view, and that was the time lag of eight hours. This meant that you had to file your cables – we were still cabling rather than phoning in the late fifties – as soon as the cable office opened at seven in the morning, already three o'clock in the afternoon in Britain.

An additional difficulty was that there was only a small sub-office in Santa Monica and, at that time in the morning, it was impossible to get a taxi to it from the hotel. So Desmond Hackett of the *Express* and I used to step it out right smartly in order to deliver our 'copy' as soon as the cable office opened shop.

One morning, just after seven, we were walking back a different way to vary the routine when, from behind the dingy façade of a rather broken-down building, we heard the sound of jazz being played expertly on a piano. It seemed strange at that time in the morning and we decided to investigate. We pushed through swing doors and found ourselves in one of the most bizarre settings I have ever come across.

Despite the early hour we were in a bar which was going full swing. But it had not got the smoke-laden, used-up air of a place which had been open all night. The ashtrays were comparatively empty, most of the glasses were clean or in use. And the clientèle, with the exception of ourselves (we shaved and showered when we got back to our hotel) were neat, clean and very well-dressed.

There was one striking-looking girl wearing immaculate jodhpurs and a hunting stock. The pianist, it's true, was in evening dress but he was far too well barbered and *cap-à-pie* not to have performed his toilet an hour or so before; certainly he had not been wearing those clothes throughout the night. He was, incidentally, playing, for his own entertainment, and that of others, but not as an employee.

That was the peculiar thing for this was not a club but only a bar, open at what was to me – apart from London's old Covent Garden – a unique hour and catering for clients who seemed to have only one thing in common. Every single one of them – although we did not realize it at once – was to a greater or lesser extent drunk.

The man behind the bar showed no sign of surprise at the intrusion of strangers, and was more than willing to serve us. For about the only time in my life I nearly refused a drink in a bar, but I settled for a small beer. Meanwhile the pianist continued every now and then reaching for a glass, the girl in jodhpurs sipped her Scotch mechanically. Most people seemed to be on their own at the bar, or at small tables, but even at those few where there was a group there seemed to be no conversation – only steady, passionless drinking. It was like a bacchanal of waxworks.

The bartender, as spotless as his customers in a crisp white jacket – why did I think of a mortuary attendant? – was politely communicative.

In answer to Desmond's question he confirmed that he opened at six o'clock every morning. He murmured self-deprecatingly: 'I regret I was about ten minutes late this morning, and some of the regular clients were waiting before I was ready to admit them. Fortunately they are very patient.' He really did speak like that.

He seemed vague about the time the bar closed. The customers did not seem to speak, even to him. A well-manicured finger would be raised and a glass refilled. He knew what everyone drank. The only sound was the precise playing of the piano. I felt as though someone were walking over my grave, and made haste to finish my beer. I think Desmond felt the same way. As we got up to go the pianist slid into a tune I have never heard before or since and started to croon gently. I have never forgotten the words:

> Let me go home, whisky,
> Let me get through the door,
> Let me go home, whisky,
> Don't throw me to the floor.

At the doorway I looked back. No one had moved except for a languid hand upraised, beckoning to the bartender. No one seemed to have noticed us enter. No one mourned our departure. Alcoholics unanimous did not resent strangers; it was simpler to ignore them. We never went back.

'A man hath no better thing under the sun than to eat, and to drink, and to be merry.' Ah, yes! Ecclesiastes knew the truth. But these living dead, how had they come together, how found, or founded, this strange place, tawdry on the outside, decorous within? Was alcoholism their only kinship, were they prey to any strange vices? I never learnt, and I never sought to know. I would rather have drunk rotgut, in a dockside bar full of crimps and pimps, than go again into that place of quiet, creeping decay.

No sooner was I back in England than boxing exploded into yet another international row. Cus D'Amato, manager of world heavyweight champion, Floyd Patterson, was so cautious that he didn't really like Patterson to meet a stranger in the street in case his 'tiger' were to catch a cold from him. Now, however, he had agreed upon an opponent – Brian London. Only ten weeks earlier, on my score-card, London had failed to win a single round against Henry Cooper; now he was to get a shot at the richest prize in sport.

I had strongly supported – and indeed anticipated – the British Boxing Board of Control's decision to forbid London to take the fight. But London went on television to announce that he intended to defy the ban and a number of readers wrote to me angrily, suggesting that if London went through with the fight he would never need to work again, as he would be receiving nearly £27,000.

I took the matter to a tax expert and he worked out that, at the then rate of income tax and surtax, all a boxer would get out of a purse of £26,700 would be £6,931 – the tax would have swallowed up £19,769. I didn't espouse London's cause in his fight against Patterson but I *did* – and still do – regard it as monstrous that an athlete who is at the top for such a short time in his life should be so savagely mulcted.

The Patterson–London world heavyweight title fight was eventually shifted to Indianapolis.

The odds quoted were 10–1 against London – and even with that absurdly generous offer I could not discover any betting at all. The unkindest crack of all, before the fight, came from one American critic who asserted that once Patterson landed properly it would be a case of 'London Breeches Falling Down' – together with their wearer.

Afterwards another American writer said: 'Before they met we didn't know how London could fight and after it we still don't know.'

I must say it was a sad night for the British spectators. London stood up to his punishment manfully – but it takes more than that to win a world title.

London was on the floor at the end of the tenth round and was knocked out after fifty-one seconds of the eleventh. He had never thrown a really damaging punch.

I had now made about thirty trips to the States but it still never ceased to amaze me how the naked face of violence not only appeared but was seen to appear time after time on the American boxing scene. I came across another example at this time.

Under oath, Jackie Leonard, who promoted at the Hollywood Legion Stadium, told the California State Athletic Commission that underworld leaders threatened him in an attempt to take over the management of the world welterweight champion, Don Jordan, whom I had just seen defend his title successfully in St Louis, immediately prior to the Patterson–London fight.

The men named by Leonard were Frankie Carbo – known as 'Mr Grey' he had been named in almost every boxing scandal in the States for years – and Frank 'Blinky' Palermo, a well-known fight manager, operating out of Philadelphia, with whom I had had at least one run-in in the past and whom I was going to come into contact with, indirectly, in the future. Both he and Carbo later got very long jail sentences for offences connected with boxing.

Retribution followed Leonard's revelations. A telephone threat had told him: 'It's to be with a pipe wrapped in a paper sack. You'll be standing in a crowd. You'll never know what hit you' and then he was admitted to a Los Angeles hospital, critically injured with a head wound.

The only thing which hadn't been blue-printed in the telephone threat was the place of the cowardly attack. It happened in Leonard's garage.

Depressing news also came from Santry Stadium – a gloomy harbinger of the horrors to come – where three explosions damaged the new stand, the recently constructed cycle track and part of the dressing rooms.

I had long known that there was bitter ill-feeling between the two rival athletic factions in Ireland. The three-day international meeting which had started at Santry was under the auspices of the Amateur Athletic Union which was affiliated to the International Amateur Athletic Federation – the ruling body of the sport throughout the world. Their rivals, the National Amateur and Cycling Association claimed jurisdiction over athletics in all of Ireland while the AAU were content to run the sport in Eire.

The person for whom everyone in sport felt sorry was Billy Morton creator of the stadium where once only sheep had grazed in his determination to bring 'big' athletics to Dublin.

Over to New York and up to Grossingers where Ingemar Johansson, who had finally got the world heavyweight title fight against Floyd Patterson after constant finagling, was training.

It was a strange contrast to the Grossingers I knew when Rocky Marciano trained in almost hermit-like isolation. Johansson, as well as the normal entourage of a fighter, had with him his beautiful fiancée, Birgit Lundgren. He had with him also his father and mother, his trainer and his physician – a pensive gentleman who had said he regarded boxing as a degrading business which ought to be stopped.

Instead of living in the lonely cabin by the aeroplane hangar where Marciano had shut himself away, Johansson had moved into the guest house of a local multi-millionaire.

Johansson's training seemed to be somewhat derisory for he rarely let his right hand – his one real justification for a title fight – go against his sparring partners. He explained this quite logically by telling me: 'If I use the right on my sparring partners, either I knock them out or I hurt them so much that they run away from me. That is no good for me. When I use the right that is for serious. Only in a fight.'

Patterson was a 4–1 on favourite when, after the open-air fight had once been postponed by bad weather and again threatened the next night, the two men finally crawled through the ropes.

Nothing much happened in the first couple of rounds but in the third Johansson let go with that right hand of his, his 'toonder and lightning' about which he talked as though it had a separate existence of its own. Half the crowd, I swear, didn't see it and Patterson certainly never knew what had hit him. What I remember chiefly is Patterson getting up the first time just before the count of ten and then turning, almost dreamily, with his back to Johansson and moving towards the Swede's corner.

In fact the second knockdown was a right-handed blow delivered somewhere behind Patterson's ear as he walked away. In the normal way that might have been construed as a foul but, of course, as Patterson had turned his back it was he who contributed to where the punch landed. After seven knockdowns referee Ruby Goldstein stopped the fight – and Johansson was the first Swedish heavyweight champion of the world.

I was back in time for the second week of the 1959 Wimbledon. It was memorable chiefly because an unseeded player reached the final of the men's singles for only the fourth time. His name was Rod Laver – and like every other unseeded player to get to the final of this event he failed to win a set, his opponent being Alex Olmedo, the Peruvian.

Had Wimbledon been 'Open' before 1968 Laver probably would have put up an all-time record as a finalist and champion. He was finalist in 1960, won in 1961 and 1962 then turned pro but came back to win in 1968 and 1969. For a man to be in the final in 1959 and then again ten years later is a wellnigh incredible performance in this day and competitive age.

The women's singles saw the first triumph of Maria Bueno, then aged nineteen, the Brazilian bombshell who, with the exception of Suzanne Lenglen whom I never saw at Wimbledon, was the most graceful of all the women players.

Sports frontiers were certainly widening: a Swedish heavyweight champion of the world, Peruvian and Brazilian Wimbledon champions, all first-timers, and Gary Player the second South African to win our Open golf championship.

And now it was time for Billy Wright to retire from the football he had so much enriched, after having been capped a record 105 times for England whom he had captained on ninety occasions. He had also, of course, been captain of Wolverhampton Wanderers during some of their greatest days.

Billy was twenty-two when he was first picked for England. Some idea of the 'iron horse' qualities of the lad from Ironbridge, Shropshire, came through when it turned out that from 1946 to 1959 he had missed only three internationals, playing fifty-one times at right-half, forty-six at centre-half and eight at left-half.

Although I was pleased that the man from Shropshire had decided to retire before shrivelling age demanded it, I wondered if he had ever come across the lines in 'A Shropshire Lad':

> That is the land of lost content,
> I see it shining plain,
> The happy highways where I went
> And cannot come again.

Time for another 13,000-mile round trip to take in the return world light-heavyweight title fight between Archie Moore and Yvon Durelle at Montreal, then on to Los Angeles to see whether Hogan 'Kid' Bassey could regain the featherweight championship from Davey Moore.

The trip to Montreal was hardly fun. We came down at Goose Bay, Labrador and were grounded there for hours, because of a threatened outbreak of fire on the plane. It felt like the edge of the world.

Yet that was forgotten when the fight started, for Moore gave one of his vintage performances. The Moore of Montreal was, I summed up, 'a greater Moor than Othello if you give him the stage of canvas and ropes in place of grease-paint and footlights'.

Archie floored Durelle three times in the third round and then knocked him out with just eight seconds of the round remaining.

The MC, by a slip of the tongue, instead of proclaiming the usual formula when a champion retains his title, 'The winner and still world champion', summed it up best when in not-too-fluent English he intoned: 'The winner and *always* world champion, Archie Moore.'

The second fight between Davey Moore and Hogan 'Kid' Bassey at Los Angeles was, like so many return engagements in the ring, nothing like as good as the first. I think now, looking back on it, that the first one had taken more out of Bassey – he had not fought in the intervening five months – than we realized.

Bassey was probably ahead when the tenth round started but in the last minute of this session he took a lot of punishment which nearly closed his right eye – his left had been nicked in the very first round – and in the interval before the eleventh round the referee was called to the Nigerian's corner and his retirement was announced.

It is always difficult 'from the safe side of the ropes' to criticize a boxer for not going on when he has been hurt, but I could have wished that Bassey hadn't, after the fight, said: 'He who fights and runs away lives to fight another day.'

It is hard to write harshly about a man whom I had watched so often and admired so much, and what I really felt was that Bassey, who had now made more money than he had ever dreamed existed, had had the spur of necessity removed from his flanks.

Now I had to cover the first Grand Prix motor race held in the USA to decide the world championship. It took place at Sebring, Florida.

There were drivers from Britain, Argentina, Australia, France, Germany, New Zealand, USA and Venezuela. But owing to the fantastically complicated points system the only three men who could win the world championship, in this, the ninth and last race of the year for it, were Stirling Moss and Tony Brooks of Britain, and Jack Brabham, the Australian.

This was how it worked out. If Moss were to win, with Brabham second, the Englishman would have $32\frac{1}{2}$ points and the Australian with 33 points would be the overall winner. Moss would have needed the extra point, awarded for the fastest lap, to get a total score of $33\frac{1}{2}$ – and a half-point winning margin. If Tony Brooks, placed third overall, were to win at Sebring, with Moss second and Brabham third, Brooks would have had 31 points. Moss 30½ and Brabham 31 and, again, the one point for the fastest lap would be decisive.

Never had the points been so close for a world championship – and you didn't have to be a motor racing expert (which I most certainly was not) to realize how the three leaders would be giving everything they had got for that vital bonus point.

Moss I found very aloof and disinclined to talk at all, but I have never known anyone more considerate and helpful to a newspaperman whom he had never met before than Jack Brabham was. He explained that the Sebring circuit was a particularly winding one which meant even more than usual gear changing so that a more than usually rigorous testing of the engine was necessary to see that it would stand up to the additional strain.

Whoever had chosen the town of Sebring for a Grand Prix – they also, of course, had a twelve-hour race there – certainly had a curious sense of location. For this was one of those 'elephants' graveyard' towns where senior citizens go only to fade away. It made prewar Bournemouth and Eastbourne, with their bath-chairs and retired relics of the First World War, look like swinging Las Vegas by comparison.

What this sleepy town down South made of the influx of foreign sports cars which zipped around the slumbering streets, driven by weather-beaten men in plaid shirts and caps that shrieked to the high heavens in green, scarlet and purple accents, I cannot imagine. It was as out of character as if those old bath-chairs had been fitted with hot rod engines!

The Sebring race had its sensations. First of all Moss, who had already completed the fastest lap of 100·7 mph, had to retire during the sixth lap with gearbox trouble and then, with some three to four hundred yards left in the forty-second and last lap, Brabham, who was in the lead, ran out of fuel because of a leak.

As he coasted to a complete halt it reminded me uncannily of a motorized version of Devon Loch's Grand National disaster. But the quiet Australian was not going to surrender. Although his team-mate, Bruce McLaren, then Moss's French partner, Maurice Trintignant – who after Stirling's enforced withdrawal had achieved the fastest lap – and finally Tony Brooks swept past him, the dark, powerful Australian actually pushed his car, weighing over 900 lb, for the remaining distance, being paid almost exactly £1 for each sweating yard for his efforts as the prize money for fourth place was £355. But of course it was the world championship, not the placing, which mattered.

It was fair to say that the Australian 'walked away' with the world championship. Moss, who had been runner-up for the world crown four times, slipped to third place on this occasion, behind Brabham and Tony Brooks, whose third place in the race gave him a $1\frac{1}{2}$ point lead over Moss but left him 4 points behind the Australian.

When Brabham finally wheeled his car over the line he was engulfed by a mob of photographers, well-wishers and motor-racing enthusiasts. At first it looked as though he had fainted as he sank from view among the milling crowd.

Actually, the exertion of pushing some three-sevenths of a ton of car – the rules forbade any assistance – on top of the strain of nearly two and a quarter hours of driving at an average of nearly 100 mph, had drained him both physically and mentally.

Just before the end of 1959 it was the turn of Althea Gibson to run into the colour bar. The former two-times Wimbledon singles champion had turned pro earlier in the year and was now giving lawn tennis exhibitions, in the intervals of the Harlem Globetrotters basketball matches, with Karol Fageros of the golden knickers. The match that caused the trouble was to be played at Norfolk, Virginia. But, as she was walking on to court, Althea noticed that the white and black spectators were segregated.

Before the match she said: 'I don't like it. I didn't know this sort of thing still existed.' After playing she continued: 'This is sport – an international thing – and yet you have some people sitting here and some people sitting there. There's only one difference between us – our colour. Our eyes are the same. Our mouths are the same. Just what the hell is the matter? Do these people [the white spectators] think there is such a big difference that they have to sit by themselves?'

Curious that, almost exactly 360 years later, a largely untutored black athlete should have paraphrased Britain's greatest poet for, if you substitute the word 'Negro' for 'Jew' and 'White' for 'Christian' was not Althea's outburst an echo of Shylock's?

Hath not a Jew eyes?
Hath not a Jew hands, organs, dimensions, senses, affections, passions?
Fed with the same food, hurt with the same weapons,
Subject to the same diseases, healed by the same means,
Warmed and cooled by the same winter and summer as a Christian is?
If you prick us, do we not bleed?
If you tickle us, do we not laugh?
If you poison us, do we not die?
And if you wrong us, shall we not revenge?
If we are like you in the rest we will resemble you in that.
If a Jew wrong a Christian, what is his humility? Revenge.

If a Christian wrong a Jew, what should his sufferance be by Christian example, Why revenge.
The villainy you teach me I will execute, and it shall go hard but I will better the instruction.

Those who introduced apartheid, whether in South Africa or in the southern USA, or anywhere else that poisonous racial weed may flourish, should ponder that passage, particularly the final words, for very surely the last few years have taught us what 'blacklash' can do, and what horrors can be unleashed after generations of oppression.

Round about this time Sally and I were guests of the Tug-of-War Association but I did have enough prescience to warn her not to shake hands with any of them, for these are men who, in the old cliché, really 'don't know their own strength', and a handshake from one of them is like getting your fingers caught in a carpenter's vice.

Tug-of-war was an Olympic sport from 1900 to 1920, and why Britain did not strive to maintain it instead of welcoming such non-sensical tarradiddles as hop, step and jump, I shall never understand.

The exercises these block-of-concrete men go in for are alarming even when you read about them. Chris Gregory, then just about the best known coach in the sport, who had achieved most of the top honours for his team, New Haw and Woodham, described just one of them to me.

When the men are in strict training – and it's a six-nights-a-week undertaking, rivalling even the steely self-martyrdom of most long-distance runners – they get to a stage where they gradually, with the rope slung over a projection, raise a tank weighing eighteen hundred-weight to a height of thirty feet. Then, 'If one man were to let go the other seven would probably find themselves in hospital. . . .'

From tug-of-war to the Derby, which that year might have furnished a film script. Angers, the favourite, broke a leg and had to be destroyed – after Exchange Student had done the same thing the day before at Epsom. It was the saddest thing I had seen on a racecource since Devon Loch's fantastic 'paralysis' in the last twenty-five yards of the 1956 Grand National.

Thousands of racegoers had left the course without knowing of Angers' tragedy. It wasn't announced over the loudspeakers. But earlier happenings were; among them the withdrawal, after an accident, of Vienna, the entry of the greatest living Englishman, Sir Winston Churchill. Then the Royal train was delayed by a fainting signalman. And a radio announcement said Scobie Breasley couldn't ride. That was less than four hours before the 'off' – and Scobie finished second on Alcaeus.

But dwarfing it all, was that astounding twenty-four-year-old genius of the racecourse, Lester Piggott. An older generation used to roar 'Come on, Steve'. They meant Steve Donoghue who won six Derbys. Now there was a new Wizard of Epsom, for so far Piggott's record in the world's greatest flat race stood as follows: Second on Gay Time in 1952 (aged sixteen); winner on Never Say Die in 1954; winner on Crepello in 1957; and now his win on St Paddy completed the hat-trick.

Incidentally, Piggott's comment was: 'This was the easiest of my three wins.'

The Patterson–Johansson fight for the world heavyweight title took me to the States again.

Patterson had been living with his rather sombre trainer, Dan Florio, in a disused, semi-derelict night-club, which looked as though it had strayed out of one of Charles Addams' drawings, in the vicinity of Newtown, Connecticut.

Patterson and Florio had been there over nine months, certainly living ruggedly for the £215 a month rent Patterson was paying. For instance, there was the time, as Patterson confided, that 'during a snowstorm we lived on eggs for three days'.

It was a place to which I wouldn't have consigned my worst enemy – gloomy, morgue-like. I don't say it was festooned with webs spun by tarantula spiders. It just felt that way. Patterson, looking very unimpressive in his sparring, did not create confidence when he said: 'It's been a long year – but not for Johansson. He's been making money.'

When I asked Johansson at Grossingers whether he thought the year's lay-off since he had upset the odds, and Patterson with them, would handicap him he answered slowly: 'Patterson has been looking forward to this fight for a year. I've done so much it's seemed like only two months.' All this is not an excuse but merely an explanation why most of us – and certainly myself – plumped for the Swede to retain his title.

But on the night when it mattered the black ghost came out of his haunted house and made boxing history by becoming the first man ever to regain the world heavyweight title, when he knocked out Johansson in the fifth round.

Johansson, I shall always believe, was *too* confident. In the second round, with Patterson attacking like a black fiend, the Swede landed his 'toonder and lightning' right hand. It did not land flush on the jaw or I really believe that the fight would have been over then, but it hurt Patterson so much that he cringed under it, almost like a dog under the whip.

But Johansson was so confident of ultimate victory that he did not follow it up properly and Patterson was allowed to escape with only another glancing blow to the jaw. It was the only time the Swede looked a winner.

192

In the fifth Patterson floored his man with a left hook. Johansson was on his knees at five, on his feet at nine. But not for long. One of the most explosive left hooks I've ever seen from a man of Patterson's size stretched his opponent out flat on his back. By the time the count had reached six Patterson began to caper up and down like some unshackled animal. Johansson lay there motionless – the canvas could have been a mortuary slab – except that one leg continued to shake ceaselessly as though it had an independent life of its own.

He was so completely shattered that, after long moments of growing dismay, when the doctors couldn't get him to his corner they brought his stool to him in the middle of the ring. It must have been a good ten minutes before he was escorted back to his dressing room.

Everything important in sport was now geared to the 1960 Rome Olympic Games. By now it was established that, in the overall count, the USSR would almost certainly be victorious. Russia with her huge population and an all-seeing State eye which spreads through the sixteen republics of the Soviet Union, had been able in less than fifteen years of international competition to reach the top in a formidable fashion.

Some of Russia's plans for space-age competitive recreation read like an excursion into sci-fi sport. Clearly the phenomenal advance of the USSR could not be put down to luck, or even a large healthy population. There had to be some considerable method behind their multiple successes in so many sports. There was.

'At 5,000 ft is he all right? At 7,000 ft can he do a simple addition sum? At 10,000 ft can he write his name legibly and fluently?'

These tests had been used to establish the potential of air crews and, obviously, cosmonauts but the Russians were by now employing them to establish the potential of athletes. The end product of the 'computerized' athlete was seen in the 1972 Olympic Games, at Munich, when a Russian, Valeriy Borzov – I always thought that with his speed he should have been renamed 'Borzoi' – broke the domination of the Americans in the sprint events. He had definitely been picked, from hundreds of candidates with approximately similar qualifications, by a computer. To some people this was frightening; almost appalling.

Without again going into the complex argument of State-sponsored sport it seemed clear to me as long ago as 1960 that it was virtually impossible for us ever to match, let alone catch, the Russians except when you got the odd freakishly endowed athlete; and, even then, more facilities would have to be available.

One final highly personal thought about the Russians. I have always believed they could be so much more popular if only they could have introduced a little of the Marx Brothers lifestyle into their way of living instead of relying only on Karl.

Conversely, while Britain remained wedded to the proposition that top-class sport was the prerogative of gentlemen, or at least the sons of wealthy men (by no means always the same thing) we were never going to overhaul the giant. Perhaps Russia used compulsion too much, drove her stars too hard and used their victories for questionable propaganda. But at least the Russians did not pretend that they did not care whether they won or lost. They made every endeavour to see that the former category was achieved – and if we did not believe that this was important we had no business competing against those who did.

Amid all that was so serious it was good to read one fairly frivolous footnote. The fences surrounding the girls' quarters in the Olympic Village in Rome had been increased in height. In previous villages a fence of 6 ft 6 ins separated the girls from the boys. But in the meantime a certain John Thomas – the American high jumper, that is – had cleared 7 ft $3\frac{3}{4}$ ins, so the Olympic officials decided to make the Rome fence 8 ft 2 ins. Perhaps they overlooked the fact that the world pole-vault record was now 15 ft $9\frac{1}{4}$ ins.!

The Rome Olympic Games were fun. Sally had driven me from England to the Italian capital where she was going to act as chauffeuse, not only for me but for other members of the *Mirror* staff.

'Cassandra' was in Rome during the Opening Ceremony and when I had a word with him to make sure that we did not 'double', i.e. write two identical or over-similar stories on the same subject, Bill assured me that I need have no cause for alarm, as he did not intend to write about the Games at all.

Nor did he. While I was waxing lyrical – well, 'waxing' anyway, for Rome was sweltering in a heat-wave – about the Opening of the Games, Bill had discovered that there is a bar actually within the precincts of St Peter's, and having availed himself of the refreshment there purveyed, he wrote one of his typically brilliant columns about it.

But if I gave you a thousand guesses I doubt whether you would get right the name of the first competitor who was mentioned to me in the Olympic Village, by one of the gamest, and not unskilled amateur boxers I had ever come across, Tony Madigan, of Australia.

I was reminding him of the Commonwealth Games in Vancouver and Cardiff, in both of which he had competed. He now had a job in the States but had flown back to his native Australia to prove that he was the man who should represent his country in the light-heavyweight division.

He proved it all right. He stopped the previous official Australian choice inside the first round and now he was talking about his possible rivals in Rome.

'Cassius Clay,' he mused. 'I know him. He beat me in the States but I must say . . .' He paused, then, 'Good-on-you Tony,' he said. 'No, I won't say it because every boxer has an excuse for being beaten. But how about that Pole with the unpronounceable name, Pietrzykowski?' In fact, in the final, it was Clay who beat the Pole after outpointing Madigan.

The heat struck with tragic suddenness. During the 100 kilometres (approximately $62\frac{1}{2}$ miles) team time trial race, held in a temperature of over 90° Fahrenheit, the Danish cyclist Knud Enamark, a twenty-three-year-old bricklayer, crashed, in a coma, and died in hospital from that scourge of so many sports, particularly boxing, brain haemorrhage. One of Enamark's team-mates, Jorgen Jorgensen, was also taken to hospital – with heat exhaustion. When he could talk Jorgensen said: 'I just felt so sick that I could not go on. The sun was simply too hot. I could not stand it any longer.'

Poor Enamark. The investigations into his death went on for months after the Games ended and, in my opinion, it was never satisfactorily established whether the illegal stimulus of drugs had been used.

I shall never forget 29 August 1960. Not that anything very memorable happened in the Games, but it was my birthday and those who say that sportswriters lead such glamorous lives should have shared mine that day.

Very little happened during the day, for the athletics had not yet begun, and the evening sessions of the boxing did not start, in that superb, pillarless, air-conditioned Palazzo dello Sport, until 9 p.m.

On my birthday night, when I had promised Sally a treat – she was working at least as hard, if not harder than I was – ill-luck decreed that Dick McTaggart, the Scottish southpaw who had not only won a gold medal at Melbourne but had been voted the 'stylist' of the entire competition, should come on round about midnight. By the time he had dealt with his Thai opponent, to the obvious delight of Princess Grace of Monaco – even her somewhat glacial calm seemed to be shattered by some of the boxing – and by the time I had got my story over to London, and 'signed off' for the day, it was past one a.m.

Anyway, eventually we started back to Rome and a night on the town. We didn't particularly want to go night-clubbing – the Olympic schedule was too tough for that – but we were dreaming of luscious viands and the wine to go with them. Medallions of lobster for me, perhaps, followed, maybe, by some wild boar from the Abruzzi, strawberries Romanoff, Verdicchio, Frascati, perchance a mighty Barolo, with a Strega as a night-cap.

The traffic was still fairly thick and, by the time we got back to that coruscating thoroughfare, the Via Veneto, much of the sparkle had gone and many of the shutters were up. From dreams of boar and Barolo we descended to eggs and bacon and beer – only there wasn't any. Finally, about half-past two, we settled for the last curling-edged cheese sandwich, meticulously divided between us. I drank a glass of *vino* which no self-respecting grape would have acknowledged and Sally had some cola drink, surely the foulest liquid ever devised.

But if that was a gloomy day personally, it was equalled for Britain two days later when, with the athletics now under way, Gordon Pirie finished eighth in his 5,000 metres heat, Arthur Rowe, the European shot-putt champion, failed to qualify for the final of his event and Mary Bignal, later Mary Rand, who had led the qualifiers with a leap only three-quarters of an inch short of the women's Olympic long jump record, 'no jumped' twice in the final and finished ninth. Brian Hewson, who had won both the 800 and 1,500 metres against the Russians in Moscow and was the European 1,500 metres title-holder, couldn't even qualify in Rome in the 800.

It was one of the blackest days of all time for British athletics. Often when we were beaten we had known beforehand that we had no real chance, but on this occasion both Pirie and Mary Bignal had been strongly favoured and Rowe was expected to make at least one British field event less of a joke (in dubious taste) than it had been previously.

There were stories that Mary had an unfortunate love affair with a Dutch athlete, but the competitor for whom I was really sorry was Pirie. When he failed to qualify in the 5,000 metres it wasn't so much a defeat on the track that we were watching but the temporary ruin of a young man's life. He had tried so hard; he had failed so abysmally.

Later we were to have some successes but the most outstanding, perhaps, that of Dorothy Hyman, the nineteen-year-old daughter of a Yorkshire miner, who won the silver medal in the 100 metres and the bronze in the 200, was even more of an indictment of British training facilities than it was a tribute to her guts.

Training presented tremendous problems. Dorothy was advised through the post by the northern AAA coach, Denis Watts. She managed to see him only three or four times a year. During the winter the grass track she used became too sticky to run on and the cinder track was only sixty yards long. There were no girls to help her train, but the boys of the Hickleton Main club trained with her for company. As a working girl she had to practise at night, and once when she was running the floodlights used by the local footballers were accidentally turned off.

Game Dorothy decided she could not afford to skip her training,

196

even for one night, and carried on. Result: bang, into an iron post while she was at full speed, which for her was about 20 mph. Her forehead was laid open and eight stitches had to be inserted. Such was her pluck, and the medals were her achievement.

A few days earlier I had had my first view of a strong, dark New Zealander. The programme told me he was Peter Snell. The name meant nothing to me but his time, even in a preliminary heat, had been so good that I made a mental note to keep an eye on him. I remember someone, presumably a New Zealand journalist, bringing the slightly farouche twenty-one-year-old to one of the Press rooms. Someone twitted Snell about his show of speed in the heats and in a rich, ripe New Zealand accent which you could have cut with a chain-saw – if it was a sharp chain-saw – he said: 'We-e-ell, yew can't hang around here, can yew?'

I thought it was the best summing up of the Olympic running I have ever heard.

In the final Snell, powerful as a black Angus bull, created one of the upsets not only of these Games but of all the Olympic festivals I have ever seen when he won in 1 min 46·3 secs. It was not so much the time – although this broke the Olympic record by 1·4 secs. It was not only that Snell beat the Belgian policeman, Roger Moens, who had held the world record for over five years – although I shall never forget the look of sheer, physical agony on the highly strung Belgian's face as, try though he might, the New Zealander rampaged past him. A brick wall wouldn't have stopped Snell that day. But perhaps the most remarkable achievement of all was that before he left New Zealand Snell's best had been 1 min 49·2 secs, which meant that in Rome he had run something like 23 yards faster.

That same day I saw athletics history made, and one of the greatest Olympic records finally expunged from the books, when Ralph Boston, from Mississippi, finally cleared 26 ft 7¾ in to increase the distance which I had seen Jesse Owens clear twenty-four years earlier in Berlin. Boston jumped just 2½ in further.

And Jesse was in the stands to witness a bitter-sweet moment in the ever-changing history of sport.

But to me the incomparable performance at Rome was put up by Herb Elliott in the 1,500 metres. This performance had absolutely everything that a truly wonderful, memorable and unsurpassable race should have.

There were nine competitors in the final and all of them, except Jim Grelle, the second-string American, had run a sub-four-minute mile or its metric equivalent. I had already been lucky enough to watch Elliott in some of his great races, at the Empire Games in Cardiff and

in Dublin when he broke the world mile record with an unbelievable
3 mins 54·5 secs. But never had I seen him run with more of the look of
a soaring eagle than he did that day. His time (3 mins 35·6 secs) converted into a mile was well over a second better than his Dublin
performance.

I quote my impressions then – and now:

So they line up like nine, lean, hungry greyhounds and the bang of the
pistol releases them like a starting gate going up.

Elliott is leading when he comes round the last bend of this third lap and
now the contest is not between men and men – it's the superman against the
most ancient and remorseless enemy – time. Can Elliott beat the clock – the
clock whose hands he himself stopped at 3 mins 36 secs two years ago?

There's a beaky, scraggy little man in the crowd, with a wispy beard like
a white exclamation mark, who thinks he can. He is Percy Cerutty – Elliott's
unquenchable coach. As Elliott passes the tunnel through which the
athletes enter the arena from the so-aptly named 'Street of the Gladiators',
Cerutty is waving a white towel.

It means that the sun-wizened little man is passing the news to his Herb
to give it all he's got – that the record is his for the breaking. And break it
Elliott does.

He is showing strain at last in the final 50 yards – and I am almost glad.
It proves that he is human, like the rest of us, with lungs which heave, a
coppery taste in the mouth, legs which shake and muscles which cry a mute
protest at the intolerable strain.

But although he is fighting at the end, he wins by nearly 20 yards from the
cream of the world's milers, the first six of whom all beat the Olympic 1,500
metres record set up by Ronnie Delany of Ireland in 1956. And Herb keeps
an incredible record – in his twenty-two years he has never been beaten in a
mile or a 1,500 metres race.

Just one other memory of the Rome Games lingered. That of the
Ethiopian marathon runner, Abebe Bikila.

In those days African runners were virtually unknown. The odds are
always grotesque against picking the victor in the longest run of the
Olympic Games – I would think it easier to pick a Grand National
winner. Certainly I should think you could have got 100–1 against the
Ethiopian – from anyone who had ever heard of him.

It remains one of my greatest regrets that I did not manage to follow
the Rome marathon, owing to the pig-headed obstinacy of the IAAF
who cancelled the coach which the Italians had been willing to provide.
It was the only Olympic marathon, in my knowledge, which did not
begin and end in the main stadium, but from various sources it seems
obvious that Bikila, who ran barefooted, was never out of the first six
after about six miles.

Bikila, a member of the bodyguard for his Emperor, Haile Selassie, had, in fact, been 'on the wrong side' in one of the many revolutions which have racked that strange country. But as he was then a non-commissioned officer it was held that with many of his comrades he had been misled, and he was spared the execution which was the fate of a number of the ringleaders.

I think it is fair to say that a vast majority of the crowd (including myself) had no idea of the geography of Ethiopia or of the fact that Bikila had done much of his training at the fantastic altitude of his country's highlands.

From the halfway mark the race was between Bikila and the Moroccan cross-crountry star, Rhadi – neither of whom would, I'm certain, have been picked out as potential winners when the sixty-nine starters congregated under the Capitol. Fortunately, the organizers had taken cognizance of the potentially killing heat and the race did not start until dusk was approaching. After about eleven miles Rhadi opened a lead of some fifty yards over Bikila but the Ethiopian, his plucked-chicken legs driving remorselessly, drew level again. Rhadi made his final effort about a kilometre from home and I am indebted to John Hopkins who wrote in *The Marathon* (Stanley Paul, 1966) for this description:

Rhadi again tried to break loose from Abebe, but the Ethiopian replied with an even stronger sprint and Rhadi was soon a hundred yards behind, and Abebe was never again in danger.

A convoy of motor-cycles and cars was accompanying the runners and at one point Abebe's career was nearly finished by a Lambretta which veered too close.

The imperturbable Ethiopian finally broke the tape in the incredible time of 2 hrs 15 mins 16·2 secs, nearly eight minutes faster than Zatopek's winning time in the 1952 Olympics and point eight of a second inside the world best set by Popov in 1958.

Abebe Bikila had been three years old when his country was raped by Italy and it was a strange 'revenge' that the Ethiopian soldier should come to Rome to achieve a triumph which left him the second most famous man – as far as the outside world is concerned – ever produced by his country. Perhaps the final twist of the knife was that Abebe made his final effort just as he was passing an obelisk towards the end of the course. This obelisk was taken from the Holy City of Axum and was presented to Mussolini by his conquering troops after they had defeated Abyssinia.

Inevitably there were a few postscripts to the Games. The lists of nations who had won medals was published; inevitably the USSR and the USA were far ahead of the rest. But there *was* one triumph for

Britain. Don Thompson, a twenty-seven-year-old Middlesex fire insurance clerk, pounded away with his wiry legs to win the 50 kilometres road walk in 4 hours 25 mins 30 secs.

Thompson, like so many outstanding champions, had made special plans for the conditions which he so rightly expected to experience in Rome by rigging up a contraption in his bathroon at home which roughly reproduced the humid heat in which he would have to compete.

It was a new Olympic record but, in the end, Thompson won by only 17 secs – a fantastically narrow margin of victory between two brave men after over thirty-one miles of competitive walking – against John Ljunggren, of Sweden. The Swede, who was forty-one the next day, had had a wonderful record in this punishing event. He had won it in the Wembley Games in 1948, retired (because it wasn't warm enough!) in Helsinki in 1952 and finished third at Melbourne in 1956. By gaining second place in Rome he had filled an 'inside straight', adding the silver medal to the gold and bronze he had already won.

But Thompson's triumph was not just that of winning. In all the Games there is always one competitor who captures the public imagination.

And for days after Don had strode alone into the stadium, you saw the 'young hopefuls' of Rome going about their lawful – or not – occasions, in a kind of crouched lope, their bottoms waggling from side to side like maniacal concertinas as they imitated 'Il Topolino', 'the little mouse'.

Even greater performers have had less acclamation.

9

1961—4
The World Gets Larger

Europe I obviously know well, and each year I was travelling to new sections of the USA. Australia I had toured with Len Hutton's successful cricketers and I had covered the Olympic Games there. But in the next four years Asia was going to mean much more in the world of sport; so far I had been only to Japan for the world table-tennis championships but soon I was to go further afield in the Orient. And Africa, too, was to come into the scheme of things.

However, it was back to Britain – briefly – after the Rome Olympics, and one evening at that time I particularly remember. I had persuaded Archie Moore and his lovely, red-headed wife, Joan, to break their return journey from Rome at my London home. My stepson, Raymond, then a rather shy pre-teenager, had arrived back from his prep school. Archie asked him if he was interested in sport and Raymond said that, among others, he liked boxing. That was all Moore needed. I don't think I have ever felt closer to a professional athlete than I did to Archie that night. He said to Raymond:

'You goin' to be a boxer, you gotta be a *good* boxer. Now you go and get that stick your pappy always carries.' (For a variety of reasons I used to carry a sword-stick.)

Raymond trotted off, got the stick, and Moore holding it, said: 'This cane, it's a kind of projection of your left hand. Now you try and get close to me and I just poke it in your chest . . . see? an' you can't get close to me. Now you take it. You're littler than me but when you poke out that ole stick I can't get close you, nohow.

'Now that stick – that's your left hand. That's what you use a left hand for, to keep your 'ponent away from you. But boxing would be pretty dull if it was just stickin' out an ole left hand. So we got to find a counter for that left. Now you poke that ole stick out, that's right, you got it stuck in my chest and I can't get at you nohow.

'But I got to, if I'm gonna win this fight. So what do I do? I knock that ole left of yours aside and then you see I cross my right hand over your left that I've knocked aside and I've got your jaw and I'm on top of you despite that long left of yours. So, now, how do you counter that?'

For a quarter of an hour he went on explaining the basics of boxing to a youngster who was floating on 'Cloud Ten – and Out'.

The footnote to the story was that Raymond won the prize for the most improved boxer of the year at his school. Maybe it was because the others knew that he'd been coached by the world champion.

Archie was – is – one of those characters whose colour is not only unimportant but who makes you forget that yours is different from his. He's a true citizen of the world and when noisier characters of his race try to make it hard for people like him to mix with whites by calling them 'Uncle Toms' I know which side is doing the greater good for humanity.

There was one splendid, spontaneous example of this in our home. Our boxer dog, Joe (named, of course, after the greatest of all boxers, Joe Louis) was wandering around in his usual haphazard fashion when he came up to Archie. The boxer (human) cupped the head of the boxer (canine) in one huge fist and remarked feelingly: 'Man, have *you* got a black face!'

So it was fascinating to read in the colour-unconscious Archie Moore's book (*The Archie Moore Story*, Nicholas Kaye, 1960) the following profound apophthegm: 'The white men say all men are created equal and then they hate the black man for believing it.'

Meanwhile back in the States, Senator Estes Kefauver was now heading the Senate Committee investigating the alleged control of professional boxing by gangsters, which I had myself publicly attacked back in 1951.

According to evidence given, in one division alone, the welterweight world champions for nearly ten years – except for one brief ten-week spell – had been manipulated by Frankie Carbo, then serving a two-year jail sentence, often with the active assistance of my old 'friend', none other than 'Blinky' Palermo who was then under indictment in California for attempting, with others, to take a share of the earnings of Don Jordan, the sixth welterweight champion of the world whom 'Mr Grey' had attempted submarinely to pilot! An additional tasty morsel was produced by John Bonomi, special counsellor to the Senate Committee, who said that Palermo was the behind-the-scenes manager of Sonny Liston, then beginning to loom as the most dangerous heavyweight in the world.

The extent to which professional boxing was under fire in the States amazed even me – and I had seen more of the racketeering than most people on this side of the Atlantic. A fortnight or so before Christmas I received a form from the US Treasury, asking for information about my tickets for the return heavyweight championship fight between

Ingemar Johansson and Floyd Patterson which had taken place in New York about six months earlier.

This apparently, was in connection with an examination by the US Inland Revenue of the affairs of Rosensohn Enterprises Incorporated (Bill Rosensohn was the promoter of record in the first Patterson–Johansson fight) and Feature Sports Incorporated, which promoted the return. The US Treasury wanted to know what kind of tickets I had. How many, whether I paid for them, and, if so, how much. If they were purchased by cheque they wanted me to furnish the cheque for photographing and, if the stubs of the admission tickets were retained, they wanted to see those too.

Fortunately I kept most of my Press tickets as souvenirs and I was able to send them winging their way back across the Atlantic, with the information that I had had only one Press seat, for which I did not have to pay.

But it gave me an insight into how thorough the investigation was becoming when the US Treasury went to the trouble of contacting one of literally hundreds of sportswriters from all over the States and the rest of the world to see that there had been no hanky-panky about Press seats – as, indeed I knew on occasion there had been, with less scrupulous promoters selling seats in the working Press section on which they did not have to pay State or Federal Tax.

Every day the investigation in Washington grew more intense. The committee heard evidence from Ike Williams – about the best lightweight I ever saw.

Kefauver had kept Williams' identity secret earlier, for fear that he might be harmed by gangsters. Williams testified that he received absolutely nothing for two world fights in 1948. His manager, 'Blinky' Palermo – yes, that man again, a stand-in, of course, for Frankie Carbo – according to Williams took every penny of the purses of nearly £24,000 The fights were against Beau Jack, in Philadelphia, and Jesse Flores in New York.

But, Williams claimed, he still had to pay income tax on the amount he should have received. When he asked Palermo for the money he was told he wouldn't be getting any because the ineffable 'Blinky' had hit 'tough times'. . . . Palermo, as Williams' manager, was supposed to receive only a third of each of his purses.

Sonny Liston shambled on to the witness stand after Palermo; when asked about a slip with Palermo's telephone number on it which police had once found in his pocket he said, rather pathetically: 'I don't write.'

On my visit to the States in 1961 I noted a statement from Senator Estes Kefauver that: 'We found boxing to be absolutely riddled by mobsters from top to bottom. I like boxing. I think every American boy should know something about "the manly art of self defence". But its professional side is rotten to the core. It will either have to be abolished or regulated so strictly that the mobs that control the fighters have no chance of operating.'

Progress was being made. A number of the top boxing hoodlums had been by then convicted and were awaiting sentence. Gone, I felt, were the days when a millionaire like Jim Norris could write a letter to a court of law in support of a fight manager, Eddie Coco, subsequently convicted of shooting and killing an unarmed car-park attendant. On this occasion, as it happened, one of the best-known of all fight managers also wrote a would-be helpful letter – which unfortunately concluded with the words: 'I'd like you to know that Eddie has always been a straight shooter.' With friends like that who needs enemies!

In the end time ran out for Frankie Carbo, but in another sense it had only just begun, for he was eventually sentenced to twenty-five years in jail for, among other things, extortion and conspiracy.

Towards the end of 1960 trouble in soccer flared up and it looked as though there really might be a strike, with League clubs carrying out their programmes represented by amateurs or recalled veterans – there simply could not be a break because of the ever-open maw of the pools, whose promoters were contributing £300,000 annually to football.

Thousands of readers of my columns filled in a ballot and the closeness of the voting proved that the dispute about whether footballers should or should not strike had split the sporting public right down the middle. The percentages were: against the strike 52·85; in favour of the footballers: 47·15.

1960 had ended on a familiar note. My old sparring partner, with whom I had crossed pens, and tongues, in newspapers, on TV and radio and in front of a legal society, Dr (now Baroness) Summerskill was in her sixtieth year but still a bonny fighter, contradiction in terms, as applied to her, though that might be. She was still trying to get boxing banned but was refused, in the House of Commons, leave to introduce her Bill designed to prohibit the sport by 120 votes to 17.

In January 1961 it was off to an old stamping ground, Boston, Massachusetts, where Terry Downes was to meet Paul Pender, one of the only two men ever to beat Sugar Ray Robinson twice, for the world middleweight title.

The difference in character between the two men was about the only thing which made this championship at all memorable. Extrovert Downes was living up to his role of the 'Paddington Whizz-Kid'. But although it was good to see a British fighter completely unawed by the Yankees, in the end it did Downes no good.

He was dropped for a count of seven in the very first round and by the fourth the American, using his left hand like a whip, had scarlet fountains spouting from cuts over the top of Downes' nose and above his right eye. Downes continued to batter away at the body, hurting Pender, but the American's left jab seemed to have prongs in it and fifty-seven seconds after the start of the seventh round the referee, Billy Connelly, a local policeman, decided, quite rightly in my opinion, to stop the fight, although on points there wasn't much in it.

After this fight Pender entered the ring a firm favourite for the return match in London, with Terry Downes for the world middleweight title.

I could hardly believe my eyes when, at the end of the ninth round, in which he had done quite well, Pender indicated that he could not go on. I have never believed that a man who has been desperately punished or who has no chance of victory should plod on through pain to an inevitable defeat. But at the end of the ninth I had given four rounds to each man with one even.

It was particularly strange to see an American abdicate in his corner for up to that time (it was before the dismal Clay–Liston affair) only three US world champions, in all the eight weights in over sixty years, had lost a world title in this fashion.

Financial returns for world heavyweight contestants showed a marked change from earlier years. Floyd Patterson and Ingemar Johansson had now signed for their 'rubber' match, to be held at Miami Beach in March and with the receipts falling not far short of four million dollars, it represented the greatest single pay night in the history of all public entertainment!

Then it was hey! for Wales – and the last match of the Springboks' tour, in which they came to Cardiff Arms Park to play the Barbarians, with a record which read: twenty-eight matches won, one drawn!

The whole meeting was a kind of new Haydn symphony for the two men of the match, as far as I was concerned, were Haydn Morgan of Abertillery, who scored the second and conclusive try, and the late replacement at full-back, Swansea's Haydn Mainwaring.

Certainly it was Mainwaring who provided *the* moment of the match which anyone who saw it will never forget – certainly not the South African captain, Avril Malan. He came charging down the touchline and the Welsh full-back met him, almost it seemed casually, with a kind of body-check rather than a tackle.

When the collision came I truly thought that Malan's collar-bone had gone and, with it, a handful of his ribs, for his whole side seemed to cave in, even as he shot in the air. No wonder he had to call in at the hospital afterwards. Meanwhile Mainwaring carried on as unconcernedly and unselfconsciously as a Welsh sheepdog which has foiled a fox's raid on the lambs.

At home the Wolfenden Report (no! not that one, the one on sport) was debated in the Lords. The report had recommended a £5,000,000 cash grant and another £5,000,000 for capital expenditure. The Lord Chancellor, Lord Kilmuir, announced, somewhat frostily, that there would be *some* increase in capital expenditure by local authorities for facilities in sport; but he declined to say how much this would be and he doubted whether such a radical innovation as the setting up of a Sports Development Council would be acceptable to the Government.

For a nation so passionately interested in so many forms of sport Britain has always been singularly disinclined to spend sufficient money on any of them. . . .

One view of apartheid at that time was expressed by Ferdy Bergh, manager of the Springboks Rugby team, who said at London Airport before beginning his journey home to South Africa that he had found no overt expression of anti-apartheid. He added: 'We saw only a few demonstrators and they were nearly all coloured people.'

You couldn't credit it if it hadn't been put down in black and white – almost literally speaking!

Another view of apartheid came from an American Negro, Floyd Patterson, who was quoted as saying that he would hire personal guards while preparing for his third fight against Ingemar Johansson. 'I've never had to do that before, but that is the South and I have to protect myself,' he said. Ironic words, indeed, from the heavyweight champion of the world.

He continued: 'I'll tell you another thing about the South. When Ingemar knocked me out in our first fight, I made 125,000 dollars (approximately £44,640) from the films shown in the South. They pay good money to see a coloured boy get knocked out. But when I knocked out Ingo in the second fight, do you know how much I made from films in the South? Four dollars and seventy-three cents.'

For the Patterson–Johansson fight Sam Leitch, then of the *Sunday Mirror*, and I were staying at the Fontainebleau at Miami Beach, one of the most expensive hotels in which either of us had ever lodged. Sam and I were so appalled at the cost of living in the 'Fountain blue', as it was known locally, that one night we decided to economize by having a snack in our room. We had two hamburgers each, and four bottles of beer between us. With the tip, at the current rate of exchange, it worked out at £4 18s. od.! And that was sixteen years ago!

Outside the hotel was one of the greatest indictments of boxing, as it had been conducted in the States, I ever came across. There was a black shoe-shine 'boy' by the main entrance whose face seemed vaguely familiar. I asked someone about him and he nodded: 'Oh, yes. That's Beau Jack.' Beau Jack (Sidney Walker) had been recognized as the world lightweight champion by at least one governing body in 1942–3. Now, eighteen years later, he was a bootblack. This is what Nat Fleischer had to say about Jack in his *Boxing Encyclopedia and Record Book*: 'Beau Jack fought twenty-one main bouts in Madison Square Garden from November 1942 to December 1949. He drew a total of 355,092 people for a gross gate of 1,578,000 dollars.'

I did not have my shoes shone by Beau Jack. I preferred to go out looking scruffy rather than have at my feet a man who had had 111 fights, had been regarded as a world champion and who was later to be voted into Boxing's Hall of Fame. Instead I turned my head away in shame.

The local promoter, Chris Dundee, older brother of Angelo, who had become world-famous through his association with Muhammad Ali/ Cassius Clay, pulled a very smart stroke just five days before the Patterson–Johansson fight. With the sporting Press of the world assembled to see the heavyweight championship, Dundee produced the heavyweight threat, Sonny Liston, against Howard King, a Nevada heavyweight who was good enough to win his next fight against Dick Richardson. Against Liston he couldn't last three rounds!

Liston had been nicknamed, without the friendliness a nickname usually connotes, 'Old Stone Face'. He had been called, not facetiously, 'the grim reaper of the heavyweights'. A lot of nonsense has been written about the 'killer instinct' in the ring. But Liston had it, all right, even when sparring. When they set him to train with a gangling coloured heavyweight called Wendell Newton, despite repeated admonitions from his corner to go easy, he crushed and crunched and hurt his un-talented spar-mate. In the second round Liston smashed him in the mouth and I thought for a dreadful moment that I should see a full-grown man crying in the ring.

Afterwards Liston did not suffer from that delayed remorse which often affects a triumphant fighter. Another man had shared another ring with him and had left it broken. It had all happened so often before.

This monolith was a strange contrast with the other black, Floyd Patterson, whom I had come so far to see. Liston was a brooding giant with the mark of the jail heavy upon him, a one-time strike-breaker who terrorized fellow blacks trying to improve their lot, who didn't give a foul word for what you might think of him; Patterson was so anxious for people to think of him as a *great* champion, a man who sat after a work-out in a little box room, hot as the inside of a fur-lined glove, sweating and saying, as he discussed the aftermath of the first Johansson fight: 'I must have stayed in the house for a month – too ashamed to step outside. One night my wife talked me into going to the movies. We sneaked out of the house. But when she saw what was playing – "Johansson–Patterson Fight Film" it read – I made a U-turn and drove home. I don't intend to make any more U-turns.'

Johansson, as usual, was training in the glossiest section in which I had ever seen boxing penetrate, Palm Beach, some seventy-five miles from Miami Beach.

I have never disliked writing a preliminary as much as I did on this fight. If you're wrong once you can try to laugh it off with a 'Well, you can't win them all.' If you're wrong a second time, with the same gladiators involved, it becomes distinctly serious.

But the worst thing of all is loss of faith in yourself. Can it be, after all these years, that you really *don't* know anything about it? If so, talk about the years that the locust hath eaten. . . .

And if you're wrong three times on the trot the savage criticism turns to derisive laughter which is the hardest of all to take. I had to make this vital 'pick' and, I suppose, subconsciously, I was wondering how many more of these trips there would be if I picked the loser three times in a row.

Finally I wrote: 'I take Patterson to win on a knockout or referee's intervention inside the halfway mark, which means before half the eighth round has been contested.'

I swear I was as tense as either of the fighters as I sat waiting for the first bell in the 17,000-seater Miami Beach Convention Hall plastered with posters saying: 'Next week Come and Be Saved by Billy Graham!' Looking over my shoulder was a very pretty girl, a Western Union employee who would dispatch my words, as I touch-typed them, straight into our London office where, of course, it was something like three o'clock in the morning. She was, I'm convinced, the best operator in the hall. She had been chosen by Joe Caly, whom successive generations of overseas sports writers had learned to bless and to whom Western Union should always feel indebted for his constant work and public relations, on their behalf.

I know I shall never be able to repay his practical help across the length and breadth of the USA and, of all the people alive whom I met 'in the line of business' Joe stands supreme for unfailing kindliness, willingness to do anything to smooth the working hours of newspapermen constantly fighting that damnable cross-Atlantic time gap, and a quiet enjoyment of our company when the day's work was done; not that his ever seemed to be.

My operator nearly fainted during a particularly gory preliminary bout, and *I* nearly did so almost before the first bell of the main fight had died away, when a left and a right from the Swede put the heavyweight champion of the world flat on his back! I admit that I was nearly sick. My 'no hedging' tip down inside a minute.

Worse was to follow. When Patterson got up Johansson floored him again, hurting him considerably more than he had the first time. I had just enough of a breather to ask my pretty operator if she knew how much they paid street sweepers in Miami Beach – a remark which, I'm sure, made her more convinced than ever that she had been translated into a world of lunatics but, at the time, this looked like my most likely form of future employment. But then it was Johansson's turn to go down, from Patterson's best weapon, a left hook.

That more or less exhausted the first round – not to mention at least one journalist!

Curiously enough all this action, easily the most pulsatingly seesaw round in the sixteen world heavyweight championships I had already seen, provided all the real drama the fight was to furnish.

At the start of the sixth round it looked as though Johansson had got his second wind – and one composed of equal parts of oxygen and champagne. He was whisking his man in front of him with a prodding left, and then shaking him with old 'toonder and lightning' right-handers when, with no warning, he got caught.

Patterson landed a left hook and two rights – one on the angle of the jaw, just below the ear, the second behind the ear. Even so the blows did not seem enough to beat Johansson, but he fell forward and although the brunt was taken by his right knee and elbow he ended with his nose and forehead buried in the canvas and this, possibly, sent his senses whirling. Even so, by the count of six, I would have laid any money that he was going to get up again, but at eight his legs melted beneath him and although he was getting up at ten, he was pitching forward into the referee, Bill Regan. Immediately there were shouts of protest from Johansson's corner that he had got a 'short count' and the Swede himself seemed to object.

Regan himself was not in doubt, however, and the knockdown time-keeper, Jim Levenson, shouted 'Ten' and spread his hands wide in boxing's most definitive gesture before Johansson was fully upright. Although the Swede's gloves may have cleared the canvas, he was still rising, and so in no position to defend himself. The referee was, therefore, right to count him out, though I was surprised Johansson did not make it to his feet earlier.

The time of the knockout was announced as being 2 mins 45 secs of the sixth round which meant, praise be, that my prediction had come true with 4¾ mins of actual fighting time to spare!

But now it was time, in April 1961, for, perhaps, the most fascinating trip I was to make in my whole career. The world table-tennis championships had been awarded to China – 'Red' China in popular jargon – and I had managed to get the assignment. With me were Desmond Hackett and Jim Manning.

The championships were staged in the Peking Workers' Indoor Stadium, which was an almost exact replica of the stadium in Dortmund, West Germany, where the last world championships had been held. As a German journalist remarked to me: 'It is a copy of our Westfalenhalle – but I must admit the copy is better than the original.' It was. And this stadium was completed in just fifteen months. It was astonishing to see this glass, marble, concrete and granite palace towering over the lowly, grey-tiled dwelling places where nearly seven million people laid their heads in greater Peking.

What made the pandemonium inside the Workers' Stadium seem particularly shattering was the almost complete silence in the rest of this City of Whispers. In the teeming, sprawling capital almost everyone wore felt-soled slippers so that, apart from the occasional honk of a car or a taxicab – both of them rare enough – and some public transport, which seemed to be confined largely to the morning and evening rush hours, there was only the slightest, shuffling susurration of the slippers, and any loud noise was as rare as seeing a Chinese blonde.

Here again Peking was different from any other city I have ever visited for everyone was dressed alike, in blue jeans and high necked tunics, and, believe it or not as you like, at a range of ten yards or so you genuinely could not tell whether someone walking towards you was a man or a woman.

Particularly fascinating was the trip we made to the Great Wall of China, about 4,000 miles long, originally constructed as a defence some 2,250 years ago, which at its nearest point is some thirty to forty miles north-west of Peking. Our hotel made us up a very reasonable picnic lunch and, as well as being provided with a car and a chauffeur we were given, for the day, a special interpreter who, thanks be to Confucius, was for once more of a scholar than a propagandist.

The impression of everyone striving for the common weal was reinforced when we stopped for lunch after exploring some of the sinuosities of the Great Wall. We sat down in a kind of squat stone tower which had doubtless in the old days been some form of strongpoint but now, furnished with rough chairs and a table, was used as a kind of *al fresco* restaurant by tourists like ourselves.

I noticed that our scholarly guide sat apart from us and produced his own all-too-scanty-rations. There were enough for half a dozen between Desmond, Jim and myself and we invited him to come and share our food and the very reasonable bottled Chinese beer. At first he demurred, fearing himself, I think, patronized. But in the end he joined us – and capital company he was. His was not the mechanical patter and chatter of the tip-hungry courier.

He made the Wall and its ancient defenders and besiegers come to life. He told us of the old China – and the new. Two of his remarks I shall never forget. One of us had commented that he was unique in our experience of guides. He replied that it was not his real job; that he and his wife were both schoolteachers but as they could both speak English they had volunteered to show their country to such strangers as could come to it.

Rather brashly I queried the 'voluntariness' of his occupation. He looked at me gravely. 'You are wrong. There was no compulsion. There was no need for it. I, and my wife as well, would do anything to help our new nation grow in strength and unity.'

It was said with a dignity which precluded propaganda. I felt abashed and more so when a few minutes later, after we had been chatting about various trips to different countries which we had made in the past, our Chinese friend commented gently: 'I know you gentlemen who have seen so much of the world must think that much in the China of today is very primitive by your standards. All I can say is that before "the great leap forward" the China of then was as primitive to us as the China of today is to you and the industrialized countries of the world.'

He was a fine and mature citizen of the world which we hope will come tomorrow. A patriot who did not need to wave flags.

As we drove back I thought of his words as we looked out of the car's windows and saw, not once but many times, a horse, an ass and a man, yoked troika-fashion, and pulling what looked like wooden ploughs which made shallow scratches across the vast landscape.

Yet this modern China was not all solemnity. I used to be a heavy smoker in those days and with unhappy memories of the Japanese sweet-tasting 'Peace' cigarettes – cynics used to say 'Smoke enough of them and you'll be at Peace – for ever!' – I approached my first Chinese cigarettes with trepidation. Yet the most popular Chinese brand, 'China', which cost half a yuan (the yuan was then worth almost exactly three shillings) for twenty, tasted closer to the popular English brands than the cigarettes of any other country I had visited.

When I commented on this to one of our interpreters he replied slyly: 'Well, they should be alike; after all you used to own all our tobacco factories!'

This was one trip where the sporting *raison d'être* became subordinated to the strangeness of the environment: *everything* was so different.

Two traditional pursuits seemed to have been entirely eliminated – gambling and prostitution. The Chinese were (and, abroad, still are) perhaps the world's greatest gamblers. But now, although the traditional game of Mah Jong – I was told that in Chinese its literal meaning was 'sparrows' – still existed it was as harmless as English children playing beggar-my-neighbour. At the same time I asked if there were any night clubs in Peking. My guide replied gravely: 'Oh, yes; we have one. It closes at nine pm.' A slight pause, then he continued: 'Now I come to think of it, it closed for good two years ago!'

'Good,' I felt, was the operative word.

There were, I was assured, pubs in Peking but I must confess that after the most diligent search I was unable to find one. In any case, I was told that the lifestyle of a publican was distinctly precarious as, at any moment, a Government official was liable to come up to him and announce: 'We are behind in the rice harvest and, perhaps, it would be a good idea for you to go out to work in the fields.'

Maybe that was the reason why my search, although so diligent, was fruitless. They must have had a terrible rice harvest.

As for prostitution, once rife in China, according to the officials this had been abolished. Certainly I saw no signs of it. Prostitutes were 're-educated', which the Chinese admitted was a lengthy and arduous task, but, according to Government spokesmen, it had been necessary to jail comparatively few.

In a superbly appointed theatre, I attended a modern Chinese ballet, *Maid of the Sea*. The music seemed to derive largely from the West. It was a delightful presentation, if a little childlike – almost as though Walt Disney had turned choreographer.

There did not seem to be a lot for the young Chinese to do in the evening. There were no dance halls, as we understand them, but occasionally a factory or an office building would organize dances with both Western and modern Chinese music. But there was strictly none of the jitterbugging or rock-'n'-rolling which was the Western style at the time. Factories also organized concerts, sometimes of gramophone records, which included recitals of modern Chinese and classical Western music.

Television had arrived but there were few privately owned sets. Most Chinese watched, in their spare time, at their place of work. I may have been unlucky, but every time I looked at a set in the Press Centre it was clearly some sort of propaganda being pumped out – with a monotonous emphasis on such exhilarating subjects as heavy machinery!

Cinemas were extremely popular – I saw more queues outside them than outside food shops – and in those days the film industry promised to be a big one.

Apart from the table-tennis championships I was naturally interested in all manifestations of Chinese sport. Because of the participation of Formosa – now, as Taiwan, another stormy petrel of sport – 'Red' China had not entered the Olympic Games and, apart from a few matches in different sports against Albania, she had not, as far as I could find out, competed internationally at all. Yet the facilities were there.

As well as the Peking Indoor Stadium there was the outdoor Workers' Stadium, not covered but with windbreaks protecting the higher seats and holding 100,000 people. It was completed in August 1952 having taken eleven months and thirteen days to build! It included a sports arena, an exhibition hall, a large cinema, a swimming pool, practice rooms and living accommodation, including Eastern and Western kitchens, for 1,500 athletes and 200 resident staff. The primary idea, at that time, was not so much to turn out champions – although the Chinese, even from table tennis, were quick to realize the prestige value of internationally known champions – as to produce high-class performers who could then go back to their own districts, and even villages, and pass on their expertise to the young.

I was tremendously impressed with what I had seen and I said as much to the official who had shown me round. Then came the bitter pill. He said: 'Oh, yes. We sent our experts round the world to examine the most modern stadiums in all countries and to bring back ideas which we could incorporate from all nations.' There was a pause. 'I'm afraid they did not find anything very modern in Britain. . . .'

How could they? Our 'National' Stadium, Wembley, was even then nearly forty years old.

Another complex which fascinated me was the Peking Sports and Physical Culture Academy.

To my astonishment I found they had a 100 metres straight indoor running track, under cover; unique, I imagine, in the world. By 1961 there were nearly 2,500 students and about 400 teachers. The students could take two-, three- or four-year courses, entering the Academy at eighteen.

My first example of a 'Chinese blush' came after I had studied a chart showing times and distances for various events – something comparable to the 'standards' set by our own Amateur Athletic Association. Although I could not, of course, read the Chinese characters I could figure out most of the events by the times and distances (in metres) required. But one distance puzzled me: too far for shot-putting, much too short for the discus.

What could it be? I asked.

And then came the 'Chinese blush'. After a certain amount of circumlocution my guide explained what this unusual distance was for. Grenade throwing.

Although most of the activities were genuinely and purely athletic there was just a touch of military proficiency about some of them; later I learned, unofficially, that some of the men's swimming tests had to be accomplished in a military uniform and with a rifle strapped to the swimmer's back.

But the most revealing thing I saw in China was an urban commune.

I visited some of the factories – although, to be candid, to Western eyes most of them looked more like holes in the wall than factories. Two scenes are tattooed in my mind. One is of an old man with a long grey beard tapering down to his waist, beating on a sheet of metal with a hammer, surrounded by women and girls in the inevitable blue jeans and high-necked blue tunics, all of whom seemed to be a quarter of his age.

The other scene was symbolic of the lusty, young China; an electrical apparatus factory, staffed only by women. There were two of them, frantically sawing through some metal, almost like performers in a futuristic ballet. Women like these had a saying: 'Formerly we were people with palms upwards; now we are people with palms downwards.' This means that previously they had to beg for the necessities of life and now they were beginning, with their own hands, to construct for themselves.

One other thing was astonishing in this strange land: even though it is the second largest country in the world, not one inch of earth was wasted in Peking. Outside the last commune house, containing heaven knows how many teeming, industrious 'ants', I saw a patch of dry soil. It was no more than a square yard. But in it three different kinds of vegetables were growing. Nothing, nothing, but nothing, was wasted in a Chinese commune.

Apart from the size and enthusiasm of the crowds – including the opening ceremony and the thrice-daily playing sessions between 350,000 and 400,000 spectators attended – there was nothing particularly memorable about the championships themselves, at least from a British point of view.

Among our girls, Diane Rowe justified her place as seventh seed, and Ian Harrison played 'over his head' beating, in the Swaythling Cup, Ichiro Ogimura, the Japanese who had twice previously won the world singles championship.

Some idea of our relative standing, however, came with the ITTF rankings at the end of the championships, when the England men's squad (the home countries entered separate teams) were placed equal sixth and our women's teams also shared sixth place.

The real struggle was, of course, the Sino-Japanese one. And, in front of their own hysterical crowds, China did magnificently, not only retaining the men's singles title but adding the women's singles and the team Swaythling Cup to it. Japan won the men's and mixed doubles and the Corbillon Cup (the women's equivalent of the Swaythling).

Just to hold the balance, Europe did manage to get a toe in the door when the Romanian pair, Maria Alexandru and Georgetta Pitica, took the women's doubles.

During the course of the championships, there were some justifiable accusations against the Chinese players of gamesmanship; but it would be churlish to end on a grudging note. By the prowess of their players, the enthusiasm of the spectators and the supremely slick and efficient presentation of the world championships, the Chinese had proved themselves a new force in the world of sport.

I took one final memory of China, and her people, with me which had absolutely nothing to do with 'ping-pang', the Chinese version of ping-pong.

Desmond Hackett and I were travelling back to England in the same plane, and to catch it we had to leave our hotel while it was still quite dark. As we drove to the airport and the sun rose we could see battalions of the inevitably blue-clad workers on their hands and knees in the fields, cutting the pasture with what looked like little more than glorified scissors – to have called them shears would have been to exaggerate. Mother China was, even in the dark, using the one inexhaustible wealth she had – the number of her children.

Back in Britain there was no time to settle down to the difference between East and West; after leaving Peking on the Saturday there was a preliminary for a world title fight in London to be written on the Monday. It was the return lightweight championship between Joe Brown and Dave Charnley.

I tipped Brown, but Charnley, though wickedly cut across the nose by a right-hand counter from Brown as early as the fifth round, so that his face was like a pillar-box with Brown trying to post letter bombs in it, staged a truly magnificent rally in the thirteenth and fourteenth rounds. It was not enough to offset Brown's previous lead, but the thirty-five-year-old New Orleans Negro knew that he had been in a fight.

British boxing seemed to be looking up, for only a fortnight after Charnley's plucky performance we saw the first national professional title won by the man I consider to have been the most scientific boxer Britain has produced since the war, Welshman Howard Winstone.

I am convinced that had he not lost the tips of three fingers of his right hand in an industrial accident in a toy factory, where he was working as a youth, he would have won a world title earlier and, moreover, it would have received universal recognition; as it was the Americans refused to accept Winstone's just (in my opinion) claim to the championship. In his fight for the British nine-stone title with Terry Spinks, once the so-proud winner of an Olympic gold medal, Spinks reeled to his corner at the end of the tenth round after taking six lancing lefts to his face without a return, and gasped: 'I've had enough.'

The 'winter' season ended with a magnificent Rugby League Cup Final in which St Helens beat the favoured Wigan by 12 points to 6 with a midfield temperature of 79 degrees Fahrenheit – taken just before the start of the match.

The game contained one of the two most memorable tries I have ever seen, executed with a shuttle-smooth movement between Tom Van Vollenhoven, a Springbok with a crewcut, and the frequently under-estimated Ken Large. I can only compare it with that run at Twicken-ham when the late, great Alex Obolensky must have covered a good seventy yards on his own for England. Vollenhoven and Large, surging like an irresistible tide down the wing at Wembley, probably ran twenty yards farther than that.

The South African carried the ball, passed inside, and then trailed Large like a Derby winner on a short rein, until he was perfectly placed to receive the return pass and gallop on, leaving the opposition grasping at nothingness – men trying to imprison swirling smoke within their clutching fingers.

In the end it was, of course, speed which beat strength, as the fried egg in the sky boiled the lard out of the heftier Wigan stalwarts until even heroes such as sixteen-stone Brian McTigue were reduced to no more than ordinary mortals. . . .

The European Amateur Boxing Championships were held in Yugo-slavia and we won two gold medals, only Russia winning more. Our heroes were Frankie Taylor, a prime favourite with us at the ringside as, at eighteen, he was an apprentice journalist, and the elegant Dick McTaggart.

I always had the idea that Taylor could have made a world champion. In a professional career which lasted four days short of four years he had thirty-one fights. He won twenty-seven of them, drew another, lost one on a disqualification, one on points and one inside the distance. He gave up fighting for writing when he was only twenty-three. An accident in the gym when he was sparring left him with incipient eye trouble and, thank sanity, he was sensible enough to put his sight in the proper per-spective compared with the transitory glory of boxing.

But oh! how good he was. He had the real aggression of the best American scrappers, yet he could box well. The dream featherweight title match which was mooted – promoters with open cheques, fans with open mouths – was a contest between him and Howard Winstone.

Who would have won? Over eight rounds: Winstone. Over ten rounds: Winstone. Over twelve rounds: Winstone. Over fifteen rounds . . . I always thought Taylor. It would have been Eric Boon and Arthur

Danahar all over again. The puncher wearing down the infinitely better boxer. (Apocryphally, I am sure, it was alleged that the two fighters once came face to face and Taylor said: 'You can win the first fourteen rounds – but I'll win the fight!')

As well as the threatened damage to his eyesight I always felt that Taylor had certain mental reservations about boxing as a whole which may have added to his determination to give it up so early. But he was a truly great prospect.

At Wimbledon 1961 we had the sensation of two British girls, Angela Mortimer, now Mrs Barrett, and Christine Truman, now Mrs Janes, contesting the women's singles final – the first time this had happened since 1914 when Mrs Lambert Chambers beat Mrs Dudley Larcombe in two sets.

I have always thought Christine was one of the unluckiest losers of a Wimbledon final I have ever seen. She won the first set 6–4, led 4–3 in the second and in the next game, in which Angela served two double faults, was within a point of gaining what would surely have been a winning lead of 5–3. Then the big twenty-year-old Essex girl slipped and fell heavily. With her weight any fall was bound to shake her, but worse than this was that earlier in the year she had had thrombosis in one leg and that for a time, while the match was still in progress, she thought that her fall had caused a recurrence of the earlier trouble.

As a result she lost five games in a row which meant that instead of being a set up and leading in the second she found herself trailing 0–2 in the third. She had one more chance when she caught up to 3–3, but again the luck was against her for, having had the advantage point called in her favour and started the next rally the umpire, who apparently hadn't heard the linesman call 'out', interrupted the rally and made the girls play the point again.

That did it. Christine lost the point and then double-faulted to lose the vital lead. The only crumb of comfort was that if Christine had to lose then the girl from Devon who had really dedicated her life to lawn tennis was a worthy winner. But it was impossible not to be biased in favour of Christine who typified everything we so often wrote about 'sportsmanship' – but all too seldom came across in the higher echelons of sport.

At midnight I danced with Cinderella at the annual LTA ball at Grosvenor House which rounds off the championships. Before we went on the floor I promised that I would not talk of the sport which had made world-famous the girl who eight hours before should have won the world's major lawn-tennis title. I kept my word, but what I should like to have told her was that when she followed Angela Mortimer, to give the traditional interview expected from the runner-up after the champion had expressed her views, it was the only time I could remember the loser getting spontaneously applauded as though she had won.

You can't buy that sort of appreciation from those of us who spend our lives – and earn our livings – writing about sport. And phoneys don't get it.

Now she's a mother herself, and when I see how much money some of the little madams and bitches of all sizes and sexes, can now make, while Christine's great days were in the supposedly amateur era, it proves once again what a froward mistress sport can be.

The annual Wightman Cup match was held that year at the Saddle and Cycle Club in Chicago.

If ever there were a tie we should have won this was it. We had a team which included the Wimbledon champion, Angela Mortimer, the runner-up, Christine Truman and Ann Haydon, a semi-finalist the preceding year. The Americans had dropped their leading player, Darlene Hard, and were represented by the youngest team ever to play.

Its members were Billie Jean Moffitt, later of course Mrs King, who was then seventeen, Justina Bricka, aged eighteen and Karen Hantze, later Mrs Susman, also eighteen. There was, it was true, a very minor leavening of age in the playing captain, Mrs Margaret du Pont, and Margaret Varner, a player who had the distinction of being picked to represent her country in three different sports – badminton, her forte, and squash rackets as well as lawn tennis.

But the 'veterans' were not called upon to play for, unprecedentedly, they were given a walk-over in the last doubles match by Miss Mortimer and Miss Haydon. Not that it mattered by then as we had already lost the tie and the final score of 6–1 to the USA merely emphasized our inferiority.

I also covered the US lawn tennis championships, and here the most memorable incident involved my oldest friend in Fleet Street – Lance Tingay, of the *Daily Telegraph*.

As far as I can remember, he and I were the only two British journalists covering Forest Hills that year, which meant that we could come to a 'gentleman's agreement' about what time we would send our final messages for the day, and knowing Lance, I could be sure the agreement would be kept.

Sure enough, one evening at six pm (eleven pm in London) we looked at each other, agreed that neither the *Mirror* nor the *Telegraph* sports desk would thank either of us for cables arriving around midnight, closed up our typewriters and called it a day.

As we left the West Side Club 'Chuck' McKinley, who a month or so earlier had reached the men's singles final at Wimbledon, was involved in what looked like being a distinctly tough match.

Joe Nicholls, who wrote boxing and racing so accurately for the *New York Times*, had tipped me off about an uncommonly pleasant little bistro within walking distance, even for me, of Forest Hills. Thither Lance and I repaired, reminiscing about how we had first met at another West Side club – that one was in the London suburb of Ealing and was run by the family of that English girl prodigy, Betty Nuthall – when we were both in our teens.

It *was* a nice 'local'. Down a few steps, into air-conditioned peace, undisturbed by TV or juke-box. Just a few serious drinkers, getting on with the important business of the day. We were on our second gin and tonic – or whatever we were imbibing – when the door opened and a man came in.

I don't know about extra-sensory perception but on occasions I *can* perceive when trouble is going to rear its not only ugly but unexpected head; this was one such occasion.

Not that the newcomer was in any way a trouble-maker. Not that Lance, bless his heart, has ever deliberately started trouble of any kind in the over forty-five years we have known each other. But I knew that this was going to be a D – for Disaster – evening.

For the man who came in had a remarkable resemblance to one of the Forest Hills officials. Don't ask me how I knew it wasn't the same man; don't even ask me how I knew Lance was going to think it was. I just knew – that's all. And furthermore I knew that it could lead only to trouble.

The bloke sat down. As usual during the US championships the weather was so hot and humid you could have stuffed a turkey with it. The bloke had probably had a hard day at the office. He almost certainly had had a lousy ride back in the subway.

Now he was in his own friendly neighbourhood pub. He didn't even have to order a drink because the barkeeper knew what he wanted, down to the last cube of ice and the exact splash of soda. He relaxed.

And then, so help me, it was all ruined for him.

For Lance, lovable Lance said brightly: 'What happened to McKinley?'

The bloke looked round: to one side of him – behind him. No. It was no use. This utter stranger with an even stranger accent was indeed addressing him with what seemed, not to put too fine a point on it, the query of a lunatic.

Gruffness, he thought, might be the solution. 'McKinley?' he growled. 'McKinley got shot.'

Lance beamed at him. 'You must forgive me,' said he, courteously. 'I'm English' – as though the bloke after hearing his accent might have thought he was a Hottentot – 'yes, I'm English and that's a new phrase for me. McKinley was "shot", eh?'

The American closed his eyes, as though that would make everything go away and restore the nice, calm evening caesura he usually enjoyed between the earlier aggravations of the office and the still-to-come tensions of the home.

But Lance, fine newspaperman that he is, was not going to be fobbed off as easily as that. 'What,' he asked keenly, 'was the score?' Then, as an afterthought: 'And who won?'

The bloke opened his eyes again. Yes, the bar was its old, friendly, familiar self. The drink was what he always had. The bartender had left the change from the five-dollar bill, with which he had paid for his drink, in front of him. Everything was its wonderful, normal, sane self except for the raving maniac with the goddam loony, limey voice who had this obsession, for heaven's sake, about McKinley.

Speaking very slowly and distinctly he said: 'There wasn't no score. No one won. McKinley he lost. He got shot – dead.'

Whereupon he drained his glass at one go, nearly missed the bar while replacing it and, completely ignoring his change, stumbled out into the stifling evening – a man for whom things would never be quite the same again.

When I could stop laughing, I tried to explain to Lance, between whoops, that I thought the bloke wasn't really referring to 'Chuck' McKinley, the lawn-tennis player, but to the twenty-fifth President of the USA, William McKinley, who was assassinated by an anarchist of Polish descent in 1901.

But I'm not sure that he really believed me. . . .

Soon afterwards the professionals were again playing lawn tennis at Wembley and it was now clear that Ken Rosewall, at nearly twenty-seven was ready to take over from Pancho Gonzales who would be thirty-four next birthday.

On this occasion these two players, so dissimilar in style and temperament, paid generous tribute to each other. After Rosewall had beaten Lew Hoad, conqueror of Gonzales in the semi-final, for the Wembley championship he said: 'The toughest man I've met? No question about it – Gonzales. All of us can "get hot" for a day or a night and beat any of the others. But if you take Gonzales on for a tour you're always under pressure, match after match, with that tremendous service of his.'

Gonzales put Rosewall, by a shade, as the most difficult man he had had to beat and he thought the future of the game would continue towards attack but 'with the back court security of Rosewall' becoming more and more important.

Gradually things were beginning to move in sport as the new decade started to get into its stride. The garrotte around the throat of South

African sport was given another turn when it was announced that FIFA, soccer's world governing body, had suspended the Republic and, at the same time, the South African FA was told that as their country had ceased to be a member of the Commonwealth it could no longer be a member of the FA or be represented on the Council.

Next came the shortest British title fight ever recorded, when David 'Darkie' Hughes was knocked out by Dave Charnley, defending his British, Empire and European lightweight titles, exactly forty seconds after the first bell had sounded.

There were two remarks I remember about this. Benny Jacobs, Hughes' manager, was quoted as saying: 'I thought my man was ahead on points when it finished!' The other was distinctly at my expense. Obviously, for a late night affair like a fight, a certain amount of space has to be allocated in the paper. With great glee, one of the compositors remarked, knowing my appalling habit of over-writing: 'Well, let's see how he goes about filling the space on *this* one, then.' Three-quarters of an hour later he said disbelievingly: 'By God! 'E's gone and stuffed us again! Eight bleedin' inches of overmatter!' – this being the length of the type surplus to the space provided. . . .

Meanwhile my old mate Archie Moore had plenty to say to an American writer, Jack Murphy – a friend of his – in the November issue of the *New Yorker*.

His most acid remarks were reserved for that other black gladiator, Sugar Ray Robinson. Explaining how he beat Robinson out of the part of Jim, the runaway slave, in the film version of *Huckleberry Finn* Archie said: 'Ray lost the part because he was too sleek. They didn't have sleek slaves in those days.'

I remember seeing the film. At the start Moore, untutored in the art of acting, was almost embarrassing to watch. But in the most extraordinary way as the film developed so Archie improved and I defy anyone – well, anyone as basically sentimental as myself – not to have to blow his nose, trumpet-fashion, when the dialogue, right at the end, went something like:

Jim, sitting on the 'freedom' bank of the river: 'Don't forget to write.'

Tom, rowing out to one of the big paddle-steamers and vanishing into the distance with his voice dying away: 'I don't write too good.'

Jim, speaking barely audibly, to himself: 'I don't read at all.'

My first trip in 1962 was to a new country for me – Brazil. São Paulo was the precise destination.

My journey had boxing as its *raison d'être*. John Caldwell, the cold-eyed kid from Belfast, whom Europe regarded as the world bantam-weight champion, was to meet Eder Jofre, the Brazilian, accepted as champion in both Americas and various other parts of the world.

In those days I found São Paulo an enchanting city. On the surface, anyway, there seemed a complete absence of a colour bar and never have I seen such a concentration of truly gorgeous girls; when they walked by they seemed to jiggle in places where other girls didn't even have places.

I reckoned that this was the fifty-ninth world title fight, at all weights, that I would have seen. But there was one thing about this which made it unique. I had the honour to be asked to be one of the three judges.

The referee was the brilliant former featherweight champion of the world Willie 'The Wisp' Pep. But he would only control the fight. If it came to a points decision it would be up to the three judges to give it. One was a Brazilian, Edmar Teixira, director of the Federation of Brazilian judges, the second was Tony Petronella, of the USA. He was supposed to be neutral, but as he was a former President of the National Boxing Association, which already recognized Jofre as world champion, it was felt that his leanings might be in the Brazilian's direction. I was the third arbiter.

On the eve of the fight I thought I must make my position clear to Sammy Docherty, Caldwell's manager. He was a small but very tough little Scot who, it was alleged, on one occasion when he found it necessary to sort things out with a considerably larger rival went after him with not a brick in one hand but two half-bricks in each hand, on the grounds that the 'haufs' fitted the size of his hands better and that a half in each hand was as effective as a whole brick in one fist!

As you can imagine Mr Docherty was not a man with whom to trifle, but I was determined to make my attitude towards judging crystal-clear.

Without beating about the bush I said: 'I know the judging set-up here looks as though it's one for Jofre, one 'neutral' who, I suspect, you think isn't exactly on Caldwell's side, and myself to act as some sort of counter-balance. Well, so that you've got time to change your mind if you feel differently after what I'm going to say, that's not how I view this judging job at all.

'Of course, I'd like to see Caldwell win. We're both British and we're all a long way from home. But if Jofre wins, even if it's only by one point' – we were using the ten points to a round system, unlike the quarter point one then in vogue in Britain – 'then he's going to get my vote.'

Docherty looked at me, long and hard. Then he said: 'Why d'ye think I acceptit you as a judge?' There was a pause. Then he added: 'An' wha' happens if it's John that's ahead by jist yin point at the end?'

'Well, *he* get's my vote, of course.'

'Aweel, tha's a'richt then.' Again a pause. 'But if it *should* be John . . . jist see you do your addeetion richt!'

Unfortunately the fight was too 'one-way' for it to be regarded as great.

I gave the first two rounds even, the fourth to Caldwell and the eighth even – with all the rest to Jofre; I was very glad when Sammy Docherty, in the tenth round, got on to the apron of the ring to signal that his man was finished, causing Willie Pep to wrap his arms protectively round the Irishman in token of the fact that he had taken quite enough punishment.

I was rather pleased to compare scoring with Tony Petronella later. He had Jofre ahead by eighty-eight points to eighty-two at the end of the ninth round; my score was eighty-nine to eighty-three, so we had exactly the same points spread. I was told the Brazilian judge had Jofre eighteen points in the lead – just three times greater than Petronella's and my assessment!

While I was in São Paulo I took the opportunity of getting in touch with Maria Bueno whose home town it is. Maria had already won Wimbledon twice, in 1959–60, the first time when she was only nineteen, but in 1961 she had been forced, by ill-health, to scratch from the French championships and this was the first time I had seen her since.

She had been much more ill than anyone had known at the time. In France they had not at once diagnosed her illness as hepatitis and they told her she could go on taking exercise for a couple of hours a day. She felt terrible and when she got home to Brazil the doctors told her to go to bed immediately, and she stayed there for four and a half months.

We walked together through the tepid rain until we came to a larger-than-life-size statue near the entrance of the magnificent Tiete Club with its superb athletics facilities and its Olympic-sized swimming pool. Maria looked up at the statue which the club had erected in her honour and, all feminine, asked me: 'Do you think it's like me?'

I said: 'No, the backhand shot is yours, but the statue isn't as attractive as you are.'

She got into the car which the Jockey Club gave her when she won Wimbledon and we drove across to the house almost opposite the club, where she had been playing since she was nine years old. When we got into the small, slightly garishly furnished house where she lived with her father, mother and brother, it staggered me how this girl could have kept her head following the adulation she received.

First of all they issued a special set of six-cruzeiro (then roughtly $1\frac{1}{2}$d.) stamps to commemorate her two Wimbledon wins. The stamps were engraved with a picture of Maria making her graceful forehand, and inscribed: 'World champion of women's tennis, Wimbledon 1959–60.'

There was a small replica of the statue, in bronze, in their living room and Maria told me: 'They were going to rename the street in which my house and the club stand "Avenida Maria Esther Bueno", but unfortunately they discovered a law which says that a person has to be dead before you can do that for them. I couldn't oblige, although this last year I sometimes thought I might!'

The reception she received when she returned dwarfed anything I have seen provided for world heavyweight champions, Cup Final winners or victorious Test teams.

The Tiete Club gave her two of the most magnificently bound and collated scrapbooks I have ever seen. In one of them there was a picture of Maria, crowned with a tiara, wearing a flowing white robe, seated next to President Juscelino Kubitschek in the presidential helicopter, hovering a few yards above a crowd, which must have numbered literally hundreds of thousands, all of them staring upwards as though at a fairy queen.

It would be untrue to say that she was unaffected by all this. She was still as naively and unspoiledly excited about her globe-girdling fame, which transformed her from the unknown daughter of a São Paulo veterinary dietician into one of the world's sporting celebrities, as a kitten is with a new ping-pong ball.

But the kitten couldn't obscure the tiger girl of the courts.

If you asked any knowledgeable sportswriter to name perhaps the greatest daily sports publication in the world I should be surprised if the answer wasn't that magnificent French paper, *L'Equipe*. One of the real stalwarts of English Rugby football at this time was that whalebone and whipcord scrum-half, Dickie Jeeps, who that year represented his country against Scotland, Ireland and Wales. When the French match was coming up *L'Equipe* proved that it had wit as well as authority by commenting: 'There was a time when the English Rugby footballers used to go around in their carriages. Nowadays they content themselves with Jeeps.' Great.

Athletics I regret to say – for it has always been one of my three favourite sports – is more riddled with hypocrisy than almost any other popular sport. Never was this more cruelly illustrated than in the case of a long-distance runner named John Tarrant.

His overriding ambition in life was to wear an England vest as a marathon runner, but from the word 'go' he was doomed by a rule which, I am convinced, was introduced for one purpose but applied for a very different one by a set of pettifogging 'barrack-room lawyers'.

As a very young man John Tarrant decided he might make a few quid as a boxer. He wasn't licensed – the British Boxing Board of control, whose lists go back to 1940, when Tarrant would have been eight, have no evidence of his record. He fought eight bouts against other unlicensed boxers for an unlicensed promoter at local unlicensed shows, all in Buxton, Derbyshire. For these eight bouts, a total of twenty-five rounds, he received the princely reward of £17, and, as he said rather pathetically: 'I did not show a profit from my boxing because four times a week I travelled to Stockport to a gym (fare 4s. 6d. return) for training.'

The original idea of banning anyone who had competed in any professional sport from competing against amateurs in other sports was (privately) snobbery and, for public consumption, the idea that the pro might have gained a physical advantage by pursuing a sport as a full-time occupation.

But how vindictive, how unfair, how utterly against the *spirit* of the law was this IAAF ruling. By no stretch of imagination could those eight 'pro' fights have given Tarrant an unfair advantage over other amateur runners – great heavens, he won only three of them!

The rubber match between Terry Downes and Paul Pender for the world middleweight title was due to take place in Boston, but I broke my journey in New York to see the man whom I regarded as the best middleweight in the world – Nigeria's Dick Tiger. Tiger's real name was Ihetu, and not a bad one for a fighter!

It was ironic to see him win so one-sidedly that he almost took eleven out of ten rounds against one of the then leading middleweights in the world, Henry Hank, and then go on to Boston to see the man whom he had beaten in half a dozen rounds less than five years earlier, Terry Downes, defending the world title.

In fact, the last Downes–Pender fight was the least attractive of their three; and none of them, for differing reasons, was truly memorable.

In the end Pender's superior boxing skills regained him the title. Downes fought the roughest fight I ever remember him producing. I don't think he liked Pender – or even respected him which, in boxing, is a rather different thing. Pender, particularly in the later stages of the fight, was a pair of handcuffs on legs as he held more and more. But he did score more points.

The 1962 French championships that year provided plenty of drama, for Rod Laver was trying for the 'grand slam'. In the end Laver got it – thus becoming the only man since Don Budge, in 1938, to have brought it off – but twice, in Paris, it looked as though it were going to elude him.

In the semi-final Laver's match against Neale Fraser, the Wimbledon champion of 1960, was suspended at 2–2 in the fifth set when the light got too bad, Laver, who was 3–4 and 4–5 down in the final set described what it was like beginning again with the score so close: 'Starting at two-all was the toughest spot I've ever faced in a big championship. If Fraser had won that first game I might not have got another.'

In the final Laver beat another Australian, Roy Emerson, who by then was about the only remaining amateur who could consistently extend him. But 'Rocket' lost the first two sets and only won the fourth 9–7. So close did the record-breaker come to defeat.

The great sensation at Wimbledon was the first-round defeat of Margaret Smith, still only nineteen but seeded No. 1, by an American with whom she was to fight to the death for years afterwards, but who was then an eighteen-year-old college kid, Billie Jean Moffitt, later Mrs King.

It was a disastrous blow for Miss Smith who had already won the Australian and French championships and was to go on to take that of the USA.

But it led to a simple but curiously moving gesture. David Shure, a London curio dealer, had read my comment after the match that: 'Everyone was sorry to see the girl from whom so much had been expected so publicly humiliated.' He got in touch with me and told me that he had a medal which used to be presented to the loser in the All-Comers' final before the Challenge Round was abolished. 'I was deeply moved by Margaret's story,' he said, and on the medal he had the simple message inscribed: 'For determination, sincerity and effort. June 1962.'

I gave it to the young Australian on the players' terrace at Wimbledon and Margaret said: 'I'll always treasure this medal.' And then like a real fighter: 'And I'll be back next year.'

And she was to win the final, by a strange quirk, from – Billie Jean Moffitt!

This was the year that Larkspur won the most disastrous Derby in living memory. Seven horses down, one shot, six jockeys taken to hospital – the Derby, you know, is a flat race not a steeplechase.

How few people at the end of the 2 mins 37·6 secs which it took Larkspur to win, *knew* how many horses were down. A lot of people didn't know that *anyone* was down or hurt. This was the Derby which everyone who loves horseracing would want to forget.

But now it was time to go to Yugoslavia where the European athletics championships were being held in Belgrade.

There were two highlights for Britain – who finished second only to the USSR in the gold medal tally – which I still remember.

One was the magnificent sprint of Dorothy Hyman in the 100 metres in which the daughter of a Yorkshire miner who had died suddenly four months earlier beat the powerful blonde Jutta Heine, daughter of a West German millionaire. This was fairy-tale stuff. And then there was the triumph of Brian Kilby, a Coventry draughtsman, who won a marathon which had been begun in a temperature of 81 degrees!

No sooner was I back in London, on the Monday night, than it was time to take off for Chicago for the world heavyweight title fight between Floyd Patterson and Sonny Liston for which the publicity drums had been beating in earnest.

Liston, asked whether he had seen any of Patterson's fight films, summed up his opponent in twenty-one succinct words: 'I saw him fight in person and he was always on the deck. So what can I learn from his movies?'

Interviews with Liston, at the disused trotting-race track which he was using as his training headquarters, were like pulling teeth from an unwilling patient. The answers came, if they came at all, like someone spitting pebbles.

A Swedish journalist asked: 'What do you think of Ingemar Johansson?'

Liston's answer: 'He should be locked up for impersonating a fighter.' After the inevitable roar of laughter had subsided he added: 'I'd like to meet him in a warm-up fight before I meet Patterson – like in the dressing room on Tuesday.'

Someone remarked that he had been quoted as saying that his fight against Patterson would be over by the fifth round. He nodded. 'It will be – either him or me.' And was he worried that he had boxed only four competitive rounds in the past two years? 'No. In future, as champion, I'll only want to box ten or more rounds in the next twenty years. The fights will last thirty, forty, fifty seconds.'

It is difficult, years later, to convey just how baleful Liston appeared and the feeling of having survived mortal combat which you experienced at the end of an interview with him. But this is part of what I wrote at the time:

Sometimes he takes so long to answer a question, and has so much difficulty in finding the words he wants to use, that it's rather like a long-distance telephone call in a foreign language.

But the man is fascinating. While his scarred face is immobile and his enormous painted-saucer eyes have the fixed glare of an octopus, his hands compel attention. The palms are soft and white, like the inside of a banana skin. The fingers are the unpeeled bananas.

Instead of the talons you expect to see sprouting from such massive engines of destruction, there are perfectly tended, varnished nails. It is as though the hangman had had a manicure before going to work.

One question has been worrying me. Can Liston be hurt by an unarmed man? I asked the man the question. He said: 'I've never been hurt in the ring.'

I persisted: 'When you were outpointed by Marty Marshall, in 1954, they say he broke your jaw.' Liston nodded: 'That's right. But it didn't hurt – not at the time. I didn't know it had happened until afterwards.'

How did it happen? 'I'd knocked him down. When he got up I was laughing at him. He was a clown fighter. My mouth was open when he hit me.' A pause. 'Taught me one thing. No one ain't ever seen me laugh in the ring again.'

While Liston trained brutally in a broken-down, overgrown racetrack, champion Patterson prepared quietly, and often behind locked doors, in a Roman Catholic centre for underprivileged children, set in bland farming country. This was one of those incongruous places which champions sometimes choose for training centres. The indoor training ring was in a one-roomed building where, presumably, in normal times the children congregated to sing hymns.

But it was the same old Patterson, the way he had been five years earlier, still really longing to be accepted as a super-champion but now more reconciled to the compensations. For instance, he said: 'I am satisfied with what I have – the title. I was the only man to regain it after losing it. I was the youngest man to win it. That's enough. I still don't feel I've been accepted as a good champion. I'd relish that opportunity, but I don't think it will ever happen.'

I asked him why he felt that way and he replied: 'I don't think you gentlemen would ever accept me as a great champion.'

And, of course, he was absolutely right. A few nights later he was to reach the lonely eminence of being the only heavyweight champion never to hear the bell ring twice. When he leaped at Liston it was like a kitten playing games with a bull mastiff. When Liston struck, first with a brain-numbing right then a left hook, it was like that same bull mastiff snapping off the kitten's head. The whole thing was over in just two minutes and six seconds.

What happened afterwards had the elements of tragedy, for those with compassion, or of farce for anyone who gets kicks out of pulling wings off flies.

When he left Comiskey Park – where a quarter of a century earlier I had seen Joe Louis dethrone game Jim Braddock – Patterson was so sick at heart that he got into a car and started to drive the 800-odd miles from Chicago to New York, where he was then living. So humiliated was he that he put on a false beard to hide his face of shame from the world. Had he had a premonition of the destruction to come? – for he had brought the beard to the stadium. Then, as though he had not suffered enough, he was stopped by a cop and asked for his driving licence. He could not find it. The policeman threatened arrest. In desperation Patterson removed his beard.

'Are you some kinda actor, or sump'n?' growled the cop.

Then he took a closer look at the man who, until a few hours earlier, had been perhaps the most universally known athlete in the world – and waved him on. . . .

After the fight I attended a most remarkable party given by Harold Conrad, a friend even then of twenty-five years, who somehow managed to bring a touch of class into fight-huckstering or – as I'm sure he would phrase it – the dissemination of information to the media. He was, and is, in fact, a first-class PRO.

As well as Hal and his lovely, blonde dancer-wife, Mara, there were in the suite Norman Mailer, Budd Schulberg and Gerald Kersh, all long-time fight fans, and James Baldwin and, to crib Damon Runyon, assorted guys and dolls. My old friend Sam Leitch came with me.

It was quite a party. The fight was re-fought for at least four hours – that was when I left – which was rather remarkable as it had lasted only 126 seconds; still, to be fair, I wrote several thousand words about it.

Among the guests was one of the loveliest *café-au-lait* coloured women I have ever seen. One of the celebrities was determined to make her. Someone knocked him down. They needn't have bothered. She had a tongue even more wounding than the blood-red talons into which her slim, sinewy fingers merged and which could, I imagine, have eviscerated the out-of-shape Lothario. In fact, it would have been rather interesting to allow him to try to continue his experiments. She was a notorious lesbian!

In the November of 1962 I left for one of the longest tours I ever made, London to Los Angeles, to Perth, Western Australia, to Brisbane, to Fiji, to Honolulu, to Seattle, to New York and back to London – some 32,000 miles all told.

The main purpose of my trip was to cover the Commonwealth Games at Perth but the first stop, at Los Angeles, provided in some ways the most sensational part of the whole journey. The occasion was the sixteenth professional fight of a young man still known to the world – or the small part of it that had heard of him at all – as Cassius Clay. And he was meeting my old friend Archie Moore, now deprived of his world light-heavyweight title by all the boxing commissions and now within a month of his forty-ninth birthday. 'Ol' Arch' was having his 227th pro fight – almost exactly twenty-seven years after he had had his first.

You have to remember how unknown Clay then was to realize how his predictions – 'Old Archie Moore, he'll fall in four' – astounded, delighted or provoked people, according to their temperament.

The fight? There was no fight. Clay was the blur of speed which was to become famous. Archie was an old grey man, his chubby knees tinged as white from the dust on the canvas as the hairs on his head and chest. As Clay had predicted they stopped it in four rounds and never was a contrast in two dressing rooms so vivid.

In Clay's there was a blackboard chalked: 'Moore in four. Liston in eight. Next champ, Cassius Clay.' Clay was talking, almost singing, when I got into the room. He carolled 'Sonny Liston said he'd give me eight seconds. I said I'd give him eight rounds – he didn't like that. I've predicted twelve of my sixteen fights right – to the round. You *must* admit I'm the greatest ever. I name the round.'

You couldn't dislike a youngster like this – you could only marvel at him, he was so incredibly naïve, brash . . . and *right!*

'If it was left up to me I'd fight Liston now. I'd put my pants on again' – at this stage he was unembarrassedly new-born naked – 'and I'd beat him as easy as I beat Moore.'

In my report I suggested four fighters whom I thought Clay should meet and added: 'If he succeeds in this pugilistic pilgrimage, then in two years, I think Liston might have a real fight on his hands.' It was an underestimation. Clay took three fights and just over fifteen months to give Liston his come-uppance.

The following day Sydney Hulls of the *Daily Express* and I went to get the first 'in depth' interview with Clay ever printed in England. We found two huge bronze young men lounging easily in a rumpled Los Angeles hotel room, their tartan luggage packed for the long haul to Louisville, Kentucky.

They were respectively Cassius Marcellus Clay, a great-grandson of a Negro slave, twenty years old and the fourth generation to bear this odd name, and his brother Rudolph Valentino Clay, named after guess who. (The world now knows Clay as Muhammad Ali and he refers scornfully to 'Clay' as his 'slave name'. Yet the original Cassius Marcellus Clay was a long-lived – 1810–1903 – American politician who urged the abolition of slavery. He joined the Republican Party in 1856, and in 1861 was sent by President Lincoln as Minister to Russia.)

On the surface Cassius Marcellus Clay was just another young heavyweight, albeit of outstanding talent. I found him much more than that: the most exciting young athlete I had seen since the days of the young Joe Louis a quarter of a century ago. I believed then that he could be the saviour of boxing, for the sport depends on the heavyweights, and particularly the heavyweight champion.

What sort of man was Clay then, in November 1962? Twenty years old, he had never done an ordinary day's work in his life – and never aimed to. He was extremely good-looking by any standards – fantastically so for a boxer. His Mephistophelian eyebrows, his burning eyes the colour of liqueur brandy, and his spectacular physique looked likely to cause as much havoc among the girls as his spade-like hands created among the contemporary heavyweights.

Clay on girls: 'Take a look at this telegram. . . . It says: "Good Luck, sweetheart. I love you" – and I don't even know her. So far I've never met the girl of my dreams. She'll have to be pretty and fall in one round. But I don't like to say what my ideal is because it upsets all the others.'

Clay on his beginnings: 'When I was eleven someone stole my bicycle. I said I'd beat him up. So I thought I'd better learn how to box. I never did find who stole my bicycle, but I liked boxing from the start. I was taught by Fred Stoner, a poor coloured man who didn't have nothing going for him.'

There's something very interesting in that. Every book about Clay and many articles and TV interviews that I've read and seen credit Patrolman Joe Martin as being Clay's original boxing mentor. But Martin was white – and a policeman. Clay's father, whom I subsequently found rather difficult to take, was alleged not to like white policemen, perhaps Martin in particular. It was not until *after* he had won the world heavyweight title that Clay announced his adherence to the Black Muslim beliefs and way of life. But, perhaps because Sydney Hulls and I were the first foreign journalists to interview him at length, he was already determined to identify only with his black brethren – interesting, though, that he called the shadowy Stoner 'coloured'. In my view the Black Muslim creed has always been basically anti-white – although Clay has never objected to using the expertise of Angelo Dundee, his chief corner man and, of course, a white man. Clay's conversion to the Muslims was supposed to have been effected by Malcolm X, later allegedly killed by Muslims for breaking away from the sect's leader, Elijah Muhammad, but Clay once said that he had originally been attracted by a Muslim speaker in New York. At the time I was interviewing him I did not know that he was an incipient Black Muslim – I had heard only vaguely of the sect – but he had, in fact, by then appeared twice in the ring in New York, in February and May 1962, so perhaps the seeds had already been sown.

Clay on his role in sporting history: 'I'm going to be the perfect heavyweight champion – like the young Joe Louis. I'm single – I think the champion should be single, the public likes it. I'm clean living, I haven't got a prison record. I think you've got to be an idol for young people.'

In this day of the gimmick, it was obvious that anyone as 'with it' as Cassius must have one. His was predicting how long his fights would last. It all started when a fighter called Lamar Clark came to Clay's hometown of Louisville. He started sneering at Cassius who went on TV and said: 'He must fall in two rounds.' He did.

Clay on Sonny Liston: 'I've told Liston I'll take him in eight. Even if I could beat him in the seventh, I'd keep him dazed and then get him in the eighth.'

When I wrote up this interview I concluded: 'A show-off? A loud-mouth? Clay has been called worse than that. But, in this country dedicated to the proposition that you either put up or shut up, he has consistently put up. And most of what he says about himself is true. Except when he compares himself with the young Joe Louis. *He* was a most modest young man.'

Then it was on to Perth and the Commonwealth Games. I think it was on this trip that, flying from Sydney to Perth with George Whiting, we were forced by head winds to make an unscheduled stop at a weather-station-cum-emergency-refuelling centre. It's only when you get away from the coastal belt of Australia that you realize just how much desert they have to spare.

It reminds me of the story of the debate in the House of Lords when one speaker had made a lengthy speech extolling the merits of the Commonwealth, ending up with the peroration: 'All Australia needs is a better type of immigrant and an improved system of irrigation.'

To which an elderly and testy peer replied: 'Good God! You could say the same thing about hell!'

Perth, with Las Vegas, was at times as hot as anywhere I've ever been – shade temperatures of well over 100 degrees Fahrenheit were not that exceptional. But this was a dry heat which is infinitely more supportable than twenty, or even thirty, degrees less with attendant humidity.

The city is quite different from any other part of Australia which I have visited. There is a kind of Victorian charm about it and, to a large extent, its people who seem happily lacking in that 'damn your eyes, I'm as good as you – or, if the truth be known a bloody sight better' attitude which is such a sign of the 'Strine' elsewhere.

I was looking over the list of the entries for the boxing competition when someone told me that the Australian flyweight Eddie Barney was in fact the son of the legendary aborigine fast bowler, Eddie Gilbert. Gilbert was once, inevitably I suppose because of his speed, accused of 'chucking' whereupon he offered to perform with his bowling arm in a splint. His critics pondered this and then decided against it – because the splint might give him additional leverage!

I remember a lovely story of him told me by that king of Australian cricket writers, Jack Fingleton. It was in Jack's playing days and he was at the wicket while Gilbert was producing one of his most witheringly fast spells. Finding himself, fortunately, at the bowler's end Fingleton remarked: 'You're bowling pretty fast today, Eddie,' which was, I understand, one of the masterpieces of understatement of all time.

Gilbert gave him a look of some dissatisfaction and then grunted: 'Then let me take these blurry boots off, Mr Jack, and I show you some *real* fast bowling!'

There were personalities galore at Perth. In some ways the most outstanding was swimmer Dawn Fraser. When she retained her 110 yards freestyle title, with a time of 59·6 secs, she clipped three-tenths of a second off her own world record time, and broke a world record for the *thirty-second* time. How good she was is proved by the fact that over twelve years later in two polls, one restricted to sportswriters and one open to the public, she was voted the No. 1 outstanding sports star, man or woman, in Australia for the past twenty-five years – in both polls.

Brian Kilby, whom I had seen win the European marathon title just under eleven weeks earlier in Belgrade, brought off a wonderful double by taking the Commonwealth marathon as well. He, and all the super-long-distance men, were lucky. The temperature was never more than 65 degrees, whereas five days earlier it had reached 103 degrees – and that was in the shade. What it was like in the sun was impossible to estimate accurately. Because of the way different surfaces reflect the heat there could be a difference of 20 degrees in as many yards. But it had been as high as 148 degrees!

There was one truly wonderful scene in the boxing. In my opinion, and that of the vast majority of other spectators, former Olympic gold medallist, Dick McTaggart, had outpointed Clement Quartey of Ghana in the final of the light-welterweight division. Came the moment of verdict and – they lifted Quartey's hand.

Everyone was astonished but, just as some people can be more equal than others, the most astonished of all was the Ghanaian. For as his arm was raised so he fell forward, stiff as a board, almost like some human woodpecker trying to drive a hole in the canvas with his nose – out like a light, in a dead faint. Despite the enormity of the decision it was one of the funniest things I have ever seen in the ring.

The next stop was Fiji, still to me in those days one of the world's remaining fairly unspoilt places. I think it was on this visit that I was in the Defence Club at Suva talking of this and that with among others members of the Fiji Parliament.

We were chatting idly when, from behind me, in one of the most pronounced 'Oxford accents' I have ever heard came the query: 'And how is the Old Country getting on these days?'

I looked round, expecting to find some relict of Somerset Maugham's

South Seas. Instead I found myself facing one of the most magnificent physical specimens I have ever seen. He looked, although I suppose memory exaggerates, nearer seven than six feet tall with the kind of frame which made his height seem in no way freakish. He was dressed in native fashion, wearing the endemic long grey kilt-like garment.

He was one of the Paramount Chiefs who, even though Fiji was then still a colony, wielded considerable power. I was told that in certain circumstances if a notorious wrongdoer and troublemaker persistently refused to mend his ways one of the Chiefs could order him to be flogged, almost literally to within the proverbial inch of his life. But there was no hint of such violence about this perfectly spoken, handsome giant of a man who, while he drummed on the bar, reminisced, after I had assured him of the well-being of the 'Old Country'.

'Ah! good, good. It's some years since I was back. I remember I was invited to a Burns Night supper. A splendid affair; but later in the evening a gentleman – I think it would be fair to say that he had, perhaps, indulged a little too freely in the, er, "wine of the country" as you might say' – he really *did* talk like that – 'this gentleman came up to me and said: "Wha' are you dewin', yew wi' your great blaaack face, wearrrin' the kilt?" Well, it was a bit difficult for me, you know, because we're rather proud of our own dress, so I was constrained to answer: "Well, sir, I probably have as much Scottish blood in my veins as you have."

'Of course, it wasn't the most tactful answer and it really made him very angry indeed. So much so that he shouted: "Hoo can tha' be? Yew wi' your great blaaack face?" ' (The Chief's imitation of a furious Scot was far better than anything I can convey even approximately phonetically.) 'So finally I was bound to justify my claim to Scottish blood by saying: "Well, sir, the truth of the matter is that my great-grandfather *ate* the first Scottish missionary to come to my country!" '

And he laughed like one of his native volcanoes before they became extinct.

But the most interesting character to me of all those with whom I renewed acquaintanceship in Fiji was a one-time six-round Cockney scrapper, Harry Charman, who had, more than almost anyone I ever met, made a dream come true. He had found the treasure trove which eludes so many men all their lives – a really worth-while job.

Years earlier I had found myself in Suva's bare parish hall, meeting some of the members of Charman's All Races Sports and Social Club. Then I had lost touch with him, until our paths crossed again during the 1956 Melbourne Olympic Games. Now I was again aware of his work in the club which numbered among its members Europeans and part-Europeans, native Fijians and Indians whose families had been there for three and four generations. There were Polynesians, Melanesians, Micronesians and Chinese. Their colours ranged from the yellowish ivory of old piano keys to faces the shade of the black snooker ball. But all had smiling faces – and Harry treated them all the same, patting a head here and smacking a backside there and calling them all impartially 'silly monkeys'.

Everybody agreed on the value of Charman's work but he received only a modest grant for it. Sometimes donations came from places as far apart as Singapore and London – and Harry welcomed them. Eventually he was awarded an MBE. I have known life peerages go to people who have done a great deal less for the human race.

I finally got home as I had, six years earlier after a similar journey, in 1956, in the early hours of the morning of Christmas Eve.

I had travelled 32,000 miles and written, I suppose, about 20,000 words in forty-one days.

Oh well, a few years later Kissinger became a good contender!

South Africa once again hit the unwanted headlines in sport with the affair of Sewsunker 'Papwa' Sewgolum, the South African-born Indian golfer.

Ironically Sewgolum had already twice won the Open championship of Holland – the descendants of which country were largely responsible for his persecution at home. He had played in the British Open at Muirfield – and had called his white caddie 'sir'. He could not read or write and he played golf in the most extraordinary cross-handed fashion, putting his left hand below his right on the club shaft, although he was a right-hander.

When Sewgolum became the first non-white golfer to win the Natal Open championship he had to receive his prize in the pouring rain because club officials ruled, on legal advice, that he could not enter the clubhouse.

Sewgolum returned a 293 total, was given the £400 winner's cheque and a silver trophy outside the clubhouse, while the rest of the prizes were presented later, inside. He had been given special permission to compete in the Natal Open, provided there was no conflict with South Africa's racial laws.

As though to pretend that the 'disaster' had never happened the South African Broadcasting Corporation refused to broadcast a commentary on the tournament, and national news bulletins did not give the result. The director of programmes explained that the Corporation's policy was never to broadcast multi-racial sports meetings and that sport was broadcast for the five [*sic*] different racial groups on their own separate radio services!

The following day P. W. Botha, the South African Minister for Community Development (and what a fine, farcical appointment that must have been!), said in Johannesburg that Sewgolum did not have a permit to take part in the tournament. Quoth he: 'The question of what steps should have been taken is under consideration.'

I commented that this was like pretending the whole thing never took place at all and that South Africa was colour blind.

I made it clear that I would love to debate this nauseating and anachronistic and almost universally detested South African form of 'sportsmanship' with anyone whom the Republic thought would have a chance of holding his own with me. I didn't expect to get many challengers.

I got none.

There was certainly a lot of travelling that month for after flying visits to Copenhagen and Vienna I was off again to Las Vegas to see Dick Tiger who, because of the inactivity of Paul Pender, was generally recognized as world middleweight champion, defend his 'title' against Gene Fullmer, the Mormon.

Tiger had beaten Fullmer previously and I thought he did so clearly once again, but the verdict given was a draw which, although it left Tiger as champion, also left the question of individual superiority in the balance.

If ever I loathed a place it was Las Vegas. I am neither a very respectable nor, certainly, a very religious person but I remember leaving 'Lost Wages' on this occasion at about 7 am on a Sunday.

I walked through the main gambling hall to change some traveller's cheques – it was deliberately arranged that you could not get to the cashier or more importantly, when your pockets were full of money you could not leave him, without passing by the one-armed bandits, the roulette wheels, the blackjack tables and the crap games!

Even at seven o'clock on a Sunday morning there was still a hard core of gamblers in the casino. God knows how long they had been there; certainly none of them had been to bed, the men with their faces the colour of paste, relieved only by black pads under their eyes; the women, their make-up either run or caked, only the eyes feverishly alive and their fingers instinctively curling to grab their winnings or lying like white worms as the croupiers raked in the stakes.

The prostitutes are available morning, noon and night. But only the 'unionized' ones, so to speak. Of course, there are 'freelances' by the score, but they are the ones whom the police will pick up to give an air of spurious respectability to the whole set-up.

I am not, as I've said, either very respectable or religious but, as I turned to take a last look at the gambling room and the zombies in it,

I did have a feeling that Sodom and Gomorrah hadn't unfortunately been completely wiped out.

Cassius Clay continued to be hotter than a stove-lid and in March I was back in New York to see him meet someone who proved to be a much underrated fighter – Doug Jones, who lived in Harlem.

Bobby Gleason, who for years had managed that scourge of British heavyweights, Nino Valdes, was running a gym in the 'Spanish Harlem' section of the city, and he told me that normally he charged 25 cents admission to watch sparring sessions – and was lucky if he took four or five dollars – thirty bob or so. The last time Clay had worked there Gleason had doubled the admission fee – and had got the equivalent of over £50.

Days before the fight Madison Square Garden – that was the old Garden on Eighth Avenue – was sold out for the first time in years. As Clay himself was the first to admit that was entirely due to his appearance; only he put it rather more picturesquely when he said: 'They goin' to have to git a squad of men to scare off all those pigeons that been roostin' for years up in them top seats!'

At 14 st 6½ lb he outweighed the chunky but solid-looking Jones by a stone and half a pound. But rarely was he to have a more difficult fight.

The first round was almost disastrous for him. After the first minute Jones landed a right cross which was just too high to be decisive but which left Clay shaken and open-mouthed. Then a left hook nearly put him through the ropes.

Until the end of the eighth round it was pretty even but although both of them were tiring at the end Clay took the ninth and tenth rounds and deserved the verdict. But not according to some of the crowd, who threw paper cups and peanuts into the ring.

Even then Clay was unperturbed. They had taken the gloves off him and when one peanut landed near him he bent down, picked it off the canvas and chewed it reflectively while they bayed round him, shouting what at first sounded like 'Clay, Clay, Clay' but which eventually made itself heard as 'Fake! Fake! Fake!'

In Los Angeles, a triple title bill had been postponed because of bad weather for nearly a week – which cost the co-promoters Aileen Eaton and George Parnassus £25,000 in forfeited TV fees. Would that the whole thing had been cancelled.

Most of the evening was run-of-the-mill. Luis Rodriguez, far busier inside, convincingly outpointed Emile Griffith for the welterweight title. In the junior welterweight championship Roberto Cruz, of the Philippines, knocked out Battling Torres, from Mexico, in 127 seconds. But those are facts I have to look up in the record books. What will never be expunged from my mind is the featherweight title fight between the holder, Davey Moore, and the Cuban-born 'Sugar' Ramos.

Even for the States it was a bitter, bitter battle. Although both men were well-above-average boxers they elected to stand toe-to-toe for long periods, and the punching was accurate and hurtful.

Past the halfway stage, that's to say at the end of the eighth round, I made Ramos ahead by the slenderest possible margin – a quarter of a point. In the tenth round Moore was beaten to one knee, almost like some reluctant knight awaiting the black accolade of defeat.

He got up before the ex-fighter referee, Frank Latka, could think of a count, but he was driven clear across the ring and finally beaten down incredibly with a left jab – the rarest knockdown punch of all.

Moore seemed almost to shimmy back up, like the rope does in the Indian rope trick. The count was only two but the compulsory count of eight was in force. So he was given an extra six seconds in which to recover while Latka wiped his gloves, and Ramos, in a far corner strained against the invisible bonds of the rules.

The referee waved them together. Ramos came in, a tawny tiger striped with black bars of the bruises he too had suffered. He swirled Moore before him to the ropes near the champion's corner and Moore folded over the middle one like you might hang a wet towel over a clothes line.

With scrupulous fairness, Ramos retreated from his opponent who presented only a defenceless back to him.

Slowly Moore revolved and pulled himself upright. And again the sabre-toothed left was at his face. And again he spun half-circle and folded over the middle rope as the bell sounded. The referee went to Ramos' corner and raised his hand to show that he was the new champion of the world.

Willie Ketchum, Moore's manager, came over to me and said: 'Davey's mouthpiece was split. Then one of his teeth was loosened. He couldn't hold the mouthpiece in. I retired him. No, he ain't going to quit the ring. We've got a return match scheduled.'

The programme went on and then we all drifted back into the stadium building. I saw Willie Ketchum again. And now he said: 'Davey's not too good. He's complaining about a headache.

I said: 'What about that return match?'

Ketchum replied: 'It's inside ninety days.'

Suddenly a man came into the clubhouse and, with the bush telegraph of boxing, you knew he had something vital to say.

'They've packed his head with ice and strapped him on to a stretcher to take him to the hospital,' he gasped.

I went back to my hotel. Then I rang the hospital. I spoke to co-promoter Aileen Eaton. Her voice was like a scratched record: 'Moore's condition is very serious. There's damage to the brain stem. Surgery is unlikely.'

I asked: 'Is there a fifty-fifty . . .'

'No.'

We rang off.

From then on it was the most terrible job in sport and sportswriting. They call it the 'Death Watch'. Newspapers wait for no man, alive or dead. All I could do was type the story in my silent hotel room over-looking the vast city of Los Angeles, sprawled out like a broken egg, with only the shimmering lights alive at half past two in the morning.

At 4 am I walked across the room and dialled Angelus 99131, the number of the hospital, to try to get some reassuring news. The informa-tion was that George Parnassus, the other promoter, was with Moore and that he would phone me back in half an hour.

He did. He was in tears. Davey Moore was unconscious and desper-ately ill. You thought of him in his moments of triumph – against Hogan Bassey and a one-round win over Bobby Neill.

Surely it couldn't happen again. For exactly a year (less two days) earlier the first-ever world champion to die defending his title was Benny Paret. Beaten by Emile Griffith – who had been on this bill, too.

Alas! Tragedy did strike again. After being taken to hospital late on the Thursday night Moore never regained consciousness and died on the Monday. For Ramos this was a particularly ghastly occasion for it was the *second* time that an opponent had died after fighting him. In November 1958, before he had exiled himself from Cuba, Ramos met a Cuban lightweight, José Blanco, whom he knocked out in the eighth round – and the following day Blanco died.

When the news of Moore's death was broken to Ramos he said: 'I'm speechless . . . I don't know what to think.' Then he buried his face in his hands and sobbed.

From the tragedy of the ring in Los Angeles to the fresher breezes of Aintree was a welcome change, and I had only two regrets about the 1963 National. One was that I did not back the winner, Ayala. As an ignoramus on form or the technical side of racing the only time I ever win is with 'hunch' bets and if ever I should have had a 'hunch' it was over that year's winner, 66–1 Ayala.

Luis Ayala of Chile was one of the world's leading lawn-tennis players at about that time; in 1960 he had been ranked No. 7 in the world, had reached the final of the Italian and French championships and I knew him quite well. But not well enough to help myself to a piece of 66–1!

The other regret was for one of the gay Corinthians of our time, John Lawrence, now Lord Oaksey, who was second on Carrickbeg. Rarely have I known such sympathy for a beaten rider as there was for this gallant amateur. Lawrence – not of Arabia, but of Aintree – was sport's new title.

Lawrence and Carrickbeg had negotiated all thirty strength-sapping jumps of the Grand National and with 4 miles and 800 yards unspooled behind them, they still led. Two and a half cricket pitches to go! Could defeat so long delayed be more cruel as Ayala, like some chestnut crocodile, eventually engulfed his rival? Only Devon Loch's last collapse is a sadder cameo in my memory.

But if he could not win Lawrence, who was and is a very fine journalist, achieved the next best thing – one of the very finest descriptions of the race, in the *Sunday Telegraph*, that I have ever read. It used such phrases as '. . . the stands looming ahead like the promised land. It was a sight that has been with me day and night for months – and now, seen in reality, will never, never be forgotten. You can only just hear the crowd, a murmur from afar . . .'

He wrote about that torturing time which racks every imaginative athlete before the moment of truth: 'The hours and minutes before a National are always hell, and today when we left the warm dark haven of the weighing room a cruel wind bit through thin breeches to drive one's heart deeper still into one's boots.'

And then the final agonizing seconds: 'It still seemed possible – but then, like Nemesis, the worst sight I ever expect to see on a racecourse, Ayala's head appeared at my knee.'

As I commented at the time: 'Only a rider could experience things so personally. But it takes a *writer* to convey them so vividly to the vast majority of us who will never straddle anything more obstreperous than an easy chair.'

I remember only one phrase as vivid, also written about the National by another famous amateur, John Hislop, who after finishing third in the greatest steeplechase commented that: 'For ten minutes or so the whole world narrows down to the V between your horse's ears.' I trust I have quoted him correctly, for I am writing from memory.

At a time when English soccer was in one of its all too frequent doldrums a Scotsman, Denis Law, put on one of the greatest solo performances I have ever seen in the FA Cup Final to make the match between Manchester United and Leicester, won by United 3–1, a truly incandescent memory. Law, who had such an uncanny resemblance to Danny Kaye, dominated Wembley's green stage as we had seen the great clown mesmerizing stage and audience at the Palladium.

I commented then that W. S. Gilbert summed it all up (although I

Right The name's the same but — even at Wimbledon — there *is* a difference between two Wilsons.

Below A League of Notions at the 1966 World Cup: myself representing England; Jim Roger (Scotland); Svend Nielsen (Denmark); Sally (USA); Brim Brimble (Jamaica) and Ken Jones (Wales).

Opposite top The greatest of modern men lawn tennis players — Rod Laver at his incomparable best.

Opposite bottom A medal for a mighty player — Margaret (Smith) Court at Wimbledon.

Above Perhaps the greatest sportswoman — in the truest sense of of the word — Britain has ever had: Christine Truman.

Right With Pancho Gonzales, Ken Rosewall was one of the two greatest players of my time who never won Wimbledon — although he got to the final in 1954, 1956, 1970 and 1974!

Above left Basil d'Oliveira who featured in the great apartheid row which culminated in MCC calling off the South African tour.

Above right And now to bowl them out. Sobers, in the same match, playing one of his many other roles.

Left Dennis Lillee, the last of the truly great Australian fast bowlers I saw in my Test-match-watching years — which began in 1921!

Opposite The greatest all-rounder? Gary Sobers in the process of making 150 not out against England in 1973.

Opposite top left Joe Frazier's happiest hour as 'The Greatest', Muhammad Ali/Cassius Clay, becomes 'The Flattest' in the first of their three fights.

Opposite top right The destroyer destroyed. 'Indestructible' Smokin' Joe Frazier loses to George Foreman for the first time.

Opposite bottom George Foreman takes less than a round to defend his title against Joe 'King' Roman in Tokyo.

Right Ali/Clay's greatest achievement – giving George Foreman six years and his first professional beating.

Below Two fighters and a writer. Eddie Thomas, former European champion and sometime manager of ex-world lightweight title holder, Ken Buchanan.

Above left Not ANOTHER bloody Alp! The Winter Olympic Games of 1956 at Cortina d'Ampezzo.

Above right Red Rum who became the first horse ever to win the Grand National three times.

Right Not the grace of his Austrian predecessor Tony Sailer, but oh! the power of France's Jean-Claude Killy winning one of his three gold medals in the Grenoble Winter Olympic Games of 1968.

doubt whether he really had Wembley in mind) when he wrote in *Iolanthe*:

> The Law is the true embodiment
> Of everything that's excellent,
> It has no kind of fault or flaw.

Denis Law had one of those days of which most men can only dream. Never a foot wrong, never a moment when he wasn't the inspiration of Manchester and the threat for Leicester. I am not forgetting that one man can't make a side. I'm not forgetting that soccer is a team game.

I'm not forgetting great colleagues like Crerand, the carpenter of success; Quixall and Giles, valiant and true; Bobby Charlton with a good day; and Noel Cantwell, Captain Courageous.

But this was more of a one-man Cup Final than even Stanley Matthews', previously the greatest solo effort. This was the peely-wally son of Aberdeen fisherfolk who came to Huddersfield in his sixteenth year, bespectacled – with one lens blacked out – so that they thought the scout who had sent him must have been out of his mind.

And this was the kid who, when he played in a car-park kick-about at Huddersfield, showed such amazing talent that the club's then manager, Bill Shankly, called out all the office staff to admire genius.

Huddersfield got him for nothing and sold him to Manchester City for £55,000 – then a British record. Torino grabbed him for £100,000 – cheap at the price. And Manchester – but United this time – got him back for another record, £115,000.

So to the long-awaited meeting between Cassius Clay and Henry Cooper – unique in British boxing for its mixture of pantomime, drama and eventual tragedy. The weigh-in was held at the Palladium, and somewhere Clay had got hold of a stage crown, all gilt, false ermine and fake jewellery, which he eventually wore into the ring. I have it still.

The interest was not so much in the outcome, for no unbiased critic could make Clay anything but an overwhelming favourite. But, master showman that he is, Clay kept on repeating: 'Following all the jive, Cooper will fall in five.' Even at the weigh-in he held up four fingers, like great brown bananas, and a thumb, to indicate how long the fight would last.

My prediction was: 'I reckon he will win, just as he said, in five rounds – although he may have difficulty in making it last that long.' And it is still my opinion that his determination to prove himself not only the master boxer but the supreme prophet of the ring, damn nearly cost him the fight.

The ringside was as star-studded as any I can remember. Politics were represented by Lord Brabazon of Tara and Ernest Marples; there were stars of almost every sport, including what looked like every jockey in the country. Prominent among the show-biz greats were Jack Hylton, Bud Flanagan, Norman Wisdom, Shirley Bassey and, inevitably, Richard Burton and Liz Taylor.

Miss Taylor, a dazzling figure in turquoise, figured in one somewhat hilarious incident on her way to her ringside seat – where later she was to be heard screaming 'Stop it, stop it!' as Cooper looked as though he were going to bleed to death. As Burton and she were pushing their way through the mob one distinctly over-excited Welshman flung his arms round the delectable Elizabeth. Pushing him away, Burton said gruffly: 'Get hold of yourself, man!'

To which the reply came: 'Oh, I've tried *that*, boyo!'

Those people who stayed away missed what turned out to be one of the most pulsating fights I can remember. Cooper never fought better. In the very first round he took Clay out of his stride and if there was a suggestion of hitting on the break – a tactic which by now had been outlawed – by the British champion, Clay in subsequent fights was to bend the rules on more than one occasion.

But by the third round it looked as though everything were going according to plan – Clay's plan. He had opened Cooper's always suspect left eyebrow with a succession of accurate right-hand punches, and I still believe he could have increased the damage so much, either in that round or the next, that the referee would have had to intervene. But Clay had spoken. Five he had said – and five he meant it to be.

And that was where he nearly, oh! so nearly, came unstuck. For, towards the end of the fourth round, with Clay backing towards the ropes, Cooper leaned forward behind the one classic weapon in his armoury – a left hook. Clay, for once, was more or less stationary and the force of the punch, from a man whom he outweighed by over a stone and a half, could be judged by the fact that it took him completely off his feet and threw his 207 lb upwards and backwards into the ropes.

And that was the first great piece of luck he had. For the ropes gave him the leverage to get himself upright halfway before the count had reached the definitive ten. His second immense piece of luck was that coincidentally with his getting to his feet the bell sounded, ending the round.

For if there was one thing Cooper did like a real world champion it was finish off an opponent once he had got him, literally, on the hook.

Instead, the bell having sounded its protective tocsin, Clay's seconds were able to surge into the ring and get their man back to the haven of his corner while Cooper, poor frustrated, half-blinded Cooper, trudged, melancholy, back to his, enough of a fighter to know, I suspect, that his great chance had come and gone – and that he would not much longer be allowed to continue under his handicap of spurting blood.

The crowd had already had enough to drive them half-delirious with excitement for, let's face it, even professional observers like myself had lost their cool when finally, in the best *Boy's Own Paper* tradition, the braggart had been made to bite the dust by the clean-cut – well, very definitely cut! – hero.

Now there were more alarums. For the men working in Clay's corner were indicating to the referee that something was wrong with one of their man's gloves. Inevitably the story was bruited later that a quick-thinking second had deliberately slit the glove, so that Clay should have more than the statutory minute's rest while a new one was procured.

The following year I was to see Angelo Dundee, the genius behind Clay's genius, save a world champion from the very jaws of defeat. But on this occasion my colleague, that outstanding sports photographer Monte Fresco, happened to have taken one shot in the *fourth* round which showed the beginning of the split in Clay's left glove, although I'm not saying that some enthusiastic member of Clay's entourage might not have made it a little worse in the interval; neither, incidentally, am I saying that anyone did.

All I do know is that when the bell finally sent them on their way for the fifth round a great ball of horsehair flew out of the ring and landed between the typewriters of Desmond Hackett and myself. Desmond, in fact, put it in his raincoat pocket – we had all been soaked right at the start of the big fight – and he may have it still.

And that, of course, was virtually that. For another seventy-five seconds Clay continued to pound away at the gash over Cooper's left eye, which gaped like a harlot's mouth: when his left landed there he was virtually punching with bare knuckles. Sickening though Henry's luck was, his injury was even more ghastly and Tommy Little did not act a moment too soon when he ended the bloodbath.

Afterwards a serious Clay summed it up by saying: 'Cooper's not a bum any more. He's the toughest fighter I've ever met and the first to really drop me. I've never been hit so hard by anyone. I underestimated him definitely.'

In later years I talked at length to Henry about Clay whom, of course, he met again with very much the same result. He conceded that Clay was far and away the fastest heavyweight he had ever met but he has always maintained that he was never badly hurt by any of Clay's punches – the cuts notwithstanding.

Among the mob which forced its way into Clay's dressing room after the fight was Jack Nilon, Sonny Liston's adviser, who said: 'I came 3,500 miles to see you tonight. You fought a great fight – and we are ready to take you.' I wonder if that fourth-round knockdown had any influence on Nilon!

Liston and his connections may have been 'ready to take' Clay, but, before that, they had to fulfil quite one of the most senseless return matches ever made, against Floyd Patterson. As though that weren't stupid enough the venue was the detestable Las Vegas and, just to make everything even more bloody, Vegas, when I arrived, was in the throes of a scorching heat wave which made it more than ever like hell.

It was nine o'clock at night when we touched down and I got some idea of the unbelievable heat from the desert when I stood aside to let a lady passenger off first and she stepped on to the platform at the top of the plane's steps, raised her arms like someone faced with a pistol, and sank senseless at my feet.

An airline official scooped her off the metal frying pan on which she had melted, and carried her back into the comparative cool of the plane. I stepped out and recoiled; I thought something was on fire. Out of the darkness, a man said: 'Come on down, bud – it's only 97 degrees. You shoulda been here at two pm. It was 113 then!' Vegas was like a red-hot roulette wheel.

Over at Liston's headquarters, aptly at the Thunderbird, I saw him lose the equivalent of £50 in half as many minutes in the casino there; but, as he stood to make three times £50,000 in about as many seconds in the ring three days from then, £50 was the equivalent of a tip to a taxi-driver.

I think it was then that Liston told the only 'funny' story I ever heard him retail. He grunted: 'There was this guy, see, an' he happened to know how he could get into an ice-box that belonged to the local butcher. So he keeps on gettin' in there an' stealin' steaks an' roasts an' ever'thin'. So fin'ly the butcher he gets wise an' he hides hisself in the ice box. An' when this guy comes reachin' in again – *wham!* – a hand like a black ham made the table shake – 'the butcher he bring the cleaver down on this thief's wrist an' instead of the guy gettin' away with a steak or what-all he only got time to grab his own hand and stuff it up his sleeve an' run for his cotton-pickin' life.

'An' outside he meets someone who knows how he's bin thievin' an' this other guy he asks: "You got yours?" An' the first guy says: "Yeah, I got mine, okay. Now you go in an' get yours." '

And Liston laughs. I don't. I can see him – as the butcher, waiting in the dark for the next victim.

The 'fight' was as pathetic as the first one had been – almost a replica of it, in fact, except that this time Patterson did get up, twice, and the whole thing lasted four seconds longer than the Chicago fiasco – 2 mins 10 secs to be exact.

Life was good at this time for now it was time to break new ground – as far as I was concerned – by going to Nigeria in August 1963 to see Dick Tiger defend his world middleweight title against his most persistent challenger, Gene Fullmer.

The fight was almost unbelievably one-sided. After an even first round Tiger fought like – well, a tiger.

This was the only time he was to defend a world title before his own people and whether in front of that unbelievably colourful crowd – flowing Nigerian robes next to black and white dinner jackets, jewelled headdresses of women next to the nodding ostrich plumes of some of the chiefs – whether all this produced some sort of atavism in Tiger I shall never know, but certainly in the many tough fights of his I saw he never produced the absolute savagery with which he destroyed the over-brave Mormon in front of him.

I have never been happier at a fight than when Fullmer's corner called Jack Hart over to tell him that their man had suffered enough, for I'm sure that if the fight had gone on any longer Fullmer would have suffered permanent injury. As it was he never fought again.

From Ibadan to another colourful occasion – but in what a different setting! – at the Kennington Oval, London, SE11. It was there that the West Indies, winning by eight wickets, took the series against England by three rubbers to one, with one drawn. This is how I described it at the end:

For hours, we had known the West Indians were going to win – and how deservedly. The police had been patrolling the boundary, waving back the kinky-haired, jinking youngsters, the man in the green and yellow Jamaican robe, the scores waving the West Indies flag, the lovely chocolate girls, teetering on their stiletto heels or bounding on their flat soles.

England played it seriously right up to the end. No comic gesture. No batsman going on to bowl. Not this time.

Test veteran Brian Statham, who had taken the new ball only a few overs before, was still hurling them down.

Four runs to win. . . . The West Indian fans surge forward. Go back! Go back! Still two to go. Statham was yet bowling as though it were the last wicket he was aiming for, instead of the West Indies having eight in hand.

It's Statham to Basil Butcher. Butcher pierces the on-side field.

Before Butcher and centurion hero, Conrad Hunte, can get started on the two victory runs, the crowd are across the ground like a sea swamping King Canute.

Let joy be unconfined. This was the moment of truth and happiness for perhaps 10,000 folk who don't have too much colour and gaiety in their day-to-day existence. This was the Caribbean calypso to end all victory marches, dances of triumph, celebration rites and conquering heroes' receptions.

The time came when the cheering had to stop. When the crowd seeped out – out of fairyland and into the tangle and scribble of mean grey streets.

The time when they had to return to conducting buses, sweeping roads, humping baggage and doing all the other day-to-grey-day tasks which enable a man to pay the rent and support his family.

The details are unimportant. This was the day when old men recovered their youth, and young men had a vision. The day when the rainbow of the Caribbean lit up the greyness of Kennington. A day – oh, such a day to remember!

Although it was now the autumn of 1963, 'open' lawn tennis seemed as far away as ever, and it might be interesting for some of today's spoiled babies to realize what they would have been playing for in those days – if they'd been good enough to get into the indoor professional championships at Wembley.

With five past Wimbledon champions Frank Sedgman (1952), Tony Trabert (1955), Lew Hoad (1956–7), Alex Olmedo (1959) and Rod Laver (1961–2) as well as Ken Rosewall, finalist in 1954 and 1956 who now had the beating of all of them, the winner's prize was only £1,000 and a first-round loser got just £50.

Yet less than twelve years later at Wimbledon the men's singles winner was to get £10,000 and a first-round loser £150. It was a measure of the gulf that still yawned between the tiptop amateurs and the established professionals that Laver, who the year before had become only the second player to achieve the 'grand slam', was beaten 6–1, 6–4 in his first singles match at Wembley by Earl Buchholz, the American who, at twenty-three, was two years his junior, but who had been a professional for nearly three years.

On the still amateur side of the game Britain had now reached the Inter-Zone final of the Davis Cup – the furthest we had ever progressed since the war – in which we were to meet the USA.

In the event, however, we went down ingloriously 5–0 to the Americans – Chuck McKinley, Dennis Ralston and Frank Froehling – Mike Sangster having at least one day when he seemed to be disturbed by the noise of the clouds overhead and Billy Knight running out of both ideas and stamina.

Once more I began to feel that the third of my great sporting wishes – to see a British-born fighter win the world heavyweight title, a British runner win an Olympic marathon and Britain regain the Davis Cup – was as far off as ever. . . .

From America came a prediction from Sonny Liston which, in retrospect, had a more than unfortunate connotation. Talking to airmen at a US missile base at Cheyenne, Wyoming, about his forthcoming fight against Cassius Clay, the world champion said: 'If the bout goes past the fifth, I'm going to quit.'

Well, no one can say he didn't warn us.

Some of the abuses rife for so long in American boxing were beginning to filter over here. A Negro middleweight, Bill Pickett, came over, outpointed the useful Harry Scott, and was then left here alone by his manager, Al Rachman, although it was known that he was not due to fight again for another four weeks.

In the meantime he was fined £150 for indecently assaulting and hitting a twelve-year-old girl and ordered to leave Britain within twenty-four hours.

He was sent over here by the well-known New York agent, Lew Burston, who told Barrie Harding, a colleague of mine in New York: 'Some time ago Pickett was put in an institution by his mother because he was an alcoholic. His trouble was that he got into a few fights because he thought that every man he saw was an opponent in the ring. However, they dried him out and he came out apparently completely cured. I saw Pickett in my office before he went to England. He struck me as being polite, courteous and quiet.'

Nevertheless, before sending Pickett to fight Scott, Burston had written to a British promoter saying: 'If his manager, Al Rachman, is with him he will behave himself. In fact, Pickett is rather a nice kid but irresponsible if left alone. That was why trying to send him alone was out of the question.'

How was it that Pickett, with his known record, *was* left alone in Britain?

Early in 1964 two of the most entertaining men who ever wrote about sport – although neither was trammelled by the limitations of insulated sportswriting – wrote their last stories. They were A. J. Liebling, an internationalist but basically as American as Mom's apple pie, and John Macadam, as Scottish as the great amber drink he so appreciated.

One story of John's will stay with me always. It was of the man on his way to borrow a lawn mower from a nearby neighbour. As he walked to the other man's house, he began to think. 'Supposing he doesn't want to lend it to me. Suppose he starts making excuses. Suppose he says I kept it too long the last time I borrowed it. Suppose he's downright insulting.'

By the time he had got to the neighbour's house he had worked himself up into such a state that when the other man answered the bell the would-be borrower, without giving him the time to open his mouth, punched him in the nose and shouted: 'You can keep your bloody lawn mower! *I* don't want it!' and stormed away back to his own home.

Dear John . . .

Now it was time for the 1964 Winter Olympic Games, held in Austria, at Innsbruck and surrounding centres.

They had started with a tragedy when, in the new event of tobogganing or 'lugeing', a naturalized Pole, Kazim Skrzypecki, a member of the British team, died in the Innsbruck hospital.

When trying, with a complete lack of success, to do something to help Skrzypecki's widow, I discovered that there was no insurance covering the men and women trying to bring honour to the country of their birth – or adoption. I protested about this, and insurance was later introduced.

The start of the Winter Olympic Games was characterized by something which so often seems to happen to a venue once it is chosen for the Games – lack of snow. At Innsbruck I was told that the conditions, for the time of year, were the worst for shortage of snow since 1906!

From a British point of view we did outstandingly well in winning a gold medal in the two-man bobsleigh event, our team comprising twenty-seven-year-old Tony Nash, a bespectacled company director who ran an engineering business with his uncle in Buckinghamshire, and Captain the Hon. Robin Dixon of the Grenadier Guards, a year older.

These were only the fourth gold medal awards achieved by Britain up to that time. Yet we might never have won at Innsbruck at all had it not been for an example of outstanding sportsmanship displayed by one of the very experienced Italian riders, Eugenio Monti, during the two preliminary runs.

This was what Nash, still sweating from the jolting second run – from my one unforgettable experience I know that it's like being a piece of ice in a cocktail shaker – told me: 'At the end of our first run we discovered we'd broken a back axle bolt. We were looking desperately for another one. But, as soon as he heard about it Monti, who had completed his second run, took one out of his bob and sent it up to the start so that we could race again.'

To help the one foreign entry who had a real chance of beating you seemed to me the quintessence of what sport should be, but alas so seldom is, all about, and I was glad to nominate the Italians for a newly created international award for sportsmanship which, I believe, they received.

Undoubtedly the outstanding performer at Innsbruck was the Russian woman speed-skater Lidija Skoblikova who took all four medals (for the 500, 1,000, 1,500 and 3,000 metres) in this event. This was a titanic performance when you equate it, for instance, with a runner winning every event from a little over a quarter of a mile to nearly two miles. And the fact that many people felt that too many medals were being awarded for one branch of sport – as is the case with gymnastics in the Summer Games – did not detract from the brilliance of the Russian star.

Lidija, with whom I had a long talk after her fourth victory, was someone whom you could really describe as being 'two-faced' without intending any insult. She was twenty-four and blonde with blue eyes – but they were ice-blue; she had two most beguiling dimples – but set them off with a chin like the prow of an ice-breaker . . . instead of a mere ice-skater!

But for me, the 'Girl of the Games' was Marielle Goitschel, at eighteen the younger by a year of two French sisters who filled the top places in the slalom and giant slalom events, her older sister, Christine, winning the slalom with Marielle second, and the positions being exactly reversed in the giant slalom.

Although she could finish only tenth in the downhill – because of a leg broken in the past this was the event of the three she most disliked – her time was still good enough to give her the overall Alpine ski championship.

This youngster was the daughter of a professional footballer and, with Christine specializing in cooking, she did much of the book-keeping in her parents' hotel at Val d'Isère, where so many British Olympic skiers trained. The strongly-built Marielle struck at least one doughty blow for the freedom of the individual. As I wrote at the time: 'The trouble is that the vast majority of police, attendants and Army personnel seem to think that they are little Hitlers – and it's scant comfort to remember that Adolf Schickelgruber had his origins in this country!'

But stronger than my words was Marielle's action after one of these bully-boys assaulted her quite small coach, who was accompanying her when she was due to be presented with her gold medal. With the innocent air of someone who might say: 'Sorry, me 'and slipped', she dealt him a fourpenny one just where it was likely to do him the least possible good for, one hoped, a long time. Then, most demurely, she accepted her medal. I'd have liked to have given her another one!

Although it is only realistic to acknowledge that our competitors in the skiing events stand little or no chance of getting among the medals because of geographical and climatic conditions, it was rather hard to wave the Union Jack over-enthusiastically when it came to an examination of the *British* girls' team.

Divina Galica was the daughter of a Polish officer; Jane Gissing lived in Switzerland; Wendy Farrington lived in Monte Carlo and rarely even visited Britain; the father of the British champion, Anna Asheshow, was a naturalized Russian.

To cap it all the team manager, Sue Holmes, was German-born and her address was given in the official British handbook as *Zeppelin* Allee, Frankfurt, Germany! It all seemed to be a case of 'Land of Hope and Glory . . . wider still and wider shall thy bounds be set . . .'

The one event which particularly caught my imagination was the ski-jumping, culmination of the Winter Games – as the marathon is of the summer Olympics. I had seen ski-jumping before but the event on the slope overlooking Innsbruck impressed me particularly – perhaps not least because of the magnificent use of one of the truly great ski-jump pictures I have ever seen which Don Bate, now assistant editor in charge of sport on the *Mirror*, made – as a superb make-up man – to illustrate my final article from Austria.

In passing, never trust a journalist who boasts: 'I don't need make-up.' Make-up – or the attractive layout of a page – is as essential to a newspaperman as it is to the most beautiful woman.

This is what the ski-jumping was like at Innsbruck.

The tens upon tens of thousands thronging the slopes of Bergisel watched as fifty-two heroes from fifteen nations hurled themselves off a platform over 480 ft high, down a precipitous slope, and then took off at some 60 mph to sail for slightly over three seconds through the air. They flew – birds without wings, men without fear – at over 67 mph and finally landed 313 ft away from the spot where they had lost contact with the ground.

The dangers to a ski-jumper are fog and wind: jumping into fog is like being a pilot without instruments flying blind. Wind caused one or two brief delays even at Innsbruck when conditions were generally fine.

I enjoyed Innsbruck; but, of course, any connection between the Winter Games and amateurism wasn't so much tenuous as coincidental. Within a week of the Winter Olympics the three winners of the men's Alpine events – the downhill, giant slalom and slalom – Egon Zimmermann of Austria, François Bonlieu of France and another Austrian Josef Stiegler (nicknamed 'Pepi'), had already turned professional and were due to race in Toronto on 23 February – in the same month that they had won their Olympic gold medals!

A week after returning from Innsbruck it was bags-packed-and-typewriter-at-the-ready for the trip to Miami Beach to see Sonny Liston defend the world heavyweight title against the man who still called himself Cassius Clay.

From the start this was, in many ways, the zaniest heavyweight championship I had ever covered. My first view of Clay was in the gym surrounded by the four Beatles, all prostrate in the sparring ring at the feet of the only man in the world who was probably a greater show-off than they were.

However, perhaps they were not over-impressed because when Ringo Starr was asked by American boxing writers who he thought would win between Liston and Clay he answered: 'I'll let you know when I get outside this gym!'

But far more interesting in the long run was the announcement on the same day by Clay's father that Cassius was a member of the Black Muslims. To a younger generation, which has grown up with that knowledge, this may not seem particularly sensational, but in those days Clay wasn't quite the worldwide figure he subsequently became and, outside the USA, the Black Muslims were virtually unknown.

I had seen garish posters advertising the sect and its leader, Elijah Muhammad, pasted up in New York and one or two of the other larger American cities but frankly, to an outsider, it seemed just another quasi-religious organization like previous cults from the hot-gospelling of Aimée Semple McPherson in California to Father Divine's 'angels' in Harlem and the vicious fascism of Father Coughlin.

All anyone could tell you about the Muslims – except the members themselves, and they were keeping pretty mumchance at the time – was that they comprised a sect which wanted to operate apartheid in reverse and set up an independent enclave within the United States. People who loathed and feared the Muslims said they were the Ku Klux Klan in black.

Clearly membership of a suspect group was not going to help Clay's image in boxing, run traditionally by whites, even if the blacks now made up the majority of the successful fighters. It was very difficult to get any statement about the Muslims themselves, whether Clay was in fact a member and, particularly, what role an extremely sinister-looking character, Malcolm X, played in the whole set-up. Some people said it was he who had inducted Clay into the sect; others that the youngster had been influenced by a speech he had heard made in New York's Columbus Circle – something like Speakers' Corner in London's Hyde Park.

In those far-off days no one quite understood what the idea of these black revolutionaries was in substituting 'X' for their surname until it was pointed out that it would not be exactly healthy for them to be publicized individually; so they kept their first names and tacked on an anonymous 'X'. In Malcolm's case it seemed only to be a question of 'X' marking the spot, for it was not long before he met death in as violent a way as he had lived.

He was, of course, Clay's biggest booster, but everyone at Miami Beach was very cagey about whether he would be allowed to buy his way into the £90-a-seat inner circle of privileged ringsiders. Not long before he had made a particularly shocking remark about President Kennedy's assassination which brought the movement so much adverse and unwanted publicity that Elijah Muhammad had forbidden him to make any public statements.

The only time, years later, after Malcom X had been shot, that I saw Clay genuinely angry as opposed to the synthetic rages which he can turn on and off to order, was when I asked him what had really happened to his erstwhile friend – and was it true that he had been killed by Black Muslims?

Clay glared at me and then rasped: 'He went against Elijah Muhammad' – as though that explained everything.

On top of all this there was the question of when Clay would have to go into the armed services. He had already taken his medical examination, preparatory to being called up, and there was normally a four-month delay before a recruit was assigned to the branch of the service where he was needed.

Even the most routine questions suddenly assumed a new and twisted significance.

For instance, after that wonderful trainer and psychologist, Angelo Dundee, had been asked what his charge was going to eat on the morning of the fight, he replied that his man needed a lot of fuel and that he would have five poached eggs, rye toast and tea with lemon.

With elaborate unconcern the questioner asked if Clay would not be eating any bacon with his eggs. Angelo, giving a wry smile – to match the fighter's toast! – replied that Clay hated bacon or any kind of pork.

The hidden barb in the question was, of course, that for the Black Muslims bacon or any kind of pig product is forbidden food.

A cynic remarked that with Liston's past reputation and the one Clay was rapidly earning boxing history would be made when *both* men were booed into the ring. Yet the odds remained solidly at 7–1 on Liston – the longest since Floyd Patterson had fought Brian London.

In case, with thirteen years' hindsight, you think that we were all mad, let me take you to one of Liston's last training work-outs at the Surfside Civic Centre.

'Formidable, menacing, horrifying, scarifying, choose your own adjective. The man is like something that has strayed out of a horror movie. Sonny Liston, the human hammer.' Such was my description of him then. His most spectacular act of all was when his trainer, Willie Reddish (a useful heavyweight of the Joe Louis era now blown up to over seventeen stone), took the $12\frac{1}{2}$ lb medicine ball. From two or three yards he threw it with all his strength at Liston's mighty midriff; incredibly after every three or four throws the champion's stomach muscles so distorted the ball that Reddish had to knead it back into shape. And Liston never took a backward step, gasped at the impact or even blinked.

I go into such detail to prove that, whatever else was adrift, Liston was in as good physical shape as human hands and his own apparent determination could get him. His record was nearly perfect.

Yet there was one man, better qualified than any of us, who wasn't so impressed with the lowering giant – Eddie Machen, the last man to go the limit of twelve rounds with him, three and a half years earlier.

At Liston's last-but-one workout Machen caused a flare-up by suggesting that the champion was disinclined to meet him again. 'I had no respect for him. I kept asking him: "Where's that big punch?" and calling him names.' Machen said that Liston could not handle name-calling in the ring and he added: 'He isn't used to being called names and no one can calm him down either. The trainers can't say: "Look, Sonny, cool it," because he won't listen to them.

'I talked to Liston a lot when I fought him. I cursed him every time I got a chance. It kept him confused. It kept him from concentrating. He ain't the smartest guy in the world, you know. He still hasn't forgotten.'

Clay turned the weigh-in into a pantomime. Subsequently we have learned to regard these outbursts as all part of the psychological warfare which Clay has always used so brilliantly against a variety of opponents, but at the time everyone there was convinced that he was teetering on the verge of insanity.

Screaming, 'Tonight I'll upset the whole world', he was led away to strip and the tension mounted and the minutes lengthened while Liston refused to take his place on the weighing-in platform until Clay had reappeared.

When the two men finally came within a few yards of each other, under an operating-theatre bank of lights and a battery of microphones, Clay seized his opportunity.

Shrieking: 'This is *my* show,' he fought and wrestled with police and handlers, including Sugar Ray Robinson, seemingly determined to get at Liston. Bill Faversham, representing the board of millionaires then behind Clay, who normally looked rather like an English country squire, was sweating like a shower bath and seemed on the verge of a stroke.

Clay was screaming: 'Someone's gonna die at the ringside tonight,' and then to Liston: 'Hey, chump, you haven't fought anyone good yet. I'll eat you up tonight.'

On and on went the insults, the shrieking and the struggling, so that a man next to me said: 'It's all very well having a physical examination, but what this guy needs is a mental one.' I couldn't have agreed more and, if we were all wrong, we were in good company, for the Boxing Commission's chief physician, Dr Alexander Robbins, after examining Clay said: 'This is a man who is scared to death. He is living in mortal fear. He is emotionally unbalanced and burning energy at a furious rate.'

The Miami Beach Boxing Commission, when they had partly recovered themselves, fined Clay $2,500 – then roughly £890 – for 'putting on an act', with the money to go to charity. At least one British newspaperman wanted the doctor, on the basis of what he had said, to call the fight off at the last moment as it might prove fatal to Clay.

What happened in the ring that night I shall never properly understand – and the Lord knows I've been over it in my mind times without number.

Clay boxed brilliantly. He cut Liston – as he was to rip and slash so many more opponents later – under the left eye in the third round and, at last, we knew that 'Old Stoneface' was made of flesh and blood as a scarlet ribbon unspooled down his cheek.

But according to Angelo Dundee: 'Cassius said to me at the end of the fourth round: "Cut the gloves off." But I said: "Come on, this is the big apple, don't louse it up!"'

Personally I got the impression that it was after the fifth round that Clay, having been driven into the ropes with a series of eviscerating body blows, after blinking frantically at the beginning of the round, had wanted to surrender. Certainly later the referee, Barney Felix, indicated that it had been in his mind to disqualify Clay for slowness in answering the bell for the start of the round.

He seemed to be temporarily blinded, much as Rocky Marciano had been in his first fight with Jersey Joe Walcott, and both Marciano's and Clay's corners claimed that some ointment administered to their opponent's cuts had, in fact, got into their own man's eyes. But even under that handicap Clay didn't forget to box and, once, to bewilder his man by leaning forward, placing his left hand on the big man's head, long left arm extended, so keeping Liston out of distance.

Came the bell for the seventh round . . . but cometh the hour no cometh the man. Liston had quit stone cold in his corner!

Despite Clay leaping around the ring like a madman – with some justification now – shouting 'I *am* the greatest. I *am*. Will you all admit it now?' it took minutes for what had happened to sink in properly.

True there were bumps, lumps and cuts on Liston's face. But I had seen almost all the other ten world champions whom I had previously, at one time or another, watched in a worse state at the end of a fight, either as winners or losers. Liston just sat there like some chipped and age-encrusted statue – at times during the fight he had looked at least five years older than his purported thirty-one years – and let the championship drift into limbo.

Later he was to claim (or it was claimed for him) that at the end of the first round he was feeling pain in his left shoulder and then, as the dramatic story continued, a sense of paralysis crept down his left arm to his hand and eventually he had no feeling in his hand at all. His mentor, Jack Nilon, and his trainer, Willie Reddish, stopped the fight before his own physician, Dr Bennett, advised that he should not continue.

That was the story – and I couldn't believe it then and I still don't believe it now, these many years later. How close the fight still was came in the disclosure of the score-cards of the referee and the two judges. The referee, Barney Felix, scoring on a ten-point-a-round system, made it dead level at 57 points to each man. Judge William 'Bunny' Lovett scored in 58 to 56 in Liston's favour, Judge Gus Jacobson had it 59 to 56 to Clay. I made Liston ahead by three rounds to two and, using the scoring system then in force in Britain, by $29\frac{1}{2}$ points to $29\frac{1}{4}$.

When he was asked later how he felt about losing his title, Liston said: 'Like I did when the President got shot. I never wanted to quit, I wanted to go on, just as I did in 1954 when Marty Marshall broke my jaw.'

It was his advisers, he said, who had insisted upon his retiring. He thought he injured his shoulder when he missed with a left hook in the first round. He said: 'I couldn't feel anything. It was as though my hand had turned to water.'

I'm sorry. I still don't believe it. One of the last punches I remember in the fight was Liston throwing a left hook which, at least, proved that his injury had not completely incapacitated him – the reason that the Boxing Commission doctor, Alexander Robbins, had given for believing the fight should have been stopped as the injury prevented Liston from defending himself. And since when had Liston's handlers made the decisions for him? – particularly one as important as giving away the world championship!

Was it the classic case of the bully meeting an opponent who refused to be intimidated and turning coward? That Liston *was* a bully is scarcely beyond dispute: his treatment of sparring partners in the ring and his strike-breaking proclivities outside it, leave that in little doubt. But, in such good company as Charles Lamb, I beg leave to doubt whether a bully is always a coward.

I think Eddie Machen may well have been right and the arrogant insolence of Clay had thrown him off beam and left him confused – 'He ain't the smartest guy in the world, you know.' But even so, for someone who had had so little to throw away so much . . .?

There were the usual stories of a 'fix'; that Liston had been bribed to lie down, or that he had bet such an extravagant sum on Clay, at the prevailing odds of 7–1, that it paid him better to lose than to win, and that he could regain the championship in a return match.

I discount both those theories completely. Not because of an ingenuous belief in Liston's honesty but in the first place how much you would have to give the holder of the world heavyweight title, the richest prize in sport, to give it up? And there had been plenty of examples from past boxing history where a victorious champion avoided, or at any rate for a long time evaded, the necessity of giving the previous title-holder a second bite at the luscious cherry.

As for the betting theory, that is even more easily discredited. Even with odds of 7–1 Liston would have needed to have something like $300,000 to make it really worth his while to lose.

Now betting on that scale can be conducted in the States through only one place – Las Vegas. And that amount of money involved, even if it were split into a number of smaller bets – which would have increased the number of people in on the 'fix' and, therefore, the risk of discovery – would have had the effect of bringing the odds down with a rush.

No, those theories simply don't hold water – or, knowing Liston and his associates, vodka.

There is one rumour which persisted and which is, of course, completely uncheckable. That is that the 'hatchetmen' of the Black Muslims, known as the 'Fruit of Islam' (rather unfortunately I always felt since 'fruit' in the States has the same connotation as 'queer' in Britain), had paid a visit to Liston and had shown him convincing reasons – most of them .45 calibre ones developed from Samuel Colt's original design – suggesting that it would prolong his health if he were to see reason and cede the victory to the latest recruit to the cohorts of Elijah Muhammad.

If such an idea seems preposterous in Britain – and these days with the recollection of such ripe characters as the Krays still reasonably recent, if not fresh, in our memories, does it? – it certainly wouldn't have been beyond the bounds of belief for someone like Liston with his background of violence and his association with gangsters.

As I've said, the story defies proof or disproof. I give it as one of the few possible explanations of one of the most baffling events I have ever witnessed in sport, and I must add that it is not a solution which was proffered at the time.

There were two footnotes to the whole affair. Flying from Miami up to New York one of my co-passengers was the man then chiefly the architect of the transformation from Cassius Clay to Muhammad Ali – one-man Ton-Ton Macoute, Malcolm X.

He refused to speak to anyone, either on the plane or when we landed, and he had a look of malevolent disdain for the 'common herd' which I have rarely seen equalled and never surpassed. All at once the old phrase 'Such men are dangerous' had a new connotation of more modern deadliness.

256

Meanwhile, evidence was given to a Senate probe committee by Jack Nilon, adviser to Liston. He claimed that Liston had not trained properly for the Clay fight – that had *not* been my impression – believing that he could not be beaten. Finally the Senate sub-committee investigating the circumstances wound up its hearings with Senator Philip A. Hart of Michigan stating that Congress wanted to give boxing 'this apparent last chance to survive'.

The National that year gave me an experience which was unique and which I hope remains that way. The *Sunday Mirror* had always chartered a small plane with which to get the pictures back to London as expeditiously as possible after the big race. I had used it for years and, on this occasion, one of my fellow-passengers was 'Teasy-Weasy' Raymond, the fashionable hairdresser and owner of Ayala, the previous year's winner, and of the 1976 winner, Rag Trade.

There were quite a few small charter planes, and when I got to Aintree I think it was Ron Clare, a talented newspaperman and an old friend from wartime days, who greeted me with: 'My God! Am I glad to see you!' Although it was some time since we'd met I couldn't understand his intensity until he asked: 'Haven't you heard? I was listening to a transistor radio in the Press room and it was on the BBC news. A charter plane crashed quite near the course and I was afraid you were on it; everyone was killed.'

It was an out-of-character role for me to have to phone Sally to tell her that the news had nothing to do with me! But in fact it nearly drove me frantic. In that slum of a racecourse (on which is run the world's greatest steeplechase), it is virtually impossible to get to a telephone.

Finally I got through and, mercifully, I had been forestalled by one of the best all-rounders in sport and one of the most generous colleagues I ever worked with, George Harley, who had guessed what Sally might have been imagining and had contacted the BBC, whose first flash had given only the news that there had been a crash, to find out if any names were yet known.

One of the victims was writer Nancy Spain who was, I think, flying to Aintree to do a story for the *News of the World*.

It was altogether a sad National. For Paddy Farrell the end of the race came when he was left lying at the foot of 'The Chair' with his spine broken, while Tim Brookshaw, crippled by the sometimes savage sport he loved, was watching from a wheelchair.

In the way that only at Aintree does a close finish become a minor tragedy, Purple Silk was beaten half a length by Team Spirit.

My next trip, in May 1964, was really one to remember – to Accra, the capital of Ghana, for a world featherweight title fight between Sugar

Ramos, the self-exiled Cuban whom I had seen win the world championship so tragically at Los Angeles, when Davey Moore had died after yielding the nine-stone crown to him, and Floyd Robertson, the Ghanaian, whom I had seen on several occasions when he had been based for a long time in Belfast.

Another win for Ramos? He is sure. He is always sure of winning. Why not? No one has ever beaten him in forty-eight bouts. That was the way I felt. Against Ramos' 'perfect' record Robertson had had thirty-five fights of which he had lost eight and drawn four more. Additionally the class of opponents he had met did not compare with those whom Ramos had beaten. I thought Robertson was bound to lose, very possibly inside the distance.

For the first half of the fight it looked as though Ramos and I had been right. One right cross from him sliced Robertson's left cheek almost to the bone. And then, from the middle of the eighth round, Ramos started to wilt and, following the seventh, he did not win a single round.

He looked as though he were going down in the twelfth and in the thirteenth he *did* go down. He tottered up but he had been unable to close his mouth from the middle of the round. His jaw looked to be broken. I described the finish: 'The fourteenth was murder – even from outside the ring. The Ghanaian was fighting the fight of his – or anyone else's – life. I cannot remember a more wickedly punishing fight, and at the bell both men were nearly out. Ramos because of what had been done to him. Robertson because of what he had done.'

I had not the slighest doubt that Robertson had won but while I was waiting for what seemed the inevitable verdict I added up my score-card. I had given eight rounds to Robertson, five to Ramos, with two even. Some of the rounds the Ghanaian had won had been by bigger margins than any of Ramos'.

Suddenly the referee, Jack Hart, leaned over the ropes and said to me: 'The blankers have given it to Ramos!' I gaped at him foolishly and he said: 'Lassman and Velazquez' – the American and Mexican judges – 'have given it to Ramos; my decision was for Robertson.'

All at once I thought how ironic it was that three and a half years earlier I had attacked Jack Hart bitterly for giving the verdict to Robertson against Percy Lewis for the Commonwealth title, and now, thousands of miles from home, we were both going to be attacked because of a verdict in the infinitely more important championship of the world.

The roar that went up as it seemed, from Hart's decision, that Robertson had won, gave us a few extra, precious seconds to get to a kind of haven before the crowd slowly, unbelievingly, realized that a majority verdict of the two judges over the referee had robbed them of having the first-ever world champion produced by their nation.

When they *did* realize it, it was not healthy to be white. There was one piece of bravery from a youngster I shall never forget. I went first to Robertson's dressing room to commiserate with him. When I left a man came for me in a way I have never been attacked before. His fingers were crooked like black meat hooks, seeking to pluck at my eyes. I should have known how to deal with an orthodox attack – whether successfully or not is a different matter – but this horrible form of would-be mutilation caught me off-guard, and had it not been for the intervention of a young Ghanaian, who had been allotted to me as my chauffeur while I was in Accra, I could have lost my eyes.

I'll never forget that youngster. He spoke tolerable English and he had understood how outraged I had been at the unfairness of the verdict. He jumped between my attacker and myself and explained that not only was I not one of the judges but that I disagreed with their decision as much as the man who wanted to blind me.

However, that wily operator Angelo Dundee, who had been in Ramos' corner, wisely decided that Accra was no longer any place for the fighter – or for him. So, in the very early hours of the morning, the two of them arrived at the airport for the only piece of light relief this fight produced. Having made sure that he was in the international section – he sure as hell didn't want any domestic flights within Ghana – Dundee went up to the desk and asked for two single tickets on the next plane.

'Yes, sir,' said the clerk. 'Where to, please?'

To which the bold Angelo made the only perfect answer, in the circumstances. 'Who cares?' he asked defiantly.

I believe they ended up in Spain, which at least had the advantage, for Ramos, of speaking the same language as he did.

But all that was later. We were still immured in that damn clubhouse . . . Promoter Jack Solomons, myself and various other characters including a couple without whom I could have very well done – the two judges! It was really difficult not to be extremely rude to the two. At least it would have been difficult for some people. For others it was just impossible. I was among the second group.

So there we were, in the dressing room now vacated by Ramos, locked in for our own protection.

In fact when an immaculate Army officer returned and said he thought it would be all right if we now left, under escort, I demurred. I suggested, I'm afraid with some warmth, that it would be even better if we left in separate groups – and that I didn't want to be in the same one as the two judges.

I left Accra on the Monday via Sabena, the Belgian airline which was then servicing Ghana.

As we arrived at the approaches to the airport there was a long line of traffic. I asked my youngster – to whom I had given all my remaining Ghanaian money, not that it was enough – to get out and discover what was going on.

He came back and, I suspect, not without a touch of the kind of relish which doubles up schoolboys when someone sits down where the chair isn't, he announced that all the cars were being searched for bombs, as it was suspected that the two offending judges were going to be aboard the same plane as I was catching and the authorities wanted to take every precaution. . . . Sky-jackers weren't the commonplace characters they have subsequently become, but bombs – thank you, very much!

Fortunately, it had been arranged that I should make a 'black' – a carbon copy – of my story for the *Mirror* available for the *Daily Graphic*, the paper with the largest sale in Ghana. Therefore my views on the verdict and who, in my opinion, had justly won the title, were available to anyone who had twopence – and thought it was worth spending on the paper.

Before we left the Chairman of the Ghana Boxing Authority had announced: 'The GBA has had a meeting and decided to reverse the decision, thus making Floyd Robertson the world champion. We shall make an official protest to the World Boxing Association. We also intend to ask all the African nations to recognize Robertson as world champion.'

I sympathized wholeheartedly with every Ghanaian who felt, as I did, that Robertson was robbed. But I couldn't and can't support the idea that you can reverse an official verdict because you don't agree with it. That way anarchy lies. The supreme irony then was that if the GBA protested to the so-called World Boxing Association, their protest would to to Ed Lassman, President of the WBA – and one of the judges who voted against Robertson! If they also protested to the World Boxing Council, their communication would probably go through the hands of Ramon Velazquez, the secretary-general of the WBC – and the other judge who voted against Robertson.

What chance did they have?

That gruelling fight, incidentally, just about finished both Ramos and Robertson as top-class boxers. In his very next fight Ramos lost his world title, inside the distance, to Vicente Saldivar, and then after a sprinkling of unimportant bouts he was beaten twice running inside the distance by Carlos Ortiz.

Robertson's subsequent career was even more brief. In 1965 he had just one fight, a victory in England. Then in 1966 he went to Mexico and was beaten, again for the world title, but this time without any controversy as he failed to last two rounds against Saldivar.

My next trip, in the spring of 1964, was a much shorter one, to Paris, to see a very different – but equally memorable – conflict, the final of the women's singles in the French championships between the Brazilian ballerina, Maria Bueno, and the champion of the Australian outback, Maggie Smith, as she then was.

The match had one of the most extraordinary starts I can ever recall in championship lawn tennis. When the two of them got to the umpire's chair Margaret discovered that she had come on to court without any rackets. It was almost as embarrassing if not, fortunately, so revealing as the time I remember a very nervous novice fighter at the old 'Ring', Blackfriars, coming into the ring, taking off his robe and discovering he had forgotten to put on his shorts!

How nervous Miss Smith was – at her peak this was her only but costly, deficiency – was shown when she started the match with three double faults and was then easily passed to lose the first game to love having, to all intents and purposes not laid an effective racket on the ball.

But gradually the tenseness dissolved and Margaret sailed home to victory like some great galleon under full sail. On what I saw that day I was convinced that the Australian belonged among the gallery of the 'greats', for she managed to reach balls to which no other woman in the world could have got her racket – and not only reach them but make winners from them.

It proved a theory, not happily but conclusively as far as I was concerned, that power will always overcome the most superb grace and skill if it is relentlessly applied. La Bueno did not play badly; she produced shots which would have beaten any other girl in the world apart from the one across the net from her, but after winning the first set she could only scrape three more games in the match.

A non-vintage Wimbledon came to a climax with yet another meeting between the reigning champion, Margaret Smith, and Maria Bueno – and this time the butterfly beat the battering ram!

It was a good final and perhaps the fractional difference between the two, that day, was that I can't remember La Bueno missing a smash or an overhead shot, so that even if she did not make an outright winner her stroke was good enough to keep her in a dominating position in the rally.

The same old weary, dreary farce continued when, at the meeting of the International Lawn Tennis Federation, Britain failed yet again to achieve 'open' tournaments. Among the nations who voted against our 'open' proposals were Australia, the United States, the East European Communist countries and West Germany.

As ever, that fine man, Herman David, chairman of the All England Club and the Wimbledon Management Committee, was to the fore when he said: 'They should all be players. If that designation was adopted open tournaments would follow naturally. It is nowadays very hard to distinguish between the professional and the amateur.'

At Wembley, in a different class of lawn tennis, thirty-six-year-old Pancho Gonzales played one of the greatest best-of-three-sets matches I have ever seen to beat Lew Hoad, now twenty-nine, 0–6, 6–4, 9–7 – and that was on the same night after, in two of those artificial 'professional set' matches, Gonzales had beaten Rod Laver 8–5 and Hoad had defeated Rosewall 8–1.

But still they were prevented from taking part in any of the world's great international championships!

However, if lawn tennis was impoverished – because of the administrators – cricket was dying of sleepy-sickness, transmitted by the players and caught by the spectators.

I've seen some uncommon dull Test matches in my time but the innings which remains for me the greatest bore I have seen in over fifty years as an intermittent spectator belonged to Bobby Simpson, the Australian captain, who batted for nearly twelve and three-quarter hours for 311 runs. Australia scored 656 for eight declared and England, to prove I suppose that anyone they could bore we could bore if not better then as well, drummed up 611.

Of course the match was drawn – it should have been hanged and quartered as well as drawn – and, of course, as Simpson had very clearly known, Australia retained the Ashes. The sackcloth was reserved for the spectators.

Another current world champion arrived in Britain around this time, Emile Griffith, who was going to put up his welterweight crown for Brian Curvis to tilt at. Griffith was a considerably better than average champion, but what really added to the gaiety of life were his two managers, Irish-American Gil Clancy and Jewish-American milliner, Howie Albert.

Talking about Albert, Griffith said: 'I was working for him in his millinery business and I was stripped down to the waist one day and he says: "Have you ever done any fightin'?" And I says: "You crazy or sump'n, boss? I don't get myself in no trouble." And he says "Well . . ." and the next thing you know I'm a pro fighter.'

Of Griffith, Albert said: 'Does he have any trouble making the weight? Of course not. The last time we fought, we only had to cut two of his toes off to get him down to the limit, and this time we plan to take off his ears!'

I thought Curvis might make some sort of a showing in the first world championship fight to be held in Britain for over three years – in my preliminary story on the fight I made him no worse than a 13–8 underdog.

It was much more one-sided than that for, on my score-card, I made it ten rounds to Griffith, two to Curvis and three even.

Before the two men had left the ring, the promoter, Jack Solomons, leaned over the ropes to tell me: 'Curvis admits he was beaten by a better man.'

What else could he say? But I was glad he *did* say it.

A considerably happier confrontation, at Wembley, was the final of the indoor professional lawn tennis championships between Rod Laver and Ken Rosewall.

Normally speaking it is only in certain sports that you can pinpoint the end of an era and the beginning of a new reign. Lawn tennis is not usually among these sports but, at the end of this match I felt as certain that Laver was set to succeed Rosewall who, in turn, had superseded Gonzales, as though he had literally knocked him out – although the match could not have been closer.

This was how it felt to me at the time:

Never, never have I seen a better *match* than the one which lasted from Saturday night to early Sunday morning, and in which Laver beat Rosewall 7–5, 4–6, 5–7, 8–6, 8–6.

In the end, with the score 30–all in the sixty-second game, with Rosewall serving, one net-cord broke his rhythm and gave Laver match point.

And that, in sober truth – *one net-cord* – was all that was between them in two hours forty minutes of superlative, sporting combat in which Laver won thirty-two games to Rosewall's thirty with, I'm sure, the points relatively as close.

The match was great . . . and, as such, a good omen for the Tokyo Olympic Games of 1964 which were now only a few weeks away.

There was the inevitable preface to the Games with a series of political quarrels involving the indefinite suspension of South Africa – already barred from the Games – by FIFA, the world-governing body of soccer. North Korea walked out of the Games because six of their competitors were banned for having competed in the outlawed Games of the New Emergent Forces eleven months earlier. Indonesia threatened the same action.

Why had the Emergent Forces Games been outlawed by international sports federations? Because competitors from Taiwan (Formosa) and Israel had not received visas allowing them into Indonesia for the Asian Games the previous year.

It was a bloody miracle anyone was allowed to compete against anyone else!

Swimming provided some of the most exciting moments in the Games. Britain had the rare distinction of producing one of the favourites for the men's 100 metres freestyle in Bobby McGregor of Scotland.

Alas! In the final McGregor was beaten into second place – by a tenth of a second – by the blond eighteen-year-old Don Schollander who thus won the first of his four gold medals. It was the first time McGregor had been beaten in a sprint for two years. It would *have* to be in the Olympic final!

But the really incredible performance was that of Dawn Fraser who won the women's 100 metres freestyle for an unprecedented third time in a Games record time of 59·5 seconds.

As George Harley, one of the great swimming experts, put it: 'The "granny" of swimming has done it again, winning the gold medal for an incredible third time, breaking her 1960 Olympic record by 1·1 secs. It is an achievement that must rank as the greatest in the history of women's sport.'

The performer who really set us off with a bang was the athletics pin-up girl of that era – Mary Rand in her 'special' event, the long jump. On a sodden, soggy day in Tokyo, the golden girl of British sport, from ten o'clock in the morning until five in the late afternoon, dominated the women long jumpers of the world.

What, in fact, did she do?

She began by leading the qualifying competition with her very first jump. That one was 'only' 21 ft $4\frac{3}{4}$ in – just seven inches below the existing world record – and the only time in the long, long day when she failed to exceed $21\frac{1}{2}$ ft. The afternoon record read: 21 ft $7\frac{1}{2}$ in (a new UK record); 21 ft 6 $\frac{3}{4}$in; 21 ft 9 in (another new UK record); 22 ft 2 in (a new world record and the first time any girl had ever cleared 22 ft without wind assistance); and finally 21 ft $8\frac{1}{4}$ in.

All through the day she was the queen of the arena; sometimes consoling or advising her team-mates, sometimes crossing or sprinting up and down the sodden green turf, sometimes lying on her back and just kicking up her legs at the grey skies with the abandon of a foal lying in summer pasture. She seemed the spirit of youth in the age of cosmonauts, and the international crowd took her to its composite heart.

Finally, after her last jump, she ran to the side of the track to join her husband and hurdler John Cooper, and they both embraced her. If I'd been there I would have, too!

Shchelkanova, the world champion, her blonde hair framing a white face, took her last jump, and when the red flag signalled it a 'no jump' her looks could have curdled milk. The rather equine-looking Irena

Kirszenstein, of Poland, who had once got within an inch of Mary's previous best, made her final desperate effort. But this was a 'no jump' too, and she accepted it with a resigned shrug.

In the sheen of the floodlights Mary marched to the victory rostrum – the first girl ever to win Britain a gold medal for track or field events since women began competing in them in the Games of 1928.

Four days later came the most remarkable 'double' I ever saw Britain pull off in the Olympic Games when Lynn Davies won the *men's* long jump.

'Tonight,' I wrote, 'there'll be a singing in the hillside, there'll be a singing in the vales – and nowhere will it be louder than at 14, Commercial Street, Nantymoel – translation The Spring by the Mill [incidentally, what a delightful *double entendre*!] in the heart of Glamorgan, where Lynn Davies was born twenty-two years ago behind the shop of Davies the Draper.'

Only once since 1896, when the Games were revived, had this event not gone to the USA and you could have hung your hat on the tension in the air as Davies took his fifth out of six jumps in the competition proper. He was sandwiched between the two men who jointly held the world's ratified record – Ralph 'Hawkeye' Boston, from East Bonbon Street, Covina, California, and Igor Ter-Ovanesyan, 'Merited Master of Sports of the USSR'.

Davies stood poised strong and powerful, defying the rain which came down like silver lances in the floodlights, and the buffeting wind. For once, experience of our much-reviled British weather was paying off. Boston was shrivelled by the cold. The Russian was rigid with tension.

And then something happened which really *was* a near miracle. As Lynn prepared for his run the wind, for something over one minute but under two, completely dropped so that, instead of having to jump, as it were, against an invisible net, the Welshman had the advantage of leaping in cold, but normal conditions.

He charged down the run-up, soggy as red porridge, took off, soared arrow-straight and landed 8·07 metres away. (In those days metrication was as far from Britain as the moon and all you could hear was the frantic rustle of conversion tables before the British sportswriters could discover that Davies had cleared 26 ft 5¾ in.)

It was Lynn the Win – and again we had that emotional moment of the old flag creeping up towards the sullen Japanese sky. Spectators found themselves singing the National Anthem aloud – which Englishmen don't often do.

By the time the track and field events were over it was clear that Britain had done better than ever before.

Robbie Brightwell, who had dedicated as much to athletics as any British star I ever knew, had the ill-fortune to be beaten out of a medal in the 400 metres – but it was this very defeat which spurred his fiancée, Ann Packer, to get her gold medal.

Ann had been favoured to win the 400 metres but in this event, after looking as though she were going to overhaul that wonderful Australian competitor, Betty 'You Beaut' Cuthbert, the English girl seemed almost to come to a dead halt in the home straight as she ran into an invisible 'wall' of wind – through which the more experienced Miss Cuthbert plunged, ducking her head into it so that she minimized its effect on her whole body. She won in a new Olympic record time of 52 secs with the English girl 0·2 secs behind.

Ann had never taken the 800 metres seriously – at least as a winner, that is. She had run only four 800 metres, or half-miles, before coming to Tokyo. And at the halfway stage it didn't look good: a blue-clad French girl Maryvonne Dupureur was leading from Hungary's Nagy Szabo, followed by Antje Gleichfeld with the black bar of Germany across her breast, then Kraan in the orange shorts of Holland, Marise Chamberlain (New Zealand) and Ann.

Coming round the bend it looked as though she might get boxed in. But she switched to the outside and, with no apparent heart-bursting effort, she was gliding along like some majestic white swan sailing down a red river.

They struggled in after her, like shrivelled leaves blown down a gutter, Dupureur and Chamberlain, Szabo and Gleichfeld. And you got some idea of the quality of the race when the announcement went up that all four had beaten the Olympic record of 2 mins 4·3 secs.

But Ann, the swan in her swan-song, with her time of 2 mins 1·1 secs had beaten the ratified world record by a tenth of a second.

You could see the exuberant health and strength of a Mary Rand but Ann Packer looked comparatively frail – the very reverse of some of the 'muscle molls' from Eastern Europe – yet she had achieved her 800 metres triumph after three days of the 400 metres – an event previously thought too tough for gentle girls.

Meanwhile some strange things had been happening in the long-distance races. The 10,000 metres was won by Billy Mills of the USA, seven-sixteenths – don't ask me how that percentage is computed! – a Sioux Indian who, from the age of thirteen, had been brought up in a Red Indian orphanage.

The 5,000 metres was only memorable in that another American, twenty-seven-year-old Bob Schul, was more or less handed it on a gold plate. Both his main rivals on paper, Ron Clarke and the Frenchman Michel Jazy, who the following year was to break the world record for the mile, were always, in my opinion, better at beating the clock than flesh-and-blood opponents.

In this race they spent so much time looking over their shoulders that they defeated themselves and Schul beat them both.

As ever I found Peter Snell, the New Zealander, who performed the magnificent double of winning the 800 and 1,500 metres (the first time this had been done in the Olympic Games since the Englishman Albert Hill pulled it off in the 1920 Games), humdrum.

It seems an absurd description of a man who held world records at 800 metres, 880 yards, 1,000 metres and the mile. Perhaps it was that after erupting on the international scene so utterly unexpectedly at the Rome Games, the New Zealander seemed to win so easily, devaluing the opposition by the lack of drama with which he conquered them.

As Chris Brasher once said, talking of Snell in the 800 yards: 'I wish somebody would stick a pin into this man and then we would really see how fast the distance can be run in.'

But, as usual as far as I was concerned, the peak of the athletics programme in the Games came with the marathon.

I really thought, at last, that one of my cherished ambitions was going to be fulfilled – and it wasn't blind patriotism. Emil Zatopek said: 'Britain has three of the greatest marathon runners in Heatley, Hill and Kilby and I don't see how they can be beaten.'

As for the time, Zatopek forecast: 'If they run 2 hrs 14 mins it will be excellent; if they run 2 hrs 13 mins it will be fantastic, and if they run under that time it will be unbelievable.' So what happened? We had all forgotten, or ignored, or disbelieved, the fact that a man of today could win two Olympic marathons in succession. We had, in fact, forgotten the 'rich jewel in the Ethiop's ear' – and the golden medal round his neck. We had omitted from our calculations Abebe Bikila. And this was the way of it:

Today Abebe Bikila, a sergeant in the Ethiopian Imperial Guards, did it just five weeks after an appendicitis operation! His time of 2 hrs 12 mins 11·2 secs (remember Zatopek: 'If they run under 2 hrs 13 mins it will be unbelievable') was the fastest ever for the marathon and was 3 mins 5 secs faster than the one he returned to win the title in Rome four years ago.

What it means is that he averaged nearly 12 mph, or almost a mile every five minutes, *for over twenty-six miles!*

After five kilometres big Ron Clarke – third in the 10,000 metres, unplaced in the 5,000 – was leading from Ireland's Jim Hogan and Tunisia's Haddeb Hannachi.

It took just 28 mins 17 secs for Abebe to wrest the lead from Clarke . . . and thereafter the Ethiopian was never to be headed.

Then, at 3.10 pm precisely, a fanfare of trumpets – the marathon champion's accolade – and the cheers from the crowd heralded the entry of the gladiator into the arena. Never varying that crocodile-gobbling stride of his, Abebe circled the red shale track to thunderous applause.

There followed an incident unique in my experience of a dozen or more marathons. After mopping his face with a small hand towel, Abebe went into a new act. In the centre of the field, he touched his toes half a dozen times; lay on his back doing cycling exercises; kicked his legs so that his feet touched the ground behind his head.

He speaks only Ethiopian, but in the universal language of sport he was telling 75,000 people how much he still had in him!

And no sooner had he finished this than the biggest explosion of applause in the whole eight days of athletics broke out as Japanese champion Kochichi Tsuburaya treaded his way into the stadium . . . only to be followed seconds later by our own Heatley.

As Tsuburaya plodded his way tensely along the back straight, the frantic cries from the Japanese thousands stilled when, 220 yards from home, Heatley ground past him. For eight long days, the crowd had been praying for a Japanese success and now their silver man was being turned into bronze before their very almond eyes.

As Heatley was crossing the finishing line Tsuburaya, twenty yards to the rear, began to waver and when he crossed the line he was rubber-legged. He was, in fact, the only one of the leading runners to show any signs of distress. Kilby, who was fourth, was quite composed, so was Hill, in nineteenth place.

The final of the heavyweight division in the boxing was an anticlimax for everyone. The then unknown Joe Frazier, a skinner in a Philadelphia slaughterhouse, had been boosted as some second Cassius Clay – an unlikely eventuality. Frazier met a monumental German, Hans Huber, who must have stood 6 ft 5 in and almost certainly weighed sixteen stone.

Afterwards I called it a dreary business, with hardly a punch landing. 'I suppose they gave Frazier the decision because he went forward and the German back,' I said.

I have just one slight excuse for that. None of us knew at the time that Frazier had gone into the fight with a broken thumb and made just enough menacing gestures to contain the German giant and land a few punches himself which, for once, justified that sanctimonious and hypocritical saying, 'This is going to hurt me more than it hurts you.'

Only four and a half years later, Frazier became the first professional ever to beat Clay in March 1971.

The Games ended with a wonderfully artistic Closing Ceremony, and I shall never forget leaving the stadium for the last time with thousands of Japanese youngsters crying their eyes out and sobbing, '*Sayonara, sayonara*' . . . 'Farewell, farewell . . .'

10

1965–8
Here, There and Any Old Where

After Tokyo and before the end of 1964 it was time for me to go to Boston to see what should have been the return Clay–Liston fight. But, with one of those fantasies which only Muhammad Ali/Cassius Clay could introduce into boxing, on the eve of the fight he went down with a hernia.

Financially the postponement was disastrous. But it could have been worse, much worse. For Clay was a very sick young man – much sicker than anyone thought when he was taken to hospital. Without immediate treatment, his doctors said, complications, even gangrene or peritonitis, could have set in. Had Clay entered the ring he might have died – and the 14,000 spectators would have believed the collapse part of his 'nutcase' act.

Back to Britain, then, for one of the few world title fights to be held in England outside London, when at Manchester Willie Pastrano defended his world light-heavyweight title against former world middleweight champion, Terry Downes.

By the end of the tenth round the American was a picture of dejection as he sat in his corner, head hung low, gulping in the smoky air with lungs which heaved like bellows. But in front of him was a bouncing, gesticulating, shrieking, gnomish man, his black eyes snapping like coals. He was Angelo Dundee, Pastrano's manager, and what he shouted at Pastrano was the sort of thing footballers get sent off for saying, and what he delivered were two full-blooded whacks across the buttocks.

From then on Pastrano went berserk – but it was a controlled, vicious, deadly kind of fury. Eventually Downes, who had seemed previously an indestructible battering-ram, went down sprawling, willing but no longer able to control the splayed legs and the nerveless arms. As he felt the canvas gritty under his knees so he began the painful crawl upwards, his fighter's heart still beating as indomitably as ever.

At eight he made it, a sway-legged, wavering target, and as the referee waved the traffic towards him he tried to square up to meet it. Slowly the referee moved across the ring until finally he came to

Pastrano and tapped him almost apologetically on the shoulder to indicate that he should stop the onslaught.

And just as he did so Downes' legs simply melted under him and he fell to the canvas like a punctured doll.

If ever a championship was salvaged from *outside* the ring this one, with its eleventh hour, rather than eleventh round, victory, was. And it spotlighted one of the reasons why the Americans retained for so long their dominance in world boxing: the infinite superiority of most of their managers, trainers and handlers.

Downes never fought again, and Pastrano was beaten in nine rounds in his next fight, in which he lost his world title and after which he, too, retired.

1965 started with an honour long overdue – the knighting of Stanley Matthews. Pelé, Puskas, di Stefano *may* have been better players. I don't know; I saw them only intermittently. But I watched Stan Matthews week in, week out, for years and I do know that he was the greatest consistent footballer I ever saw – and the greatest entertainer with a football. Now he was honoured, with his fiftieth birthday barely a month away. He remained perhaps the most modest star, in any sport, I have ever met – and he had so much not to be modest about!

Gradually the tradition of British sportsmanship – at least as far as soccer was concerned – was being eroded. A wounding comment appeared in the Zurich paper *Sport*: 'Where is the fairness, the imperturbable calm, the cool temperament so characteristic of the island which once justified and explained the respect for British football? Was it only an illusion, clever propaganda? Have we been fooled for more than half a century or has the British sporting spirit changed just as everywhere else?'

Perhaps the impending retirement of Stanley Matthews really was the end of an era. . . . His final farewell to the sport he had adorned since he joined Stoke City ground staff when he was fifteen, thirty-five years earlier, involved for me one of those journeys by air, rail and road which are so short in miles but so difficult to accomplish, from Newcastle, where I'd been covering a fight, to Stoke.

Since Stan made his League debut for Stoke on 19 March 1932 he had played in over seven hundred League and Cup games, including those for Blackpool. Jack Mee, the Stoke director, told me that they had longed to make it seven hundred League games alone, but Stan didn't think he was right for that and stopped at 699!

It was impossible to write a satisfactory tribute to such a wonderful player, but my appreciation of him tried to show that Stanley Matthews had always been to me what sport should always be. 'He had genius without ostentation . . . he walked away from trouble and he didn't foul opponents or defy authority. . . . He was a professional in the best sense of the word – in that he never gave of less than his best; he was fit; he tried; he didn't "alibi". And in the true sense of the word amateur – "one who loves the game" – he was a great amateur.'

Retirement was in the air but from Australia came the unwelcome news that Donald Campbell, holder of the world land and water speed records, was undecided whether to call it a day.

I knew Donald better than slightly and it had often seemed to me, as we sat next to each other at some sporting luncheon or other, how his prowess dimmed the 'courage' and 'gallantry', the 'guts' and 'pluck' of which we were wont to write about the other sports stars.

But, sadder than that, was the feeling when you got in a serious conversation with Campbell that somewhere, deep inside him, there was a dark seed of destruction which forced him to push his luck further and further until that fickle jade was bound, one day, to betray him . . . as, of course, so tragically happened in the end.

At last Britain was making up some of the leeway in governmental aid to sport, with the announcement in the House of Commons of the formation of the first British Sports Council. The man who made the announcement was, and is, an old friend of mine, Denis Howell, a former League football referee and the first politician really to devote himself to the welfare of sport.

Meanwhile, I flew to the States for the long-awaited – with some apprehension – return fight between Muhammad Ali/Cassius Clay and Sonny Liston. In all my coverage of sport I have never known an event which switchbacked from pure farce through potential disaster into utter disgrace.

All the 'fight mob' was staying at Poland Spring, Maine. The fight was to be held in the nearby textile township – some 40,000 inhabitants – of Lewiston, which had been officially designated 'a depressed area'. I don't know whether that was a fair description of Lewiston *before* the fight but it was certainly an accurate one after it.

The hotel buildings at Poland Spring – mineral water was bottled there and sold commercially – were set in five thousand acres. Liston's living quarters were in the Mansion House, which was built in 1794 when George Washington was President of the fairly dis-United States.

A chapel within the grounds was described in the official information sheet as 'the only hotel-owned and hotel-operated chapel in America'. Then the brochure added, in rather an odd choice of phrase, that the chapel is 'just a spade mashie shot from the Big House'. The Big House was another description of where Liston was living and considering the amount of time he had spent, involuntarily, in assorted 'Big Houses' – American slang for jails – in various parts of the USA, it seemed scarcely a tactful description of his current abode.

Just to heighten the illusion of living in a dream or, as was so often the case with Liston, a nightmare, you had only to look out of your window in the early morning, while the mist was wreathing the pines, the beeches and the willow trees and curling off the lakes, to see Liston trudging along the winding pathways accompanied by two security men.

Whether their job was to protect him from the public or the public from him was not quite clear.

An additional touch of fantasy was provided by the fact that as ill-luck – their's – would have it, some 150 Catholic priests had chosen that particular week to hold a retreat at Poland Spring. It was said that on the first day when the early morning Angelus bell was sounded by the priests, half a hundred semi-punch drunk fighters leaped out of their beds, shaping up to invisible foes and proclaiming: 'That was a goddam short interval!'

Liston looked slow and clumsy in his training but suddenly seemed to discover something of his true form in his final workout against Amos 'Big Train' Lincoln, an even bigger Negro than the ex-champion, who ended up in each of the three rounds apparently dazed by Liston's left jabs.

I write 'apparently' for after the fight it was divulged that Liston's camp *knew* the ex-champion had no chance of regaining his title. But they tried one last ploy, for before the last workout Lincoln was given $100 – in those days about £36 – to go into the ring with the sole intention of making Liston look good. The idea, of course, was to give Clay the impression that he was up against the old impregnable 'Stone Face'.

I confess that I was influenced enough to write: 'It's up to Liston. If he keeps his head he has the equipment to become the second man in ring history to recapture the heavyweight title.'

But I was clearly not very convinced about the outcome, for I also wrote: 'If Clay first bamboozles and then infuriates Liston again before the fight and then cuts him we could see the same result as before – an ignominious end with Liston surrendering in some fashion.'

And about three hours before the fight was due to start I knew that my foreboding was right. I was with Joe Caly who was to drive Don Saunders of the *Daily Telegraph* and myself from Poland Spring to the arena at Lewiston – incidentally, the attendance, at the junior ice hockey stadium which belonged to the Dominican order, was, even going back to the first heavyweight title fight with gloves in 1892, the smallest ever, reaching only 2,434.

As we were walking to Joe's car we saw one of the most prominent of Liston's entourage walking in the same direction as ourselves. There was a long line of parked cars and Liston's 'mate', as though oblivious of his surroundings, walked slam-bang into the back of the last one. He was stoned out of his mind.

And when you're supposed to be working in the corner of a man who is trying to regain the richest prize in sport you don't get yourself plastered on your way to work.

One unique circumstance was that when the affair started it was the first time that three men who had held the world's heavyweight title were operating in the ring at the same time – for the referee was Jersey Joe Walcott.

And, virtually, no sooner had it started than it was over. This is how I noted the sequence of punches. Clay dashed in and scored with a hard right to the head and then a left hook. Liston was short with two left jabs and then got through with one, the force of which Clay minimized by backing away.

Liston landed a right to the body and then Clay moved in to bang a right to the mouth which halted Liston. On reflection I believe this was the punch that won the fight. Not that it in any way dazed Liston but it was a painful blow and I believe the brooding behemoth suddenly decided that as he wasn't going to win anyway what was the point of staying there for, perhaps, fifteen rounds and just getting hurt for nothing?

I stress that this is only my own opinion but I feel it is the only one which explains, with any adequacy, what then happened. For as Liston moved in Clay came off the ropes and crossed a short right, rather high on Liston's face . . . whereupon the ex-champion went down and stayed down.

In all honesty I do not believe that particular punch would have knocked me out, although it might well have knocked me down. But to me it seemed quite incredible – and twelve years later it still does – that Liston, a supposedly fit man who had trained for months and weighed nearly fifteen and a half stone, could be taken out with one punch after little more than a minute of the very first round.

If Liston had been gradually worn down by his own exertions and the punishment sustained in twelve, ten or even eight rounds, then one punch could do it, but to suggest that this could happen in a minute, or a little more, was to try to make fools out of all of us.

As a matter of fact everyone seemed to go berserk once Clay hit Liston and Liston hit the floor. First of all Clay stood over his 'stricken' foe, apparently shouting over the din: 'Come on, you bum, get up and fight!' The lolling Liston took absolutely no notice of this compelling invitation and Walcott seemed at a loss what to do about the whole fiasco.

What he *should* have done was to force Clay to retire to a neutral corner and only then start counting over Liston. In fact, I never heard him take up the time-keeper's count at all, and when Liston did get to his feet the referee rushed over to the ropes – as we thought, to confer with the time-keeper about how many seconds had elapsed.

Later it was said that Nat Fleischer, probably the greatest boxing expert who ever lived, who was sitting next to the time-keeper, Francis McDonough, had called to Walcott and showed him the time-keeper's stop-watch which registered twelve seconds as being the time Liston had spent on the canvas.

Meanwhile back at the mill – except that there had been no 'mill' – Liston had floundered up and was, although bent double, flailing back at Clay as the champion did his level best (well, something had to be on the level) to knock him down again.

Finally Walcott came back and indicated that Liston would now be allowed to leave the ring as he had lost!

The reactions were varied and fantastic. Within minutes of the chaotic finish Clay, who had not even bothered to put his robe on, was doing a running commentary on the tele-recording of the 'fight' which was being shown to him on a small monitor set as he clutched the ropes.

Behind me infuriated ringsiders shouted and screamed hoarsely and bitterly: 'Fake . . . fake!' and 'Bum . . . bum . . . bum!' Liston was hustled out of the ring with the kind of speed which attends a pauper's funeral. I heard a sad-eyed kid cry: 'To think I was here the night boxing died.'

Later Clay was to say that the 'knockout' blow was 'an anchor punch, a twisting [!] punch which the old-time Hollywood star, Stepinfetchit, taught me, the punch Jack Johnson took to his grave with him.' 'Anchor' punch, indeed! To me it was more like a crown and anchor punch. (Yet another sidelight on the unbelievably complex character who is Muhammad Ali/Cassius Clay is the fact that he had as part of his entourage, Stepinfetchit, who used to portray the Negro as a feckless, dumb, raggedy-ass, moronic type of clown, suitable only for the most menial tasks. But Clay's own avowed ambition was to get a better image, and a better deal, for his race.)

Other people at the ringside and those who had seen the whole disaster, via TV satellite, were devastating in their criticism.

Rocky Marciano, who had sweated and strained and bled in forty-nine professional bouts, said – as simply as he used to fight – that he just couldn't understand it. George Chuvalo, the Canadian heavyweight who was to go a total of twenty-seven rounds with Clay without getting

274

stopped, was even more succinct in his summing-up. He said: 'It stunk!'

In England Henry Cooper, who had come within seconds of knocking out Clay, said: 'It couldn't have been fixed. They'd have made it look better.' But he added: 'That was no punch Clay landed. It could not have hurt anybody.' Henry's manager, Jim Wicks, declared: 'The fight was a joke.'

Tommy Farr, who gained imperishable fame by going the full fifteen rounds with Joe Louis, when Joe was 'The Greatest', said: 'It's the the blackest night for boxing.'

In America the *New York Journal-American* quoted former world champion, Gene Tunney, as saying: 'This is the worse, most offensive debasement of boxing I have ever seen. Two completely reprehensible characters . . .'

Never has a 'sporting' event been so widely criticized in newspapers round the entire world.

But perhaps the best journalistic comment appeared on the front page of the *Corry Journal* of Pennsylvania. It stated baldly: 'Due to the nature of last night's fight, the *Journal* feels it does not warrant coverage. Don't look for it on the sports page.'

In this same month of July 1965 there followed one of the saddest episodes to have occurred in my life in sport. Freddie Mills was found shot near the Chinese restaurant he ran.

It was decided that Freddie, lion-hearted Freddie, had committed suicide. I write 'it was decided' for, despite what I'm sure were the most exhaustive police enquiries, I could never bring myself to believe that this man who, among so many, was more full of life than any I knew, could have brought himself to take his own life.

I once spent an evening in Freddie's home watching the films of some of his old fights – an uncanny experience to see him getting hammered on the screen while he gave a commentary by my side, as he did on that terrible second round in the first Gus Lesnevich fight. 'You don't know much after knockdowns like those first two,' he said. 'The rest of the fight is a bit of a haze looking back on it. In fact, when I saw this film for the first time, three days after the fight, I felt bruises and cuts I'd never noticed before.'

It has always been the fashion to say that Mills never had all the boxing skills. That is a fair criticism. But he showed by his lion-hearted determination and his uncompromising fitness how a man with guts can get to the absolute top in a sport where the competition has never been more worldwide.

I was always proud to call Freddie Mills a close friend – and I like to think he felt the same way about me.

One of the reasons for the decline of professional boxing as a mass entertainment sport in Britain was the spread in London, and throughout the country, of private members' clubs where gentlemen in evening dress – some of them all too easily confused with the waiters – wined and dined while youngsters slugged it out in the ring for their delectation.

I was never quite able to stomach the contrast between spectator and competitor in this sort of club although, of course, to be logical everyone who went to an ordinary commercial show would have eaten and drunk earlier; but the combination of swiping inside the ring and sipping outside it . . .

More serious, from the sport's point of view, was that the more the clubs flourished the further boxing departed from the ordinary working men who had traditionally supported it, and whose ranks still supplied the actual performers. For instance, Ken Buchanan, the only British-born fighter to win a world title overseas, in 1971, since the great Ted 'Kid' Lewis did so in 1915, had only three more fights in Britain before retiring, as undefeated European champion, almost exactly four years later. But if boxing deserved to remain a major sport, instead of a lucrative livelihood for a few entrepreneurs and performers, it was ridiculous that perhaps the most successful of our postwar world champions should have virtually been frozen out of Britain. The trouble was that he had many of his early fights in the clubs and, as a result, never built up the sort of fans who stick with a fighter through thick and thin.

Another superb boxer, Howard Winstone, *did* get his chance of a world championship – the featherweight – in London. And, as though to disprove the idea that people didn't come to watch *boxers*, a capacity crowd of over 18,000 packed the gigantic Earls Court Arena to see him challenge the Mexican holder of the title, Vicente Saldivar.

They saw an heroic battle and, had it not been for one round – the fourteenth – in which his face disappeared into an anonymous red smear, his features creased with blood from his nose and cuts round both his eyes, I think the Welshman would have been crowned world champion.

In fact I thought Winstone had just got there for, although the sheer power and aggression belonged to Saldivar, when it came to the skills of jab and parry, footwork, turning a man, the lost art of feinting – then the honours went to Winstone.

Even in a life which was never exactly static 1965 was providing more than the usual amount of travelling for, in exactly three weeks, I was now due to see three world title fights and one European one in San Juan, Puerto Rico; Las Vegas; Tokyo and Rome.

It was my first visit to Puerto Rico. I had gone to see Ismael Laguna defending the world lightweight title, which he had won in his native

Panama, against the man from whom he had taken it, Carlos Ortiz – and Ortiz was a Puerto Rican.

How I got through that night of the fight I shall never know. There had been a downpour so terriffic that it occasioned something I had never seen before. A whole new canvas had to be relaid over the under-felt so that the fighters should have a reasonable chance of keeping their feet. This, of course, delayed matters even further, and when Bill Daly had ensured that his man, Ortiz, lasted the full distance by, quite un-justifiably, not only working in his corner but also, at the start of almost every round, accompanying him into a remote section of the ring so that precious seconds were lopped off every session, I wondered if I too were going to be able to last the night. The previous evening I had had a bad fall, splitting my skull badly enough to have eight stitches in it and, during the rainfall, the bloodstained bandage I was wearing was washed away leaving me more bloody than either of the fighters!

From the tropical heat of Puerto Rico I arrived at Las Vegas where, instead of the usual blazing skies, fresh rainfall had turned the desert town into a mud patch with the temperature down to 48 degrees Fahrenheit.

The fight in Vegas was Clay defending his world heavyweight title against the former champion, Floyd Patterson, and it afforded me the chance of having the most interesting interview I ever had with the world champion, providing the most enlightening information I ever got on the subject of the Black Muslims.

It was conducted in the small room where Clay had his massage and, as I remember, there were three white journalists besides myself, and three of Clay's supporters including his younger brother, Rudolph Valentino. The Muslims kept up an *obbligato* of 'Amen . . . that's right Muhammad . . . Amen . . . You tell them', all through the interview which, for most of the time, was the inevitable monologue.

It began with Clay announcing unequivocally: 'If the prophet Elijah Muhammad told me to stop boxing, I'd do it at once. If he came into my dressing room next Monday and told me to stop, there wouldn't be a fight.'

The 'prophet' Elijah Muhammad, then sixty-seven, was the head of the Black Muslims which, Clay said, had a membership of two million. This was not the Clay of the boxing ring even though his magnificent stark naked body was being kneaded and pummelled in preparation for the fight which was only seventy-two hours away. He continued: 'Elijah Muhammad is never wrong.'

From the background came the deep rumble: 'Amen. Elijah is always right.'

Clay persisted: 'Why would I obey the prophet? Because he knows things no one else knows. If he told me not to fight it could be that he knew there was a bomb under the ring. He is always right. It's lucky he hasn't already told me not to box. Other people have told me that if you don't want to hear something, don't ask the prophet about it. So I have never asked him if it's all right to go on boxing.

'Why did I join the Muslims? When I came back from the Olympics in Rome with the gold medal I won for America, I couldn't sit down and drink a cup of coffee in a place in my own home town of Louisville.'

When I asked: 'Is Louisville still segregated?', Clay said: 'It's not as bad as it was.' He continued:

'I don't smoke. I don't drink or go to places where there are prostitutes. There's never been a breath of scandal about me – but there are people who hate me.'

The deft charcoal hands of the masseur smoothed the heroic limbs and the giant torso and Clay went on talking, sometimes seeming to address us personally, sometimes as though preaching to the world.

He said: 'But there are people who like me. Nasser wants me to open a new stadium named after me. . . . President Nkrumah of Ghana, loves me: And in Atlanta, Georgia, they held up a plane for a quarter of an hour when I was late.'

The comparison wasn't as banal as it might read for Georgia is in the Deep South where integration was still a dirty word to most people. If Clay could have a plane held for him, it meant his message was getting through to some people even there.

I asked: 'But what is it your movement wants? Do you want a separate part of the United States? What are your aims?'

Clay answered: 'There are twenty-two million Negroes in the USA. We want two per cent of the country and its wealth. The alternative is for us to go back to Africa.'

'But surely you realize that if you *were* given part of the country it would almost certainly be the desert of Arizona and New Mexico – and Nevada, *excluding* Reno and Las Vegas!'

There was a shrug of the massive black shoulders.

'As for Africa,' I persevered, 'surely a lot of American Negroes wouldn't agree to going there?'

He nodded his head violently. 'No, they wouldn't, no, they wouldn't. But we can't keep on living like slaves in our masters' country. We can't forever be slaves to you white men. Maybe we could go somewhere in the East. Things are changing. They said Elijah Muhammad would never be heard. Now he broadcasts from Washington. Soon President Johnson will have to ask him to solve the situation of twenty-two million Negroes.'

The other Negroes in the tiny room almost anaesthetized with liniment, nodded their heads as though they were on one neck.

As Clay dressed he said: 'We don't believe in violence. How could I, as heavyweight champion of the world, be mixed up in anything violent? We don't carry weapons. Bullets can't hurt the Muslims. The only thing is, you must follow Elijah Muhammad – believe in him. Some people think they are greater than the prophet.' (In the background: 'No one greater than the prophet.') Without the words being spoken one called to mind Malcolm X who broke away from the Black Muslim movement and was assassinated by killers still unidentified.

Clay finished dressing and concluded, his voice black vitriol: 'They's nuthin' so awful as a white man in the Southern States. Nuthin'. You English ain't never been like that.'

He had been talking for over an hour – but not with the clown's bray which he so often uses in public. I believe it was the testament of a man's faith. A man gifted physically above the world, a man of quick wit and lively intelligence, if not of culture or academic education.

I believed the Negro even though I could not subscribe to his testament. I have always detested racialism whether it is practised by whites against blacks or conversely. I did not and do not think the Black Muslims' creed is right – but I am a white man, and it seems fair to put the view of Muhammad Ali/Cassius Clay, one of the world's most famous Negroes.

The fight itself came as a terrible anti-climax and was one of the more unpleasant exhibitions of Clay's cruelty towards a man whose beliefs he genuinely detested. My personal feeling was that Clay could have won any time from the third round onwards. He did in fact put Patterson down in the sixth when a mix-up over the count and the failure of Clay to go to a neutral corner gave the ex-champion a break of perhaps a quarter of a minute.

At the time Clay said: 'He took my best punches. He wouldn't fall.' But a couple of months later he admitted that he did 'carry' Patterson because he believed it was better to be 'carrying a man than killing a man'.

Clay was, of course, entitled to his opinion, but many professional boxers have told me that a clean, quick knockout is much less painful and distressing than a prolonged beating. The real responsibility for stopping a bout which has become hopelessly one-sided devolves upon the referee. And I have always wondered why the referee on this occasion, Harry Krause, a blackjack or pontoon dealer in Las Vegas, waited until the twelfth round was nearly completed before he intervened. All the more so as it was obvious that after the fourth round Patterson, who had had a recurrence of an old back complaint, was half-crippled.

Krause nearly did stop the fight – as he certainly should have – much earlier. He told me afterwards that: 'I first thought of stopping it in the third round when Patterson's legs buckled and I knew he was in for a bad night. I went over after the fourth round when I realized he was in pain and asked if there was any trouble. They said it was a back spasm.'

I can only repeat what I wrote at the time. 'It was brutal, disgusting and without excuse from either Clay or the referee.'

Then I left Las Vegas for the third fight of those hectic three weeks. The trip to Tokyo was quite a journey, finally ending in a 100 mph tornado. I shall always remember the pilot, his grey shirt black with sweat, after he had finally wrestled the plane down.

The rumours which always precede a world title fight had it that Masahiko 'Fighting' Harada, whom Alan Rudkin was to challenge for the 8 st 6 lb championship of the world, had received so much hospitality after beating Eder Jofre for the title that he had ballooned up to 9 st 9 lb – the *lightweight* limit!

The fight was a fine, clean, hard-fought contest all the way, even if it was disappointing to see Harada given the decision at the end; I had given the fight to Rudkin, but by only the smallest possible points margin, $73\frac{1}{2}$ to $73\frac{1}{4}$, and I admit that's a pretty slim difference on which to take a man's world title away from him.

The life of a sportswriter had its glamorous side – Puerto Rico, Las Vegas, Tokyo – but sometimes it was as well to get both feet firmly on the ground, and this I did early in 1966 when, having so often thrilled to the Rugby League Cup Final played at Wembley, I took the chance of seeing that most rugged sport played in its own setting, in this case Wigan. My mood was melancholy.

Looking out on to the playing pitch and its environs, thirty-five years seemed to roll away and one returned to the days of the depression and hunger marches and love on the dole. The surrounding buildings were a memorial to the days of 'where there's muck there's money' – eczema red showing through old-bruise grime. There was a church or chapel whose bell looked as though it would never ring again except for a funeral. Through the haze of industry, which seemed impenetrable, there was the forgotten uniform of cloth caps and chokers and drab headscarves.

A scratchy record played 'The Entry of the Gladiators' and the players loped on to the field. Their play was magnificent but I thought I noticed a thickening of the waists and a thinning of the hair in some cases and recognized a drawback for Rugby League: lack of recruits.

What incentive did they have? They read of soccer stars earning £100 a week in a game which is not all crunch. Rugby League stars would be lucky to get a fifth of that.

But Rugby League survives and, with savage irony, it could be that a national recession could benefit a game where only the toughest can endure. . . .

It was towards the beginning of 1966 that I was lucky enough to be voted Sportswriter of the Year. Hugh Cudlipp presented me with the cheque which went with the award, and I was able to say that this was the first time he had given me a gold handshake – and I hoped it would be the last!

In America the death of James D. Norris, reputedly one of the richest men in the world, was announced at the age of fifty-nine. Although most of Norris' real dough had come from wheat, at the height of his powers he had probably the greatest boxing monopoly that ever existed, as boss of the International Boxing Club which was supposed to have done the equivalent of five million pounds' worth of business in Chicago, New York, Detroit and Florida alone, until it was dissolved in 1955 on the grounds of monopoly.

Norris was a strange man. Tall, bulky and very quiet, I could only assume that he was more interested in power than money – his father, anyway, had left him more cash than he would ever be able to spend. But what I found so remarkable was his attitude towards a number of the underworld characters in the fight game for, instead of shunning them as a man in his position would be expected to do, he positively courted some of them.

Boxing went on, with the arrival of Cassius Clay to defend his world heavyweight title against Henry Cooper at Arsenal Stadium: the first world heavyweight championship to have been held in Britain for fifty-eight years.

Clay had never attempted to belittle what Cooper did to him three years previously, and had recently told me that the punch which floored him then was the hardest with which he had ever been hit.

The fight was similar to the first, *sans* the excitement of that Cooper knockdown, and Clay showed a lively respect for the power of the Englishman's left hook and his ability to 'hit on the break' – although by now this ploy was forbidden – by leaping clear at the conclusion of the clinches.

But sure enough, in the sixth round, at the end of a bout of close-quarter work, Cooper came away with the left side of his face looking like a map of the old British Empire – crimson everywhere. George Smith, the Scottish referee, took a look at the gash, let the fight go on for perhaps three-quarters of a minute, and then waved Cooper to his corner. It was another desperate wound above and to the side of Henry's left eye. Clay gave the most graphic description of the finish when he said: 'Man! I could *hear* him bleeding!'

But if Cooper had been just a little too old at thirty-two to win the richest prize in sport, four days later I saw someone run away with one of the most famous races in the world, the Epsom Derby, when Scobie Breasley at *fifty-two* became the oldest jockey in living memory to triumph in the great race, riding the 5–1 shot Charlottown.

Breasley had come to Britain from his native Australia, and the reason the experts gave for his successes – he had already been champion jockey four times – was that he had a built-in stop-watch in his brain. In other words, he figured that if you covered the first two furlongs in such and such a time you would have to do the last two in x seconds. The great runner Paavo Nurmi, nicknamed the 'Flying Finn', used to run with a stop-watch held in his hand. Scurrying Scobie did not need a watch – the seconds ticked away against the furlongs in his brain.

One of the nicest men in the game finally restored a world boxing title to Britain – which had been without one for over four years – when Walter McGowan lifted the flyweight crown from the swart brow of Italy's Salvatore Burruni. I made McGowan an overwhelming winner on points.

One of the unluckiest Wimbledon losers I can remember was Roy Emerson that year. He had already won the singles title twice and there seemed no one to prevent him equalling the hat-trick record of Fred Perry, which had then stood for thirty years. Alas, he injured himself so badly that he lost in the quarter-finals, leaving the door open for the popular Spaniard Manuel Santana.

Now the World Cup was upon us.

It left happy memories because – and let's be honest about this – England won. It left doubts – and let's be honest about this, too – whether the home country should have played *all* its matches at Wembley. It also left memories which, without any hedging, were utterly distasteful: the appalling behaviour of the Argentinians and the 'crippling' of the Brazilian superstar Pelé, which my colleague Ken Jones described, under the headline 'Pelé Is Butchered', as 'the worst foul I have seen in this championship'.

The *Mirror* was wonderfully generous to me during this period. I pointed out that I had travelled the five continents and that wherever I had gone I had been right royally entertained, not only by officials, promoters and others who might have some financial or personal involvement in an event, but by my colleagues of the pen round the world. Could I now, please, return some of that hospitality?

That most lovable and benevolent of editors, Lee Howard, was all in favour and the paper allowed me most generous expenses with which to make friends and fellow-workers welcome at Wembley. It had to be there because I was covering – or, to be more accurate, doing supplementary and colour stories on – all the nine matches there.

I think by the time the final was played we calculated that out of our Humber Snipe – plus the invaluable aid of Win, sports editor Jack Hutchinson's wife – we had managed to entertain between 300 and 320 sportwriters from a dozen and a half different countries.

Sally was magnificent – a female Fortnum and Mason. None of your meals-on-wheels stuff. She insisted on three courses: hot soup if we got a typical English July day, or melon hollowed out and enriched with port, or perhaps a shrimp cocktail; cold turkey, salmon, cold beef or lamb or the occasional game pie with salads and various kickshaws; strawberries and cream, chocolate mousse liberally laced with brandy, peaches in champagne, fruit salad and kirsch.

The liquid side was my responsibility. Pimm's No. 1 was the greeting drink, or sherry for the more serious-minded. Cooled white wine, or red at 'car temperature'. Lager, of course, Scotch, vodka or gin, with the various mixes. Tubs and containers of ice. 'Claret is the liquor for boys port for men; but he who aspires to be a hero . . . must drink brandy.' I think Dr Johnson would have been proud of our multi-national heroes; and our heroes seemed to find the brandy, among other things, very much to their taste.

This was Sally's show, and I'm happy to say that she was mentioned in at least four Continental newspapers, the nicest comment being by that gentle Belgian giant, Maurice Simon, who wrote in *La Dernière Heure* that he had a suggestion for a new Secretary of the United Nations for, as an American married to an Englishman, Sally had been able to assemble a galaxy of nations round one table – without anyone using the veto!

On the field not everything was quite so halcyon. The tournament in London had started drably with a dreary 0–0 draw between England and Uruguay.

There was nothing drab, however, about England's 1–0 victory over Argentina. This was before the days when shop-wrecking, setting fire to trains and stabbings became regular Saturday afternoon pastimes but, apart from the first Cup Final, it must have been the nearest time that a Wembley match came close to disintegrating into a riot.

I never had the slightest doubt that Antonio Rattin, the Argentinian captain, thoroughly deserved to be sent off, according to *our* interpretation of the rules – even though the referee, Rudolf Kreitlein, was a German – for constant and deliberate foul play. What I will concede is that basically his fouls were not dangerous and, apparently, if you play the South American way, such fouls do not merit dismissal.

The repercussions were immediate and violent. Alf Ramsey, England's team manager, referred to teams who 'act as animals' – and was promptly rebuked by the disciplinary committee of FIFA who instructed their secretary to write to our FA calling attention to 'the unfortunate remarks' and asking for disciplinary measures.

In the meantime Rattin had been suspended for the next four internationals and two other Argentinians were out for the next three. Argentina had been fined the maximum possible under FIFA rules – a derisory £83!

For me the match which above all others – even the unforgettable final – rescued this World Cup from mediocrity and meanness was the semi-final in which England beat Portugal 2–1. In case I appear a biased witness let me quote from Tass, the official Russian newsagency. 'The World Cup semi-final between England and Portugal was like a spring of clear water breaking through the murky wave of dirty football which has covered recent matches in the championship. The players played beautiful, correct football.'

My own observation supported that. I saw players not only run to help an opponent on to his feet again, but the prostrate player reaching out his hand to *be* helped up, instead of spitting and snarling at a helper who, in so many previous matches, would have been giving only a Judas hand.

Eusebio's duel against Nobby Stiles was unremitting and relentless, but it was as fair as when two men used to go out into a deserted park at dawn to duel with pistols for two, and coffee for one. Bobby Charlton, who scored twice, was of course England's hero – but much more important to me was that in this match the World Cup justified itself, and Soccer could hold up its head again.

And the final against West Germany, praise be, lived up to the Portugal match. I cannot remember a more emotional British sporting occasion. As one colleague of mine who had spent a middle-aged lifetime in football said to me at the end, his cheeks still wet: 'For the first time I've cried at a football match – and I never want to see another in my life.'

Like everyone else in the stadium I thought we had it won after eighty-nine minutes – and I shall never accept that the tackle made by Jackie Charlton, which gave the Germans a free kick from which they equalized with only fourteen seconds left on my stop-watch, was a foul one.

The scene between full and extra time really did resemble a battlefield with exhausted players sprawling on the ground, surrounded by discarded shin-pads and other impedimenta which looked like bandages and emergency field dressings. Only Alan Ball (of fire) seemed impervious to the fatigue, physical and mental, which seemed to be strangling a team which thought it had won and now had to go out and do it all over again.

Was England's third goal, and Geoff Hurst's second, valid? It would be ridiculous for someone sitting as high in the stands as I was to pontificate on whether or not the ball, after hitting the cross-bar, or, as some averred, the roof of the net, bounced down over the line.

The referee, Gottfried Dienst of Switzerland, did not know and for a dreadful moment it seemed that the Russian linesman Bakhramov, who also was not on the goal-line, was disallowing it, as he waved his flame-coloured flag laterally.

But, merciful heavens, the decision was in our favour, and so to the final rocket in the England boots when, with the hand of my stop-watch having marked off fifty of the last sixty seconds of extra time, Hurst did it for the third time – with, incidentally, some unorthodox support on the right wing, where three spectators, apparently thinking the final whistle had sounded, were capering and careering like dervishes on the sacred Wembley turf.

I defy anyone who ever cared about any sport and who was still guilty of that old-fashioned emotion, patriotism, not to have been profoundly moved at the end.

I was glad when I was firmly brought back to earth by a Russian journalist who, with a straight face but the most gentle mockery, remarked: 'Congratulations! But I 'ope you veel not mind it if I say that not for the first time you needed some asseestance vrom the Rossians to beat the Germans!'

I couldn't wait to buy him a drink. . . .

From that unforgettable afternoon to a night which could not be forgotten quickly enough – one of the most farcical (in dubious taste) mis-matches I have ever seen for the heavyweight championship of the world between Muhammad Ali/Cassius Clay and Brian London.

One thing that has always puzzled me was why the Board of Control who had banned London from fighting Floyd Patterson seven years earlier and fined him £1,000 when he defied them, now found it logical to let the Blackpool bruiser tangle with the world champion who had outclassed Patterson.

Anyway we paid for it – some, who had to fork out twenty guineas for ringside seats, more than others, but all of us in one way or another.

No one had expected London to win, but they had expected him to put up some sort of fight and, remembering some of his past performances, to try a bit of rough stuff in order to hustle Clay out of his smooth rhythm. Vain hopes.

As I said, 'Clay exposed London as a lumbering, bumbling, unskilled workman – a boxer who couldn't box. Clay floored his challenger for the first time early in the third round and London stayed down to take the full count.'

London came into the champion's dressing room, fully clad and looking as though the last thing he had had was a fight. He was all set to return to Blackpool and family less than three-quarters of an hour after the fight had *started!* Later, when he was asked if he thought the affair had been a mis-match, London replied: 'The British Boxing Board of Control sanctioned it. It was up to them, not to me. It's not my fault if it was a mis-match. I'm forty grand better off – before the taxman hits me – but that's no consolation.'

For the 1966 Commonwealth Games in Jamaica Sally and I were lucky enough to be invited by an old friend to stay just outside Kingston. This friend, who had been one of our 'picnickers' at Wembley, was Brim Brimble, famous in Jamaica for his sporting broadcasts and also one of the island's biggest bookmakers. He and his wife Marjorie entertained us regally.

Because of the London 'fight' I had missed the first sensation of the Games which was the defeat of Ron Clarke in the six miles race by the then unknown little soldier from the highlands of Kenya, Naftali Temu. Once more Clarke, genuine as he was, had failed in 'a big one', for Temu won by some 150 yards but his time of 27 mins 14·6 secs was 27·6 secs outside the world record which Clarke had established a year earlier.

These Games were, in fact, to complete a hat-trick of international sporting successes for black athletes from America, the Caribbean and Africa.

First Clay had destroyed the two leading British heavyweights in a total of fewer than nine completed rounds; then the West Indians, at Leeds, had beaten England by an innings and 55 runs in the fourth Test, clinching the series with a winning lead of 3–0; in Kingston the 100 yards went to Harry Jerome, the coloured Canadian, the 220 to Sam Allotey, of Ghana, the 440 to Wendell Mottley, of Trinidad and Tobago, the mile and the three miles to Kipchoge Keino and the six miles to his team-mate, Naftali Temu, of Kenya. The only white man to get a gold in the flat race events was Noel Clough, of Australia, in the 880 yards.

Where thirty years earlier Jesse Owens had been christened 'The Black Arrow', the Kenyan Keino became known as 'The Black Train'. Not only did he win the mile in the fine time of 3 mins 55·3 secs but he dragged the next five runners through the four minute barrier. Running like this revolutionized not only records but possibilities, I felt, and I predicted that even those of us in middle age could look forward to seeing the 3 mins 45 secs mile, if the rate of progress was similar to that of the last twelve years, during which time Roger Bannister's Games record had been reduced by five and a half seconds. In fact it was only nine years later, to the week, that New Zealand's John Walker reduced the world record to 3 mins 49·4 secs at Gothenburg.

The highlight in Kingston was Keino's double, for Clarke was again beaten into second place in the three miles, although the time was seven seconds slower than the world record which Clarke himself had established in Stockholm less than five weeks before.

One of the most popular wins was that of the Jamaican-born Louis Martin in the weight-lifting. He was a citizen – and sportsman – of the world. The night of his victory I was particularly glad of his company, however, for it would be dishonest to pretend I did not recognize a strong feeling of the colour bar in reverse in the Jamaica of that time.

After years of dependence on – and exploitation by – the white man the Caribbeans were beginning to feel their muscles. When I walked into the Ward Theatre that night with Sally we were greeted with a battery of looks which it would be an understatement to describe a 'dour'. But as soon as it was seen that we knew Louis Martin we too became honoured guests.

The undercurrent of violence was, at times, quite frightening. Every time Brim Brimble left the house he would make certain that not only were the valuables locked in a big, modern safe but that this part of the house, which had barred windows, was sealed off from the rest by locked wrought-iron gates.

I myself saw only one example of naked violence. One night when we were driving back from a late session at the Games Brim, Marjorie, Sally and I saw three or four men attacking another. As he went down they started to put the boot in.

'Don't get out, whatever you do,' Brim said. 'I know where there's a patrolling policeman.' He drove on at top speed and, sure enough, round a couple of corners we came upon an officer of the law. Brim explained what we had seen and where it had happened. The policeman nodded gravely and walked off slowly – in the opposite direction.

Almost as horrifying from my point of view was an experience I had while I was 'on the air'. Brim, as I have said, was one of Jamaica's best-known sportscasters and, as well as proving as generous a host as anyone whose hospitality I've been lucky enough to enjoy, he had arranged for me to do a number of broadcasts on the boxing.

Most of the time he was there too, but on the night of the finals he had told me that, because of other commitments, he might be a little late.

Sure enough, when the flyweights got into the ring I was, in the classic phrase, 'on my Tod'.

To my absolute horror I heard the announcement that the final would be contested between a Jamaican, one K. Campbell, and a Ghanaian named Sulley Shittu.

My throat went dry. I tried to lick lips, all at once cracked, with a tongue which had become paralysed. My fevered imagination conjured up a thousand families listening as I introduced that awful name into their hearth and home, and rising as one to bellow back defiantly: 'And Shittu, too!'

I took the coward's line. The BBC's pronunciation department would not have faulted my enunciation of the Jamaican's name, but when it came to his opponent I lied in my false teeth and, granting him an honorary – and temporary – knighthood introduced him as 'Sir Hittu'. As I have said, it is the commentator's business to be as strictly neutral as is within his powers, but I frankly admit that never in a lifetime spent at the ringsides of the world have I ever wished for such a summary extinction of one fighter as I did for S.S.

But it was not to be, and never have nine minutes' boxing and the intervals of a minute each, plus the time necessary for the announcement of the winner – yes, you've guessed correctly, it was Sulley – dragged so abominably. I never spoke his second name again. The pride of the Campbells might be coming, but 'you know who' never. 'The Ghanaian has done this, the Ghanaian has brought off that', or occasionally 'Sulley has got home with a snorter'. All I could thank heaven for was the creation of Ghana. What a fine old mess I should have been in if I had had to euphemize with 'The Gold Coaster has just landed a fine left jab'.

When the verdict was given I breathed freely for the first time for nearly a quarter of an hour; and things weren't improved by the arrival of Brim who, with his customary *bonhomie*, inquired cheerfully: 'Everything been going all right?'

As I write this S.S. is ranked fourth among the Commonwealth bantamweights – he was only eighteen when he won that flyweight in Kingston – and I hope he progresses so well that one day he will come to Britain for a major title fight, for I am sure he is a most deserving young man. But I confess I have an ulterior motive behind my wishes for his success. Should he appear on TV – BBC or commercial – I'm looking forward to seeing how either of my two old friends, Harry Carpenter or Reg Gutteridge, will surmount the phonetic dilemma, particularly if the bout lasts, as I hope it will, for of course I want the customers to get proper value for their money, for the full fifteen rounds!

On three successive Saturdays I had seen England win the World

Cup, my twenty-fourth world heavyweight championship – if you could call it that – and the conclusion of my fourth Commonwealth Games. It seemed a good time to take a breather.

So Brim and Marjorie took Sally and me on a brief tour of the island. The weather was sweltering and I seem to remember a tidy number of stops to purchase huge blocks of ice from various factories to replenish the ice-box in the back of Brim's car; picnics with exotic drinks under the palm trees which swept down to the water and swimming in the Caribbean. A night when I was able to return some of Brim's hospitality because the man who ran the hotel was a former reader of mine, from Leicester, and he presented us with some really first-rate French wine which had travelled splendidly.

Estates, staggering in their opulence – I believe one was Noël Coward's – and a night at a Playboy Club where the black Bunny Girls were endowed with almost topheavy charms. Montego Bay and more swimming in the Caribbean – and then it was time to head for home via New York.

Almost immediately I went to Budapest to see Lynn Davies make athletic history by becoming the first man ever to win the three long-jump titles – Olympic, Commonwealth and European.

Our only other European Championships medal – we did not win a single silver or bronze – came in the marathon through the efforts of Jim Hogan, the Chiswick groundsman who had represented Eire before becoming a naturalized British subject two years earlier.

Thanks to the good offices of my incomparable friend Dezso Vad, easily Hungary's best-known sportswriter, I was the only journalist able to follow the whole course in the official camera car.

It was now off to Frankfurt to see Cassius Clay in action, again defending the heavyweight title, against the German southpaw, Karl Mildenberger. No one had anticipated Clay having any real difficulty with this one although that shrewd, very shrewd, trainer of his, Angelo Dundee, had told me that the champion hated meeting southpaws.

In fact everyone had Clay a 'mile' ahead on points at the end, when British referee Teddy Waltham intervened halfway through the twelfth round. Nevertheless Clay had made heavy weather of part of the fight. In the tenth round the German hit him with a shot to the body which was the only punch under which I had seen Clay quail since his first bout with Sonny Liston two and a half years earlier. Clay wasted as little time as possible after that but an example of the speed with which not only his legs and fists move in the ring but also how his brain reacts was told me, years later, by Teddy Waltham.

During one of the exchanges Teddy had said to the champion:

'You're holding'. And Clay, without ever stopping his efforts, replied: 'Which hand?'

Three days later on September 20, 1966 it was the end of the road – as far as the world title was concerned – for Henry Cooper, when he was knocked out in four rounds by Floyd Patterson.

For two rounds Henry more than held his own, with Patterson chiefly concerned in holding Cooper. Then at the end of the third round two left hooks dropped the British champion briefly, in the fourth Henry went down twice more and the second time there was no chance of his getting up. Afterwards Patterson generously said: 'I caught Cooper with a lucky punch.' Cooper, as ever, was more honest, saying: 'I don't remember the punch that put me down. I didn't see it – it must have been a good one.'

There was now a trip to the States, to Houston to see Muhammad Ali/Cassius Clay defend the world heavyweight title for the fifth time in twelve months.

Clay's opponent was Cleveland 'Big Cat' Williams, who was a lucky man to be alive, let alone fighting for the richest prize in sport. Some two years earlier he had been shot in the belly by a cop during a dispute, and after four operations he still had a bullet between his pelvis and his hip, and his left leg looked leaner than his right.

I have to record that on this one night Clay was up among the truly great heavyweights I have seen, Joe Louis and Rocky Marciano.

For once, without sacrificing his dazzling speed, he punched his true weight – and that night his weight was 15 st 2¾ lb, the second heaviest he had scaled up to that time.

I described the carnage: 'In the seven minutes and eight seconds of fighting, Clay scarcely missed a single blow. His jabs rammed Williams' head back on his shoulders. His hooks sent the red-tinged hair on the Negro–Cherokee Indian's head flying from side to side, pendulum fashion. And every punch, after the halfway mark in the first round, drew more and more blood from Williams' nose.'

'The Cat' had used up four of his nine lives, hammered to the canvas three times in the second round and once in the third, and so hard was Clay punching that I was delighted when Harry Kessler, the referee, moved in to cry 'Enough'.

It was a tremendously aggressive performance by Clay – and one which I was never to see him duplicate.

It was a little more than a month after this that I took one of my longer trips, to Bangkok, to see Walter McGowan defend his world flyweight title against Chartchai Chionoi.

The fight, to all intents and purposes, was over in the second round. Despite the fact that McGowan, boxing beautifully, once put his opponent down and twice half-dropped him, the immensely powerful Thai came back from the knockdown to rush McGowan to the ropes. And to my dismay I saw, as he ended up just over my head, that blood was cascading from a cut on the Scot's nose.

Round after round McGowan strove to keep the exchanges at long range, but after fifty seconds of the ninth round the referee stopped the fight.

I spent New Year's Day, 1967, in Tokyo having a massage – no, not from one of the 'pretty ladies' but from one of the blind Japanese masseurs who discovered aches and pains in part of my body I didn't know I had, and then assuaged them.

The reason for my trip to Japan was to see the Fighting Harada, conqueror of Alan Rudkin, defend his world bantamweight title against Mexico's Joe Medel. The fight itself was one of those curious ones where, all along, you are sure who the winner is going to be, but at the end when you add up your score-card you find that it has been much closer than you thought. Harada, the only man ever to win the world fly and bantamweight titles, won all right, by virtue of his non-stop aggression.

My next assignment was to go back to the Astrodome in Houston to see Muhammad Ali/Cassius Clay defend his world title against Ernie Terrell, also called the world champion by the self-styled World Boxing Association.

This, with the first fight against Patterson, revealed the unacceptable face of Cassius – or, perhaps, Muhammad. Hindsight indicates that even he must have been under still more than the considerable strain which always builds up before a world heavyweight fight for, week by week, the shadow of the call-up was approaching.

Terrell made no bones about his deep dislike of Clay. This very dark giant – at a shade over 6 ft 6 in he was, ironically, too tall to be called up! – gave an inkling of his feelings when I asked him: 'You obviously dislike Clay intensely. Have you ever felt like this before any of your previous fights?'

He paused for a moment and then said slowly: 'Most guys I've fought I've known beforehand, or got to know afterwards. One of them was a real good friend I was at school with. I've never had any malice. This one is different. I wouldn't . . . I wouldn't care to socialize with Clay in any way.'

Clay had previously deeply mortified Terrell by calling him 'an Uncle Tom' – the biggest insult one Negro can bestow upon another, suggesting that he is a servile slave, kowtowing to white men.

I summed it up by commenting: 'If Terrell has the ability, this could be a bitter, bitter fight.' But I still forecast Clay to win – 'about the twelfth'.

Maybe he could have, and held back only to prolong the torment as he did in his first fight against Floyd Patterson – but I don't think so. Terrell was bigger and stronger than Patterson – and he did not have a bad back. He also, like Patterson, had immense courage; but that was about all he had going for him.

In my opinion the referee, Harry Kessler, was grossly at fault for not stopping the fight any time after the end of the eleventh round, the fight which I then described as 'for long squalid segments one of the most distasteful prostitutions of boxing I have ever watched'. I had never seen Clay box so dirtily or, apart from his performance against Floyd Patterson, so cruelly.

In fact both men broke the rules so flagrantly, with virtually no remonstrance from the referee, that it was difficult to believe that there was an official in the ring. I commented: 'He allowed both fighters when they were not openly fracturing the rules to distort them to the point of ridicule. He never checked Clay who, for at least half the fight, was taunting, jeering, sneering, reviling and blackguarding the man he had sworn to torture and humiliate.'

Outside the ring Clay's brother, Rudolph Valentino, was constantly shrieking savagely: 'You fight like a girl, Terrell. You haven't got a face. It's turned into a hamburger.' Altogether an unsavoury, unsporting affair. Even so I missed the foul about which Terrell and his handlers complained the most – an incident in the third round in which Terrell claimed that Clay had rubbed the challenger's eye along the top rope.

The taunts and jeers and baiting by Clay were, of course, all to do with one thing. 'What's my name?' Clay would shout – for Terrell refused to call him Muhammad Ali, sticking to the original name which, as far as I know, he has never legally changed.

It was another magnificent display of the diverse weaponry, offensive and defensive, which makes up boxing of the highest class; but it was sadly marred by the questionable use of hands and tongue.

Clay was to have only one more fight – the following month against the veteran Zora Folley whom he beat in seven rounds – before his refusal to join the US armed forces came to a head and kept him out of the ring for three years and seven months. He was twenty-five when the enforced break to his career occurred and undoubtedly at the height of his career, just as Joe Louis at twenty-seven, equally on top of the world, had a break of over four years after joining the US Army.

It became increasingly obvious that Cassius Clay, as Muhammad Ali, was coming to a crisis in his affairs with the military authorities – ironically just as Joe Frazier, now unbeaten in fifteen professional fights with fourteen wins inside the distance, was coming to the fore. Clay's proposed return bout against Floyd Patterson was cancelled in Las

Vegas and then, under pressure from the State Governor, thrown out from Pennsylvania. After a two-day trial by an all-white jury Clay was found guilty of refusing to be called up into the US Army and he was sentenced to five years in jail and a fine of the equivalent of £3,500.

It was clear that Clay, who had claimed exemption from military service because he was a Black Muslim minister, would appeal, and he left court on a £1,500 bail.

One of the most revealing books about the suspended world heavyweight champion came on the market later that year, *Cassius Clay* by Jack Olsen, a senior editor of America's world-famous *Sports Illustrated*. I was particularly intrigued by Olsen's statement that '[Elijah] Muhammad's book *Message to the Black Man* is studied by Cassius like a Bible. The dominant theme of Muhammad's book is hatred of the whites.' He quoted 'a professional observer and friend of Clay' as saying: 'That kid has a sincere, true, deep hatred of whites, that goes all the way back to his childhood and the way his father brought him up. He set up an environment that made the Black Muslims or some other hate-white movement perfect for the kid.'

Olsen revealed that Elijah Muhammad served three years in prison during the Second World War for urging his flock not to go to war, and that, according to a close relative of Clay's, 'Clay was searching for a father and Elijah Muhammad is it. If Elijah told him "Don't go to war, go to jail", he'll go to jail. That man have Cassius by the nose.'

I could confirm his father's detestation of whites for on one occasion I was at an airport in connection with one of Clay's fights and was talking to Howard Bingham, the very agreeable Negro photographer who always seemed to accompany Clay. Suddenly Clay's father appeared, seized the photographer by the arm and pulled him abruptly away from me, saying in a loud voice: 'What you doin', talking to a *white* man?'

Racial intolerance is always a tragedy.

Still with boxing, the Ninian Park football ground in Cardiff was the scene of another world championship, this time the world featherweight crown which Howard Winstone was again trying to lift from the swarthy brow of Vicente Saldivar. Once again the referee, Wally Thom gave it to the Mexican by half a point, and once again I thought Winstone had won, this time by a quarter of a point.

I would not have minded if Thom had stepped in and called a halt in the fourteenth when Winstone was first put down and then nearly put clean out of the ring by the fury of Saldivar's attack until his clutching hands, like trapped moths, managed to grab at a restraining rope and keep him in the canvas world of carnage and courage. But since Thom let it continue I felt that Winsone had built up such an enormous points lead in the first half of the fight that he could only lose through a knockout. Britain was really unlucky around this time with world titles for the little men – flyweight McGowan, bantamweight Rudkin and featherweight Winstone. Once more the curse of cuts, which seemed to affect British fighters more than almost any others, intervened to prevent that brave and sporting little fighter Walter McGowan from regaining the world flyweight title from the man who had taken it from him, Chartchai Chionoi. The Scot was stopped in the seventh round with a cut eye.

Wimbledon opened with a sensation unique in my experience – and these were my thirty-first Championships – when Manuel Santana, the holder, was beaten on the first day in four sets by twenty-three-year-old Charlie Pasarell, born in Puerto Rico. I found it odd to see Santana, formerly 'Mr Quicksilver' himself, caught so often on the wrong foot. The truth was that after an operation on one of his ankles, which left him with an artificial ligament some seven and a half inches long, Santana was never again the same agile player he had been.

At last the first crack in the bastion of 'amateur' lawn tennis appeared when the first professionals were allowed to hold a tournament on the hallowed lawns of Wimbledon. They had of course been playing for years at Wembley but the traditionalists would not dream of trekking out to that dreary suburb at night and, although some of them regarded the breach with alarm and disfavour, those of us who wanted to see the best players in the best setting for the game were delighted when Rod Laver became the first winner of a pro tournament on the grass where he had already won the 'amateur' championship of the world twice.

In the final he beat, inevitably, Ken Rosewall; poor old 'Muscles' was still unable to overcome his Wimbledon jinx when, as a pro, he was again allowed to play there.

But if the lawn tennis authorities were beginning to live in the last third of the twentieth century cricket was not going to be stampeded into anything so revolutionary – by Gad, sir, no!

Brian Close, later to get the CBE for his services to the game, was sacked as the England captain. The charges were that he had deliberately wasted time against Warwickshire to gain two points for Yorkshire in the county championship; that he assaulted a spectator at Edgbaston (this part of the affair was shrouded in mystery); that he had expressed no public contrition for his time-wasting tactics which the Advisory County Cricket Committee stigmatized as not only being 'against the best interests of the game' but as constituting 'unfair play' – a unique allegation in my recollection.

As a substitute for Close Colin Cowdrey was chosen.

My comment was: 'I hate to write this, but in my opinion the elegant committee of the MCC, headed by Sir Alec Douglas Home and largely joined together by the indissoluble knot of a variety of old school ties, has preferred the gentleman to the player, the urbane ambassador from the Garden of England to the abrasive, pugnacious, bellicose, irritating-as-a-piece-of-grit-in-the-eye Roundhead from the dales of Yorkshire.' (There is no one in cricket whom I personally liked, and like, more than Colin Cowdrey.)

I would be the last to condone time-wasting or alleged cheating, but Close's own statement that he was guilty only of playing to the best of his ability and that his sole concern was to see English cricket climb to the top again, must have appealed to anyone who knew the tensions and the savage disappointments of big-time sport.

To be fair to Cowdrey I must record that England did win by the one victory scored by either side with the other four matches drawn, in the series against the West Indies.

Internationally cricket was still trying to strangle itself – and Pakistan was among the stranglers. It was apt that during the Test match at Lord's, because of construction work on the new stand, the first notice you saw as you walked through the gate was 'Danger: dead slow'. That was surely the motto of the Pakistani captain, Hanif Mohammad, who in the first innings had made 187 not out, occupying the crease for nine hours and two minutes. Brian Close declared at lunch on the last day, leaving Pakistan to make 257 to win, at a rate of fractionally over 73 runs an hour. A tough target – much faster, in fact, than England had scored in the morning.

But there wasn't even the gesture of chasing the runs. Instead Pakistan scored 88 for three in sixty-two overs and were, legitimately, booed off the field.

England seems to have a genius for getting rid of the best coaches and/or leaders in sport, rare as they are. Shortly after the Close affair it was announced that Bert Kinnear, one of the top-notch swimming coaches of my time, had resigned after a disagreement with the Amateur Swimming Association over a coaching appointment.

When I interviewed Kinnear for a TV programme I was tremendously impressed – not so much with his technical ability, for I am not sufficiently expert to judge that accurately, but with the blazing sincerity of the man's character. He was one of the few people in big-time sport who had seriously queried to himself the propriety of taking youngsters at the extremely early age which swimming demands if they are to get to the international summit and, as it were, brainwashing them into thinking that the sport is the be-all and end-all of their lives.

Obviously no sport could afford to jettison a man with the moral fibre, inspirational ability and wholesome integrity of a Kinnear; but he disagreed with authority and . . . he had to go.

I was on holiday, in my beloved Majorca, when Howard Winstone went to Mexico to try for yet a third time to take the world featherweight title from the powerful Vicente Saldivar. But what Winstone had been unable to do in London or Cardiff he was certainly not able to achieve in Mexico City, with the additional handicap of oxygen shortage in an arena nearly a mile and a half above sea level.

The contest came to an end when Howard's manager, Eddie Thomas, threw in the towel, not a moment too soon, in the twelfth round. Then, while the beaten Welshman was being sponged and cosseted in his corner, came this amazing announcement: 'Vicente Saldivar has fought his last fight. He has retired permanently from the ring.'

No one there could believe it, but in his dressing room Saldivar said: 'I decided to retire in the middle of the fight. I knew I'd win – but I've had three hard fights with Winstone. We've both taken a tremendous amount out of each other. Winstone could be the next world champion.'

In fact Howard did claim the world title when, three months later, he stopped the Japanese, Mitsunori Seki, in nine rounds, but he was only a shell of his former self. Six months later, with weight troubles as well, he lost his newly gained championship when the Cuban-born, Spanish-domiciled José Legra stopped him in five rounds; it was Howard's last fight. Another little gentleman of the ring and, with Nel Tarleton, the most skilful British nine-stone boxer of my time.

I feel I must mention Brian Lochore's All Blacks and their last match against the Barbarians, which brought their overall total to fourteen victories in fifteen matches with the fifteenth drawn. Twickenham on a fine December afternoon was as honey-coloured, crisp and spirited as a champagne cocktail and the New Zealanders, after drawing level half a minute before full time, won the match in injury time. Despite a lot of dropped passes earlier on they seemed like gigantic black-clad butlers, dispensing with the formality of silver salvers as they passed the ball to each other as though it were a brimming glass with a minimum period when it was not under one or another's control.

There was even a story-book ending when, I swear, there were not half a hundred in a crowd of 40,000 who did not instinctively, with shifting shoulders, twitching legs and mesmerizing fingers, lift over the bar the very last kick of the match, Fergie McCormick's culminating conversion of the final try. That gave him exactly his century of points during the European section of the tour: altogether a memorable occasion.

In soccer there was a magnificent drawn match (2–2) at Wembley between England and the USSR in which not only was the football skilful and thrilling, but the first approach to a 'foul' foul came after sixty-three minutes play, and that was the only one in the match.

Perhaps the best summing-up was from Rudolf Kreitlein, the West German referee, who had officiated in England's infamous World Cup clash with Argentina and whose last match before retirement was the Russian one. He said: 'I couldn't have asked for a better last match. The teams made it easy for me.'

And so to the great day, 14 December 1967, when the Annual General Meeting of the Lawn Tennis Association carried by an overwhelming majority an amended motion of which the vital words were: 'That . . . all reference to amateurs and professionals be deleted from the rules of the Lawn Tennis Association and that the Association itself should legislate only for players.' There were only five dissenting votes in a total of nearly two hundred.

The date for implementing 'open' tournaments was put off until 22 April 1968 – the first day of the British Hard Court Championships at Bournemouth, so that the management committee of the International Lawn Tennis Federation, who were due to meet in Paris on 19 and 20 April, should have a chance to come up with some form of house-cleaning.

Ben Barnett, the former Australian Test wicket-keeper, made a menacing speech on behalf of both Australia – or rather a minuscule portion of it – and the International Federation, threatened us with bell, book and candle if we pursued what was, in effect, a course of honesty.

This, probably the most important day in the history of modern lawn tennis, was the climax to a campaign which I had been pursuing ever since the first reigning Wimbledon champion, Bill Tilden, turned professional in 1930.

And I was a very happy man.

That some of that happiness was eroded by the fast-growing greed of so many players and the revoltingly ungrateful walk-out in 1973 of so many men players from Wimbledon, the showpiece of the country which had made their new-found and previously undreamed-of wealth possible, could not obscure the fact that people who did not stand to benefit financially from it had decided that honesty must be the best policy. . . .

1968 was barely a week old before Giorgio di Stefani, president of the International Lawn Tennis Federation, announced that from 22 April (the date given by the LTA for implementing 'open' tournaments) British players were to be outlawed from world-class tournaments, stating: 'Britain will not be suspended until then.' He added, no doubt whimsically: 'If God puts a finger on their head, maybe they will change their minds before then.'

The best remark I read came from the former Australian Davis Cup star Adrian Quist, one of the greatest doubles players of all time, who commented in the *Sydney Morning Herald*: 'For sheer hypocrisy the decision of the ILTF can have no equal.'

Wimbledon, unperturbed by the worldwide reactions, announced that its prize money would be £26,150, with the winner of the men's singles getting £2,000 and the lady champion £750; a distribution which was to cause repercussions in the future.

And now it was time to go to Grenoble for the Tenth Winter Olympic Games. I have rarely known a more lavish presentation; later I was told that the French had spent 1 per cent of their entire national income on ensuring that these Games would glorify *la patrie*.

There was, for instance, the bob run at Alpe d'Huez some forty miles from Grenoble itself which, unfortunately, had been so sited that the sun beat down on it melting the run and making it unusable until midnight or the early hours of the morning. Even then three of the bends had to be artificially refrigerated at a cost of tens of thousands of pounds a *day*!

The imagination boggled at the idea of freezing an Alp!

When competitive racing did start, around midnight, on the top of a mile-and-a-half Alp in cold as frigid as a mother-in-law's kiss and under amber lights as artificial as a callgirl's blonde hair, there was an announcement after approximately every four runs that because of damage to the track there would be a delay, varying from ten minutes to half an hour. Each time that happened it meant that iron men from Austria had to handle blocks of ice a metre long, with their bare hands, easing them back into place so that the compressed-air gang could seal up the track. Additional delays were caused periodically when the lights failed.

In the end Tony Nash and Robin Dixon did not have a lot of luck defending their 'boblet' title, finishing fifth.

But if we couldn't win, the next best thing happened for at last Eugenio Monti, who had won nine world titles but had always been cheated of an Olympic gold medal, steered his boblet into first place – Monti, the forty-year-old red-headed Italian, with the eyes as blue as a frozen sea and the battered look of an old fighter, the same Monti who had looked like winning that elusive gold medal at Innsbruck but who had ensured victory for Nash and Dixon by lending them an essential bolt for their boblet – a gesture which won him the European award for sportsmanship.

The highlights of the Winter Games are the Alpine skiing events – and this was particularly true at Grenoble, for a Frenchman, Jean-

Claude Killy, rather laughingly described as a Customs official, was the hot favourite to bring off the triple of downhill, slalom and giant slalom and so get his skiing MA – Master of Alps.

He won the downhill – by eight hundredths of a second. He made this race of over 3,000 yards, with a vertical drop of over half a mile, in 0·15 second under two minutes – and he didn't fall!

To me Killy never had the grace of his triple-winning predecessor, Toni Sailer. The Frenchman seemed to prod himself down the courses as untidily as a chicken with outstretched wings traversing its run. But, my God! his attack – *that* was championship material of the highest order.

Killy won his second gold medal, the giant slalom, more easily than he had the downhill; his winning margin over a course of about a mile and a furlong, with a drop of nearly 500 yards and the necessity of negotiating fifty-seven gates, was 3 mins 29·28 secs.

Alas! Killy's hat-trick, in the slalom with the even tighter gates, was achieved in conditions which did much to tarnish the eventual result, for although Haakon Mjoen of Norway and Karl Schranz of Austria beat Killy's combined time for the two runs, both men were disqualified for missing gates. What happened, however, must remain in doubt for, in a desperate attempt to finish the Alpine competition, the two runs were held in a sort of freezing fog, where even spectators' hair turned white with the rime and visibility was usually down to less than twenty yards.

The memory of Killy's frenetic stick work – it was almost like watching Gene Krupa on the drums! – lingers yet, but his final victory left the blue Chanticleer's feathers distinctly bedraggled; popular opinion was summed up by the typical, if unfair, remark around Grenoble: 'I suppose if Killy had finished tenth, they'd have disqualified the other nine!'

But there were other unsullied memories: the skating of the Russians, thirty-five-year-old Olyeg Protopopov and thirty-two-year-old Lyudmila Belousova, who retained the pairs title in figure-skating which they had won at Innsbruck and came as close to achieving a perfect artform as is possible in sport.

There was the almost unbelievably good performance, for a British-born skier, of Gina Hathorn who was only three-hundredths of a second from winning a bronze medal in the women's slalom.

There was also a form of disqualification new to me: three East German girls, including the world champion Ortrum Ederlein, were ruled out of the women's single toboggan for illegally heating the runners of their sleds over a fire before racing!

As a footnote to the Games, this was turning out to be quite a year for French sport for, towards the end of March, by beating Wales 14–9,

I saw them finally achieve what they had been trying to do since they entered the five nations competition in 1909–10 – beat all four home countries in one Rugby season.

Although I had a date in Oakland, California, I could not bear to miss at least the start of the new era of 'open' lawn tennis when I saw Mark Cox, that rather negative personality, cause a sensation by beating Pancho Gonzales.

In Britain the signs were that any major future for lawn tennis would have to be for the 'open' variety. In 1968 Bournemouth had taken over £12,000 for the first 'open' championships; yet a week later, at the same venue, in a Davis Cup tie in which we beat the French with all the first three rubbers going to five sets, I doubt if there were more than 500 cash customers during any one of the three days of the meeting. Clearly the Davis Cup, after nearly seventy years, was going to have to accept a new formula or decline in importance.

Back to Paris for the final stages of the first of the 'Big Four' tournaments to go 'open', and another astonishing reversal of form by Ken Rosewall. Less than five weeks earlier at Wembley he had been able to win only one game against Rod Laver, but he now beat 'Rocket' with the loss of only twelve to regain a title which he had first captured fifteen years earlier!

I have never seen a match 'paced' better than this one was by Rosewall. As soon as things would not go right for him in the third set he let it go and then returned, after the interval, to sweep Laver off the court in the fourth. At Wimbledon, of course, there is no interval and that is the only reason I can hazard – far-fetched though it may be – for Ken never having won the greatest of all singles titles.

There was an hilarious Wightman Cup match at Wimbledon this year with Britain winning 4–3 when the two Truman sisters, Christine (by now Mrs Janes) and Nell, won the final doubles match and the deciding rubber after a three-set match.

Earlier the tie had included one incident which, macabre though it was, could have happened only at Wimbledon and despite its tragedy was, in the setting, hilarious. At a crucial point in one of the matches a man started shouting in the stands and after being angrily 'shushed' managed to stop play by crying harshly: 'Is there a doctor? A man is dying here. . . .' And, shockingly, he did die.

But Sally swears she heard two Kensington matrons, who obviously could not have heard the interrupter's words, protesting testily: 'Really! Not at game point!'

The first 'open' Wimbledon produced two worthy champions in Rod Laver, for so long to prove himself the best player in the world at the tournaments which then really mattered, and Billie Jean King, always at her formidable best at Wimbledon, who thus became the only woman apart from Louise Brough and Little Mo Connolly to win three years running since the war – a record which still stands.

I have seen every Wimbledon champion since Henri Cochet won for the second time in 1929. Laver, on his play against Tony Roche in the final bore comparison with, if he did not excel, all of them.

Now came the saga of d'Oliveira. He had been recalled, somewhat unexpectedly, for the final Test match against the Australians. After the second day's play I wrote:

At 2.43 on a glorious summer's afternoon at Kennington Oval, Basil d'Oliveira played a leg glance, off Australian 'mystery' bowler Johnny Gleeson, which was probably the most political stroke in postwar cricket.

For the single it produced completed d'Oliveira's hundred and made it virtually certain that he will be chosen for England's forthcoming tour of South Africa.

The day after England won the Test by 226 runs, but with only six minutes play left, it was announced that 'centurion' d'Oliveira, who had also got the wicket which started Australia's final collapse, had not been picked for South Africa! On my fifty-fifth birthday an article by me appeared on the front page of the *Daily Mirror* which began:

'It is a bitter disappointment. I have nothing else to say. I don't want to discuss it, thank you.'

These were the dignified words with which Basil d'Oliveira, the Cape Coloured South African cricketer, fobbed off further queries before being driven away from the county ground at Worcester, before close of play, after he had made 128 against Sussex. He was a broken man when he heard the news.

'Dolly' may have nothing else to say, may not wish to discuss it. But I do – and so will many thousands of people all round the world.

There's no need for d'Oliveira to prove his fitness. His recent play proved that more dramatically than a thousand doctors' certificates. His only 'unfitness' is one of birth not batting, background not ability.

So much for the end of one man's dream. And so much for the thought that all men, on the playing field at least, are equal in everything but ability. The MCC may continue to wield authority in cricket. But, for many, they have forfeited respect.

I have rarely if ever received so many phone calls, telegrams and letters from the public on any one subject. There were comments from cricketing countries like Australia, Pakistan and, of course, South Africa itself. My correspondence was almost exactly eight to one in favour of d'Oliveira, and more than one reader ended up with the phrase: 'For the first time in my life I am ashamed to be British.'

D'Oliveira had this to say: 'I have been so moved by the messages of encouragement and understanding that I feel I must grope around for something to say. For instance, fantastic though it seems I can, at this strangest moment, see the ball going off the bat as I turned Gleeson for a single to get my Test century at the Oval last Friday.'

Then d'Oliveira was hired to report the test for the *News of the World*. Some dinosaur from the Transvaal was quoted on the radio as saying that South African cricketers would not object to d'Oliveira commenting on the tour but whether he would be allowed to sit in the 'white' Press box was another matter. South Africa's Premier, John Vorster, hinted that d'Oliveira might not be allowed into the country to report the tour, saying among other things that South Africa could not allow 'certain organizations, individuals or newspapers to use certain people or sportsmen as pawns in their game to bedevil South Africa's relations with Britain and to create incidents to undermine South Africa's way of life'.

Less than a week later I was just getting to my feet to make a speech of appreciation for Howard Winstone, who was being honoured by the World Sporting Club at Grosvenor House, when I received the news that 'Dolly' was after all going to South Africa – as a player. It was one of the happiest moments of my sporting life.

Tom Cartwright, whose health had been suspect, had been forced to withdraw which left open for d'Oliveira the place which he should have had from the first. One day later the ineffable Vorster reacted by saying that the MCC had yielded to pressure and that 'we are not prepared to accept a team thrust upon us'.

To which my reply was: 'Now we see the nature of the Beast. White South Africa, the repressive Republic, will not accept that a man with a different coloured skin can be an equally good sportsman as one of its own kind.'

Henry Cooper, still persevering, took the European heavyweight title from Karl Mildenberger, the in-and-out German fighter. That night was one of Mildenberger's 'out' performances, and he was well on the way to an overwhelming points defeat when he was disqualified at the end of the eighth round for illegal use of his head.

By now it was time to leave for my seventh Summer Olympic Games, in Mexico City. They had had a disastrous prelude. Students protesting against the regime had been gunned down mercilessly. My old friend John Rodda of *The Guardian* had spent a terrifying period lying on the floor at the wrong end of a pistol held by a man with a glove on his hand to identify him to his colleagues as one of the official 'executioners'.

John wrote a brilliant story about his ordeal – I thought he should have got the Sportswriter of the Year award for it although, God knows, there was nothing 'sporting' about it – but the experience left him, and us when we arrived, very shaken.

And yet there *is* that recurrent four-yearly miracle of the Games, typified by the Olympic village.

Olympiad by Olympiad the Games were getting bigger, more unwieldy and financially more and more impossible to stage, except for the wealthiest or most powerful countries. I felt that soon it would be no good building an Olympic village – it would have to be an Olympic town. 'The Games need to take the Pill before the sporting explosion gets entirely out of hand,' I said.

At the head of this top-heavy pyramid was Avery Brundage, the only American who had completed more terms of office than Franklin D. Roosevelt and who had actually been born nine years before the Games had been revived in 1896.

The estimated cost of the next Games, which had been awarded to Munich, was already hovering between sixty and seventy million pounds. What chance had, say, Nairobi, the Kenyan capital? Yet the five Olympic rings stood for the five continents – and Africa was the only one which had not been awarded the Games.

Brundage, the arch-apostle of amateurism, had – through a surfeit of success ensured that only professional countries could afford to put on the amateur festival.

I don't think I've ever worked harder, journalistically, than I did in Mexico City. The journey to the main stadium was a daily traffic jam, miles long and, as you neared the stadium, there was the added tension of concentrations of troops and armour. Communications were chaotic. Eating was a problem, too, for much of the local food was liable to cause what was euphemistically known as 'Montezuma's revenge', and some of the better restaurants were excessively expensive. However, we did discover quite a lot of more than agreeable Chilean wines, which made a pleasant change from the ever-present 'cactus-juice' tequila.

Another drawback, of course, was the question of altitude. I am among other things – so many other things – a chronic bronchitic and I found the problem of breathing a perpetual hazard. I would forget and run up a short flight of stairs, to find when I got to the top that when I took a breath nothing happened. The first two or three times this occurred it was really very frightening; afterwards it became a constant harassment. What it was like for the athletes, particularly those in the more prolonged events, I really could not accurately imagine.

It was no good pretending that these Games were equitable or, really, friendly. The records were so false. When they were established in one of the 'explosive' events you felt you might have to wait until the Games were put on in the altitude of Addis Ababa, or some currently unlikely venue, for them to be broken. When it came to a long-distance affair you could very nearly be damn certain that it would go to a character born and bred to altitude – and not necessarily to the best athlete.

Some people argued, saying that running at altitude for sea-level athletes was no more unfair than running at sea-level was for altitude athletes. That was nonsense. The altitude boys had an 'oxygen capacity' advantage when they came down to sea-level. The sea-level competitors had an 'oxygen debt' at altitude. An Australian doctor, Brian Corrigan, estimated the difference between sea-level and altitude running at 2 per cent. That meant a 200-metre difference in 10,000 metres.

One of the truly great British Olympic triumphs of my time was that scored by David Hemery in the 400 metres hurdles. He not only looked a winner all the way but he clipped a staggering 0·7 seconds off the world record. This event is one of the 'killers' of the athletics programme and I have never been sure in my own mind whether altitude was a help here or a handicap which Hemery brilliantly overcame.

Meanwhile hopes were high for another English star, the delightful Lillian Board who, as she had said she would, was specializing in the 400 metres and entered the final a hot favourite for it. She was nineteen, it was her first Olympic Games and she returned 52·1 seconds, her best time and a UK record. But it was Colette Besson, a streak of blue lightning in the vest of France with, as I wrote, 'long black hair swinging and long legs devouring the last vital metres' who passed her, perhaps five metres out, and whose time, one-tenth of a second faster than Lillian's, equalled the Olympic record and won her the gold medal.

I think the golden girl, who temporarily had been transmuted into silver, summed it up best when she said: 'I felt great coming out of the last bend. My dream of Olympic gold was coming true. Then with forty yards to go I just lost something. When I came off the last bend I could not believe it – I was in the lead out there. Then Colette just beat me.'

But Lillian kept her word. All along she had said that she would not cry if she lost. She would cry only if she won. And when she mounted the rostrum for the medal ceremony, she smiled gaily and chatted while the silver – instead of the coveted gold – was placed round her neck.

But sad though Lillian's defeat was – tragic, indeed, when you remember what was to come – it was in some ways eclipsed by what happened at the end of the men's 200 metres. The race is quickly told.

At the start America's John Carlos seemed to be ripping the field wide open. But at halfway Tommie Smith looked to be gathering speed, and some fifty to sixty yards out he really put down the accelerator and, uncatchable as drifting smoke, raced on to the gold medal and a world record of 19·8 seconds.

There had been a lot of talk about 'Black Power' before and during the Games. Now we were to see an overt demonstration of it.

For Smith and Carlos, both black as the ace of spades, both bearded, marched to the podium to receive their medals. Both wore black half-stockings; both wore black scarves. Smith wore a black glove on his right hand, Carlos wore one on his left; both wore expressions of arrogant dissociation with the 99 per cent white majority of the crowd.

As the National Anthem of what they would say was not their country was played each of them bowed his head and raised a black-gloved clenched fist toward the US flag as it slowly climbed two of the three masts. Neither of them spoke to, or shook hands with, the Australian Norman who had won the silver medal.

Were they right or wrong? How can I, as a white man, put myself into their position? It all reminded me so painfully of the 1936 Games which had been set up to prove the superiority of the blue-eyed flaxen-haired Aryans – and had been so patently punctured by the flying spikes of an Alabama-born Negro, Jesse Owens. Hadn't Owens' 'protest' been the more effective?

But the black performance continued to be breathtaking. Although altitude was of course a vital factor, Bob Beamon both proved and dis-proved Lynn Davies as a good and a false prophet in the long jump. Before the Games Lynn had told me: 'If he hits the board right, he could clear 28 feet and it would be all over.'

Well, Beamon *did* hit the board right, with his very first jump in the final, and it *was* all over. But his distance was 29 ft 2½ in! Altitude alone could not account for this performance, for no one else on the day could reach even 27 feet and, as far as I know, no one to this day has cleared 28 feet.

That was a different example of black power – but we were not yet finished with the capital letter kind. In one of the most dramatic races – especially considering the Black Power machinations behind it – Lee Evans won the men's 400 metres final. Another of the most militant of the American Negro athletes, Evans won in the well-nigh incredible time of 43·8 seconds, which means he virtually ran a quarter of a mile in even time. And he ran like a man possessed.

All morning he had been under the most intense pressure, first from officials trying to discipline him and then from a crazy throng of photographers and TV men seeking interviews. He ran as though his very life depended on it – as his convictions most certainly did. As he pell-melled into the end of the home stretch, his bearded jaw agape, I thought for a moment he was going to blow up. But, like the old motto of the Foreign Legion – 'March or Die' – Evans was determined to run until his heart burst, in justification of his principles. This was more than just a foot race. It was a physical demonstration in a sports stadium of a man's belief; a manifesto in muscle; a sermon in speed. I was certain Evans was not thinking of anything like a gold medal. He was running to prove that Black Power had to be reckoned with. And, whether you agree with his ideas or not, you have to admire the man's passionate personal triumph.

African black power came to the fore, among other events, in the 3,000 metres steeplechase which was won by Amos Biwott who, in a whirl-wind finish, beat his fellow Kenyan, Ben Kogo; Biwott had run his first-ever steeplechase only seventy-four days before the Olympic final – so much for sophisticated techniques – and I still remember the way he regarded the water-jump as though it might be concealing crocodiles!

The marathon went to Ethiopia for the third time running – but not, alas, to that great-hearted competitor Abebe Bikila who, at thirty-six, had sustained such a bad leg injury that his selection for the team had been in doubt. Sure enough, shortly after the ten-mile mark Bikila's legs folded under him and he had to give up.

It did not matter as far as his country was concerned. Mamo Wolde, a thirty-five-year-old soldier from Ethiopia, won the race which started in Constitution Square with the bells in the cathedral pealing the runners on their way – it had been slightly re-routed in order to avoid the Plaza of the Three Cultures [sic] where the students had been killed just before the start of the Games and where, until a few days before the race, there were still tanks.

One other athletics event is etched darkly in my mind – the defeat of the world record-holder, Vera Nikolic, in the women's 800 metres. And what a disastrous defeat, for it was not even in the final but in the round before that the Yugoslavian girl, a hot favourite for the event, dropped out after running only 300 metres. There was no obvious sign of distress or collapse on the track; indeed, she left the stadium without even watching the end of the race. But it was possible through binoculars to see that she was in tears. Far worse was to come once she had quit the public gaze.

She went to a bridge over an outside road and whether she really meant to hurl herself from it no one can ever be sure. Certainly she was reported to have been tearing her hair as an official pulled her back and she collapsed, still screaming, to the ground. A wicked and terrible thing had been done to someone whom we had seen less than three months earlier as a happy teenager setting a world record.

Perhaps Chris Brasher who, more than any of us in the Press box, knew the tensions of Olympic competition, put it best – as he often does – when he wrote in *Mexico 1968*:

Her coach is to blame and he should never be allowed near another athlete. He has had this young Yugoslavian girl . . . out on the training track three times a day for the past three weeks, working her so hard, and reducing her to tears, that even the Australian distance runners, hard trainers themselves, wonder how anyone's body, much less the body of a woman, can stand it.

Britain did wonderfully well in the three-day equestrian event with a strangely assorted team. It was led by a fifty-four-year-old grandfather, Major Derek Allhusen, whom I had last seen in the pentathlon event which was part of the Winter Olympic Games at St Moritz twenty years earlier.

Then there was Richard Meade, described then as a property broker but later to become far more famous when his name was linked with that of an even more celebrated show jumper, Princess Anne. Next was Staff Sergeant Ben Jones and finally came Jane Bullen, a fetching lass of twenty from Hampshire who was a student nurse at the Middlesex Hospital.

At the end of the three days – dressage, cross-country and show jumping – we had won the team event so easily that it was scarcely believable, placing our top three – Allhusen, Meade and Jones – in the top five. Indeed Allhusen, a Norfolk farmer riding Lochinvar, which had now set up a world record by finishing sixteen three-day events, in winning the silver medal had ended up only 2·75 points behind the individual winner, Jacques Guyon of France.

The finals of the Olympic boxing had two memorable moments – but one of them only for the British. That was in the middleweight division when Chris Finnegan, a Buckinghamshire bricklayer, won the gold medal against the Russian Alexei Kiseliov by the slenderest possible points margin. What I really appreciated about southpaw Finnegan's victory was his own evaluation of it when someone asked him what his first reaction to winning a gold medal was and he replied: 'Oh, I thought – it's better than being a silly old bricklayer.'

Later, of course, Finnegan, having moved up a weight, was to win first the British and Commonwealth and then the European light heavyweight titles and to fight fourteen gallant rounds for the world title against one of the greatest modern 12 st 7 lb champions, Bob Foster.

The other and, from a neutral point of view, greater excitement lay among the heavyweights. The final was won by George Foreman, who destroyed Russia's Ionas Chepulis, the referee coming to Chepulis' rescue in the second round. Foreman hadn't the speed of the young Patterson or the genius of Clay. But at the time I believed he might well be the most talked-of young heavyweight in the world – if he could find a really good tutor. I really thought he was better than Frazier at the same stage of their development; but I shall always feel that he didn't find that 'really good tutor' – or, at least, not in time – or he would never have fought the asinine battle he waged against Clay in Zaire six years later. Previously his power of punch had been enough to win thirty-seven of the forty professional fights he had had inside the distance – but a bludgeon alone is not enough against Clay.

Less than two months after the Olympic Games had concluded a story came out about John and Sheila Sherwood, respectively bronze medallist in the 400 metres hurdles and silver medallist in the long jump, which proved yet again how we in Britain never learn. Sheila was a Physical Education teacher at Myers Grove Comprehensive School in Sheffield and her husband John also taught PE at Doncaster. They now had to prepare for the 1969 European championships and for their winter training they were planning to hurdle along a corridor at Sheila's school! According to Sheila: 'There are no indoor facilities in Sheffield now that the bad weather has arrived, and if we couldn't have used the school corridor it would have affected our training pro-gramme. The long jump in Hillsborough Park, where we usually train, is in a dangerous condition and it seems incredible that there are no indoor facilities or a tartan track in a city the size of Sheffield.'

No amenities for champions; no facilities to encourage youngsters to become champions. How different from a smaller and younger nation like East Germany, and so, with the disappointment so predictable in British sporting circles, the year came to an end.

11

1969–72
The Last Lap

Now it was time for my fourth trip to Australia, to see plucky little Alan Rudkin (the 'Scouser choirboy') challenging yet again on the other side of the world for the supreme bantamweight title at the Kooyong Stadium. His opponent was the Australian aborigine, Lionel Rose.

According to the Australian judge, Ron Walden, and my own score-card Alan won by one point – or, by British scoring, a quarter of a point (in Australia they do not use fractions). But the referee, ex-Australian boxer Vic Patrick, who handled the fight admirably, and the other Australian judge, Ray Mitchell, both voted for Lionel Rose, the aborigine, and thus he officially retained his title.

I was horrified by the scoring of the second judge. Mitchell made Rose the winner on points by seventy-five to sixty, which meant that he did not give a single round to Rudkin and made only one, the thirteenth, even; a verdict which I was prompted to rank with some of those handed out by 'Bloody' Judge Jeffries. I commented: 'My feeling, twenty-four hours after this monstrous miscarriage of justice, is that he should never again be allowed to judge even a baby show.' More than eight years later I still feel the same way.

Thirty-three hours afterwards it was sad to be met, in Rome, with the news of the death of Jimmy Wilde.

Wilde – I should like to have the brief of defending his right to be acknowledged as the greatest pound-for-pound or, in his case, almost ounce-for-ounce fighter of all time.

Official record. Total bouts: 140. Won inside the distance 77; won on points 48; won on a foul 1; drew 2; no decision 8; lost on points 1; lost inside the distance 3.

Unofficial record – as Wilde told it to me himself. Over 800 fights – most of them in the travelling booths where British world champions, up to the time of Freddie Mills, learned their job.

Hardest work, twenty-three knockouts in one day. A break halfway through for a bun and a cup of tea. Reward – fifteen bob, one shilling more than he had made in a week as a twelve-year-old miner! Sparring partner at the time – owing to lack of cash – wife, 'Lisbeth' who, according to the great Jimmy Butler, father of Frank the columnist and sports editor of the *News of the World*, used to wear a shield over her chest during the sparring sessions.

The four men who beat Wilde were the Scot, Tancy Lee, who caught the Welshman when he was recovering from 'flu and stopped him in 17 rounds. Wilde subsequently stopped Lee in 11 rounds.

Then, in the final of the *bantamweight* class in the Inter-Allied King's Trophy Competition, in December 1918, Pal Moore, of the USA, got a three-round controversial points decision over him.

I stress *bantam* (8 st 6 lb) for Wilde's best fighting weight was supposed to be between 6 st 10 lb and 7 st 2 lb. Sometimes he used to weigh-in wearing his beloved bowler hat and an overcoat with lead weights in it so that his opponent shouldn't know how much poundage Wilde was conceding. Incidentally, seven months later, Wilde outpointed Moore over twenty rounds.

His last but one fight was against Peter Herman, again a bantam-weight and one good enough to hold the world title at that weight for over four years. It was stopped, in the American's favour, in the seventeenth round. There was a dispute about Herman's weight and Wilde was about to put on his street clothes and leave the arena when a message came that the Prince of Wales, later the Duke of Windsor, was eagerly awaiting the fight . . . so the little Welshman went out to certain defeat.

Again I'm indebted to the late Jimmy Butler for a description of the end: 'He still tried to fight on, until at last (referee) Smith had to pick him up under his arm and carry him across the ring to his corner.

' "I'm sorry, Jimmy," he told the furiously protesting champion, "but I had to pick you up because you don't know how to lie down!" '

Finally Wilde met the Filipino, Pancho Villa, at twenty-one ten years Wilde's junior. The Welshman had been out of the ring for two and a half years and it was only the staggering purse for flyweights of those days – £13,000 – which lured him back.

Even so the price he paid was too high, for the beating which he took before being knocked out in the seventh round, stayed with him for the rest of his seventy-six-year-old life and when I last saw him, in a home for old folks just outside Cardiff, he did not recognize me and he had completely forgotten his glorious past – partly as a result of a cowardly attack on the old gentleman by some vicious lout at Cardiff station.

I was in Rome to see Henry Cooper defend his European heavyweight title against Piero Tomasoni, an Italian from roughly the same region where Primo Carnera, the world heavyweight champion produced by Italy, had been born. The promoter, Rino Tommasi, now one of the world's most famous lawn tennis writers, was hardly encouraging about Cooper's chances when he told me the day before the fight: 'This is the twenty-fourth European championship I have put on, and so far no Italian has been beaten in any of the twenty-three previous ones!'

Right nobly did ''Enery' break that sequence, for he succeeded in knocking out Tomasoni in the fifth round after being as wickedly fouled as any man I've ever seen in the ring. Cooper, never a moaner, summed it up when he said: 'I've never been hit so hard or so low in my life, and I've never been so badly hurt in the ring. Cut eyes are nothing to what happened to me tonight.'

The evidence of the iniquity which had been committed against Cooper was in his dressing room, where his protector looked like an old sardine tin which had been damaged by booted feet.

One sad footnote to the saga of Sugar Ray Robinson, arguably the greatest box-fighter of the past fifty years. In his autobiography *Sugar Ray* (Putnam, 1970) he described how in 1965, after he had announced his final retirement, officials of Madison Square Garden, scene of so many of Robinson's greatest triumphs, gave him a big gold trophy inscribed 'The World's Greatest Fighter'.

The evening ended in his apartment and, in his own words: 'I had to put it on the floor. The only table in the apartment was a beige metal card table, with thin legs, in the middle of the bare wooden floor in the dining room. We had our meals on it. The only other piece of furniture in the room was an old, scratched wooden bed.'

He may not have been 'The World's Greatest Fighter', but he deserved better of boxing than that.

A curious little story which was never pursued and which fizzled out after a few months, was the statement that Cassius Clay had clashed with the Black Muslims and was now no longer to be called Muhammad Ali by order of Elijah Muhammad, leader of the sect to whom Clay owed allegiance. The cynical, knowing that Clay had not been allowed to fight for over two years and had therefore been unable to contribute in cash or kind to the movement, suggested that it smacked of 'The King is dead – let's find a new King'. However, with the never-ruled-out possibility of a return to the ring for the man who had never lost the heavyweight title, the whole business quietly disappeared from the news.

Athens, where I had gone in the summer of 1969 to cover the Federation Cup, was as spellbinding as ever, with the open-air restaurants rising in tiers above the centre of the city, a particularly impressive *son et lumière* centred on the Acropolis with the simulated foot-beats of the original runner from Marathon particularly moving, and much gay

Grecian music with splendid ouzo, horrible retsina and generous Athenian hospitality.

But there was a reverse side to the coin. One morning when that boon companion, David Talbot of the *Birmingham Post*, and I were sitting in the lambent sunshine pursuing that most pleasant of occupations, watching the world go by, the main square in which we were sitting seemed to empty as though someone had removed the plug from a gigantic basin.

There wasn't even a waiter in sight as we sat sipping our drinks in an open-air café. Then, almost like a tank attack, a cavalcade of black limousines, either curtained or with heavily tinted windows, swept through the deserted square at breakneck speed; and the Athenians did not need to be reminded to 'Watch the wall, my darlings, while the gentlemen go by!' For this was a passage of the infamous 'Colonels'who were dragooning the country. The only time I had ever seen anything like it was the time when I had met a flotilla of Krushchev's body-guard while I was on my way to Moscow airport.

One evening when we were being entertained by the extremely agreeable officials of the Greek LTA, I was introduced to one of the Colonels who, I was assured, had 'special responsibilities for sport' – shades of my old friend Denis Howell! The official who effected the introduction, normally an amusing, urbane and civilized man, was like a cat on hot bricks. After the introduction I didn't blame him.

For I have rarely met a more ruthless-seeming individual who, with the knowledge of his own virtually limitless power, could scarcely bother to be civil to a foreign journalist who was clearly immersed in the activity for which he himself had 'special responsibilities'. I can say only, with complete sincerity, that it took me back to the bad old days of the Nazis.

As far as the Federation Cup itself was concerned, the final was the one which was customary, if not inevitable, in those days: the USA beat Australia 2–1 after Australia had eliminated Britain 3–0 in the semi-final.

And now I was being faced with one of the rare really important crises of my life. From the time I had reached fifty I had decided to have an annual medical check. When I got to fifty-five I decided to make it twice yearly. And, with later unpayable debts to other people, I owe my life to the alertness of Neville Stidolph who had treated me – and 'treated' was the operative word – for years.

I have been a chronic bronchitic since before I can remember and, like the fool that I was and – in other ways – will no doubt remain, I was an over-average to heavy smoker. Neville decided he didn't really care for the way I was progressing and he arranged for me to spend two days in the Whittington Hospital where he had been a luminary for so long, for 'observation'. I couldn't help the feeling that if anyone really wanted to observe me there must be something very wrong!

Peter Davis, another of the team of men who were to be of such inestimable help – curious how much you appreciate team-work when your life depends on it – broke the news to me. It wasn't what I had vaguely suspected, TB. It *was* what I suppose I had refused to contemplate, a growth; yes, malignant; yes . . . cancer of my right lung.

I shall always remember Peter Davis with gratitude, apart from what he had done, for one remark. He asked: 'Do you know any good thoracic surgeons?'

'I don't even know what the hell they are,' I said – and we both laughed.

In the end I was lucky enough to be sent to Lance Bromley. When Neville Stidolph, bless his heart, heard he wrote to me saying how glad he was to hear this, and adding if anyone could pull me through he was sure it was Bromley! Of course, he didn't mean it that way. But I did manage to get a message to him that if he would stick to his profession and leave the writing side of things to me I, at least, would feel very much better!

Then I saw Lance Bromley. I have no way of knowing what it is like to meet someone for the first time and tell them the simple, unadorned truth. But because he laid the cards on the table, face up; because he spoke to me like an adult in non-technical terms which anyone but a self-deluded fool could understand; because he gave the facts and left me the choice, he is someone whom for eight years I have enjoyed the reassurance of seeing.

It didn't, of course, help when, on the very eve of Wimbledon, the death of Little Mo Connolly was announced – from cancer. She was the epitome of sportsmanship, always willing in later years to encourage, inspire and coach other players – as both Virginia Wade and Ann Jones will testify.

It proved to be one of the most exciting Wimbledons with Pancho Gonzales, by then aged forty-one, winning the longest singles match ever played there against Charlie Pasarell, sixteen years his junior, and Ann Jones having her 'finest hours' as a player.

The Gonzales match had everything a great athletic contest demands. The first *set* lasted nearly two hours; the score of 24–22 to Pasarell equalled the longest singles set ever played at Wimbledon. Gonzales saved no fewer than eleven set points before conceding the set, and promptly went to the umpire to appeal against the light – quite justifiably, in my opinion.

The umpire consulted the referee, Captain Mike Gibson, whose orders were 'Play on'. I still don't think he should have given them –

but I'm very glad he did for, without them, we might well have been robbed of one of the dozen most memorable matches I have seen in over forty-five years.

Throughout the second set, which comprised only seven games and which lasted barely a quarter of an hour, Gonzales was swearing, shouting at the crowd – and being shouted at by them – and once slinging his racket along the ground so fiercely that one of the ball boys had to skip out of the way right smartish. Normally I deplore that sort of behaviour by a player but I must say I did sympathize with Gonzales this time; it was a case of *Gotterdamerung* – or, at least, the twilight for one god. At the end of the second set, won of course by Pasarell, as the veteran could hardly see the ball, Gonzales swept off the court pursued by the boos of a section of the crowd.

I guarantee the next day they were sorry for their previous behaviour when Gonzales, making one of the greatest comebacks ever achieved in lawn tennis, won the third set 16–14, the fourth 6–3 and the fifth, after being *seven* times within one point of defeat, 11–9.

The full score was 22–24, 1–6, 16–14, 6–3, 11–9, a total of 112 games spread over two days, and lasting in all five hours and twelve minutes playing time. This eclipsed the famous Drobny–Patty match by nineteen games, but that 1953 match was of course played in one day.

I sometimes wonder if the people who emasculated lawn tennis for the sake of TV sponsors (mostly in the US) have ever considered that had their bloody tie-break been introduced by the 1960s these epics, and so many that had gone before, as well as some to come, could never have been played. I don't suppose they have. If you're interested in money first and sport not at all, you don't waste time – which is money – on considering the wrecking job you have done.

Ann Jones' triumph was especially warm to me. I had seen her playing – first table and then lawn – tennis in Japan, Sweden, France, Italy and the USA. So often she had been 'Miss Nearly'; surely now she wasn't to become 'Mrs Almost'.

In the semi-final she scored her greatest victory to beat Margaret Court, who was apparently sailing serenely towards the grand 'slam' having already won the Australian and French titles, the latter by beating Ann in the final.

But there was still the final to play – against Billie Jean King, the woman who was destined to win Wimbledon more often than any postwar player. This was the eighth Wimbledon meeting, including Wightman Cup matches, between the two and, apart from the first one seven years earlier, when Mrs King had been only eighteen, the American had won every time.

It looked as though she were going to do so again when she took the first set 6–3 but after Mrs Jones took the second you had to be in good shape even to be a spectator. Ann, her features set like some marauding Red Indian and her steel racket flashing like his tomahawk, dashed to 3–1 and, continuing to play the aggressive game which had defeated Margaret Court, clinched it at 6–2. Only the second British girl to win in thirty-two years. . . .

There was one strange thing about the men's final won, as expected but only after a first-class match, by Rod Laver who beat John Newcombe by three sets to one. I had seen my first final in 1929, when Henry Cochet beat Jean Borotra, and now in 1969 it was the first time since then that two previous champions had clashed in a final!

It had been a wonderful Wimbledon to cover and now it was time for me to observe sport largely from the sidelines for a time, although I did manage to write some columns and commentaries from home or hospital.

When I started the treatment I knew, I suppose, as much – which meant precious little – as the average layman about cobalt rays and what to expect from them.

The approach was not encouraging. The equipment was in the basement of St Mary's, Paddington, largely, I was told, because its weight and the treatment room (lead-lined so that no rays should escape) came to so much that any higher storey would have had to be reinforced to support its weight. Logical enough but descending to the bowels of the hospital was not heart-lifting.

I was put in the care of another man to whom I owe as much as you can owe anyone – Dr Hulbert. He was a pragmatic character and one of his first questions was about my age. I told him I was nearly fifty-six and he nodded and remarked drily: 'Yes, old enough to know that you don't live forever.' In cold print that sounds brusque to the point of being inhuman, but in fact I preferred the astringent approach. Living away from the sunlight, with men and women coming to him day after day as virtually their only remaining hope, no doctor could afford to be emotional or in any way melodramatic; and it was better for his patients that he should be matter-of-fact.

It was curious to lie on a couch-style piece of furniture, rather like an operating table, while behind your head was a kind of huge wheel which one of the nurses would adjust three or four times, the intervals judged by – I think – a stop-watch. The nurses invariably wore a kind of meter pinned to their uniform to register the amount of exposure they had had.

You lay there on your back, shut off from the rest of the world by a glass screen. You felt nothing. You saw nothing. You heard nothing. It might all have been, in years gone by or in some other country, a kind of elaborate witchcraft. I was almost glad when some light brown stains, almost like fading sunburn, began to appear on my body.

Sally waited on the 'safe' side of the partition until she could drive me home. Every time I got there I knew that something had been happening.

I have never experienced such lassitude in my life. Everything – anything – was too much effort. I was so lucky. The weather was gorgeous. I was able to lie out in our enclosed garden, full-stretch in a kind of outdoor chaise-longue. Sally would arrange a table with a portable radio, the day's papers, and a whacking great beaker of iced Pimms on it.

I would start reading the first paper, radio in the background, and before I had got through more than a couple of pages, lulled by the music, I would be asleep – but with the Pimms finished!

The rest of the summer and early autumn went by as though seen through gauze. I went into hospital for a couple of minor operations and various tests.

But I did insist on getting back to Wimbledon to see the British team in the Inter-Zone final of the Davis Cup against Rumania.

What wretched luck it was for Graham Stilwell that year, whose career thereafter was never to match his achievements in this tie which would have seen us through to the Challenge Round for the first time since 1937. He won both his singles matches which included a win over Ilie Nastase.

Alas, to no avail! Cox lost both his singles and, partly through bad doubles selection, we had lost the four-handed match. But Stilwell's record in the Cup deserves to be remembered. In six rounds he had played twelve singles matches and won ten!

Everything for me was eclipsed at this time by something which was not only tragic but unbelievable: the death of Rocky Marciano the night before his forty-ninth birthday, when a private plane in which he was a passenger crashed at Newton, Iowa. As I wrote: 'It took a plane to knock him out. The first heavyweight champion of the world to set up the perfect record has died earlier than any of the twenty other men who have won the richest prize in sport, since the legendary John L. Sullivan.'

At the end of September 1969 it was time to take the longest holiday I had ever spent in Majorca – over five weeks. I swam in the then pellucid water of the little bay at Camp de Mar. I relaxed. I was thankful to be alive and to have had a wife whose confidence never wavered – outwardly at least. But I did not fool myself. At my age I could never be 'as good as new'. Yet, apart from a few disabilities – stairs could be protracted torture, carrying anything heavy was impossible except for the shortest distances, and on so many occasions subsequently I was indebted to rival colleagues and friends for helping with luggage or even my heavyweight typewriter, 'Old Faithful' – but these comparatively minor disadvantages apart I felt no severe physical handicaps. And fortunately the one essential without which no one can enjoy a career – enthusiasm – was still there, so for a time at least I did not contemplate retirement.

But the odious South African business was still going on. Up to the eve of the Springboks' first match no one was sure where it was going to be played. The team was meeting Oxford University but the ground at the University was deemed to be too open to demonstrators. Only just after midnight on the actual day of the match was it announced that it was to be played at Twickenham, headquarters of the Rugby Union. It was not an experience I would wish to see duplicated.

On the long walk to the East Stand – where with my colleagues I was as though in an isolation ward – it was eerie on that bright blue and white afternoon to hear behind me the echoing hoofs of a mounted policeman's horse. He walked at the same pace as I and, although I had the assurance that he was in no way interested in me, I could not forget the familiar lines:

> Like one, that on a lonesome road
> Doth walk in fear and dread,
> And having once turned round walks on,
> And turns no more his head;
> Because he knows a frightful fiend
> Doth close behind him tread.

Towards half-time the struggles in the crowd intensified, and every now and then a squirming figure, like a fly caught in blue flypaper, would be removed. At half-time there was a penetration of the pitch. A middle-aged figure trotted on to the grass and it was only when he peeled off his outer sweater to display another, emblazoned with the AA of Anti-Apartheid, and apparently kicked the ball at the referee, that I realized he wasn't part of the game. It was trivial enough but, as I noted, 'a sinister proof that, despite all security, the bomber does still get through'.

And, of course to the delight of the huge majority of the crowd, Oxford won by six points to three!

It was the same thing the following Saturday at Leicester. I was sickened; I hadn't come across anything like it ever in British sport, or indeed in all the six continents since the 1936 Olympic Games in Berlin. I thought it madness that the South Africans had ever been invited when the trouble that would accrue was so obvious.

The madness went on. At Swansea, a match I did not see, they had 'stewards' who seemed more like vigilantes and Clem Thomas, who had previously been in favour of the tour, wrote in the *Observer*: 'There followed the ugliest scenes I have ever seen on a rugby pitch . . . in my view the stewards used unnecessary violence. In some cases they brutally manhandled the young demonstrators, pulling them by the hair and punching and kicking them.' In case anyone has forgotten, Clem Thomas was himself a formidable enough international player to be no milksop, but never a bully.

That was the trouble; this utterly bloody tour was bringing out the worst in everybody; it must have been sheer hell for the touring players, too.

Writing in the same edition of the *Observer* as Thomas, Geoffrey Nicholson commented: 'After Leicester I don't think I could report any Springbok fixture as though it were just another game of rugby . . . to report the moves of the players out of this context would be like writing a review of Nero's bow technique and ignoring the smell of burning.'

Only Wilfred Wooller, whom I had last heard at Twickenham jeering at England's inability to behave well in Rugby, wrote in the *Sunday Telegraph*: 'As one supporter remarked, "For the next game, stand tickets are a pound, but they could charge £2 10s. for the privilege of being on the field to tip them off." ' I preferred the attitude of the man who was to revolutionize modern rugby when, in the *News of the World*, Lloyd Lewis reported that: 'Former Welsh international fly-half, Carwyn Jones, has refused to watch or meet the Springboks when they play Llanelli. James, who coaches Llanelli, said: "I'm making this small gesture because of the South African policy of apartheid!" '

One long threatened ban on professional boxing was made permanent. Sweden finally decided to outlaw it from 1 January 1970. Ingemar Johansson, the only non-American to win the world heavyweight title since the Second World War, was in the Upper House of the Swedish Parliament to hear the demise in his country of the sport which had made him a dollar millionaire.

There must have been times, in the less than two rounds that he lasted against Ruben Olivares, when Alan Rudkin wished that they had banned boxing everywhere. The beautiful boxer and game fighter who had grown up in Liverpool was no match for one of the greatest punchers in the history of the sport, but when the fight ended after two and a half minutes of the second round Rudkin, after testifying: 'He's the best fighter I've ever met,' added a postcript which I have heard other boxers express in different words: 'The punch that finished me was so hard and so fast that I didn't feel a thing!'

And so to the end of 1969, a year in which my priorities and values had been changed rather more fundamentally than I would have chosen, and the end, too, of a decade.

Normally I don't care much for 'gimmicks' in sport, but from a purely personal (opponents would say prejudiced) point of view, I had to confess a certain satisfaction that the much-publicized 'computer-fight' between Rocky Marciano and Muhammad Ali/Cassius Clay decided that 'the Rock' would have split 'the Lip' in the thirteenth round of their 'contest'.

Murry Woroner, who was responsible for the 'phantom fight', said that apart from the film knockdowns, there were two real ones during the various sessions. 'Rocky dropped Cassius with a right-hand blow under the rib-cage, and Cassius put Rocky down on one knee with an overhead right.'

The classic if somewhat colourless Ken Buchanan suffered one of his rare setbacks in Madrid, when an Italian referee, Piero Brambilla, decided that the Spaniard Miguel Velazquez had outpointed him over fifteen rounds for the vacant European title. My own summing-up was: 'I have certainly seen worse decisions, but this was bad enough to get on with.'

The Madrid bout was one of those fights which are so different when you see them 'live' and on TV. As far as I could ascertain no British sportswriter at the ringside thought Buchanan had been beaten. But, apparently, two-dimensional TV told a different story. To take a simple example: Velazquez launched a mighty right swing and Buchanan swayed back, avoiding it by only a matter of inches so that he was in distance to counter-punch. But the TV viewer saw Velazquez' muscles bunching for a mighty attack. He saw the punch thundering home towards its target. He saw Buchanan's head jerk back. In the transitory excitement of the relayed moment it was impossible to appreciate the fact that Buchanan jerked his own head back to avoid a blow, and that it was not jolted back by his opponent.

Of recent years when I have relied perforce on TV for world title fights this intrinsic difference has been brought home to me more and more forcibly. It was particularly apparent in the third Clay–Frazier fight when, up to the fourteenth round, I had Frazier ahead on points, whereas critics, whose judgement I respect, later made it clear that the champion had a comfortable, if not overwhelming, lead. I saw this fight on a black and white set and this imposes another veil over the truth because it is almost impossible to see the cuts and contusions – this is particularly true of a black fighter – which are the mute witnesses of the power of an opponent's punch. I did, on this occasion, towards the end remark to my companion that I guessed Frazier's face must be seamed and dented by the number of Clay's punches; but that was because I had seen so many fights in the past. The average viewer cannot be expected to have quite that expertise. Even so when this particular fight ended in the interval between the fourteenth and fifteenth rounds it still came as quite a shock.

But, in 1970, it was away to the cold and damp of a New York February to see the world heavyweight championship as satisfactorily sorted out as it could be while Muhammad Ali/Cassius Clay was kept on the wrong side of the ropes.

Jimmy Ellis, Clay's long-time sparring partner, had won the elimination tournament which included eight of the approximately best available heavyweights. Joe Frazier, the 1964 Olympic heavyweight champion, had refused to take part in the eliminators but had built up a useful unbeaten record, most of his wins being inside the distance. Now he and Ellis were meeting at Madison Square Garden, and Frazier proved himself in a different class from the man who for so many years had been Clay's sparring partner, winning at the end of the fourth round.

For once at Madison Square Garden I hadn't been at the ringside, but although my distance from the ring hadn't really mattered in the Frazier–Ellis fight I think had I been nearer I might have got a better slant on the abilities of yet another Negro giant who was to cut such a wide swathe among almost all the contemporary heavyweights – George Foreman. He was having his sixteenth professional fight in just under eight months, against the Argentinian Gregorio Peralta, then nearly thirty-five.

It turned out to be only his third to go the full distance – in this case ten rounds – and although from my eyrie I could not legitimately quarrel with the points verdict, which was strongly in favour of Foreman, I made it much closer, and I think had I been able to watch it more closely I should have been less surprised than I was – some four and a half years later – by Muhammad Ali/Cassius Clay's victory over Foreman.

I flew on to Madrid just to get a glimpse of José Urtain challenging Peter Weiland for the German's European heavyweight championship. I was not impressed. The German was beaten more through his own deficiencies than by Urtain's abilities for, although the Basque was a genuinely heavy puncher, he was woefully crude.

What I chiefly remember about the night was once more meeting 'Emperor' George Gainford, the man who for so many years had looked after the affairs of Sugar Ray Robinson. George had a fighter, Dick Hall – who the year before had scored a narrow points victory over Joe Bugner – on the Urtain bill, opposed by another German fighter; Arno Prick. Hall was a clever boxer, on the light side for a heavyweight, and although he managed to win on points he contrived to get himself knocked down in the course of the fight. They didn't print programmes in Madrid but there was a large electric sign showing the names of all the different contestants – but even this gave only the initials and not the first names of the fighters.

After Hall had showered and changed he and Gainford came back to the ringside, and I felt obliged to point out quietly to George how the sign illuminated the name of his fighter's opponent. The irrepressible George looked at it for a moment, his jaw agape, and then with a stentorian roar which could be heard all over the stadium he nudged Hall in the ribs and bellowed: 'Hey, Dick! See who you got knocked down by? A Prick!'

Later in 1970 came the tragic news that Joe Louis had been committed to a mental hospital unit in Colorado by his family. It seemed incredible that a man who had been a beacon for his own people, an example to the many other ethnic divisions with whom he came in contact and, as Jimmy Cannon put it, 'a credit to his race – the human race', should now be in such dire straits.

The Cup Final between Chelsea and Leeds United ended in a 2–2 draw after extra time – the first occasion this had happened at Wembley, and in fact the first draw in a final since 1912. Chelsea won the replay 2–1 at Old Trafford, Manchester, but once again only after extra time. This prompted me to write:

Not for the first time I find myself questioning the equity of playing extra time after a full ninety minutes – as well as the players – have been exhausted. I know that perhaps the most famous English soccer victory ever was gained after extra time – in the 1966 World Cup – but exceptional occasions do not make good law. Just apply extra time to other sports and see how ludicrous it would become.

Imagine a world title fight resulting in a draw after fifteen rounds and the referee ordering an extra five rounds to ensure a winner. Or a Derby ending in a dead-heat and the Stewards decreeing that the two horses should run a further half-mile so that a clear-cut victor could be established!

Again South Africa was coming into the 'sporting' news. One day I had to announce publicly that I would be reporting those matches in the forthcoming white South Africans' cricket tour which did not clash with other sporting events within my orbit. That would have been an unnecessary explanation had not some of my colleagues voted, in the branch of the journalists' union to which I belong, not to report the forthcoming tour. Fortunately this proposition was decisively defeated at the National Union of Journalists' annual delegate meeting.

There was no doubt, however, that a number of people whose views

I respected felt such a repugnance for the political regime which the white South African cricketers represented that they were unable to report their matches dispassionately as sporting events. But, although I detest murder and war, and the sight of starving children or agonizing terminal illness desolates me, I could not and cannot believe that not writing about any of these catastrophes is a successful way of circumventing or curing them.

Gradually, however everyone was beginning to come over to the opinion, held for different reasons but adding up to the same thing – that the proposed tour was not to be encouraged.

Although on 19 May the Cricket Council expressed their determination that the tour should continue, on the 21st James Callaghan, then Home Secretary, issued what was in effect a Government ruling, requesting that the tour be cancelled, which was naturally immediately obeyed.

So we, who had not wanted to see grounds protected with barbed wire, interrupters on the green fields, the flashing of mirrors into players' eyes, the digging up of pitches and other even more fantastic schemes – one, if I remember rightly was a threat to release a million locusts (God knows from where!) – with the very real threat of civil commotion, had won the day.

It was not a time for gloating; only grieving that sport had come to such a pass.

The World Cup was getting under way in Mexico and already we had got off to an unsteady start when it came to that imprecise area, 'public relations'. It became obvious that future football teams needed, as well as a manager, a public relations officer.

No one who had seen the players with Sir Alf Ramsey could doubt that he was the perfect inspiration for them: a disciplinarian, but one who brought out the best from a team of widely varying personalities, and a man who would fight, like a tigress protecting her cubs, in defence of his 'boys'. Unfortunately it was equally clear that Ramsey neither particularly liked nor welcomed represenatatives of the various communications media – unless he knew them well; my colleague Ken Jones, for example, described his Press conferences as 'conducted in an atmosphere of complete formality without warmth and with a hostile undertone'.

Other journalists commented on Sir Alf's 'tight-knit and sometimes off-handed treatment of the foreign Press' and 'the cold courtesy of Sir Alf Ramsey and the Mexican thirst for news' as a cause of the anti-English 'vendetta' in Mexico.

Newspapers and TV, of course, are increasingly a part of the international sporting scene, and it was not fair to Ramsey to put on him the additional burden of dealing with newsmen whom he did not know and whose problems he could not be expected to comprehend. Nor was it fair that the England team should get the backlash from frustrated overseas writers and commentators who were neither accustomed to, nor prepared to put up with, Ramsey's too often cavalier treament. Journalists, TV and radio men are not some strange breed. They are like everyone else – an average mixture. It was not Ramsey's job to understand that it is impossible for journalists from more than twenty countries, with varying deadlines, to line up at the same time for information, but he should have been able to brief a PRO who, with the aid of interpreters, would have been able to satisfy the legitimate curiosity of accredited correspondents.

Then it was Lord's – to see England *v.* Rest of the World, replacing South Africa, and to write:

I've got a better idea. Let's start a new cricket series – Gary Sobers *v.* Rest of the World. It's no good matching him against England because he has already beaten them. He spent part of the first day taking six England wickets for 21 – and, did the laws of cricket not forbid him to bowl at both ends consecutively, no doubt he would have taken the other four. He spent from 2.30 yesterday afternoon passing England's total of 127, which he achieved with an on slog off Snow at 5.55, ending up with 147 still undefeated. The game's greatest-ever all-rounder mounted a one-man baton charge on the bowling, with particular attention being paid to the unfortunate Snow who had 14 – a six and two fours – taken off him in four balls!

The substitute series produced some sparkling stuff and, ironically, no greater partnership – in the match at the Oval – than that between the black Gary Sobers and the white Graeme Pollock – from South Africa!

From tea-time until stumps were drawn, it remained high noon out in the centre as the two cavaliers, with their willow swords, competed in essence more against themselves than against the players of England. After the tea interval, Pollock had 29 to his credit, while Sobers was 0 not out. But with Pollock getting most of the strike – and Sobers was generous about this, as genius can afford to be – the race developed into whether Pollock would get his hundred before Sobers reached his half-century. And, in the friendliest contention, it was as though the South African and the West Indian were trying to outdo each other, ball by ball and stroke by stroke. Pollock won the race by one run, having hit one six and sixteen fours in his hundred!

What had been proved beyond all doubt was that, even in a relatively unimportant match, you didn't need to have 'instant', limited-over, cricket to produce the deep and abiding thrills which the game can so lavishly offer.

Wimbledon was on us again and this one proved to be memorable for me in a very special fashion. Round about six o'clock on the first Friday, the time I normally sit down to write at least the bulk of the day's play so that it will be in the office in plenty of time for the first edition, I got a message from an old chum, Roy McKelvie, who not only covered the Championships for the *Sunday Express* and the magazine *Tennis World* but is also in charge of the international Press arrangements, that the Chairman of the All England Club, Herman David, wanted to see me.

When I arrived, Herman David looked suitably grave. He said: 'I'm sure you must realize that as Chairman of this Club I have some unpleasant duties to perform.' There was one of those pauses which, I believe, are called pregnant. I was thinking furiously how you went about suing an entire committee for libel and slander. Then Herman smiled.

He went on: 'But, of course, there are compensations and it's now my very pleasant duty to tell you that by unanimous decision of the committee you have been elected an honorary member of the Club!'

The rest was all delightful confusion.

The great sensation that year was the defeat, in the fourth round, of Rod Laver by Roger Taylor, followed by the inevitable disappointment of seeing Ken Rosewall beaten yet again in the final, this time by John Newcombe, in five sets. You still got the feeling that had it been anywhere else but Wimbledon, *and* the final, Rosewall might have pulled it off.

But the great match of this year, or almost any other in my memory, was the final of the women's singles in which Margaret Court beat Billie Jean King 14–12, 11–9 after the largest number of games – forty-six – and the longest time – 2 hours 26 mins – ever played in a women's singles final.

It was, perhaps, also the *greatest* women's singles final ever played. It was, certainly, the cruellest physically I had ever watched. Because, magnificent athletes as these two were, I was not sure that this wasn't just a little too gruelling a physical test for women. I wrote:

Towards the end Mrs King was whey-faced and groaning, almost like a hospital case, as she punched the ball on her service.

Across the net, Mrs Court still looked the picture of glowing health but people who had seen her left ankle, injured in her quarter-final against Helga Niessen and heavily strapped yesterday, told me it was black and swollen.

If I had to say why Margaret won, I would say that she can make shots no other girl in the world could duplicate, because no other girl in the world could get to them. But what made it so great was that Billie Jean must surely rank as one of the world's greatest-ever *competitors* in any sport.

And now that great quadrennial occasion was on us – the 1970 Commonwealth Games, held this time in Edinburgh. Sally and I had managed to rent a house again, and this time Frank McGhee, Frank Taylor and Ron Wills were sharing it, too. It belonged to a minister and I often wondered if he afterwards had to exorcise all the spirits which remained – not evil, but alcoholic ones, I hasten to add.

There were, of course, some great performances and the inevitable personal tragedies – Ron Clarke, still able to win 'only' a silver, his fourth silver medal in three Commonwealth Games; Kip Keino, despite two letters and a telephone call threatening him with death from a rifle equipped with telescopic sights, winning a fine 1,500 metres from Dick Quax and getting a gold medal from the Queen; the collapse of New Zealand's Sylvia Potts, when leading, literally within ten feet of the tape in the women's 1,500. But these Games somehow did not produce the 'hwyl' which Cardiff had provided twelve years earlier.

There was, however, a wonderful climax when Ron Hill, a thirty-one-year-old research textile chemist from Romiley, Cheshire, scored a magnificent marathon triumph. He covered the 26 miles 385 yards course in 2 hours, 9 mins, 28 secs, the fastest time ever recorded in a major championship, dominating the race after the first ten miles – and in the process losing more than half a stone of the nine he weighed normally.

Hill himself summed up this man's race for a race of men when he said: 'After four miles today I didn't feel at all good and I was tired. But then everything clicked and it became one of the best marathons I've ever run. For the first half the conditions were perfect but on the way back it was really too hot. I would have liked a bit of drizzle over the last few miles.'

I wonder if there's another sport where the winner prays for rain!

In the boxing section of the Games a good-looking, brown-skinned youngster aged nineteen, John Conteh, won the middleweight class but did not exactly set the stadium, adjacent to Murrayfield, on fire.

The following day saw the end of two eras, for it was the last time that big athletics took place at the White City, London, which had been a world-famous stadium ever since the 1908 Olympic Games had been staged there, the setting – among other things – of perhaps the most famous marathon finish of all time when the Italian, Dorando Pietri, staggering as Jim Peters did nearly forty years later, was helped by kindly hands to victory – and disqualification.

It was sad that, because of the Commonwealth Games and the

Europa Cup, the AAA championships, which should have been the great middle act of Britain's athletics season, was played out largely by understudies to a weak final curtain, in too large an old theatre in front of too small a crowd.

But if the athletics failed to be outstanding there was one occasion which no one present is likely to forget: the final, irrevocable retirement of one of the finest men ever to stand out in bas-relief in the gaily coloured, never-ending frieze of sport – Ron Clarke, athlete not only of Australia but of the world. In his fourteen years of international competition he averaged well over a world record every twelve months and he inspired the youth of every country where he showed his dedicated but unselfish skills to an understanding of what sport is all about – or should be.

I moved on for my fifty-seventh birthday to Stockholm, to see the seven-nations final of the men's Europa Cup athletics.

Once more I could only marvel at the progress of East Germany. The descending order of the final scores were East Germany, USSR, West Germany, Poland, France, Sweden, Italy. Britain had been eliminated in the semi-final round. Considering the fact that, apart from the host nation Sweden, East Germany had easily the smallest population of any of the competing countries, it was an astonishing performance from a 'new' country.

Whether a nation alleged to be among the hardest pressed financially in Europe was justified in putting down two or three tartan tracks a year, at a cost of some £100,000 a track, depends on the value, both from a propaganda point of view and as an investment in youth, which you place on sport.

In the evening I was able to prove, not for the first time, that the Swedes knew the value of 'the good life' by downing some very palatable bottles of champagne in the pleasant company of Jim Coote, athletics correspondent of the *Daily Telegraph*. We didn't quite get up to my age but we did our best and, at the end, I felt capable of challenging any East German – at drinking champagne.

Incidentally, the phrasing of one remark by a South African athletics official, Bob van Reenen, was perhaps not wholly felicitous; referring to the suspension – for a minimum of two years – imposed on South Africa in Stockholm by the International Amateur Athletics Federation, world governing body of the sport, he said: 'Things are looking very black for us. This decision will rule our athletes out of all big meetings in Europe.'

At fifteen Chris Evert had made the international sports headlines for the first time. She had pulled off the shock win of the year when she had beaten 'Grand Slammer' Margaret Court in the semi-final of the

Carolina international tournament. And although, in the final, the schoolgirl had trouble getting her first service in and was soundly beaten, 6–4, 6–1, by Nancy Richey, it was clear that her victory over Mrs Court was no flash in the racket, for she had already beaten another top professional, the French girl Françoise Durr, with the loss of only one game.

I noted at the time: 'Chris, who never lost her poise against Mrs Court, said after the match that she never thought she had a chance of winning – and then burst into tears!'

Soccer continued to astonish and appal me. Jackie Charlton, Leeds centre-half and a member of England's World-Cup-winning team of 1966, went on record on a Tyne-Tees TV programme saying publicly: 'I have a little book with two players in it, and if I get a chance to do them I will. I will make them suffer before I pack this game in. If I can kick them four yards over the touchline, I will.

'It has nothing to do with money. You do what is necessary in the circumstances. If I were chasing a yard behind a player in an international match and thought I could not catch him, I would flatten him. I would not break anyone's leg but, if I could not stop a player within the rules of the game, I would grab him by the scruff of the neck.

'Referees try to look after players, but players have to look after themselves. It is the way of the world.'

I commented: 'What a world! Have these petulant, primping, over-paid, under-principled gladiators *no* sense of sportsmanship? Don't they care about the influence they have on youngsters in the country? Don't they care about *anything* – except cash and clogging, money and malevolence?'

It all reminded me of an exchange between a very wealthy man – the story has been 'fathered' on the late Lord Beaverbrook among others – and a very beautiful woman. The man asks: 'Would you sleep with me for £100,000?'

To which she replies coyly: 'I might.'

This prompts him to ask: 'Would you sleep with me for £5?'

Her indignation is unfeigned: 'What do you think I am?'

And he retorts: 'I think we've established that. Now it's merely a question of price!'

Such disgraceful talk by one of our best-known players seemed to me likely only to reinforce complaints about the pattern of 'brute force and bloody ignorance', which smudge the spectrum of the English game, made by some of the more skilful footballing nations.

Charlton had this to say of his future: 'People say I would make a good manager. I would prefer to be a coach for two or three years and learn about man-management. I am not very good at that.' The ironical thing is that Jackie Charlton *has* proved a good manager whereas his brother, Bobby, the very symbol of a 'parfit gentil knight' proved less than a success.

If there is a moral to all that, I must say it eludes me – unless it is that today there is no place for saints in soccer.

As someone who had campaigned for years to get greater financial freedom for footballers it was disappointing to see how some reacted when they acquired it – as though the carrot had proved too juicy and the stick too fragile. More and more the turbulent George Best, who seemed to typify everything undisciplined in sport, was in the news. I commented:

What George Best decides to do with his own life is his own business, and is a matter of supreme indifference to me. What he does to other footballers' lives comes into the domain of public criticism. Inevitably the reactionaries, who would like to see professional footballers back in shackles and with a ceiling to their wages, will point to Best's irresponsibility – to put it at its mildest – and claim that high payment destroys discipline.

They will say that Best – fined £250 by a Football Association disciplinary committee only last week and now, forfeiting perhaps another £400 following his suspension by Manchester United – can thumb his nose at such sanctions, which are financial 'flea bites' to him.

But I am convinced that it wouldn't matter whether Best were paid £25,000 or 25,000 shillings a year – it would not alter his 'don't-give-a-damn' attitude towards life in general and authority in particular. It would obviously be completely unfair to penalize the many for the immaturity of the individual.

I still believe those words; but the trouble is that far too many lesser stars, who do not even have the genius which Best had, think their limited talent entitles them to behave like unlimited louts. . . .

At last came the news that Muhammad Ali/Cassius Clay had been cleared to take part in a serious contest, as distinct from exhibition bouts, in the USA, after three years and seven months in the 'boxing wilderness' since being stripped of his crown by various boxing authorities after refusing call-up to the US Army.

For that refusal he was sentenced to five years in jail, and fined $10,000 (approximately £4,170 at that time) but never served a day of his imprisonment, nor paid a penny of his fine, for the tangled American system of justice left him still out on bail after over three years of legal escapology.

Whether boxing could afford to have Clay back as world heavyweight champion was one outstanding question; the other was whether boxing could afford *not* to have Clay back as world heavyweight champion.

It was more than somewhat ironic that his comeback, on 26 October against Jerry Quarry, should be at Atlanta, situated in the State of Georgia, part of America's Deep South and notorious for its 'nigger-baiting' and 'nigger-hating'.

In the build-up to the fight it was the Clay of old. Having watched a film of the first meeting between Joe Frazier and Quarry, made a few scathing remarks about Frazier and then, with a hand bigger than the biggest hamburger you ever saw, still failing to cover that mouth which was made for talking, he mumbled: 'Ain't gonna be no match – a amateur 'gainst a pro.'

I never had the slightest doubt about the outcome of the fight – but I was a little too optimistic, from the customers' point of view, when I said I thought that it would take Clay about ten or eleven rounds to win.

But the complement of the auditorium – gaudy, meretricious, bizarre, in grotesque ill-taste if you like – was nonetheless a tribute to Clay's magnetism and what he had achieved for 'his' people by his arrogant but fearless assertion of his 'rights' against a regime which he considered repressive and which had overwhelming numbers on its side, largely inimical to him.

I shall never forget that ringside, surrounded as it was by some of the people who wielded much of the power in the country, some of the leading stars of the entertainment world, some of the most dangerous gangsters – and all *black*. It was the first time at any professional fight I had ever attended, outside Africa, that Negroes easily outnumbered whites.

And what Negroes! Some of them in silky top-hats and black ties, embroidered with artificial diamonds, one in a sapphire suit, another with ermine tails hanging from a white cowboy hat, another with a full-length grey mink coat and an enormous trapper-style mink hat to match, smoking a great, curved meerschaum pipe and, not surprisingly, under the television lights, sweating like a leaky brown tap. There was also the most spectacularly beautiful, lacquered-haired, black girl I have ever seen, like some gorgeously enamelled beetle. And, by ugly contrast, a topless, drooping-titted chemical blonde, who could have stepped straight out of *Tobacco Road*. And the musical accompaniment was a rendering of the 'Star-Spangled Banner', America's national anthem, crooned by a Negro, accompanying himself on a guitar.

The former world champions, introduced before the fight, were all coloured – lightweight Ike Williams, who had hammered Ronnie James in Wales twenty-four years before; light-heavyweight José Torres, who knocked out the late Chic Calderwood in two rounds in José's native Puerto Rico in 1966; and Jimmy Ellis who had had his brief moment of glory, as substitute world heavyweight champion, two and a half years before when he outpointed Quarry.

The referee was a Puerto Rican, Tony Perez.

It was unbelievable to think that some of the glittering mink-clad occupants of the £42 seats had had parents, or at least grandparents, who had bent their backs in the fields to 'the white boss'. It was, in some ways, Clay's finest hour.

For sheer boxing brilliance I doubt whether Clay, even after forty-three months away from the serious ring, has ever performed better than he did in the first round against Quarry. I totalled between fourteen and twenty clean punches from Clay in the first three minutes, and just two right-hand counters from Quarry. Yet I was left with one nagging doubt: how much of Clay's 15 st 3½ lb was behind the blows? For at the bell Quarry, who had been so comprehensively outpointed as almost to be outclassed, was able to lope back to his corner with a sailor-like swagger.

But it was very different in the second round, when the procession turned into a fight, and just before the bell Quarry really hurt his man with a left hook to the body.

However, in the third round Quarry was cut over the left eye. With the best will in the world, I could not say honestly that I saw the blow, but that fine judge Frank Butler, who was on the opposite side of the ring from me, assured me that it was a banging right-hander. Now it was like seeing a film – alas, in only one colour, red – which one has seen before.

The moment Quarry got back to his corner – and you wanted to give him a guide-dog to get there – trainer Teddy Bentham took one look, grabbed Quarry's hand and told him that this was the end of the road. I confess, for a moment or so, I thought they should have tried to work on the eye and give Quarry a chance to snatch a wildly improbable win.

But I was wrong . . . Othello had come back, rampantly triumphant!

Indeed, Clay made only one mistake in the whole proceedings. He said afterwards: 'He's a hard man to fight. You have to move and hit against him. I was never pressed, but if it hadn't been for the cut I was figuring it would go ten rounds. Joe Frazier is going to be easier.'

Oh, no, Cassius! No, Cassius! No, Cassius! No!

Soon it was off to New York again to see Clay in the second of his comeback fights, this time against Oscar Bonavena, the Argentinian heavyweight.

I wrote that, to my mind, Bonavena was either the bravest or the stupidest man alive. When he met Clay this was the ex-champion's version of what happened:

This man Bonavena he come up to me. He touch me. He says: 'Me white, you black; you stink. You need deodorant. You're a big coward, nothing but a big coward. That's why you didn't join the Army.' Then he says something to me in Spanish and he pinches my cheek. I ask him what that means in English, and he says I'm a 'faggot' [American slang for a homosexual].

Now he's in real trouble. I've never wanted to whup anyone so bad. Open up all the centres for television. Ain't gonna be no arena in the world big enough for all the people to see me give him the whupping of his life. Don't think I'm saying this just to sell seats. I've sold all the seats already. I just want to beat this, this man who says he's a 'white hope'.

This one may not have been a story dreamed up to sell seats, but it was not a very tasteful one. However, to be honest, 'tasteful' wasn't exactly the adjective I would have applied to Bonavena – later to come to a violent end – who was known as 'Ringo' because of his supposed likeness to one of the Beatles but who, in fact, was much more like a giant version of that great British lightweight of times gone by, Eric Boon.

It was almost like old times when Clay produced his traditional prediction: 'When the sign shows nine, he'll be mine.'

As it turned out, it was a hell of a good fight.

Of course the ninth was the one for which we were all waiting. This was the one in which Clay had predicted he would win. Instead, Bonavena landed a left hook to the belly and Clay was down. The referee said a slip. I wonder. Was Clay really groggy? He took some dynamite to the body and, at the bell, he didn't seem sure which was his corner.

In the interval before the twelfth, Clay asked what round was coming up. When the bell went he scored with jabs, but there was no power behind them and, for the first time, he looked as though he hated his work. The round was even. So was the thirteenth. The referee was allowing Clay to hold uninterruptedly.

Often Clay bore down on the stockier Bonavena. Clay was scarcely punching, but Bonavena was scarcely landing. Clay's lips looked as though he had been at the strawberry jam. Bonavena was forcing but not really effective.

Fourteenth coming up. Angelo Dundee was saying: 'Jab, jab, jab.' Bundini Brown, the assistant trainer who coined the phrase 'float like a butterfly, sting like a bee', was in tears. This was really feet of Clay. So to the last round. They shook hands with their lefts. Bonavena was chasing. Clay was wrestling. Then, almost exactly halfway through the round, both men seemed to be moving away from each other and Clay threw the sort of huge, almost lazy, hook with which you catch a shark.

Bonavena went down and Clay was magnificently remorseless – the medieval headsman in black cowl and sable vest. He followed the jittering, lurching Bonavena and again he landed boxing's most damaging punch, the left hook. And Bonavena went down again. This time his corner knew he had lost. They threw in the towel, which sailed against the lights like a seagull with a broken wing. The refereee ignored it, and Bonavena reeled round the ring like a blind man who has lost his white cane.

Black Nemesis was after him. Perhaps four more punches were welded on to that prognathous jaw and as Bonavena went down for the third time – which by New York State rules meant the automatic end of the fight – Clay lowered over the beaten buffalo and raised his hands, with what effort I know not, in his own version of the victory sign.

But what a bull was Bonavena. Within a couple of minutes of being one of boxing's broken dolls, he was sitting on the apron of the ring, with the ropes at his back, talking, half-laughing, on the radio to Argentina.

Afterwards with honesty Clay said: 'That ninth round . . . I thought I'd predicted against myself. We were both shook up. He is the best man I have fought.'

From New York I flew straight to Majorca. The previous winter of 1969–70 I had been so ill from Boxing Day (ironic that) to well into the New Year, with influenza slipping into pneumonia, that I had been warned not to spend another winter in Britain. Sally and I rented a villa in the romantically named and beautifully situated 'Nido de Aguilas' ('Eagles' Nest') and I began to ease myself into the time when I would not be writing day by day in Fleet Street; for by now I knew that I was not going to be able to go on in daily journalism until the Commonwealth Games of 1974, my original intention. My new target was to remain competent enough to cover my eighth Summer Olympic Games at Munich, in 1972.

Meanwhile I had made arrangements with Hugh Cudlipp and sports editor Jack Hutchinson, to telex two columns a week, working from the offices of the Majorca *Daily Bulletin* in Palma.

The reason I was able to function like this was that years of experience enabled me, frankly, to flesh the bare bones of facts with the background of nearly four decades in 'The Street' and travelling the world.

The first significant sports news of 1971 came with the announcement that Joe Frazier was to defend the world heavyweight championship he had won, by a process of elimination, against Muhammad Ali/Cassius Clay, the man who had never lost it. It was only logical to match the 'dreadnoughts' – which made the fight something of a rarity in itself –

for, while the other was still active and undefeated, neither man could call himself 'undisputed' champion.

Hot on the heels of the fight every boxing enthusiast wanted to see came the announcement of the death of the champion no one had wanted to know – Charles Sonny Liston. In the same way that his origins had been shrouded in poverty so his end was surrounded by mystery belonging, in fact to 1970 rather than 1971. The *Ring Boxing Encyclopedia and Record Book* records it laconically: 'December 30, 1970 in his Las Vegas, Nev. home. Died. His wife found him a week later, January 5, 1971.'

When he died his solitary death Liston was still officially a few months short of his thirty-ninth birthday, although personally I always thought he was two or three, or even more, years older. I wrote at the time: 'It was, perhaps, fitting that the man who in four title bouts amassed about £1,600,000 should end up sprawled out on a gold bedspread like the dice which roll, day and night, on the green baize in Las Vegas where he died.'

Afterwards there were many theories – but no real facts – about how he died. The simplest explanation was an overdose of drugs, although I had never heard that he was an addict. Another story was that he had been silenced by the Mafia because 'he knew too much'. Yet another was that it was members of the Black Muslims who had given him his final knockout because he had threatened to tell the 'inside story' of the Clay fights.

Anything was believable – or unbelievable – about the sombre Sonny, who died, as he had so often lived, lonely and mysteriously. . . .

Back to New York, then, for the no-longer-to-be-postponed umpteenth 'fight of the century' – but this time the confrontation between Joe Frazier and Muhammad Ali/Cassius Clay did have some justification for the label; it took me back over thirty years to the prime of Joe Louis, and fifteen to the supremacy of 'Rocky Marciano; it was a battle which would span the world, transcending race and creed and colour.

Not only would this be the first time a heavyweight title had been disputed by two undefeated boxers, but Frazier had the highest inside-the-distance percentage wins of any heavyweight champion – 88·5 – and Clay, with 80·6, has been surpassed only by Rocky Marciano, whose record stood at 87·7.

Frazier was training in Philadelphia. The first time I went there Frazier wasn't training. He was with his black manager, 'Yank' Durham, seeing their lawyer about the tax problems involved in the £1,000,000-plus purse which Frazier was to be paid for what might have been only a few minutes' work.

Durham talked a lot of sense. About the contest: 'There's no mystery about this fight. It isn't a war with secret weapons. It's a prize-fight with gloves. Clay can't change his style and Joe can't change his. No, Joe won't be laying on him. He'll be *punching* on him. No, I wouldn't say Joe is a black Marciano. More like a bigger Henry Armstrong. He just never stops. I don't predict rounds. But Clay won't get up.'

Then came a bombshell: 'Win or lose this fight, I'd like Frazier to quit.'

I sometimes wonder whether if Yank hadn't died so quickly and unexpectedly, Frazier's career would have been different. . . .

Frazier made one memorable remark.

'You hate a guy in the first round when you don't know what's gonna happen. But after two or three rounds, when you've had his sweat in your mouth, and when he's been all over you and you've been all over him, well – how can you hate a guy after that?'

Clay was as ebullient as ever. 'You fellows sit at a typewriter all day and have a drink every night and boxing looks rough, real rough, to you. But it isn't. It's easy when you are young and fit like me,' he said and when he was asked if he meant to use 'the anchor punch' to beat Frazier (the mystery 'blow' under which Sonny Liston had collapsed in their second, one-round, fiasco) Clay shook his head: 'No, I got a new one, now – the ghetto whip.'

Frazier was very impressive in his sparring, and I asked another interested spectator what he thought the outcome would be on Monday. He was Jersey Joe Walcott, former heavyweight champion of the world. He shook his head and said: 'This is too close a one to forecast.' The trouble for Negro fighters was that if they chose Frazier they were liable to be called 'honky lovers' or 'white niggers'. Racialism even within black boundaries. . . .

Then came that recurrent moment of truth – the only time when it's worse being a writer than a fighter. The moment when you have to try to pick the winner. In the heavyweights I always string along with the puncher. I wouldn't have bet an old penny on the outcome; Clay's 'cutting edge' might, I knew, make a mockery of me and a mess of Frazier – but 'I'm going to take Smokin' Joe,' I said.

So to the fight itself. It wasn't the *greatest* heavyweight championship of all time. But it was certainly one of the most emotional.

Joe Frazier, the brown tank from Beaufort, South Carolina, won so easily that the most novice fan could have scored it. But Clay in defeat made more friends, and was much more of a man than he had been in some of his own more famous victories, those 'picking-the-wings-off-a-fly' affairs against Floyd Patterson and Ernie Terrell, for example. The 'atmosphere' – the feeling you used to have in the great days of Joe Louis that 'thunder was always lurking in his gloves' – was always there.

Clay started well, just winning a hell of a good first round for a world heavyweight championship. He won the second more decisively. He was beckoning Frazier to come in; shaking his head mock-sorrowfully as Frazier appeared to miss; waving derisively at his opponent's back as the bell rang. But, towards the end of a fairly even third round, Frazier suddenly slammed in a body punch. A terrible, eviscerating body punch. I was perhaps ten yards from the apron of the ring, but this punch threw *me* back in my chair as though I had been skewered through my guts.

From the sixth round I felt the fight was slipping away from Clay. He prodded; Frazier cudgelled. Once Clay lolled on the ropes and Frazier plucked him off them. Clay hadn't the stamina, the spring in his legs which he had had before the three-and-a-half-year banishment. On the ropes he was Frazier's meat.

The doctor examined Clay between the eleventh and twelfth rounds and I doubt whether Clay had ever up to then had to suffer more than he did in the thirteenth. He was taking a savage beating to the head and body and his face was swelling. Nevertheless he managed to win the fourteenth, scoring with long-range flashes, and by the fifteenth there was a lump like an egg on Frazier's temple. But, like a thunderbolt, a terrific left hook sent Clay sprawling. For a few seconds he lay supported by one forearm, like a dying gladiator, a dazed, glazed look in his eyes which I had seen only once before in the fifteen previous amateur and professional bouts in which I had watched him – the first time round against Henry Cooper.

But he got up, the right side of his jaw distorted like some monstrous dark melon so that I was sure that it had been broken. So frantic was Bundini Brown, Clay's friend and second that, crying, while his hero was down, he sprayed him with water from a soaking sponge–for which he later got fined, I think $2,500.

After Clay had taken the compulsory count of eight they continued, with a left and right to Clay's jaw. He was quite gone. Frazier thrashed him, leaving Clay dazed and helpless and hopeless. And all the time Frazier, cut, bleeding round each eye and from the nose, lumpy as a cheap mattress, still kept bicycling forwards, that set, sharky grin on his face – that face on which you can wear out your knuckles.

Afterwards, although his face was a black relief map of bumps, cuts and bruises, Frazier said happily, justifiably: 'I'm champion of the whole wide world. I've fought everyone they've put in front of me and, God knows, I whupped them. Clay took some good punches. I went right back to the country to get them punches.'

This wasn't the only 'first' for Clay. Uniquely he didn't turn up for a post-fight interview. He had been taken to the Flower and Fifth Avenue Hospital, to see whether his jaw had been broken. Later

Frazier had to spend some quite considerable time in hospital with ailments described variously as kidney damage, internal injuries and complete exhaustion.

As though we hadn't had enough ructions in the ring for a time, I ran into another one almost as soon as I got back to England. This was the clash between Henry Cooper, then approaching thirty-seven, and twenty-one-year-old Joe Bugner, involving almost all the other worthwhile heavyweight championships – apart from the supreme one for which Clay and Frazier had fought – the British, Commonwealth and European.

I had gone out on a limb, unequivocally picking Cooper – and to this day I think I was right. I scored $74\frac{3}{4}$ points to Cooper to Bugner's $72\frac{3}{4}$. But Harry Gibbs, whom I still regard as one of the best six referees I have seen all over the world, incredibly, to me, made it $73\frac{3}{4}$ to $73\frac{1}{2}$ in Bugner's favour.

It wouldn't have been so incredible if the verdict had been delivered by anyone else but Harry Gibbs. Yet, when I think how many times I have seen him in action, not only giving eminently fair decisions but handling bouts strictly but with the minimum of interference, one terrible bloomer (in my opinion) isn't too bad a record. I wish I'd had as high a percentage with my columns!

The real tragedy was that win, lose or draw Henry had determined that this was going to be his last fight – and it would have been nice to have gone out on the crest of a wave. . . .

So now, where it had once been 'bread and Bugner' it was Bugner Regis!

Little did I know it but Dick Richards and I went out for the last time together to do a joint story on the film *The Great White Hope*, a better-than-usual film based, roughly, on the life and hard times of Jack Johnson whom the late Nat Fleischer, boxing's greatest historian and one of the few people then living who had ever seen Johnson in his prime, considered to be the best heavyweight of all time.

We met in a Soho pub before going to see the film in one of the private cinemas in Wardour Street and, as always with Dick, it was as though we were still sharing the same flat and the same office – as, for so many years, in the past, we had. As ever, too, Dick not only seemed to know but to attract all the characters in show business and after a wonderfully vinous session we made the film just in time for 'the first bell'. He was in great form and rang me up the next day to say jokingly that, because I'd been given more space, he wasn't going out on any more 'dual' jobs with me again. Thank God, I didn't know how true that was. . . .

Then: 'They brought me bitter news to hear, and bitter tears to shed.'

Now let's look at that again — watching the film of one of his fights with Muhammad Ali/Cassius Clay.

Right The greatest
competitor. Mrs Billie
Jean King whose six
singles wins at
Wimbledon is a post-
World War II record.

Below At least Arthur
Ashe raises only one
finger — at a time! — to
me during our
controversial TV
'confrontation' before
Wimbledon 1973.

Left Hands, knees and, apparently, boomps-a-daisy for two of the stormy petrels of lawn tennis – Jimmy Connors and Ilie Nastase.

Below Bjorn Borg, the Swede who, at just over 20, became the youngest winner of the Wimbledon men's singles for 45 years.

Above Evonne Goolagong (Mrs Cawley) whose happy-go-lucky disposition has prevented her winning even more championships than she already has.

Right Even at 17 Chris Evert had the determined look of the potential champion. By the time she was 21 she had won Wimbledon twice.

Left Is Gareth Edwards passing one — or taking one!

Below With one of the immortals. Jack Dempsey, in his eighties the oldest living ex-world heavyweight champion — and the crowds still lined up in Broadway to look into his restaurant windows.

Opposite top Receiving, at Wimbledon, a medal and a scroll from the International Sports Press Association and sharing the moment — and the awards — with Amy, widow of Jim Manning, who had received them posthumously.

Opposite bottom Surrounded by three former world champions who held five titles —Gus Lesnevich (light-heavyweight), Henry Armstrong (feather, light and welterweight) and Max Baer (heavyweight).

Peter Wilson
of Great Britain
for DISTINGUISHED SERVICES
to SPORTS JOURNALISM

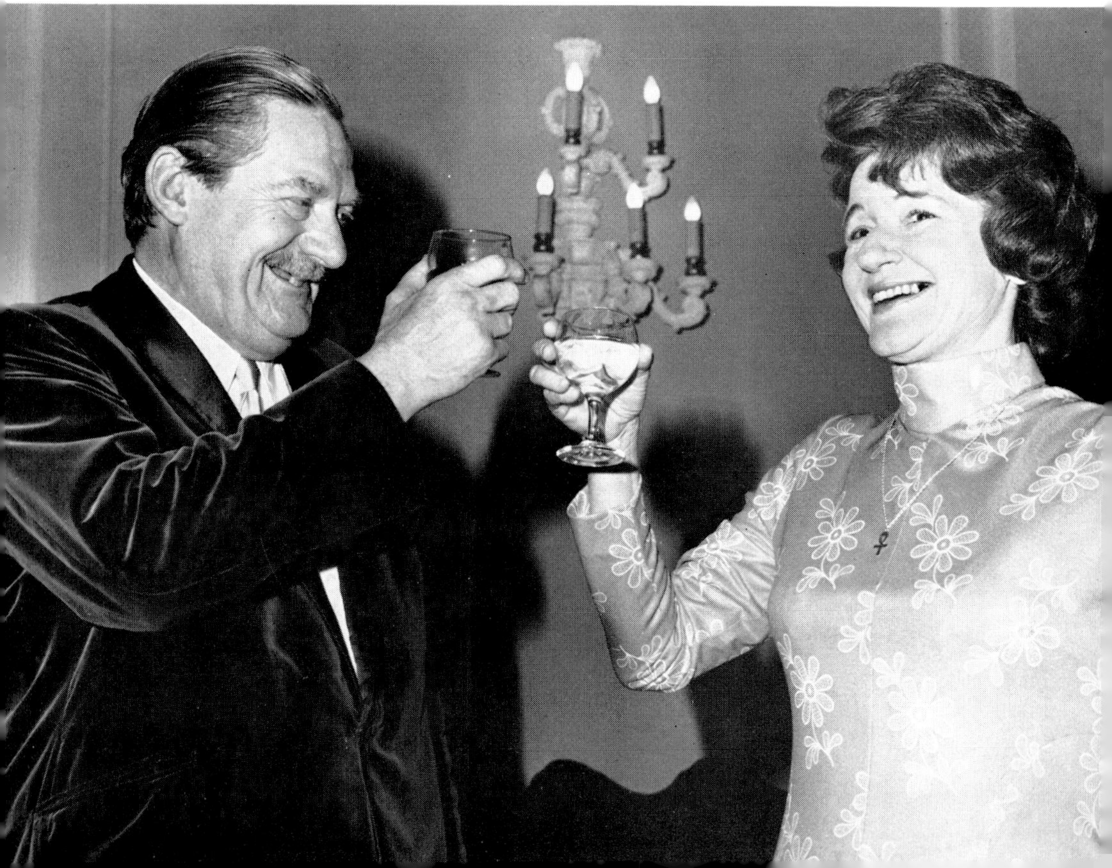

Opposite top When shall we three meet again? Bill Connor (Cassandra) left and Hugh Cudlipp with both of whom I joined the *Mirror* on the same day in August 1935.

Opposite bottom Sally and I get 'all lit up' at my final farewell party.

Above The astonishing Lester Piggott does it again winning the Derby, in which I first saw him victorious as an 18 year old, for the seventh time on Empery in 1976.

Overleaf 'Seconds away' – Henry Cooper giving me a heavyweight farewell at my leave-taking party.

Dick had died, suddenly, not unpredictably but unexpectedly. He got two paragraphs in the *Daily Mirror* and I – I could have written two columns about him. But what was the point? Men grow mawkish when they try to express their deepest feelings about other men. All I could think – I didn't even write it – was that life could never be quite the same in a world which Dick had left.

1971 was to be a sad spring for, quite unexpectedly, another man with whom I had, from time to time, circled the globe, George Whiting of the *Evening Standard*, died. No one wrote more felicitously about boxing although, as is typical of the waste of talent to which Fleet Street is so prone – as though it had, a likely thought! an *embarras de richesse* – he was never used on what I suspect was his favourite sport, cricket.

Sad to see anyone as great as Rod Laver, who lost in the quarter-finals at Wimbledon to Tom Gorman, start the slippery slope of disintegration but, from his point of view, how comforting to think that no one is ever likely to equal – certainly not to beat – his record of two 'grand slams'.

But, if it was sad to see the decline of a great champion, the women's singles made up for it with Evonne Goolagong, still just short of her twentieth birthday, beating Mrs Billie Jean King in the semi-final round and Mrs Margaret Court in the final. Neither was a great match, for both Mrs King and Mrs Court were far from their best, but it was real fairy-tale stuff to see this brown elf from the 'out' of Australia's outback, descended from a time before history, winning the greatest championship of them all two years before even her greatest booster, her coach, her foster-father, Vic Edwards, had predicted she would do so. But I'm still not sure that, in the long run, it paid her as a player. Sometimes afterwards she played as though there were nothing left to win. . . .

The vagaries of cricket were never better illustrated than in the Test which decided the England–Pakistan series at Leeds. But, even at the start, how times had changed. Perhaps in an age when men can get to the moon in five days, any sport which is scheduled to last the same number of days – with a forty-one hour break in the middle – is foredoomed to failure. For I regard it as failure that for the first day of a decisive Test in a series there were just 8,000 spectators.

The match, after all, was played at Headingley, deep in the heart of Yorkshire, and in the England side were three Yorkshiremen. Geoff Boycott – reckoned a failure if he didn't score a century! – scored his eleventh hundred for England that first day. There was Ray Illingworth, the skipper, only the second man to lead England to victory in Australia since the war, and finally, Richard Hutton, son of Sir Len, the first lancer to pierce Australia's hide in their lair during the postwar period. It was Yorkshire's day – but Yorkshire didn't seem to care. In the past they would have had the gates closed by lunchtime at Headingley, with the prospect of Yorkshire yet again coming to the aid of England.

You could not have asked for much more cricket entertainment on a day as warm and full of sunny hours as you can expect to get in England, with 309 on the board and one wicket to fall, and a pitch which promised to become more interesting – and testing – as it and the match wore on.

Despite the promise of the conditions the next three days were abysmal: on the Saturday Pakistan added 142 runs in approximately five and three-quarter hours for the loss of their six remaining first innings wickets and England, in roughly forty minutes, scored 17 for the loss of one wicket; the product of this death of a thousand nudges was, I was assured, the second lowest day's Test total ever recorded in England. (The lowest was also at Headingley, in 1953, when England on the first day against Australia, lost one more wicket, seven, than Pakistan did, for exactly the same total of 142. But eighteen years earlier thirty-five minutes had been lost because of bad light whereas against Pakistan the only break apart from lunch and tea intervals, was the ten minutes between innings.)

After a second and third day of almost unrelieved dreariness and a fourth of bitter disappointment for England, Pakistan, with all their wickets in hand and 25 on the board, started the final day with only 206 to make to record their second win over England, and their first since 1954. Yet they were beaten by 25 runs!

Every cricket enthusiast round the world must have said, in green-eyed envy: 'I wish I'd been there.' The fourth wicket fell at 65 and England looked to be sitting pretty but then, with the sun high in the sky black shadows were creeping over England. As for the Pakistanis they must, metaphorically speaking, have been putting the champagne on ice. After lunch it was worse for England. Sadiq went on his inexorable way. Asif bore him brave company. 160 runs were on the board with still only four wickets down – it looked hopeless for England.

Then Asif went, tempted down the pitch by Norman Gifford's spin, stumped by Alan Knott. The stand had been worth 95. Pakistan still needed 71 to win, with five wickets in hand. Captain courageous Intikhab came in – and was caught in the slips off the first ball of d'Oliveira's new spell. With 184 for six and 47 needed, like some sacred and immovable frog-like deity, Sadiq still squatted there.

He was joined by Wasim, the wicket-keeper, whose catches in this match equalled the world Test record. And then, in sight of the twin Himalayan peaks of Pakistan's second-ever victory against England and his own individual century, Sadiq was caught and bowled by the wonderful, invaluable, reliable, ageless d'Oliveira. Three wickets still stood, and Pakistan needed 44 runs; England began to taste the elixir of victory while the Pakistan dressing room must have been like the Chamber of Horrors.

Now the close fielders were like a white spider's web around Wasim. The new ball was taken at once after 85 overs . . . a few snicks and Pakistan would be home and dried. Oh no, oh no! Richard Hutton dropped Salim off the first ball of his own bowling. The 200 went up – 31 to win – in 260 minutes. Then Wasim was caught at the wicket off the almost forgotten Peter Lever – 8 runs from victory; and Massood was next to be caught in Lever's next over.

Pervez went in; the umpire's finger went up for an appeal for lbw; Lever took the last three wickets without conceding a run.

So to the end of what had been transformed from one of the most boring sporting exercises I had seen into a crown of golden endeavour, riven only by the diamond hardness of a team which would not give up. But performances like Saturday's drive away the customers and their cash. On the final day there were barely 3,000 to watch something which would be worth the telling to the cricketing grandchildren of the future . . . if there were any.

Back to the nation where track and field athletics really is the national sport and where I would rather watch it than anywhere else in the world – Finland; and its capital, Helsinki, splendidly geared, as ever, to present the European championships.

They started off with one of the greatest 10,000 metres races ever run, which ended with Dave Bedford going down to a defeat which was the next best thing to victory. And, as he had to lose, the gold medal could not have gone to a more popular, exciting and deserving winner than the local pride and joy, Finland's Juha Vaatainen.

The final lap was like something out of an old-time movie thriller, with the heroine bound to the railway track and the express thundering down upon her. At the bell, Bedford – who eight laps earlier had looked a beaten man – had gnawed his way to the front again, head rolling, body drooping, but heart as high as ever. Shortly after the start of the last lap but one, Bedford had put in the last of several sprints with which he sought to grind the opposition into the red track.

But he could no more lose his opponents than a kite can free itself of its tail. In a matter of seconds, he was like a lonely white skier caught by the rolling surge of an avalanche; and now there were eyes only for the front two. The Finns exploded with sheer delight, letting off rockets, as the final lap was fought in an unbelievable 54 seconds between Vaatainen and East Germany's Jurgen Haase, winner of the last two European 10,000 metres titles. Vaatainen's face was a boiling beet under the blond thatch of his hair; Haase's was contorted as if a dentist's pincers had him in their grinding grip. Haase fought the Finn step by fighting step, stride by unfaltering stride, breath by gasping breath. For the last three-quarters of a minute it was impossible to tell who would win, although 50,000 Finns were screaming, willing, almost blowing their champion home.

Right royally did he serve them. He gave an inch and gained a foot. He was reeled back and elastically stretched his lead again. In the end the new 'Flying Finn', bringing back the glory days of Paavo Nurmi, raced home in a new European championship best time of 27 mins 52·8 secs. Haase, after nearly six and three-quarters miles, was just 0·6 seconds behind.

These were the first championships in which the old rigid idea of segregation of the sexes was largely relaxed. One of the more glamorous competitors told me that married athletes were certainly sleeping together – and that even that preliminary wasn't strictly necessary. Moral considerations apart, it seems, of recent years, that the doctors who have specialized in sports investigation are very much divided in opinion on whether sex before an event is, in fact, a handicap for all athletes or whether it can stimulate some.

A fine marathon with the three British runners, Trevor Wright, Ron Hill and Colin Kirkham finishing second, third and fourth behind a twenty-two-year-old Belgian office worker, the pale Karel Lismont, running in only his third marathon.

I liked the way our trio summed it up afterwards. Hill, very upset: 'I'm very disappointed. I ran like an idiot letting them get away from me. I should have known better.' And Wright: 'It's nice to get a silver medal. I'm going out for a gargle tonight.' Then, asked what this, only his second marathon, was like, Wright answered in a gradely Yorkshire accent: 'Well, it's better than work, isn't it?' Kirkham? He fainted.

I loved them . . . I loved them all.

My next trip was one right down nostalgia lane for I went to New York, as I had twenty years earlier, to the very week, to see a British boxer defend his world title and a new girl star in American lawn tennis. In 1951 it had been Randolph Turpin and Little Mo Connolly. Now it was Ken Buchanan and Chris Evert.

As usual the US lawn tennis championships were being played in ghastly heat and humidity – that heat and humidity had been responsible years earlier for one of the worst gaffes of my life.

I was staying with Burris and Georgia Jenkins and no sooner had they left, early on the Saturday, not to return to New York until Tuesday, than the portable air-conditioner, which you could wheel from room to room, broke down. No chance of getting it mended, even if I'd known who to contact, for it was the weekend of Labour Day, the mis-named equivalent of one of our Bank holidays.

Fortunately they had a wonderfully stocked refrigerator, specially well provided with cans of ice-cold beer and, as the thought of any solid food was dispelled by the ghastly, inescapable heat I contented myself with taking a shower every hour on the hour and another can of beer. Then, after some time, as I wandered round the apartment with a large bath-towel tucked round my equator, I began to feel lonely and neglected. Only one thing for it. I rang up a very lovely lady, whom I had known for many happy years, and asked her if she could come round to solace my lonely hours.

Some time later the front door bell chimed and never has music sounded so sweet. Still girdled with my towel and with a beer can, beaded with moisture, in one hand, I flung the door as wide open as my arms and exclaimed: 'Darling!'

On the threshold, with a collecting box in *her* hand, stood a nun in her black habit.

And, as we stood regarding each other with mingled horror and disbelief, my towel fell off. . . .

But, back to Forest Hills, 1971. Before I had arrived the incredible Miss Evert, at sixteen three months younger than Little Mo had been when I first saw her in the US championships, had scored a wellnigh incredible victory over Mary Ann Eisel in which she survived six match points against her and won a tie-breaker! She had been largely responsible for the USA's victory over Britain in the Wightman Cup and, in only her second appearance on the Stadium Court – the equivalent of Wimbledon's Centre Court – had now beaten America's fourth ranked player, on grass, a surface almost completely strange to this youngster.

But, infinitely more important, 'young Chrissie' had brought lawn tennis to the American people at last. One of the things for which I disliked Forest Hills was the difficulty of getting there. I refused to take the subway – I have an uneasy feeling that I'm going to experience enough hell in the next life. And to try to get a taxi to the championships meant that you started off every day with a shouting row. Forest Hills is not in the centre of Manhattan; it's in Queen's, one of the five boroughs which make up New York City. So the drivers used, first of all, to deny that there *was* such a place and, when you insisted, you were in for a hair-raising drive, behind a surly Jehu who ended up by nearly spitting on the tip which, being a moral coward, I felt compelled to give him. Not one of them would ever pass the stringent test without which a London cabbie cannot get a licence.

But when I got into a cab this time, and prepared for the inevitable slanging match, I no sooner mentioned Forest Hills than the driver's unshaven face creased into what passes for a smile from a New York taxi-driver and he replied: 'Oh, yeah! You mean that place where that little goil is playing.'

I confess that there have been many times when Mrs King has been less than my *belle idéal* in sport, but I never admired her more than the way she dealt in the semi-final with this new 'pretender' to her eminence. Her opponent had won forty-six successive singles matches when they stepped on to court, including one against Mrs King who retired at one set all when they had met on clay courts the previous April. I wrote:

'Clay courts' is the operative phrase. Miss Evert may have the idea how to play, but she certainly hasn't got the shots to win against the top opposition on grass. This was a very good match up to 3–2 in Miss Evert's favour in the first set – and thereafter something of a rout. Not for a very long time have I seen Mrs King play as well as this.

You could not help admire Mrs King, for although I don't know how many thousands were round the court, she was playing all of them as well as Miss Evert. The youngster caught up from 0–3 to 2–4 in the second set, but then Mrs King pulled everything out with her thunderous overhead smashes and won the vital seventh game for 5–2.

Miss Evert was disintegrating and she did not have even the satisfaction of saving one match point.

For the record Mrs King went on to beat Rosemary Casals in the final. She had also disposed of any serious comparison between Chris and Little Mo which some ignorant critics had made.

Buchanan, with his then manager, Eddie Thomas, had been training at the traditional Grossingers and just to bring the memories flooding back more vividly one of Buchanan's entourage was Jackie Turpin, Randolph's nephew. Buchanan, still remote and difficult to know, was supremely confident and in the upshot I made the fight much closer than did the American referee and judges. My report went:

At the end of the twelfth and thirteenth rounds, Dr Edwin Campbell had clambered into the ring to see whether it was safe for Buchanan's future eye-sight to allow him to go on. Each time he decided – 'Yes.'

Buchanan, the strange aloof Caledonian who can sometimes be as cold as a polar bear's nose, had fought some thirteen out of fifteen rounds with one eye a winky, blinky lantern, red-curtained with blood. Now Buchanan has won. He is in the dressing room, propping up the wall – or is it the wall which is propping up him?

I was the only newspaperman there, to tell him how proud I am to have seen the only British fighter to have remained a world champion in the States since I first came there over thirty-four years ago.

And then, Lord help us, after the Lord Mayor's show came – Jack

Bodell and Joe Bugner at Wembley, which Bodell won overwhelmingly against the man who, to my utter astonishment, was later to fight for the world's heavyweight title.

On top of this fiasco came news which I found hard to credit, having seen them work so well together – a split between Ken Buchanan and his manager, Eddie Thomas, with the announcement that the Scot's father was to take over his management. I doubted whether he could get much better terms for his son, who had probably made around £85,000 for his last five fights – and I could scarcely see him performing the corner surgery on Buchanan's eye which had almost certainly saved Ken's title for him in New York.

It seemed so sad – and so unnecessary. . . .

There was a spate of boxing news at this time – not all of it good, by any means. At the London headquarters of the British Boxing Board of Control it was announced that the general secretary, Teddy Waltham, was to retire from what is, virtually, the most important executive job in British boxing. I could only say that 'if there has been a decline in boxing it can't be attributed to Teddy Waltham, good sportsman, firm legislator and loyal friend'.

Then came something even worse. Jack Bodell, who had outclassed Joe Bugner, was matched with Jerry Quarry, who had failed to last three rounds with a Cassius Clay who had been out of the ring for over three and a half years. And what happened?

In just sixty-four seconds Bodell was flat on his back and counted out! It was as utterly depressing as going back some forty years to the bad old days of the horizontal heavyweights, epitomized by 'Phainting' Phil Scott.

I was assured that Quarry had, in fact, been shown a videotape of Bodell in action, before their fight and had said incredulously: 'You're putting me on! No champion can be as easy to hit as that.' He certainly fought as though he felt it was easier to land than to miss – and he needed virtually only three punches to win.

On looking back on that night I am, at least, glad that I recorded: 'One of the more promising of the younger British boxers, welterweight John Stracey, from Bethnal Green, met some strong opposition in Guy Vercoutter, a red-headed Frenchman from Dunkirk.' But although this was Stracey's nineteenth professional fight, without a defeat and with only one draw, I confess I did not expect him to be the 10 st 7 lb champion of the world after barely four more years. . . .

In the meantime a quite appalling year for Joe Bugner came to an end when he not only dropped a decision to the not-very-highly-regarded Larry Middleton but got his jaw broken into the bargain. Among his other fights he had been hard put to it to draw with the amiable Labrador heavyweight, Bill Drover, had been fantastically lucky to take the European title from Henry Cooper, fortunate to defend it successfully against Jurgen Blin, lost it to Jack Bodell, and then came this débâcle against Middleton. I did not even bother to go to Nottingham to see it. And nowadays people have journeyed to Kuala Lumpur to see Bugner appear in a bout for the heavyweight championship of the world.

The fight game is certainly a funny old business . . . particularly nowadays.

The beginning of 1972 brought a very curious feeling to me. It was, I imagine – and imagination, fortunately, is as far as I can go – rather like the first time a lady becomes pregnant. You know that something is going to happen to you in nine months' time – and you hope it's going to turn out all right. In my case it was nine lunar months and four days – but then I always had difficulty in catching the first edition!

I had now made up my mind, firmly, that the end of the Summer Olympic Games at Munich was to signal the end of my job as chief sportswriter on the *Daily Mirror*.

The year started with a trip from my winter base in Majorca to where the whole business of modern-day heavyweight championships started – New Orleans. I went there not so much to see Joe Frazier defend his world title against Terry Daniels, but to see whether the champion had suffered any ill-effects from the punishment he had absorbed, while dishing out even more, against Muhammad Ali/Cassius Clay.

I found New Orleans fascinating although, alas, Basin Street, the nest of jazz, had been transformed, I was told, into a succession of anonymous warehouses. But there were plaques and monuments to remind you of the city's historic past, and one particularly delighted me, for I had not known that New Orleans had at one time been under Spanish domination, and I was delighted to see an inscription on one of the old buildings stating that it had originally been the residence of the Governor – who had been born in Palma, Majorca!

There was splendid food to eat – I remember with delight one meal at Brennan's and another at, I think, Antoine's; although, as ever, the difficulty was what to drink to complement such splendid repasts: for either the Americans do not import the best French wine or it just does not cross the rough Atlantic any more comfortably than I did when I had to go by ship. But there were the lovely wrought-iron balconies of the *vieux carré* district looking like Méchlin lace, the remnants of authentic jazz, and always the Crescent City bend of the mighty Mississippi, bringing back thoughts of Mark Twain and the great paddle steamers of the past.

I met a legendary boxing figure, Pete Herman, former bantamweight champion, who had beaten our own immortal flyweight, Jimmy Wilde, and who was now quite blind.

Everything about this trip was wonderful except – the fight. *That* was slaughter on Canal Street. Daniels was nearly knocked out in the first round – and it would have been better for him had he been. As it was, the referee finally intervened after 1 min 25 secs of the fourth round when Daniels had been floored five times. I had noted George Foreman as a ringside spectator at recent title fights and I asked him how he felt about it, feeling myself that he would be well advised to wait another eighteen months. (In fact, in one of the greater upsets of recent years he stopped Frazier in two rounds just fifty-three weeks after the Daniels fight.)

I wrote: 'Personally, if I were to be going to see only one more world heavyweight championship I'd settle for Frazier and Foreman. For Foreman, at least, is a new face.' In fact I *was* going to see only one more 'dreadnought battle' before semi-retirement but, unfortunately, it wasn't to be between the two 'Fs'. . . .

Back to lawn tennis: in line with general behaviour which a few years earlier would not just have been unacceptable but unimaginable, it had suffered 'a she change' – but not all of us could accept that it was 'into something rich and strange'. Strange, perhaps. But not rich if you believed in older values.

For instance, it was revealed that Mrs Billie Jean King, almost certainly the best woman player in the world at this time, had put her name, with other prominent American women, to a statement in the US Women's Lib magazine, *Ms* indicating that she had had an abortion. In her autobiography *Billy Jean* (W. H. Allen, 1975) Mrs King is very honest about it all. She writes how, after telling her husband Larry that she was pregnant:

I took the usual tests, and when they came out positive, there was absolutely no question about what I would do. We agreed on an abortion from the beginning, and there was very little thinking about the morality involved in our decision.

It was the simplest operation I've ever had. I went to the hospital, was knocked out, had the abortion, spent two hours in a recovery room, and then Larry took me home. Done. It didn't begin to compare with either of my knee operations, and later that year when I had some wisdom teeth yanked, the pain and the agony were much worse. There was no trauma at all. I just wanted to get it over with.

It could be said that an athlete is entitled to his or her private life, and not so long ago this was a generally accepted tenet of sports journalism. But when increasing cash awards meant that the stars were not restricted to the sports pages but, because of their film star incomes, became more and more 'hot news', they were bound to suffer the 'goldfish bowl' treatment.

To quote Mrs King again: 'I know I've talked a lot about money, but let me say again that it's by no means at the top of my list of priorities.' That may well be so, but when you become the first sportswoman in the world to earn over £100,000 in a year – that was back in 1971 – and when you could not have done it without having an abortion, the observer is entitled to think that money must be fairly high up on the list.

There was an obverse side of the coin, however. While a few players were making a rajah's ransom – Rod Laver had just become the first player to pass the million-dollar mark, having made some £117,500 in 1971 alone – the Green Shield Stamp Company started a scheme in Britain which, considering its implications, has never really seemed to get the publicity is deserves. The bulk of the money goes towards the development of the junior game and I wrote: 'By the mid 1970s some 150,000 boys and girls who might otherwise have had no opportunity to take up the game will be given the chance of being coached. The scheme, which began last year, goes nationwide in 1972, when it's expected that at least 20,000 youngsters will learn to play lawn tennis with the help of Green Shield sponsorship.'

This seemed to me a far better investment than giving extra money to the stars, some of whom – not Laver, I stress – were grossly overpaid and under-mannered. But. . . .

World fame in sport is, of course, in direct ratio to the number of people who can see a star play. Squash rackets was now the fastest growing participant sport in Britain, but because of gallery limitations it was witnessed by comparatively few people. That was why the fame of Heather McKay, from Canberra, who lost only nine points in reaching the final of the 1971 British women's squash championship was not as great as that of any third-rate footballer. Mrs McKay had not lost to a woman player anywhere for over ten years and she won that British title for the eleventh time to set up a new record – and a record surely unique in any sport. And Mrs McKay is still going strong!

London was lucky to get a glimpse of one of the more brilliant of modern champions, José Angel Napoles, known as 'Mantequilla' (Spanish for butter) because he was 'smooth as butter', who but for a brief break of six months, held the world welterweight title from April 1969 to December 1975. When he appeared in London the news got round that here was someone who could practise the almost forgotten arts of boxing, and the gym was crowded with young boxers. I have a picture of an up-and-coming youngster of Napoles' own weight looking

346

on as the champion exercised. His name? John Stracey. His destiny?
To dethrone 'Napoleon' some three and three quarter years later.

But when Napoles stepped into the Wembley ring against the then
British champion, Ralph Charles, the day of eventual defeat was still
wreathed by the far-off years.

Towards the end of the seventh round the counter punches came so
quick and in such poisonous clusters that I swear Charles never felt the
last one, because he had already been knocked out by the penultimate
blow. It was a champion 'kill'. I was glad to add Mantequilla to the
gallery of the immortals I had seen, even if he had passed his peak by
the time I watched him.

Joe Bugner had another win, at the Albert Hall on a disqualification
against an inept opponent, Leroy Caldwell from New Orleans.

Much more interesting was the fact that John Stracey, on the same
bill, lost his unbeaten professional record to a small, young, neat,
chocolate-coloured Canadian, Marshall Butler. I must say I did not
agree with the decision of the referee, Mike Jacobs, but I would not say
anything which would in any way detract from this splendid eight-
round scrap.

Sport often seems to go in cycles – and Britain was certainly going
through a bad one at the moment. When we lost 1–3 to West Germany
in the first leg of the European Nations' Cup, at Wembley, I wrote: 'To
face the facts honestly, the play of the England side is nowadays really
dull – the ultimate sin in sport.'

Now it was off to Omaha, on the Nebraska–Iowa border, to see Joe
Frazier against the little-considered Ron Stander, as it turned out,
Frazier's last title fight as champion. I got to know 'Smokin' Joe' better
on this trip because, for once, I was able to interview him on his own.
It was clear, although he did not express it in so many words, that he
did not like Muhammad Ali/Cassius Clay: 'The man say he belong to
the world but he only like part of it.' He mused on: 'Don' matter to me
whether someone black or white, jus' so long they behave right. I take
a guy the way he is to me. I don' like to get mixed up with the politics
of boxing. But I don't understand how them boxing commissions let
Clay announce he gonna have two-three fights in a row. You never can
tell what's going to happen in any one fight. That's why I take them one
at a time. That's why I don' sell anyone short or underestimate them.
Clay's announcements of two-three fights in a row turn boxing into
show business – or wrestling.'

It hardly seemed tactful to point out that meeting opponents like
Terry Daniels and then Ron Stander, whom many more people *didn't*
know than did, scarcely enhanced the prestige of the world heavyweight
title, so I didn't point it out!

Rightly they wouldn't let Stander come out for the fifth round.

There was blood on my typewriter, blood on my notes, blood on my programme. And, however long I live, I shall never forget the face of Ron Stander. The face of courage in tears.

Stander muttered a few words, tried to say how good Frazier was – much better than Clay (curious, this, how opponents beaten by either of the two great rivals were wont to say how much better he was than the other) . . . and then broke down completely. Broken, like all the rest, by Frazier.

Then, once I had got my story away, it was – hey! for England in one big hurry. The fight had been on the Thursday night, Nebraska time, which was the early hours of Friday morning in Britain, and I had to be in Carlisle for the wedding of my stepson, Raymond, by midday Saturday.

How do you do it? Plane to Montreal, I think. Terrible kerfuffle there about getting my luggage transferred from one side of the airport to the other. Night flight with considerable draughts of such medicaments as cold champagne and warmed cognac. Land at Prestwick round about 8 am. Met by the superb Sally. Drive to Carlisle. A memorable bath with the Bollinger feeling all the more chilled among the wreaths of steam. Shave and – get me to the church on time!

By the next Tuesday I was in Paris for the French lawn tennis championships. My interest was to see whether Mrs Billie Jean King could prove herself the *complete* great player. She had won the Australian title in 1968, Wimbledon in 1966, 1967 and 1968, and the US in 1967 and 1971. But the French, as difficult to 'fill' as an inside straight in poker and, in some ways the most difficult of all in the 'grand slam' of championships, for it was then the only one not played on grass, had always eluded her.

But it didn't this time. Meeting Evonne Goolagong, strangely enough for only the third time, Mrs King achieved a 'rubber' victory over the young Australian. But although the American was efficiency personified I wrote at the time that I was 'looking forward to the time when Miss Goolagong again plays as though life was once more full of roses'.

East Germany, as usual, made track news when in a women's tri-angular match between them, Britain and the Netherlands they won ten events, leaving us two and the Dutch girls one. How did they do it? What was the motivation – and the method? East Germany is a nation of only 18,000,000, overlooked by much of Europe. As someone put it succinctly: 'In another century they would have gone to war to prove they existed. Now they can get recognition through sport.'

Less than four weeks after I had left Nebraska I was back in the States – this time New York, thirty-five years to the day after I had reported my first world heavyweight title fight from Chicago. It wasn't a world heavyweight fight this time but a lightweight championship between Ken Buchanan and Roberto Duran from Panama.

From the start I feared for Buchanan. First of all, some nine months earlier, while he was about to take part in his successful title defence against Ismael Laguna, I was watching Duran impressing me as much as anyone I had seen for the first time since Ruben Olivares, when he knocked out his opponent in just seventy-three seconds. I was even more concerned by the reappearance, as Duran's trainer, of Ray Arcel, a quiet, scholarly looking man who could have passed as a rabbi, who had been forced out of the game years before by a villainous attack at a time when the gangsters were really running American boxing. For Ray, one of my oldest friends in the States, to come back meant that Duran must be something rather extra special.

I went up to see Buchanan training at Grossingers (where else?) but although the Scot was more communicative than before he had won the world title I still found it hard to get through to him – the more so because I had publicly expressed my view that he had made a mistake in parting with Eddie Thomas, which naturally did not endear me to his father who had now taken over. At least neither of them seemed superstitious for the first sign I saw at Grossingers read: 'The National Burial Casket Co. invites you to a reception' – whether a permanent one they did not say! Only underneath the undertakers' communication did you learn that Buchanan was training there, too!

In the event the fight was never close. It was ended by the referee before the fourteenth round could begin and of the thirteen concluded I had given Buchanan only the ninth with the sixth even – perhaps I was ungenerous to him in the third. Had it been in Britain I was convinced that Duran would either have been disqualified or found that his tactics were so severely curtailed by the referee that he would never have been able to dominate the fight as he did. But the way it was allowed to be conducted by referee Johnny Lobianco, made it a racing certainty for the street-fighter from Panama – and the official score-cards emphasized how one-sided it was.

The thirteenth round caused pandemonium with everyone apparently seeing the ending in a different way. It's true of course that if you ask ten people what happened in a street accident you're going to end up with ten different stories. The way I saw it Duran came in head-first for perhaps the fiftieth time – for which I never saw him warned – and bored Buchanan back into the ropes. Almost certainly, Buchanan hit Duran after the bell. And, absolutely certainly, Duran hit Buchanan after the bell. For my money – and this is *my* story – the final punch was a low right from Duran, which apparently displaced Buchanan's protector.

Later a doctor was to say that one of Buchanan's testicles showed signs of swelling. And, in a masterpiece of understatement he added: 'This might have been quite painful.'

If it had been a disastrous trip from the point of view of British boxing, I retained some abiding memories of it. First of all, Madison Square Garden threw a lavish party for me in the Penn Plaza Club over the arena.

It was a moving occasion for me: the end of thirty-five years of visiting the States comprising some seventy round trips, made all the more poignant for me by the death, that very day, of Nat Fleischer, boxing's greatest historian, a valiant defender of what he believed to be right and the greatest international champion the sport ever had. He was in his eighties. He was my friend.

He was a little man, but he had the heart of a lion – even if towards the end it had to be kept going with a pace-maker. Although his voice rasped like a cinder under the door he was not a loud-mouthed belliger-ent and in an atmosphere which could often be coarse I never recall an obscenity coming from him. But I *do* remember once when a couple of so-called 'friends' were blackguarding me, although I couldn't under-stand what they were saying, Nat came up to me, translated their remarks, and then added, in a tone of utter scorn: 'Those *schlemiels*: I could talk Yiddish before they were circumcised!'

But Nat's death did not destroy the party, for everyone who had known the little man knew that he would not have wished that. Kind speeches were made and I was given an extremely capacious travelling bag and a two-foot long gold-coloured boxing glove signed by sports-writers, cartoonists, radio and TV commentators, promoters and managers from both sides of the Atlantic, headed by Harry Markson, for so long the boxing boss of 'the Garden'. I am staring at it now as it hangs in my study overlooking the Mediterranean. . . .

I did perhaps my fiftieth transatlantic broadcast, reviewing the championship and then reminiscing about lawn tennis – Wimbledon had started on the day of the fight – with the delightful Sarah Palfrey Danzig whom I had known for some forty years since she first appeared at Wimbledon as a teenager. She was never at her absolute best in England, although she won the women's doubles title twice, but in the US championships she won the singles twice and the women's and mixed doubles no fewer than thirteen times.

It meant something of a dash, though, to catch the night plane from New York and be in my seat at Wimbledon in time for start of play at 2 pm on Wednesday afternoon.

The women's final was an anti-climax. Miss Goolagong admitted that for her *the* match had been the successful confrontation with a younger, newer star, Chris Evert. When she met that supreme competitor, Mrs Billie Jean King, in the final there was just not the inspiration there and although the crowd, as always, was behind her – sometimes quite outrageously applauding double faults and mistakes by Mrs King – there was no way that they could will the cuddly koala home.

For the first time ever the men's singles final in 1972 was played, because of Saturday rain, on a Sunday and, as I wrote, it was worth waiting until then to see the towering American, Stan Smith, beat the raven-locked Ilie Nastase 4–6, 6–3, 6–3, 4–6, 7–5 in the greatest final I have ever seen since the Jack Crawford–Ellsworth Vines upset of 1933. If ever there were a triumph of character over wayward genius this was it. The Rumanian won a good first set, then I wrote: 'The fatal flaw in the steel blade of Nastase's rapier-like game showed itself for the first time. He objected to a fault call on his service. He lost the game badly – almost the first he had played really poorly – and although he broke back to 2–3, he was beginning to niggle and fidget.'

Nastase changed his racket once in the middle of a game, and generally gave a visible example of the grasshopper mind at work, losing the second set but getting off with a rush again in the third. Then, when he was leading 2–0:

The fatal flaw again. There was a dubious baseline call against Nastase. I thought he was unlucky. But, in the name of sporting sanity, if you've been robbed of one point, why compound the error by giving away another half dozen?

He couldn't forget it. He lost the set in twenty-four minutes.

By the fourth set Nastase was still rejecting rackets like a gambler discarding unwanted cards. Up to 2–2 it seemed not to be a question of who would win but just how long it would take. Then the Rumanian settled down. All at once, in the fifth game Smith, presumably feeling the extra 'bite' in his opponent's shots, began missing easy volleys again.

Smith made a great stretching volley, like a salmon leaping a waterfall. But Nastase broke him with an oblique passing shot, crafty as an assassin's dagger in the dark. Smith survived two set points at 5–4, but on the third he put a backhand return of service out. Nastase, after exactly two hours' play, was as level as he had been at the start!

Let no one play Nastase down in the fifth set. He had conquered himself now. He kept striving to conquer Smith. I think, in the end, it was Smith's greater strength and almost unbelievable fitness which just tilted this so delicately balanced scale. In the tenth Nastase was making unforced errors and not getting his first service in.

The Rumanian saved two match points in the tenth game, another in the twelfth and then missed an easy backhand. A guy named Smith was the champ.

There was a delightful postscript. Smith, with a grin so wide that it threatened to meet at the back of his head, joyfully displayed the gorgeous golden cup to the crowd. Then it was Nastase's turn. The reward for the runner-up is a silver medal – not a very large one. Nastase displayed that and, even in the doldrums of defeat, the inherent clown in him came out. He did not speak, but the look on his face, the imperceptible twitch of the shoulder, the droop of the mouth, all said: 'After two and three quarter hours, all I get is *this*?'

I felt there was a touch of Charlie Chaplin in Nastase the Rumanian.

Before the Olympic Games there was a quick trip to Eire to see Muhammad Ali/Cassius Clay in action against Al 'Blue' Lewis, a Detroit Negro heavyweight with a considerably better than average record. In the end I summed it up by writing: 'I believe Lewis will do well to answer the bell for the ninth round.'

In fact, Lewis lasted into the second half of the eleventh round before the referee flown over from America, Lew Eskin, rightly stopped the bout. Clay had nearly finished it in the fifth when he floored 'Blue' and the giant 15 st $3\frac{1}{2}$ lb Negro just got to his feet with only one second of the round left. Angelo and his brother Chris, the promoter from Miami Beach, insisted that Lewis had been on the floor for over twenty seconds. I didn't think it was anything like as long as that although I did record at the time: 'I thought referee Eskin took rather a long time to get to the count of nine.'

My abiding memory of that trip was Harold Conrad, who had been very much involved in the promotion, giving a post-fight party at which John Huston, the famous movie director, was one of the guests. Huston had made a magnificent film version of Leonard Gardner's fight novel, *Fat City*, which we had all seen in a small side-street cinema in Dublin and which was so moving that it was the only occasion I ever knew even to silence Clay. . . .

With Munich now less than four weeks away I was beginning to have fears for some of our more favoured athletes. In the last major track and field meeting before the Games David Hemery, who had done us so proud in Mexico City, was having trouble with his stride pattern in the 400 metres hurdles. I feared for his gold but the real storm-petrel was Dave Bedford. Twelve thousand people had come to the Crystal Palace, largely to see him and Ian Stewart clash in a much publicized mile race. Neither man appeared. Both were suffering from the complaint which necessitates numerous short indoor dashes rather than a prolonged outdoor run, and no one but a fool or a sadist could have expected either to appear in those circumstances. But the crowd should have been warned before they paid their entrance money.

I just had time to get to the Oval – in the normal way anything but an event to celebrate – for the fifth England–Australian Test match. In some ways it was a *Boy's Own Paper* match with the two brothers Greg and Ian Chappell each scoring a century and sharing in a 201 partnership, with their parents from Australia there to watch. But what I was really grateful for was the chance of packing in my memory the sight of one of the game's all-time great fast bowlers – Dennis Lillee.

In that far-off Test match, over fifty-one years ago – the first major international sporting event I had ever seen – Australia had had one of the greatest 'quickie' combinations in cricketing history in Gregory and McDonald. Now they had one (but what a one) in Dennis Lillee. I wrote on the fourth day that: 'The thought of a fresh Dennis Lillee with the new ball is enough to make even the most stalwart apprehensive. In his first spell – certainly in the first three overs – I think Lillee was as fast as anyone I've watched since I saw 'Typhoon' Tyson so materially assist Len Hutton to retain the Ashes during the 1954–5 tour of Australia. And I'm *not* forgetting Wes Hall.' Lillee's thirty-one wickets in that series set up a new record for an Australian bowler here and – Heaven help us! – he was only twenty-three.

Next came a stop-off in Copenhagen. This gave me the opportunity of seeing one boxer whom I was determined to assess – Carlos Monzon, of the Argentine – successfully defending his world middleweight title against Denmark's Tom Bogs.

Monzon was the seventeenth world middleweight champion I had seen and, although this was the only occasion when I watched him 'in the flesh' – I had observed him previously only on television – I would certainly have put him in or around the top half-dozen.

Then it was time to go to Germany, where the Olympic curtain had risen for me just over thirty-six years ago and a million miles back, for my final tragic Games.

I arrived fortunately too late for the invitation to tour the former concentration camp at Dachau which some of the German hosts seemed to think suitable as a kick-off for the world's greatest festival of youth and the mingling of the nations of the world.

The athletics did not start for several days and, although Britain had had a very good start in the boxing competition, I never felt that the Games were properly under way until the track and field events were in full swing. When they *did* begin it was the first time *heats* had been run in the 10,000 metres – and Dave Bedford and Emile Puttemans of Belgium shattered the Olympic record by over half a minute to come within fifteen seconds of the world record. The two rivals spent almost the whole of the twenty-five laps chatting and gesturing to each other and it was only in the last twenty metres that the Belgian slightly lengthened his stride to win by a fifth of a second.

Bedford appeared to have timed his preparation perfectly – but never have appearances been more deceptive for, from that moment, everything seemed to go wrong. He permitted his name to be associated with one of the stupidest articles with which an active athlete has ever been involved, in which he more or less urged everyone to drop what they were doing and somehow get in front of a TV set in order to see him win a gold medal. Even Muhammad Ali/Cassius Clay, trying to sell tickets for one of his many mismatches, had never been quite as brash as this; and there *is* still a difference between promoting professional boxing and running for an Olympic title.

Meanwhile David Hemery was not hurdling with the perfection he had found in Mexico City although he was never pushed to get to the final.

But, even more exciting from an international viewpoint, was the continuing sprinting successes of the powerful Russian, Valeriy Borzov who, once I had seen him in action I christened 'not Borzov but Borzoi' after that most elegant and fleet breed of Russian dogs. He it was who had been picked when the Russians, tired of American domination in the dashes, went to a computer to discover the perfect build for a sprinter. When the answer had been given they combed through the available athletes – and came up with Borzov.

Unfortunately because, I was told, of the US track coach's unfamiliarity with the twenty-four-hour clock, he misread the times of the heats in which the Americans, Rey Robinson and Eddie Hart, were competing as 6 pm instead of 1600 hours so his two charges were scratched when they did not show up on time!

But Borzov made no mistake about completing the 'double' by winning the 200 metres with all his rivals competing and thus becoming the first man to take both events since America's Bobby Morrow at Melbourne in 1956. It was also the first time that Europe was able to claim the two dashes since the German Armin Hary won the 100 metres and Italy's Livio Berruti took the 200, suitably enough in Rome, in 1960.

Then came the tremendous let-down for Britain – Bedford's ignominious defeat in the first of the two long-distance races for which he had entered, the 10,000 metres. Bedford plodded home like a ploughman in sixth place after the Finnish policeman, Lasse Viren, had clipped exactly a second off Ron Clarke's world record of 27 mins 39·4 secs which had stood for seven years.

Gradually the issue had narrowed down to just four men, the tall, almost brooding Finn, with his neat beard, the swarthy Haro from

Spain, the fresh-faced, curly-haired Belgian, Puttemans, and that little bundle of energy and courage, Ethiopia's Yifter. At the bell Yifter was still third behind Viren and Puttemans who, having finally shaken off the rest – Viren had started his final burst some 600 metres from home – were now like two duellists with their shots finally to fire. It was the bigger man who won. His stride was just too much for Puttemans, but the Belgian was only 1·2 seconds behind him as they crossed the electronic beam. Seven yards, perhaps. So near and yet so far after 6 miles, 376 yards.

One hundred and fifty yards behind the winner, came Bedford. As the photographers converged upon him, he pushed their lenses away and vanished down the tunnel, tears streaming down his face, a man for whom the occasion had been too big and the opposition too good. As he ran for cover, someone threw him the top of a track suit and, still weeping, he ran all the way back to the Olympic Village, like a wounded animal seeking to hide.

To complete a disastrous week for Bedford, although he qualified for the final of the 5,000 metres he then finished last but one – Viren completed the long distance double – and, ironically, the only man Bedford beat, when it didn't matter, was Juha Vaatainen, the Finn who had won so decisively in the European championships!

So far the Games had been predictable; some fine performances, some bitter heartbreaks; rows and reconciliations. The recipe as before.

The second Monday belonged to Borzov, who completed his sprint double, and Kenya's Kipchoge Keino who won the 3,000 metres steeplechase in the Olympic record time of 8 mins 23·6 secs. After that I, for one, felt no inclination to back against him in the 1,500 metres, for which he already held the title – though in fact he 'failed' (!) by getting only a silver medal in the metric mile which was won by yet another of those fantastic Finns, Pekka Vasala. And this was, in a way, poetic justice for the steelplechase, which had been a battle between the Kenyans and the Finns. In a field of only twelve, 50 per cent of the competitors came from those two countries, and it was the strength and virility of the Africans which overcame the technique and 'know-how' of perhaps the most sophisticated European athletics nation. In the end Kenya had not only the winner in Keino, but also the second in Ben Jipcho and the sixth in Amos Biwott, who won the gold four years earlier.

In the rare moments when I was able to get away from the various stadia I was having, at this my last Olympiad, an extremely pleasant time. With Chris Brasher, Olympic steeplechase gold medallist in the 1956 Games at Melbourne, and subsequently such an adornment to the *Observer*, I had spent a very pleasant luncheon at the British Consulate at which the Ambassador and his wife – herself an ex-journalist – were splendid company.

Then came another luncheon invitation, again with Chris, as the guest of the Prime Minister, Edward Heath, who was so flattering that I almost found myself rediscovering the forgotten art of blushing!

And then . . . and then . . . the pleasant small-talk with Ted Heath, the mounting excitement of great physical, mental, aye, even moral achievement, which after all these years, could still jerk me out of my seat, dulled, like the pulsing glow of a log-fire burning ash-grey in the small hours of the morning when the world is cold, as the news of the assassination of Israelis in the Olympic Village began to percolate.

I wish I could say that I, like younger sportswriters, disguised in tracksuits, had penetrated the perimeter of the Village. But I had entered my sixtieth year one week earlier – I had a birthday card from the Olympic Committee to remind me of it, mockingly – and, as so often happens when the magnificent, memorable or, as in this case, the unforgettably tragic events of your life occur you are doing something utterly mundane. When someone gave me the first garbled news – because for a long time no one *knew* what had happened – I was, of all things, queuing up for one of the services in which the vaunted German efficiency had almost completely broken down . . . trying to collect my clean laundry and also deposit some dirty clothes.

Gradually, unbelievably, the hideous news seeped out, polluting everything it touched. I still feel the shock of disbelief, the illogical feeling of moral leprosy as though all of us who even attended the Games (*sic*) were tainted by association as, years later, I re-read what I wrote then:

> I came to Munich as a sportswriter. Today I'm a war correspondent.
>
> What happened here today is the ultimate obscenity in sport.
>
> The Olympic Games were a soaring vision of internationalism, conceived in the dying years of the nineteenth century, striving to achieve a brotherhood of Man, through sport, where the power politicians had so signally failed.
>
> There were just five Games before the bloodbath of the First World War. Another five between the wars. This is the seventh since the end of the Second World War.
>
> But still men of faith kept the Olympic flame alive. Britain put on a patchwork Games in 1948 because war-ravaged little Finland, which was supposed to be the host nation, could not organize them in time. The flame burned ever more brightly from Europe to Australia, to the Orient and Latin America. Of course, it wasn't the ideal that Baron Pierre de Coubertin had visualized when he recreated the Games in 1896.
>
> There was nationalism.
>
> My God! was there nationalism. My first Games were in this very country

in 1936 when Adolf Hitler, the wickedest man who ever lived, tried in the towering stadium in Berlin to prove the supremacy of the Aryan race.

Negro athletes proved the absurdity of the philosophy inherent in the creed of the crooked cross.

But the flame burned on.

But today's abomination must put at risk all future Olympic Games. Apparently the Israelis had been warned not to accept any unexpected parcels. Presumably soon there will be checks on the food and the liquids provided for competitors. Cars will have to be tested – but by whom? – to see that they do not blow up when the ignition is switched on.

Can any Games, any festival of youth, any congregation of the sporting youngsters, boys and girls of the world, continue in circumstances like these? Today in Munich men were boxing and playing basketball; equestrian stars, elegant in immaculate habits and top hats, were competing in the Grand Prix de Dressage at Nymphenberg; others were fencing with the épée, playing football, and handball, and volleyball.

And none of it made a blind bit of sense, for instead of the kick-off times, the ring of a bell, the bark of a pistol, at hours from eight in the morning until past midnight, the only hours which were significant were those in which nine Israelis suffered and sweated in the shadow of the gunmen, under the muzzles of the assassins, with each successive hour threatening to be their last on Earth.

Had the Games not been suspended there would obviously have been the fear of a counter-attack by Israeli guerillas against Arab competitors. What the complacent are pleased to call 'a little war' could have broken out in, of all places, the Olympic Village, where the youth of the world are supposed to congregate in friendly rivalry. . . .

To add filth to obscenity, for this to happen in Germany, almost in the shadow of the abortion which was the concentration camp at Dachau, makes one despair of the future of the entire human race.

The Olympic flame is still alight – just. But never has it flickered so fitfully since 1896.

For long confused hours the full horror of the situation was not known or, rather, was deliberately obscured by the German police and politicos. We *did* know that two Israelis had been killed within the village. We did *not* know for a long period that a further nine Israelis had been slaughtered at the airport, when a 'rescue' job was bungled, and that five of the terrorists and a German policeman had also been killed.

And then, so help me, with the representatives of the world, performers and spectators alike, assembled in the Olympic Stadium to hear words, moving though unavailing, from the President of the Federal German Republic, Avery Brundage, that monolithic President of the International Olympic Committee, horrified many of the thousands who listened by equating the exclusion of the Rhodesians with the murder of the Israelis. I wrote:

Today there is only one topic in Munich. Are you for or against the Olympic Games continuing? Let me beg the question for one moment. I am a professional journalist. That is the way I have earned my bread for over forty years. I have been sent to cover the XXth Olympic Games. And this I shall do to the best of my ability until the final fanfare signals that these ill-starred Games have come to an official end.

For me, they ended with the massacre of the Israeli athletes.

The day this appeared the *Mirror* ran a leader saying the Games should go on. But – and I doubt if anyone knew how much I appreciated, right at the end of my full-time career, working for a truly liberal newspaper – they pointed out in the editorial that I held utterly opposed views and they cross-referred readers to my article, which could not have been more strikingly displayed, appearing under the sub-heading 'Peter Wilson expresses a personal view'.

But what I had written was true for me: the Games were over.

I *do* remember Mary Peters, a warm, great-hearted lass, winning that murderous test of the all-rounder, the pentathlon, and winning it so clearly as a proper woman – in contrast to some of the nauseating freaks who had competed in this event in earlier years.

I remember David Hemery, as I had feared, not being able to master the new stride-pattern that he needed but winning a bronze as magnificently as, four years earlier, he had captured a gold – and the new champion, John Akii-Bua from Uganda, having to put up a new world record to beat the old record-holder.

I remember Dave Wottle winning just about the closest 800 metres race I have ever seen, his dingy brown peaked cap apparently so far behind that there was no conceivable chance of his getting to the front – and then doing just that with, literally, the last stride as the Russian Evgeni Arzanhov, tried to hurl himself through the electronic beam and, instead, flung himself on to his hands and knees.

I remember the build-up of Duane Bobick in the heavyweight boxing class, with people already tipping him, before the competition even began, to succeed such as Patterson, Clay and Frazier; and the cash-colour-conscious muttering behind their hands: 'And, besides he's white.'

And I remember the almighty thumping he got from the big Cuban, Teofilo Stevenson, who had already once boxed a close bout with him in a previous competition and this time stopped him in the third round. There followed consternation when Stevenson said he was not interested in cash 'only in the revolution' and that he meant to defend his amateur title four years later.

But these were all things that happened before the full horror engulfed us, and even the elfin gravity-defying grace of Olga Korbut could not wipe out the feeling of dirtiness.

And then, all at once, it was over, the nightmare Games at an end; the finish, too, of my full-time career as a day by day, week by week, month by month and year after year journalist. I had hoped that one of my colleagues could take over to record the Closing Ceremony but he mislaid his ticket – and it was left to me to write it.

Avery Brundage, retiring President of the International Olympic Committee, made the closing speech. If some of us thought the phrase 'We have celebrated these days of radiant happiness with one another' was rather excessive he did follow it by saying: '[We] have borne the difficult hours of terrible sorrow with you all.' But – and I can still scarcely credit it – even in this *Götterdämmerung* atmosphere the Germans couldn't get what should have been an impressive farewell right. On the electric score-board appeared the unforgivable misspelling: 'Thank you Avery Brandage.'

I hated almost everything Brundage stood for, and I had fought him when I could for all the two decades during which he had been IOC President. His insensitivity about the murder of the Israelis had been, to me, nauseating. But he *had* done his duty, as he saw it, fearlessly and tirelessly and now, within three weeks of his eighty-fifth birthday, they couldn't even spell the old man's name right. I suppose the knowledge that I, too, was bidding farewell to the world's greatest sporting show; that, although the flag of Canada was standing proud in the evening breeze, signalling that the next Games were to be held there in four years' time, it did not apply to me, made me feel unaccustomedly sentimental; but I did think the old tyrant deserved better of the movement to which he had devoted so much of his life than that. . . .

The reason I had hoped that I would not have to write the epitaph of the Games was that, at the last moment, I was told by the office that they wanted me to hand over, as had been arranged, to Frank McGhee, my successor as chief sportswriter of the *Mirror*. I had thought that I should be able to write a farewell article, more or less in peace and quiet, once I had got back to England.

Poor fool that I have always been! Even after forty years in 'The Street' I forgot that time and newspaper production wait for no man. And, for technical reasons, they wanted my *nunc dimittis* not only from Munich but a day in advance so that, as soon as the Olympic ceremony was finished, would I, please, get a move on and write a front page piece 'passing on the baton' to Frank – which, of course, I wanted to do – and then, no messing about, write a two-page valediction.

So, as the stage-hands, so to speak, started dismantling the largest stage in the world and my friends and colleagues of one, two, three and four decades started quaffing the lovely stuff with that feeling, so well-known to me, 'Well, that's another one in the bag, what's next?' I sat down with 'Old Faithful' and started composing . . . but, to be honest, I felt more like decomposing. Because, although this one was 'in the bag' all right there weren't going to be any more for me.

The noise didn't worry me. You can't live for forty years amid the mechanical chatter of typewriters, the shrilling of phone bells, the shouting of an office perpetually in a state of pell-mell, and maintain the ivory tower of a poet. Nor was it the lights – I seemed to have lived and worked under them for ever – or the smoke which seemed to mist up my eyes.

It was the ultimate recognition that, no fooling, this *was* the final curtain. I just wanted to be alone while I wrote goodbye to millions of friends whose breakfast tables I had shared for so long although I had met so few of them; and wrote about men and women who had given me such a wonderful, wonderful life – the friends, the enemies, the good, the bad, the living and the dead.

I put my hands in the accepted position for touch typing – fingers of the left hand on a, s, d, f; right fingers on j, k, l, and ;. Right thumb on the space bar. It was all automatic – how many tens of thousands of time had I done it before?

And yet . . . and yet. Nothing happened. The page stayed white yet shadowy.

And there I was found by a colleague, a young man something like I had been over a quarter of a century ago, with plenty of big assignments and trips to far-off places to savour. And when he asked me if anything was wrong I couldn't answer and, because he was a very nice young man he went away and left me alone – with my typewriter.

And, of course, the story got written and it read:

With the quenching of the Olympic flame for another four years, the time comes for me to hand on the torch to my friend and colleague Frank McGhee.

It is now over thirty-seven years since I first joined the *Daily Mirror*, and I have been a sports columnist for nearly thirty-six.

Wonderful years they have been, too. Thirty-two world heavyweight title fights, over 100 world championships at all different weights; every Wimbledon final, bar two, since 1929; eight summer Olympic Games and four winter ones; Cup Finals, Rugby internationals, Test matches, Grand Nationals and Derbies galore.

You name them I've covered them, and loved almost every moment of them. But the pace of sport – and writing about it – gets ever more hectic, and now I feel that it's time a younger man took over. I'll take my oath, not the Olympic one, that he'll do the job not only with the competence of a true professional, but with the integrity which is the hallmark of the honourable journalist.

I shall not be completely divorced from what has for so long been my life. For some time when the weather is kinder and the clay is red and the grass green, I shall return to the very first sport from which I earned my living as a writer – lawn tennis.

This I hope to continue for some years to come. And, perhaps, when I am somewhere where they are holding a very big fight, the old itch will overcome me and I'll be allowed to write some comment on it.

It is not as difficult for me to bow out now as it would have been even a few years ago. There is a lot about sport in the past few years which has saddened me; some things which have sickened me: the continued and mounting hooliganism on the terraces and in the environs of soccer grounds. The clogging which is glossed over by calling villains 'hard men'.

The way these last Olympic Games seemed to lose all contact with the humanism and idealism which saw them re-created seventy-six years ago.

But, despite all that, there are bound to be days of nostaliga ahead, when I shall murmur to myself – and to anyone else who will listen – 'Don't think it wasn't fun for forty years in Fleet Street.'

And the best of luck to one and all!

The rest of the year really was wine and roses. Already the Sports Writers' Association had anticipated the farewell Games and using, of all unlikely people – which, of course, is why they were so successful – Henry Cooper and his pixie-wife Albina as devious characters had lured Sally and myself to a magnificent luncheon party, in a private room at Grosvenor House, where some hundred or so of my working colleagues entertained me right regally and gave me an onyx plaque with in-scribed silver inlays and facsimiles of articles I had written about Jesse Owens on the opening day of the 1936 Games and Joe Louis winning the world title in 1937.

I swear Henry was as delighted when he led me – all unsuspecting and thinking that we were going to have a *partie carrée* – into a crowded room, warm with applause, as he was when he had feinted someone into an opening for his lethal left hook! Laurie Pignon, bless his heart, who was covering the lawn tennis tournament at Nottingham, managed to get the referee to postpone the match involving Evonne Goolagong, then the Wimbeldon champion, so that he could come to the luncheon and then cover the match! Terry O'Connor, also of the *Daily Mail*, was on his way to Park Lane when he got hit by a piece of falling masonry in Fleet Street – it seemed determined to be 'The Street of Misadventure', as far as I was concerned, right up to the end. Dick Currie, of the Scottish *Daily Record* had come all the way from Glasgow. *The Times* reported the function under the neat heading, 'Surprise punch'.

The *UK Press Gazette* – the trade paper of my profession – reported the affair perhaps a little more racily, but with the authentic touch of Colin Valdar, sometime editor of the *Sunday Pictorial* and later the *Daily Sketch*. He wrote: 'It was a fast-moving occasion, chaired by the

Mirror's Frank Taylor, nostalgiaed by a Wilson world tour of his past and present rivals, and capped by Hugh Cudlipp who was conned into providing an epilogue. He couldn't complain; he did the same thing to Michael Foot at the end of the IPC awards lunch. Instead, he named the three greatest newspaper by-liners of his four decades or so in the business: Hannen Swaffer, Sir Bill 'Cassandra' Connor and Peter Wilson.

'There were no instant dissenters, just more applause for the only living survivor of that trio. And then back to the Test Match.'

After Munich:

> And thick and fast they came at last,
> And more, and more, and more.

Chums on the *Mirror* gave me such lavish gifts, if not of gold, frankincense and myrrh then of silver and electronic wizardry that I was almost embarrassed. And Sally, too, got a silver cup, inscribed: 'Sally. She drove him to it!' And after I had made my obeisances, in the huge third floor editorial room in the big Holborn Circus building, it was my turn to return a tithe of the hospitality in one of the best named of all the Fetter Lane pubs, The Printer's Devil: great heavens! how long ago was it that someone told me, when I joined the *Mirror*, 'Fetter Lane than never'?

Frank McGhee nearly knocked me out that night by embracing me for the first and last time in our lives and Ken Jones, to my delight, succeeded Frank on the *Sunday Mirror*.

The Boxing Writers' Club made the Café Royal, where we have had so many of our annual dinners, the 'ring' for my retirement 'fight'. A cut-glass decanter and glasses which sparkle on my bar was my 'treat' there.

At the Athletics Writers' dinner I was given a crystal tankard – and a hug and a kiss from Mary Peters which still (particularly the hug) makes me tingle! The tankard is reserved for Pimms.

Then there was the Lawn Tennis Writers' Association and one of the most wonderful gifts I have ever had. Half a dozen pewter goblets, each of them bearing the signature of an unforgettable champion – Maureen Connolly (taken from an old letter), Ann Jones and Evonne Goolagong; Jack Kramer, Lew Hoad and the one 'intruder' among the Wimbledon singles title holders, Ken Rosewall – who, I am told, when he learned for what his signature was needed, wanted to pay for the goblet himself! (In case anyone has observed that the people who liked me most – and knew me best! – always seemed to give me receptacles or vessels for wines or liquor the point has not escaped me . . . or Sally!)

And so to the grandest finale – although each one had brought such bitter-sweet memories that it was impossible to list an order of precedence. But the one given me by the *Mirror* and hosted by Hugh Cudlipp was really one of the unforgettable nights of my life.

The messages, in fact, moved me as much as anything in this highly emotional evening. Representatives of the *Mirror* had obviously been working overtime contacting some of the people about whom I had written and with whom I had feasted or feuded over the years.

In no particular order, except as I leaf through them Fred Perry cabled: 'Sincere regrets at not seeing the final of Wilson saga. I saw the opening and would have liked to celebrate with you but am stuck, in Europe. Good luck always.' A cable marked 'Urgent' arrived just in time from Melbourne. It was short as a world record and it read: 'Best wishes for retirement. Herb Elliott.' The next one read: 'From Santa Barbara, California, for Peter Wilson. A million thanks for all the kind words you have written about me over the years. In my line up you'll always be Number 1. Love and best wishes. Mary Rand.'

And still they came. 'From Phoenix, Arizona for Peter Wilson. A privilege and a pleasure to have known someone who deserves a special gold medal of his own. Might even run over to Spain to see you one of these days. Regards. Jesse Owens.' Then: 'From Newport Beach, California, for Peter Wilson. No one ever did more for world tennis – and tennis appreciates it. See you on the Center [Oh, Rod, how could you go American on me like that!] Court. Best wishes. Rod Laver.'

Another from Australia: 'Our sincere congratulations to our friend Peter Wilson, a top journalist, gentleman and sportsman. We will miss him. Love and regards, Evonne Goolagong and Vic Edwards.' Next one from Sydney: 'Wimbledon breakfasts will not be the same with no Peter Wilson reports. Happy retirement. Wilma and Ken Rosewall.' Followed inevitably, from Cherry Hill, New Jersey: 'Float like a butterfly sting like a bee, Peter, you're a champion, just like me. Good luck. Muhammad Ali.'

And then the one which was the greatest accolade for me: 'For Peter Wilson. You always were a champion as a writer. The sports world will miss you. Best for the future. The Brown Bomber, Joe Louis, Caesar's Palace, Las Vegas.'

But one character who spoke I must mention – J. L. Manning, sportswriter emerited, with whom I had battled on radio, TV and in print and who, I just hope, had as much respect for me as I had for the man who was gutsy enough to write and even broadcast, with a special set-up, from what turned out to be his death-bed so that he never lived long enough even to collect the OBE which he had so richly earned.

Jim, at the dinner, took the mickey out of me for having gone through the sporting alphabet – I had started by saying: 'I haven't got an 'A'

but there are an awful lot of 'B's in sport' – but omitted the 'exes', short
for expenses, perhaps the most vital contribution in a journalist's life!
But the next day he wrote to me: 'My dear Peter, I do not mind admit-
ting that I shed a few tears during the wonderful evening at the
Grosvenor House. I expect Sally did, too. It was an occasion unique in
my experience, and Amy and I were grateful to be invited. I dropped a
note to Hugh Cudlipp thanking him, and this is to tell you how I felt
and how much we wish you every happiness during what you have
planned to do. This is not a farewell, but a provisional receipt for the
eventfulness and times we have had together. Dammit, another tear!
God bless, Jim.'

I was to see him only once more, at Wimbledon, this man whom,
speaking professionally, I feared more than anyone else with whom I
had to compete. . . .

There was little more to report about the year. I had been given the
chance to see and comment on Bob Foster being taken fourteen rounds
in defence of his world light-heavyweight title – *another* world championship, after all – by plucky Chris Finnegan. And Foster's performance
made me think that, despite the oft-repeated cry that boxing was dying,
I had, in the past five years seen five world champions – heavyweights
apart – who could have compared reasonably with all but the best of the
former 'greats': bantamweight Ruben Olivares; lightweight Roberto
Duran; welterweight José Napoles; middleweight Carlos Monzon – and
now Foster. How I would have loved to see him and Archie Moore
facing each other at their best.

I saw Joe Bugner, more impressive than usual, when he knocked
out Jurgen Blin, who had given him such a hard fight some eighteen
months earlier, in the eighth round. But, considering Bugner's original
retirement, announced shortly before his twenty-sixth birthday, it's
ironic to read what I wrote then: 'Perhaps, as his manager Andy Smith
has always claimed, we shall have to wait until Bugner, now twenty-two
is twenty-seven or so before he reaches his apex.'

The year ended for me with the Commercial Union Grand Masters'
tournament which could not have been more conveniently situated for
it was held in Barcelona and, from there, it was only a pitch over the
water and a putt uphill to the place where I hoped to spend most of the
rest of my life – Nido de Aguilas, 'The Eagles' Nest', on top of a small
mountain in Majorca overlooking the village of Capdella on the one
side and the Mediterranean on the other.

12 1973–6
L'Envoi

Do I miss it all? At times, of course.

I regretted not being in Jamaica to see George Foreman's stunning upset of Joe Frazier; slightly less that I wasn't in Zaire to see Muhammad Ali/Cassius Clay regain the title from Foreman – less because, even through the medium of television, it seemed almost unbelievable that a world heavyweight champion could fight as brainlessly as Foreman did.

I was immensely sorry not to have been in Manila for what, again having to judge through the two-dimensional little screen, looked to have been one of the great heavyweight title fights of all time – the third Clay–Frazier meeting. How misleading TV can be, however – particularly when the commentary is in a foreign language – I can only point out again by saying that up to the thirteenth of the fourteen completed rounds I had Frazier ahead on points, whereas a lot of good judges who were at the ringside have assured me that Clay was comfortably ahead before that.

Ringside judges – ah! that's the rub. I get letters and visits from chums from all over the world, keeping me in touch with the sports – and, particularly the boxing – scene; bringing a certain heart-sickness by saying or writing: 'Wish you'd been there.' And, obviously, when I can pick up on the radio a commentary of a fight like John Stracey winning the world welterweight title, I wish that I were there to write it. It's hard to get sporting history at second hand when, for so many years, you had a hand in writing it.

But when I'm honest I then think of those interminable, intolerable flights with their jet-lag, their time-zone differences which left your digestion wondering whether it was breakfast time or next Tuesday; the agonies of waiting for a phone to ring when you were waiting in some faraway place for a time-call to come from the office, *willing* the bloody machine to give some sign of life; the exquisite boredom of churning out yet another training-camp story about some champion who was as bored with being interviewed as you were with asking him the same stale questions.

And I look round 'my mountain', breathe deep the unpolluted air, swim, in the summer, in my tiny pool, and account myself lucky . . . particularly as with us, for much of the year, are Jimmy and Betty Stevenson, two of the greatest friends Sally and I have mutually had since we were married, with Jimmy one of the most competent of all sportswriters.

I was lucky in another way, too, in the manner of my retirement. I don't think I could have switched off completely, like a street-lamp being extinguished by a time-switch.

Instead I was fortunate enough to be able to end where I had begun so long ago, writing about, chiefly, lawn tennis.

But all this was nothing compared with the row which was boiling up over Nikki Pilic, of Yugoslavia who was banned for one month by the International Lawn Tennis Federation as he had allegedly refused to play for his country in the Davis Cup. Wimbledon upheld law and order by saying that they would enforce the one-month ban. Pilic, with the assistance of the male-only Association of Tennis Professionals – roughly a players' union – sought an injunction in the British law courts against the ban on his playing at Wimbledon. It was refused. So a majority of the players went on strike.

Under the heading 'The Day Of The Tennis Jackal' I began my story: 'There will be a new saying in sport in the future: "As untrustworthy as a tennis player."'' I pointed out that after his original suspension, by the Yugoslavian LTA, Pilic had appealed to the ILTF – *thereby acknowledging their authority!* Then I asked:

What was the point of Pilic appealing to the ILTF if he was going to ignore their decision? Why go to a British court of justice with the intention, if the verdict went against Pilic, of the players withdrawing their 'labour'? If ever there were a case of 'Heads I win – and if I don't win you're certainly going to lose,' this is it. It's as though Judas and his friends had taken over.

For years I have been saying that of all the athletes on whom I have reported, lawn tennis players, with certain shining and praiseworthy exceptions, are the worse behaved, most selfish, bad-tempered, ill-bred and, recently, the most grossly overpaid spoiled brats it's been my misfortune to watch.

It was Wimbledon who decided, in 1968, to 'go it alone' because, as the Chairman of the All England Club, Herman David said, they could not perpetuate the living lie of 'shamateurism'.

Now these same players, despite all the mealy-mouthed protestations that 'they are sorry to do this to Wimbledon', and the rest of the hypocritical guff which has nauseated me through the past few days, are doing their best to ruin a tournament which has been going for nearly 100 years and, for at least half that time, has been far and away the best in the world.

Roger Taylor, who finally decided to play, was attacked because he is allegedly letting down his fellow-professional players. May I suggest that he has got his priorities right? He thinks first of his country, the British public – which has supported him – the All England Club, of which he is a member.

And what is on the other side? A motley, American-dominated crew, most of whose highest common factor – or is it lowest common denominator? – is folding money, crisp cash, or lovely lolly. When they talk glibly about a matter of 'principle', I fear they have their spelling wrong. It should be 'principal', which my dictionary defines as: 'A capital sum of money put out at interest.'

The blame, I think, must largely be put in Jack Kramer's court. I have known Jack Albert Kramer since blisters beat him in the first postwar Wimbledon of 1946. The following year he became one of the great amateur champions. He followed that by becoming the world's No. 1 professional, beating a succession of amateurs when they joined the pro ranks.

Wherever there has been money in lawn tennis, Kramer has been seen. There's nothing wrong in that. As Cecil Rhodes said: 'Patriotism is good; but patriotism plus ten per cent is better.'

There's one thing of which I am certain. Wimbledon will endure after the name of many of the 'rebels' are forgotten.

In the midst of all this I was involved in a televised 'confrontation' with Arthur Ashe, the world's leading black player who was destined to win Wimbledon in 1975. Originally when I was contacted by London ITV my 'opponent' was to have been Cliff Drysdale, the South-African-born President of the ATP, but he was seeing Eldon Griffiths, then Minister for Sport, and Ashe was substituted.

In one way it did not make it easier because I have an almost morbid fear of being thought anti-black but the opposition was certainly negligible. In Ashe's book, written with Frank Deford, *Portrait in Motion* (Stanley Paul, 1975) the passage appears:

Today I had a televised encounter with Peter Wilson, the tennis writer. He began most of his comments by saying: 'The recognized administrators of the game say . . .'

'Well, that's the whole point,' I finally said. 'We don't think they should be the recognized administrators. Look, you need four things to run a tennis tournament: the court, the players, a sponsor and management. What do you need with recognized administrators? What function does the ILTF perform? They do anything except sell indulgences so that the players, the sponsors and the managers can run a tournament.'

Ashe was entitled to write what he liked in his book: this one is mine and, cross my heart, I remember him saying nothing like the above remark.

I *do* remember him saying that the players were happy to see little old ladies round the court but that what was really important was the money to be got from the sponsors. Perfectly honest: but it did confirm what I had increasingly thought, that some of the players didn't give a damn about the spectators. It also rather surprised me that he thought that the sponsors would pay such vast sums unless the little old ladies – and some others – did congregate round the courts . . . and buy the sponsors' products.

It must, I think, have been successful TV for I know that Eamonn Andrews let it run much longer than had originally been scheduled, omitting two other items.

Wimbledon itself was not as disastrous as we had all feared. If ever a man saved a major sporting event it was Roger Taylor.

When he came on to the Centre Court he got the most genuinely Royal reception I have ever witnessed for the Duke of Kent, President of the All England Club, and his Duchess led a literally standing ovation, clapping as enthusiastically as any football fans.

Then there was the quarter-final match when the big Sheffield left-hander was awarded the match against the new teenage sensation, 'A Star Is Bjorn' Borg from Sweden, when everyone knew that Taylor's service was 'long'. Everyone knew it – but it was Taylor who refused to take the match on an error and won the fifty-one-game marathon only on the fifth match point!

And finally the saddest 'break' of all, when Taylor was leading the eventual winner, Jan Kodes, of Czechoslovakia, 9–8, 7–9, 7–5, 4–6, 5–4 only for the rain to come down like grey guillotine blades, the match to be suspended and, when it was resumed Taylor, a notoriously slow starter, to be unable to win another game.

Despite Kodes' determination – he beat Alex Metreveli (USSR) in the first Eastern-bloc final – the best man did *not* win the championships. For although Ilie Nastase, perhaps the hottest favourite of all time in the 'boycotted' tournament, had the guts to compete he did not have the intestinal fortitude to win a tournament which, the way he was then playing, should have been a set-up for him.

But if the men's events suffered from self-induced pernicious anaemia the women's were a wonderful triumph for Mrs Billie Jean King who not only took the triple crown for the second time, won the singles for a record, postwar, fifth time, but also brought her total of Wimbledon championships to a magnificent seventeen.

During Wimbledon I had the chance of seeing Joe Bugner for the last time against Joe Frazier, and he proved his courage and durability by surviving the sort of tenth-round left hook which had once put Clay down – and which did the same to him. But he was up inside the statutory ten seconds and, in fact, landed one right which had Frazier, who had been fighting like a gorilla with a grin, wobbling. In fact the big black man's left eye was so badly closed that, had the fight been of fifteen rather than twelve rounds, the referee might well have had to intervene. It was an insight into Bugner's character that he never fought better than when he had been most hurt.

Later in the year, I broke all my resolutions never to come back to Britain in the winter, to attend yet another wonderful *Mirror* farewell party – this time for Hugh Cudlipp, soon to be created Lord Cudlipp – a justified tribute to the greatest journalist with whom I ever worked.

And the year progressed to the gloomiest note when what I had for so long feared happened and the Challenge Round of the Davis Cup – devalued though it might be – was not played because India refused to share a court with the South Africans who, at home, regarded them as inferior citizens. . . .

In 1974 I had done a Majorca-to-London-to-Cairo-to-London-to-Naples-to-Bournemouth-to-Rome-to-Paris-to-Nottingham-to-Wimbledon-to-Majorca circuit, all inside eighty-nine days and I decided that was rather too much travelling for an elderly (retired!) gentleman and I made up my mind to cut down in 1975. But the year was ushered in with what turned out to be a rather splendid surprise although, at the time, it seemed like an inexplicable crisis. Sally was shopping in Palma and I was working on this book, with only my desk-light on, when a persistent knocking at the door interrupted my concentration.

When I got to the door there was the burly figure of a *Guardia Civil*, complete with his rather sinister, shiny tricorne hat. He had a message. But he had no English; and I, to my shame, have unfortunately the most square-wheeled Spanish, which is adequate only in a friendly bar. But 'by guess and by God' we reached an understanding. It was vital that I should ring the British Consul *muy urgente*, which I translated as immediately, if not sooner. By the time Reg Mitchell, brother of Cyril, the former well-known racehorse trainer, and my very friendly neighbour, had run me down to the village to phone – we don't have innovations like telephones up on the hill! – the Consulate was, of course, shut.

Nothing for it but to dash into Palma to find the Consul's home number and while Sally and I were running through the various disasters which could have overwhelmed our joint and several families we put a call through to it. I took over and the conversation went:

'Is that the British Consul?'

'Yes.'

'This is Peter Wilson.'

'Yes.'

'You sent a policeman round to me tonight to get me to ring you urgently.'

'Oh, yes. I've been instructed to ask if you're prepared to accept an OBE in the New Year's Honours List.'

'OBE? Er . . . yes. I would.'

M*

'Oh, good. Congratulations. Goodbye.'

He rang off. And I never did have time to ask him if he had any more good news could he please convey it in a less alarming fashion. And now he is no longer in office in Palma so I shall never be able to tell him. . . .

I still couldn't quite believe it until, for once in my life, I tuned in to the BBC's early radio show on New Year's Day and heard Simon Bate confirm that it really was true and 'that's enough for us in the media to call Peter "sir" ' – which was a very nice awakening, Simon.

Paris was my first stop in 1975 – I had even cut out my beloved Rome – and for the second year running it was Borg and Chris Evert as champions again. Guillermo Vilas reached the final and 'newish' successful names were Harold Solomon, Eddie Dibbs and the Czech girl (later to opt for American citizenship), Martina Navratilova.

Ashe's triumph over Connors in the final was one of the most remarkable – and admirable – I can remember at Wimbledon. I commented:

Ashe scarcely put a foot, a racket or a tactical idea wrong. There were two things he had to do himself: get a high percentage of his first services in, and put his first volleys away. There was one thing he had to prevent Connors from doing: getting into the rhythm of returning service which had destroyed Roscoe Tanner. Except for the run of games from 5–5 in the third set to the time when he was within a point of 4–1 in the fourth set, 'Jimmy the One' was 'cribbed, cabin'd and confined' by Ashe's strategy.

To use a boxing analogy, it was Muhammad Ali using his superb defensive skills to win against George Foreman, forcing his rival to punch himself out. Ashe's pressure – which included an oblique forehand exploiting the physical limitations of Connors' two-fisted backhand – had one other psychological effect on the champion. He tried just too dam' hard. And, as a result of his 'pressing', he got an infinitely smaller proportion of first services into court than the cool, black man across the net from him.

You could even see the difference, between the games, as they sat back to back beside the umpire's chair, Ashe relaxing in a kind of lawn tennis yoga for at least a third of the nineteen one-minute break periods, so that for six or seven minutes he was completely away from the tensions. Connors, on the other hand, was a real 'fidget-bottom' between games, unable to remain still for a couple of seconds.

There was, in fact, one incident even more memorable than the technical skills of Ashe and that was when Connors, never a real favourite with the Wimbledon crowd, went sprawling and, as he lay impotent, someone in the crowd called out: 'Come *on*, Connors.' Upon which he shouted back, as though carrying on an individual argument among 14,000 others: 'I *am* trying, goddamit!' For a space, at least, the whole crowd was on his side after that. But, at the end, how they rose to Ashe's victory which was, as I wrote, 'comparable in some ways with the surprise Cassius Clay caused when he took the world heavyweight title from Sonny Liston. Even the odds were almost exactly the same. The 'unbeatable' Liston was 7–1 on; the 'invincible' Connors started 20–3 on.' (Incidentally, I was on the players' side when they deplored the introduction of a betting tent at Wimbledon because of the obvious suggestion that matches might be 'bent' because of wagers involved.)

In contrast to the men's final which, in the best tradition, was one of the great sporting upsets of modern times, the women's singles fizzled out in the most disappointing fashion.

Evonne Goolagong had, just before the championships, become Mrs Roger Cawley – an unexpected marriage which, temporarily at least, interrupted her 'daughter-father' relationship with coach Vic Edwards. Up to the final, despite a terrific battle with Virginia Wade in the 'quarters', Mrs Cawley had played as much as to say that she would show everyone she could win on her own.

But having dealt neatly and competently with Margaret Court she came up against the greatest competitor of them all in the final, Mrs Billie Jean King against whom she could win only one game.

Mrs King's total of six singles titles put her third equal among the all-time greats with Suzanne Lenglen and Mrs Blanche Hillyard.

'Including doubles titles, Mrs King has now amassed nineteen championships in the fifteen years she has been competing at Wimbledon, which makes her the equal of eighty-three-year-old Elizabeth Ryan,' I wrote. 'Since Mrs King lost her first match to Yola Ramirez at Wimbledon, in 1961 she has played eighty singles. She has won seventy-one of them. What can you say but – *magnificent* Billie Jean! It was *your* Independence Day.'

Sally and I stayed on for a fortnight or so after Wimbledon. We spent a truly memorable evening with Don Bate as the guests of Denis Howell, the Minister for Sport, with drinks on the terrace and dinner in the House of Commons. The upshot of it was that for only the second time, as far as I know, I was mentioned in Hansard, the official report of Parliamentary debates in the House.

.The first time had been over a quarter of a century earlier and now Denis, quoting me correctly, mentioned my long-standing opposition to and loathing of hare-coursing. It was the same barbarous pursuit – I have never dignified it by the name of sport – which had caused me to be quoted a generation before.

'I hate all blood pursuits involving animals whose panting death provides a thrill for the pursuers. But at least those who hunt the fox and the noble stag do put their own limbs at some risk. I loathe bull-fighting – but the great matador is not a coward.

'Hare-coursing puts no one, save the hare, at any worse risk than over-indulgence in eating and drinking can bring.'

I shall never be really happy, nor feel that my writing was in one way successful, until this loathsome pastime is outlawed. . . .

Then, a few days after our evening in the House, through the hard work of Marion Barbieri, who had been my secretary for the last four years or so of my time as a columnist and who, bless her, carried on extra-curricula duties for me in my semi-retirement, it was arranged that Sally and I should attend an investiture at Buckingham Palace.

It was fun chatting to an old friend, that indomitable cricketer, Brian Close and there too, although I did not see him, was Alan Pascoe who had done so much for British athletics.

At one stage, waiting in one of the apparently innumerable ante-rooms, I found myself under a life-size portrait of the gross Duke of Cumberland, son of King George II and Queen Caroline, and infamous 'Butcher of Culloden'. And I thought how, even in Buckingham Palace, I could not get away from boxing – or prize-fighting, rather.

For it was Cumberland who was the patron of Jack Broughton – known as 'The Father of Boxing' – and it was 'Butcher' Cumberland who, after having allegedly wagered the then colossal sum of £10,000 at odds of 10–1 on, disowned his fighter in cowardly fashion. This defeat proved Broughton's ruin. The Duke of Cumberland could never speak of this contest 'with any degree of temper', and turned his back on the beaten man. The legislature interfered, the amphitheatre 'which Broughton had opened in Oxford Street, London' was closed, and Broughton never fought more.

I was thinking how poor old boxing had always suffered from rumours of 'crooked' fights and how bad losers had bedevilled sports for over two and a quarter centuries when it struck me that I was probably the only person who had ever been denigrating a prize-fight supporting Royal Duke while waiting to be honoured by a Queen!

And then – a few pleasant words from the light, still girlish voice; a medal representing her grandfather and grandmother hung from my lapel and a little later I was outside with Sally and a rosy-cheeked girl-reporter was announcing – had I once been as breathless? – 'I'm from the Press Association, Mr Wilson. What did the Queen say to you?' And I took my topper off to tell her. At last Sally and I were walking back, hand in hand, after having had pictures taken outside the railings, to get the car parked in the inner courtyard of the Palace.

And I thought it was a long journey from the teenage days waiting for a drunken sports editor of *The Times* to decide, at whim, whether one ate well that week; or from the fifteen shillings a day, plus four-and-sixpence expenses, of the Exchange Telegraph newsagency.

But there had been some good views along the road. . . .

Nido de Aguilas, Capdella, Majorca, 1977.

Index